Above and Beyond

ALSO BY SPENCER DUNMORE

FICTION

Bomb Run (1971)
Tower of Strength (1973)
Collision (1974)
Final Approach (1976)
Means of Escape (1978)
Ace (1981)
The Sound of Wings (1984)
No Holds Barred (1987)
Squadron (1991)

NON-FICTION

Reap the Whirlwind: The Untold Story of 6 Group, Canada's Bomber Force of World War II (with William Carter) (1991)
Wings for Victory: The Remarkable Story of the British Commonwealth Air Training Plan in Canada (1994)
In Great Waters: The Epic Story of the Battle of the Atlantic, 1939–45 (1999)

ABOVE AND BEYOND

*The Canadians' War
in the Air, 1939–45*

Spencer Dunmore

Cloth edition published 1996
Trade paperback edition published 2000

National Library of Canada Cataloguing in Publication Data

Dunmore, Spencer, 1928–
    Above and beyond : the Canadians' war in the air, 1939–45

Includes bibliographical references and index.
ISBN 0-7710-2928-4 (bound)   ISBN 0-7710-2931-4 (pbk.)

1. World War, 1939-1945 – Aerial operations, Canadian.   2. World War, 1939-1945 – Personal narratives, Canadian.   3. Canada. Royal Canadian Air Force – History – World War, 1939-1945.   4. Canada. Royal Canadian Air Force – Biography. I. Title.

D792.C2D848 1996   940.54'4971   C96-931743-3

We acknowledge the financial support of the Government of Canada through the Book Publishing Industry Development Program for our publishing activities. We further acknowledge the support of the Canada Council for the Arts and the Ontario Arts Council for our publishing program.

Set in Bembo by M&S, Toronto
Printed and bound in Canada

McClelland & Stewart Ltd.
The Canadian Publishers
481 University Avenue
Toronto, Ontario
M5G 2E9
www.mcclelland.com

2 3 4 5   04 03 02 01

Contents

Introduction

We arrived by bus, twenty-four unprepossessing youths in well-creased and ill-fitting blue uniforms with silver buttons and dog collars. We were Air Training Corps lads. Pimply faced pests. About as welcome on the average Bomber Command airfield as an outbreak of amoebic dysentery. We knew it. We had been told as much, and in no uncertain terms, on more than one occasion. Thus it was with some surprise that we watched as a smiling squadron leader jumped on the bus step and greeted us with a wave.

He said something extraordinary: "Welcome."

We stared. *Welcome?*

In our experience, squadron leaders were lofty, distant personages before whom one stood in quivering obeisance. But this one could only be described as . . . yes, one had to use the word: *friendly*.

Such was our introduction to the Canadians. We liked them. Incredibly, they seemed to like us. Officers, NCOs, erks, the lot. They answered our questions without impatient sighs and condescending smirks. Soon we were on first-name terms. Bud and Norm. Wayne and Milt. We had refreshments in their canteen, surrounded by posters advertising Sweet Caporal cigarettes, vacations in the Laurentians, the 1939 Dodge "Luxury Liner," and a department store called Eaton's. The airmen came from places called Wetaskiwin and Moose Jaw, Trois Rivières and Goose Bay. Even the names sounded adventurous. We discovered the delights of

Chiclets and O'Henry bars, unrationed here in this corner of Canada and twice as tasty for that reason alone.

None of us thought the Canadians' presence in any way remarkable. The Empire was rallying round, as it always did. We imagined muscular lumberjacks cleaning and oiling their axes and saws before putting them away, while befurred hunters checked-in their sleds for the duration. Time to pop over to the Mother Country to lend a hand. It was the natural order of things. To our faint surprise (mingled with a modicum of disappointment), we learned that the Canadians we talked to had been accountants and chemists, clerks and corporate lawyers. Not a lumberjack among them.

We discovered an interesting fact: this Canadian unit was part of something called 6 Group. It consisted of a dozen or more heavy bomber squadrons – manned by Canadians, administered by Canadians, and paid for by Canadians. 6 Group was a sizeable component of Bomber Command. So why had we – who considered ourselves expert in every area of military aviation – never heard of it? Not a whisper in any newspaper or BBC broadcast that we were aware of. Did the Canadians prefer to be anonymous participants in democracy's battle? It seemed unlikely, particularly when we heard them telling us that fully one in four of the airmen in the air force were Canadians. Those in Royal Canadian Air Force units represented less than half of their number overseas. Our new-found Canadian friends were proud of their country's contribution to the war effort. And rightly so. Canada had a population of some eleven million at that time; by the standards of the U.S.S.R. and the United States, China and Japan, it was minuscule, a minor player in the big leagues. But the Canadians had a big impact. And, to me at any rate, the very fact that there were far fewer of them than Americans or Brits or Russians endowed them with a certain exclusivity.

In those days, the notion of ever visiting a distant land like Canada had to be filed away alongside space travel and unlimited petrol for blatantly unofficial purposes. We had grown up in an era of heavy-handed restrictions, conditioned to count our blessings and stay put. I doubt that it ever entered my mind that I might one day live in Canada permanently. But that is what happened. And I'm glad. I got lucky. So I've always been grateful to those airmen on that 6 Group base who first sparked my interest in Canada. Some of them kind, a few a bit crass, some reflective and some argumentative, every one a veritable cornucopia of information about a game called hockey (although we thought at first they meant *hockey*, because they didn't specify *ice* hockey), yet curiously reticent when it came to answering questions about their country. They were ordinary Canadians, decent men possessed of a healthy lack of respect for military claptrap, including rank badges and tradition. The fastest, most efficient way was the only way that anything should be done. It mattered not a whit how the Duke of Wellington did it. They were, without doubt, the best ambassadors Canada ever sent anywhere. This book is my long overdue tribute.

Above and Beyond

PART ONE
1939

Chaos and Crisis

HAWKER HURRICANE

"The one means that wins the easiest victory over reason: terror and force." – *Adolf Hitler*

I

Monday, September 4, 1939, dawned cloudy and mild over much of Britain. The weather soon deteriorated. By noon, it had become overcast and stormy. Rain clouds scudded across the dark sky, driven by a boisterous northwesterly. Conditions could hardly have been worse for low-level flying, yet late in the afternoon, German sailors on the pocket battleship *Admiral Scheer* at Wilhelmshaven, the major naval base on Germany's north coast, watched in amazement as two groups of twin-engined aircraft flying at sea level came streaking through the murk. At first glance they looked like Luftwaffe Junkers 88s or Dornier 17s. The sailors shook their heads. Typical fliers, showing off, trying to impress everyone. If they weren't careful they'd fly right into the water, and then there'd be hell to pay . . .

As the aircraft neared, the red-white-and-blue national insignia became visible. The onlookers could scarcely believe their eyes. Those weren't Luftwaffe aircraft, they were Blenheims of the Royal Air Force!

Bomb doors open, the bombers separated and prepared to attack. Nearby, in the Elbe, the battle cruisers *Gneisenau* and *Scharnhorst* lay at anchor, their crews relaxing, confident that there would be no aerial attacks in that dismal weather.

The Blenheims, fifteen in number, from 107 and 110 squadrons, had taken off from Wattisham, Suffolk, shortly after 4:00 P.M. Flying at wave-top level over the grey ocean, they had battled mist and cloud, the crews straining to see through the frequent and heavy rain showers. As they neared their target, the town of Wilhelms-haven, conditions improved marginally. The *Admiral Scheer* and the cruiser *Emden* were clearly visible. The leader of the Blenheim formation, Squadron Leader K. C. Doran of 110 Squadron, later reported that he could see German sailors' washing hanging on lines near the stern, with crew members looking up at the intruders as if watching an air show. Eyes wide, the sailors saw the first bombs fall away from the leading Blenheim.

Doran bombed with commendable accuracy. Two of his missiles hit the *Admiral Scheer*. The first dug itself into the deck; the second bounced off. Neither exploded.

Doran's Blenheim had cleared the ship before a shot was fired by the Germans. A second Blenheim roared overhead. Its bombs fell away. They missed their target, although one landed in the sea only a few feet from the vessel.

By now the ship's gun crews had woken up. In moments, scores of guns were firing at the audacious airmen. Darting flickers of light streaked through the misty air. The *thud-thud-thud* of cannon echoed across the water. One Blenheim took hits. Flame streamed from its engines. The bomber wobbled uncertainly, then rolled over onto its back and smashed into the water, vanishing in a great eruption of spray and black smoke. None of the crew escaped.

Four more Blenheims, these from 107 Squadron, now sped into action. They roared low over the ships, braving the curtains of flak. In moments, three of the four had been hit. One hurtled straight into the bow of the cruiser *Emden*, whether intentionally or by chance no one will ever know. The impact caused the German navy's first casualties of the war. Only one of 107 Squadron's Blenheims landed safely back at Wattisham, its bombs still nestled in their racks.

A Canadian, twenty-two-year-old Sergeant Albert Prince of Vancouver, died in the shattered remains of one of the 107 Squadron Blenheims, N6240. Prince was later buried in Soltau, Germany, the first Canadian airman to die in combat in World War II.

On that same day, a Coastal Command Hudson of 223 Squadron took off on patrol and never returned. Its fate remains a mystery. The pilot was a Canadian in the RAF, twenty-two-year-old Earl Godfrey of Saskatoon.

In the context of the slaughter that would take place in the skies of Europe, Africa, and Asia during the next five and a half years, the day's events could only be rated as minor skirmishes. The fact that Canadians were involved was, however, entirely appropriate; the participation of Canadians in the aerial battles to come would be out of all proportion to their numbers. In the ranks of the Royal Air Force (RAF) and later in the Royal Canadian Air Force (RCAF) squadrons and in the naval air force, the Fleet Air Arm (FAA), Canadians became a major presence on most of the war's fighting fronts. The RCAF, which went to war with a grand total of twenty-nine modern fighting aircraft – nineteen Hurricanes and ten Fairey Battles – would burgeon at an extraordinary pace to become the fourth largest Allied air force.

The war that was to have such a seismic impact on so many lives was a clash of economies as much as of ideologies, and it had been brewing since the end of World War I. Rather than securing a long-term peace, the delegates at Versailles industriously sowed the seeds of another conflict. The German economy collapsed under an Everest of reparations. In July 1923, the German mark – valued at four to the U.S. dollar in 1914 – plummeted to 160,000 to the dollar, and it continued its downward spiral to one million in August and 130,000 million in November. It says much for the energy and determination of the Germans that by the late twenties they were well on their way to extricating themselves from the financial mess. The currency had been stabilized. Credit had been restored. Industry was hiring again. But almost simultaneously came the devastating impact of the Great Depression. Again the fragile German economy collapsed. Unemployment soared from 1,320,000 in September 1929 to 3,000,000 a year later. Within two more years, it had reached a staggering 6,000,000. Money dwindled in value hour by hour. No one could tell what the next day would bring. Would there be enough to eat? What sort of a future did a man's family have to look forward to? Where would it all end?

One man found the chaos and panic greatly to his liking. Adolf Hitler saw opportunity there. His party, the National Socialists, soon made enormous strides. Hitler became chancellor. He lived up to his election promises, engineering a complete economic, political, and military revolution. In a few years, Hitler effectively restored German prosperity and security and – perhaps even more important – German pride.

Before long, Hitler was openly displaying his new military machine as he set about reorganizing Europe. Although the Wehrmacht's generals quaked when he defied the Western powers, Hitler remained calm. He sensed that Neville Chamberlain and Edouard Deladier, the prime ministers of Britain and France, would not risk their precious peace for anything so trivial as the independence of a few unimportant nations in central Europe. He was right. The fascist governments in Germany and Italy became increasingly bellicose. Benito Mussolini's army swept into virtually defenceless Ethiopia (Abyssinia). The following year, the Spanish fascists rebelled against their country's Republican government, and the Italians and Germans supported them with men and equipment. The Soviets supported the Republicans in the same way. The West, however, preferred not to become involved, at least officially. Meanwhile, Hitler continued to press for more territorial concessions. To the shame of Britain and France particularly, he succeeded brilliantly. Only when it came to Germany's interest in Poland did Neville Chamberlain brace himself and stand up to the German dictator – and then it was probably only because he had been made to look a fool by the hollow Munich Agreement. The world war had begun.

Canada declared war on September 10, 1939. It was, as ever, a country divided. Although most English-speaking Canadians supported the government's action ("Britain's war is Canada's war"), large numbers of Québécois were bitterly opposed. As far as they were concerned, it was just another "imperialist" war of little concern to them. They remembered the Great War, in which, despite their opposition, conscription had been imposed and a coalition government formed without any French-Canadian representation. Now the prime minister, Mackenzie King, had to use every ounce of his political skill to bring this divided country into the conflict. He pledged that it would be a war of "limited liability" and that conscriptees would not be required to go overseas.

II

Almost as soon as it had begun, the conflict seemed to be in a state of suspension. In France and Belgium, there were occasional skirmishes between patrols. The opposing airmen tested their weapons and one another. A few victories were recorded; a few airmen died. The Germans rated the Allied pilots as competent, their aircraft definitely inferior. Most of the British squadrons flew early-model Hawker Hurricane fighters with two-bladed wooden propellers. The Hurricanes were pleasant to fly and highly manoeuvrable, but about twenty knots slower than the Messerschmitt 109s they had to face. Structurally, the Hurricane was an intermediate design, a sort of aerial stepping stone between the old fabric-covered biplanes and the modern stressed-skin monoplanes. A few RAF units still flew biplane Gloster Gladiators. When King George VI visited France late in 1939, the photographs of him inspecting the Gladiators and their pilots could easily be confused with shots of his father inspecting Camel squadrons in 1918. Fortunately, Hurricanes were to replace the Gladiators before the German invasion in the spring of 1940.

The lumbering single-engined Fairey Battle and the poorly armed Blenheim were the two light bomber types in the RAF's arsenal. Both would suffer horrific losses in the battles to come, taking many of the most experienced prewar bomber crews, including several Canadians, to their deaths. Another type to see service in France in the early days was the high-wing, single-engined Lysander, an army cooperation monoplane. It proved to be easy meat for the speedy Messerschmitts.

In general, French fighters were inferior to both the RAF and Luftwaffe fighters. The Morane-Saulnier 406 equipped most French fighter squadrons. It was an agile aircraft but lightly armed and no match for the enemy's machines. In the interwar years, the French had been as active as the Germans at promoting their air force, talking glibly of its enormous strength and waxing lyrical about the scores of factories daily turning out even better, faster, and more ferocious airplanes. Newspapers talked of 8,000 first-line aircraft in service, with another 750 trundling off the production lines every month. It was pure fantasy. Although France's aircraft industry was developing several first-class new designs, few reached the squadrons in time to participate in the battles of 1940. The reasons weren't hard to find: "By the middle of 1937, the national-ization programme of the Popular Front [the left-wing government then in power] – which collapsed in June of that year – had reduced the French aircraft industry to a demoralized patchwork of small factories scattered throughout the country; there was only one factory equipped to undertake mass production."[1] French bombers were so outdated that General Joseph Vuillemin, Chief of Staff of the French Air Force, would not permit them to be used in daylight operations. To make matters even worse, the French (and British) army and air force units had to operate within the tentacles of an appallingly inefficient command structure. Orders regularly took days to be implemented – by which time they had usually become redundant.

German fighter pilots quickly established themselves as first-class adversaries, despite the nonsense regularly published in the British and Commonwealth papers about their inferior aircraft and training. Many German pilots had seen service in Spain and knew their way around a hostile sky. Man for man, they had the edge, in experience, armament, and tactics. They had evolved a loose, highly flexible combat formation: two aircraft providing mutual protection, with each pilot watching out for the other's blind spots, and either one taking over leadership as the situation demanded. Unlimited numbers of pairs could be added. It wasn't as pretty as the neat V ("vic") formations with which the RAF impressed taxpayers at prewar air shows, but it was far better suited to the realities of combat.

Supreme commander of the Allied armies was France's sixty-eight-year-old Maurice Gamelin, a hero of the Great War and a dyed-in-the-wool reactionary who, claiming that radio messages could be too easily intercepted, insisted on using the telephone and motorcycle dispatch riders to maintain communications with his army commanders. Few French aircraft carried radios, but this didn't trouble Gamelin; he had no wish to stay in touch with them. The French high command saw little value in airplanes, except as devices to fight other airplanes. It was no wonder, then, that the French army had only a handful of anti-aircraft guns. No one envisioned attacks by low-flying fighters and light bombers, despite the highly successful use of such weapons in the latter stages of the Great War. Generals are often criticized for being ready to fight the last war instead of the war confronting them; Gamelin, it appears, had still not absorbed the lessons of 1918.

In terms of numbers, there was little to choose between the two sides. The Allies had 144 divisions, the Germans 141. The Allies' complement of guns and tanks was far stronger than the Germans'; on the other hand, the Luftwaffe had the edge over the Allied air forces.

The inactivity of the first few months of the war led many on the Allied side to believe that an end to the conflict was being secretly negotiated. Neither side jeopardized the fragile peace by indulging in major air raids, the nightmare of the era. For years, magazine illustrators had been outdoing themselves, terrifying everyone with depictions of the horror of it all. Meticulous formations of bombers blackening the sky while bombs rained down on defenceless cities. Wide-eyed citizens scrambling in panic to escape from the on-slaught while the dead piled up in piteous heaps. It now seemed frighteningly possible. The Committee on Imperial Defence esti-mated that the first two months' attacks on London would kill 600,000 and injure a million more.

Instead of bombs, RAF Bomber Command's Whitleys deluged the Germans with millions of propaganda leaflets. Presumably someone or other hoped these efforts would awake German citizens to the folly of their government. Since everything that Hitler had done to date had met with phenomenal success, it was a forlorn hope.

It is remarkable how little the Whitley crews knew about finding their way about in the dark. In prewar years, the RAF seldom took to the air after sundown, especially in poor weather. Apparently *no one* in authority ever considered the difficulties of finding targets – and hitting them – when everything below was completely blacked-out, and when ice, rain, snow, or uncooperative storms might be encountered. In the years leading up to the declaration of war, RAF Bomber Command was far less able to find its way about Europe than the average airline of the period.

With approach of winter, the leaflet raids became endurance tests for the Whitley crews. Grossly inadequate heating and weather-proofing in the aircraft created conditions that could only be com-pared with those endured by Napoleon's armies during the retreat from Moscow. One Whitley crew recorded these impressions:

Crystalline ice formed on the leading edges of the wings, over the gun turrets and on the cabin windows. The front gun was frozen up and rendered useless. The aircraft's trim-ming tabs were jammed by ice and the "dustbin" turret [a retractable gun position beneath the rear fuselage, eliminated on later models of the Whitley] stuck about a third of the way down its travel. The ceiling of the bomber was reduced to 16,500 feet and it was forced to remain in cloud. After two and a quarter hours in the air the oxygen supply in the cabin was exhausted. Some of the crew occasionally banged their heads on the floor or navigation table as a relief from the feeling of frostbite and oxygen lack.[2]

All this to deliver leaflets!

III

It wasn't long before Canadian fighter pilots began to take a toll of the enemy. On October 17, a Heinkel 111 bomber appeared through cloud off Whitby, on the English coast. A flight of three Spitfires of 41 Squadron intercepted. At the controls of one was twenty-seven-year-old Howard Peter Blatchford, known to every-one as "Cowboy." The burly airman was the son of a former mayor of Edmonton. He had joined the RAF in 1935.

The Spitfires attacked the Heinkel in turn, firing bursts at short range. The tracers sparkled as they darted through the sunlight, riddling the bomber. Bits of engine cowling broke free and went fluttering away like wounded birds. For Blatchford, it was the supreme moment, the culmination of years of training . . . at last, real combat! A fine marksman, Blatchford could see his shots striking the crippled Heinkel. Striving unsuccessfully to reach cloud cover, the German aircraft streamed smoke; oily, black stuff. In a few minutes it was all over. The enemy aircraft toppled into the sea about thirty miles off Whitby. Circling over the spot, the Spitfire pilots saw two crew members scrambling out onto the Heinkel's wing. Blatchford heard later that the pair were washed ashore and captured.

Another successful Canadian fighter pilot of the early war years was also a westerner. Mark Brown of Glenboro, Manitoba, had joined the RAF in 1936. To his delight, he was posted to No. 1 Squadron, a unit widely regarded (at least by its members) as the "premier" fighter squadron. Soon after war was declared, the pilots were ordered to remove the squadron badges from their flying suits. Then, in a scene that would have been perfect for *Mrs. Miniver*, they waved to relatives and friends watching from the dispersal, clambered into their Hurricanes, and flew off to France to become part of the Advanced Air Striking Force. On one of their first patrols over France, French Morane fighters attacked them. Fortunately, they inflicted no damage or casualties. Brown – known to his colleagues as "Hilly" – was the first Canadian fighter pilot to go to France in World War II. On November 23, he scored a victory, a Dornier 17, which he shared with his British CO, Squadron Leader P. J. H. "Bull" Halahan. Afterwards, the squadron entertained the pilot of the Dornier. Brown described him in a letter to his sister as "quite a good chap." Hilly Brown would eventually become the first of many Canadian fighter aces.

Blatchford and Brown, like all Canadian prewar volunteers, journeyed to a land that wasn't at all sure what to make of them. Stout-hearted chaps, agreed most Britons, but a bit rough and ready – like all "colonials." Frank Harley of London, Ontario, sailed for Britain in April 1938, intending to join the RAF. On arrival in Britain, he changed his mind and joined the Fleet Air Arm. He recalls that some of the ex-public school (that is, private school) "snobs" referred to the recruits from the dominions as "Bolshie colonials."

The Canadians' first impressions of Britain's armed might were less than encouraging. In January 1939, the trainees went to Portsmouth to join the carrier HMS *Courageous* for sea training in the North Sea. A trio of Blackburn Aircraft's Skuas, the FAA's latest dive-bomber/fighter, carried out deck landing trials. "The first one caught a wire at an angle, blew a tire, and nearly went over the side,"

Harley says. "The second one caught the last arrester wire and swerved into the island superstructure and its airscrew [propeller] and reduction gear came off and cartwheeled over the side. The third and last machine landed on deck, catching the last wire, and the pilot jammed on the brakes, standing it on its nose. . . . We were not very impressed or reassured for our future."

It took time for some of the initial prejudices to disappear. Herb Hallatt of Windsor, Ontario, had a poor initial impression of England and the English. He went overseas in 1941, one of the first pilot graduates of the British Commonwealth Air Training Plan (BCATP). Aboard the troopship, the captain called the Canadian airmen "a bunch of colonial pigs," *all* of whom would find themselves in irons if *any* of them disobeyed any rules while on his ship. Later, in Bournemouth, a flight sergeant SP (service policeman) demanded that Hallatt, then a sergeant, stand to attention while the two men spoke. A Canadian navigator, John Harding, of London, Ontario, encountered an RAF officer who censured him for not wearing gloves: "You Canadians will never know how to wear the King's uniform. You're improperly dressed." Harding promptly retorted, "You bloody RAF types, you blow your nose on your hankie, then tuck it up your sleeve!"[3]

Yet, where it counted, aboard the aircraft, relations between the British and Canadians were, with few exceptions, outstandingly good and remained so throughout the war.

IV

On the morning of December 18, 1939, the crews of 9 Squadron, RAF Bomber Command, congregated in the briefing room. Their chatter was a little strained, their chuckles a little too loud. Nerves were taut. Everyone wondered what the target would be, and everyone pretended not to care one way or the other. Nonchalance was expected. With a clatter of skidding chair legs, the airmen got to their feet as the commanding officer came in. His two flight commanders followed close behind. One was a Canadian, Archie Guthrie of Reston, Manitoba. A slim man with a moustache, he wore on his sleeve the two rings plus "scraper"* of a squadron leader. He had been in the RAF since 1934.

The CO announced the operation: a daylight reconnaissance on enemy warships at Wilhelmshaven – "with the object of attacking by high-level bombing from not lower than ten thousand feet with 500-pound SAP [semi-armour-piercing] bombs in sticks, any battle-ships, battle cruisers, or cruisers found there or on the way out, or, failing these, any small warships."4 At this period, the business of war still possessed a rather Alice-in-Wonderland quality. Sink the ships by all means, the aircrews were told, but don't damage anything on the shore or any merchant ships that might happen to be in the vicinity. Whatever the assembled aircrew thought of their orders, they made no comment. They never did.

Three squadrons were involved: Nos. 9, 37, and 149, the entire force to be led by Wing Commander Richard Kellett of 149 Squadron.

Earlier that month, three attacks on shipping had been mounted. On December 3, Kellett had led a force of twenty-four Wellingtons in tight formation to the Heligoland and Wilhelmshaven area. Low cloud cover spoiled the attack; no hits on battleships were scored, but a minesweeper was reported sunk. While the raid could hardly have been counted a triumph of precision bombing, one signal fact had to be recorded: all the bombers returned safely. German fighters had put in an appearance, but they seemed reluctant to press their attacks against the Wellingtons (universally known as "Wimpies"). The reason was perfectly clear, the senior air force officers had told

---

*   That is, suggesting the thick and thin piston rings of an engine.

themselves. Well-disciplined formations of bombers equipped with power-operated gun turrets were the equal of any fighters. Here was proof indeed of the lessons the air force had been preaching for years. The RAF could strike at will.

But could it? A few days later, another raid on Wilhelmshaven had cost five Wellingtons of a twelve-strong formation.* A sixth crashed in England attempting to land. Air force "brass" had shaken their heads in disbelief. Fifty per cent casualties with nothing of significance achieved? It was unbelievable. Clearly the airmen had failed to carry out their orders. The official conclusion was that the bombers had pressed home their attack too low, making them unnecessarily vulnerable to the highly efficient German flak. Although enemy reports declared that fighters had been responsible for the bombers' casualties, the RAF denied it. Fighters were no match for their tightly disciplined formations. Hadn't the earlier attacks proved it?

With scores of squadron personnel watching, the Wellingtons thundered across the grass airfield and took to the air, disappearing into the brilliant sunshine. The crews huddled in their vibrating, draughty aircraft. They had strict orders: Do not bomb at less than ten thousand feet. The briefing officer had assured them that at that height, they would fly above the flak and their 500-pound bombs would have maximum impact on the German ships. But even if the bombs found their mark, would they go off? Every airman had heard stories of dud bombs bouncing off their targets like ping-pong balls.

The Wellingtons flew in four sections of six aircraft each, with Kellett leading the front section. Shortly after reaching the coast,

---

* A Canadian airman, John Griffiths, of Niagara Falls, Ontario, won the Distinguished Flying Cross (DFC) for his part in this action, the first to be awarded to a Canadian in the war. Two other Canadians flew on the op: Fred Lambart of Ottawa, and John Dyer of Minnedosa, Manitoba. Both returned safely, only to die in action within the next few months.

two aircraft of 149 Squadron turned for home. Their captains were Flight Lieutenant Duguid and Flight Sergeant Kelly. Duguid had begun to lose power in his starboard engine. His observer used an Aldis lamp to inform his two wingmen of his decision to return to base. Inexplicably, Kelly followed.

Not long afterward, Kellett was dismayed to see the cloud cover breaking up. The forecast had promised a convenient layer of cloud, and Kellett had intended to use it to make good the formation's escape after the attack. Ahead, the sky was now dazzlingly blue; not a cloud could be seen. A more cautious commander might have abandoned the operation there and then. Kellett pushed on.

Archie Guthrie and his crew shivered as their Wellington climbed. Freezing air screamed into the fuselage through the gaps around the nose turret. The sunshine flooding the cockpit provided no warmth. The airmen worked their toes in their flying boots and pulled their scarves a little tighter. Crew comfort had been of little concern to the designers of British bombers. Numbing cold and ear-splitting noise were constant companions. Machine-guns often froze solid and wouldn't fire. Coffee in Thermos flasks became brown lumps of ice.

The Danish–German coast appeared as a dark streak in the distance. Not long now. Observers left their navigation tables and took up positions in the nose, preparing their bombsights for the task ahead. At that stage in the war, the trade of air bomber had not yet been created; bomb-aiming was one of the observer's many duties. The crews' nerves tightened and mouths became dry. Aircraft captains told their air gunners to be especially vigilant; enemy fighters could be expected at any moment.

The plan called for the bombers to fly south of Wilhelmshaven, then turn and attack from inland. Once they had completed their attack, the Wimpies would be heading straight for home. Privately, many of the airmen thought the route ill-conceived, for it ensured that they all spent an unnecessarily long time over enemy territory before they unloaded their bombs.

Although none of the RAF crews knew it, they were flying into an area covered by an early form of radar known to the Germans as *Freya*. Two installations were involved: a naval unit on Heligoland and a Luftwaffe experimental station on the Wangerooge sand dunes, off Germany's northwest coast. The naval station spotted the approaching Wellingtons first, estimating their number at more than forty. The word went out to the German naval HQ, and from there to the Luftwaffe. At first no one believed the radar report: the British wouldn't be so stupid as to attack in these conditions. The Luftwaffe thought it likely that the naval operator was plotting a formation of seagulls. But then a naval report arrived. A visual sighting! Now there could be no doubt. The fighter pilots ran out to their aircraft.

In the meantime, the Wellingtons had crossed the coast and, after flying inland, had turned 180 degrees. They approached Wilhelms-haven, their bomb doors open, the 500-pounders packed neatly like metallic sardines.

The sky became scarred by flak bursts. The anti-aircraft fire did no damage to the bombers, but its intensity caused the tight formation to spread, a little at first, then more.

Looking down, Kellett saw two battleships. Damn! The ships were moored, their flanks nudging the massive wharf. His instructions had been explicit: Do not bomb if there is any likelihood of hitting the shore. Frustrated, Kellett ordered his formation not to bomb. The bomb doors on the Wellingtons' bellies folded inward as the aircraft overflew the docks and headed for home, their formation meticulous no longer. The Canadian squadron leader, Archie Guthrie, was later criticized for letting his section become badly scattered. At one point, according to reports, he was a mile ahead of his wingmen.

As Wilhelmshaven fell behind, the flak eased off. The worst seemed to be over. Aboard the Wellingtons, the aircrews relaxed, no doubt thinking what a total waste of time the whole operation had been. Imagine coming all this way and then taking your bombs home! More experienced operational airmen might have been slower to relax. That they were not yet out of the woods became glaringly obvious when a force of Messerschmitts – single-engined 109s and the recently introduced twin-engined 110s – roared in to attack. In earlier engagements with Wellingtons, German fighters had usually attacked from the rear. They had soon discovered, however, that that was the best-defended part of the aircraft, with twin Brownings (later, four) in a power-operated gun turret. On this occasion the fighters concentrated on beam attacks, having noted that the Wellington's turrets could turn only to right angles, leaving the fuselage sides completely unprotected. Another of the aircraft's deficiencies soon became glaringly apparent. The Wimpies had been allowed to go into battle without self-sealing fuel tanks. This was criminal stupidity on a par with the sailing of *Titanic* with too few lifeboats. Even if hits on a fuel tank didn't cause fire, they could all too easily result in the precious fuel pouring out – a particularly unappealing prospect on the far side of the North Sea. Within minutes, a Wellington of 149 Squadron staggered out of formation, trailing an ugly plume of smoke and flame. The bomber nosed down, turning, broad wings angled almost vertically. It plunged into the sea. No parachutes were seen.

The slaughter had begun. One after another the hapless Wellingtons went down, aerial torches painting smoking patterns across the sunny sky to the accompaniment of rattling guns. Safely beyond the range of the Wimpies' light machine-guns, the German pilots could use the fabric-covered bombers for target practice. One by one, they fell out of formation, streaming fire, hitting the sea with great eruptions of spray, and sinking, leaving only patches of oil and pathetic bits of debris to prove that they had ever existed.

The Canadian, Archie Guthrie, died early in the fight. After a beam attack by an Me 110, his Wellington spun into the sea, its fuel tanks ablaze. Neither he nor any of his crew survived.

If the leading elements of the Wellington formation suffered badly, the rear echelon, principally the aircraft of 37 Squadron, RAF, was almost wiped out. A member of Flying Officer Lemon's crew inadvertently activated the flap lever during the combat. Abruptly, like some airborne horse rearing on its hind legs, the Wellington soared heavenward, stalled, engines bellowing, then plummeted. In the cockpit, the two pilots struggled to regain control. Sweating despite the icy conditions, they succeeded in dragging the bomber back to straight and level flight only a few feet above the sea. Immediately, several fighters dived in pursuit. One misjudged its height and speed and flew straight into the water. The Wellington managed to escape to Britain, hugging the waves all the way, the only one from 37 Squadron to get back to base.

Incredibly, one of 37 Squadron's pilots, having been shot down in flames, survived the crash into the sea and was picked up by a German patrol boat. He was the sole survivor of his crew. Another of the unit's pilots became the only airman who dropped bombs in anger that day. He had spotted a German ship a few miles west of Schillig Point and tried to sink it. His bombs missed. When a German fighter attacked the Wellington, the RAF rear gunner couldn't respond. His turret was frozen solid; so were his guns. The Wimpy made a remarkable escape, managing a chaotic wheels-up landing on the sand dunes of Borkum island, the crew injured but alive. They became prisoners for the duration.

Forty miles from the English coast, a Wellington of 149 Squadron ditched. The aircraft and crew vanished. The occupants of a 9 Squadron aircraft were luckier. Their aircraft managed to keep going until it was close to the coast. Then its engines spluttered into silence. The pilot, Sergeant Ramshaw, succeeded in putting his plane down on the water, and four of the five aircrew escaped.

Of the twenty-two Wellingtons that had flown over Wilhelms-haven, only ten returned to England. All had suffered extensive damage. It was a catastrophic operation, although no one could have guessed from the newspaper reports, which claimed that fully half the enemy fighter force had been shot down. The operation itself was described as a "security patrol," whatever that meant. The senior

officers involved immediately sat down and wrote detailed memo-
randa to one another, blaming the aircrews for everything, with the
Canadian squadron leader, Archie Guthrie, coming in for particularly harsh treatment. Air Vice-Marshal "Jackie" Baldwin, the Air
Officer Commanding (AOC) 3 Group, criticized Guthrie's "poor
leadership," which, he claimed, had resulted in his formation
becoming scattered. If aircraft didn't maintain tight formation, they
would be picked off. It was a basic tenet of Bomber Command.

Apparently none of the senior officers ever considered that the
concept of daylight incursions by unescorted formations of
bombers might be flawed. At least none said so. Edgar Ludlow-
Hewitt, the Commander-in-Chief of Bomber Command, seemed
to be in a pedagogical mood when he wrote to his group commanders after the dismal operation:

> The maintenance of tight, unshaken formations in the face of
> the most powerful enemy action is the test of bomber force
> fighting efficiency and morale. It is the Air Force equivalent
> of the old "thin red line" in the Army, or, if you like, of the
> Greek phalanx or of Cromwell's Ironsides, and it is that
> aspect which should be brought home to all captains of
> aircraft. The great and unforgivable crime is for the leader of
> the formation to fly away from his followers. It is his business
> to keep them with him, to collect them and hold them
> together, and you cannot stress the vital importance of this
> too strongly. In fact, it may be necessary to hint that a forma-
> tion leader who makes it difficult or impossible for his forma-
> tion to keep position should be liable to disciplinary action
> on his return. It is absolutely vital that there should be no
> doubt in the mind of any formation leader on this point.
> Similarly, any other member of the formation who breaks
> formation for any reason under his control, is guilty of
> betraying his trust and prejudicing the safety of his comrades.
> We have got to make these things clearly understood . . .

From my interviews with the crews and from the answers I received to questions, I am not at all happy at the existing standard of crew training. It is evident that there is still much to be improved in crew drill. Many crews have not thought out the means by which they are going to deal with the various conditions which arise in active operations, and many of them, I fear, are still ignorant of their equipment. Many captains of aircraft do not seem to be ensuring that their air gunners are being taught the proper use of tracer. Now that we are actually at war we must, I think, take drastic action to ensure that crews do actually understand what is required and do organise themselves efficiently for active operations.[5]

The senior officers lost little time assuring one another that none of them was to blame for the débâcle over Wilhelmshaven. Air Vice-Marshal Baldwin wrote to Ludlow-Hewitt, saying that he knew all along that the raid was going to be "expensive." Baldwin likened the raid to the Charge of the Light Brigade, surprisingly adding, "considering the weather conditions and the opposition the formations met, they got off well."[6]

Tight, disciplined formation flying was the answer, these distinguished officers kept telling each other. They blithely ignored the truth: that the Wellingtons still operated with non-sealing fuel tanks and the gunners had rifle-calibre machine-guns of considerably shorter range and far less destructive power than the 20-mm cannons carried by the enemy fighters. The most meticulous formation flying could do little to compensate for such deficiencies.

Possibly Baldwin was harder on Guthrie than the others because he was Canadian. It wasn't uncommon in the RAF of those days for senior officers to look askance at the brash young men from the senior dominion, all of whom seemed to have a dangerously independent streak and a lack of respect for rank and tradition. These characteristics of Canadians had furrowed air-force brows for years. Eighteen months before war broke out, the president of the

Vancouver branch of the Canadian Legion offered to act as an unofficial recruiting agent for the RAF in British Columbia, where, he declared, hundreds of potential recruits were available. In a minute of April 23, 1938, Wing Commander Hargrave of the Air Ministry commented: "We shall have to watch these Canadian recruits very carefully if we decide to have a recruiting agency over there, because as a rule they are not very keen on discipline."[7]

Guthrie was not the only Canadian serving with 9 Squadron at the time of the Wilhelmshaven operation. John Challes of St. Catharines, Ontario, had joined the RAF in 1936 and was the captain of one of the unit's Wellingtons. He and his crew vanished into the North Sea, shot down by a fighter.

A third Canadian pilot was on 9 Squadron's strength and became one of the few survivors of the disastrous operation. Short, fiery Bill Macrae, from Regina, had joined the RAF in 1936. He rapidly acquired a reputation as one of the squadron "characters," more than a little fond of alcohol in almost any form and obviously a fighter pilot at heart, for he liked to hurl his Wellington about the air as if it were a Spitfire. After the slaughter over Wilhelmshaven, he succeeded in bringing his severely damaged Wellington back to England. He won a DFC. He was killed early in 1940.

The weather precluded most flying in the last days of 1939, although there was the occasional patrol and sometimes a skirmish between opposing fighters. In writing up such combats, newspaper reporters invariably declared "our" aircraft triumphant and "our" airmen infinitely superior to the enemy. The airmen at the front knew better.

PART TWO
1940

Tragedy and Triumph

SHORT SUNDERLAND

*"War involves in its progress such a train of unforeseen
and unsupposed circumstances that no human wisdom
can calculate the end." – Thomas Paine*

I

It was the worst winter in living memory, everyone said. The weather caused more deaths and injuries than the enemy. RAF airmen gulped tots of rum while they serviced their tarpaulin-draped Battles and Hurricanes. Gracie Fields came and sang to them about hanging up their washing on the Siegfried Line, bringing tears to many an eye with "Wish Me Luck as You Wave Me Goodbye" and "Sally of Our Alley." The famous comedian and strummer of the ukulele, George Formby, paid a visit to the air force. A 242 Squadron pilot, Dale Jones of Dinsmore, Saskatchewan, an amateur ukulele player himself, joined Formby on stage for a duet.

Meanwhile, in London, Winston Churchill, the First Lord of the Admiralty, tried in vain to convince Chamberlain that Swedish iron-ore fields should be captured without delay. Chamberlain was reluctant to take any action that might snuff out the last flickering hopes for peace. It still wasn't too late to patch things up and negotiate a settlement. A few words between men of good will would solve everything. There was an almost-palpable feeling that it had to be done now. By the spring it would surely be too late; the fighting would start in earnest, as if ordered by some inevitable, immutable law of nature.

II

In December 1939, Britons had cheered when they heard about the scuttling of the German battleship *Graf Spee* in Montevideo, Uruguay, after the Battle of the River Plate. Britannia still ruled the waves, the newspaper editorials trumpeted. Whereupon Hitler decided that Norwegian territorial waters must be denied to the British; he wanted access to Swedish iron ore and other materials. Besides, Grand Admiral Raeder needed the northern bases for his navy. Hitler's advisers recommended that Denmark be occupied at the same time, since the country provided a "land bridge" to Norway. By early March, 1940, eight German divisions had been assembled for the task.

The British had been preparing an expeditionary force to seize control of Narvik, on Norway's northern coast. Churchill, still First Lord of the Admiralty, wanted to mine Norwegian territorial waters in preparation for the landing in the region. Whereupon Chamberlain informed the War Cabinet that the Labour Party leaders, Clement Attlee and Arthur Greenwood, had taken the view that Britain was not justified "in taking action that would injure a third party."[1] Besides, Chamberlain pointed out, the United States might object to mine-laying in neutral waters. Churchill was furious. Vacillation and invertebracy seemed to pervade the British government at its highest levels.

Later in the month, however, the War Cabinet reviewed the situation and finally agreed that action had to be taken; Germany must be prevented from getting Swedish iron ore. Minefields would be laid in Norwegian waters on April 8, and the Royal Navy (RN) would sail in to keep things under control. Chamberlain crowed over the BBC that Germany "had missed the bus." Wishful thinking. On April 8, while the RN laid its mines in the fjords near Narvik, German forces were already on their way to invade the country. They lost no time in capturing all the available airfields. They understood the importance of controlling the air, something the Allies had still to grasp.

Totally unprepared for the German onslaught, Denmark quickly fell. The Norwegians proved to be a tougher proposition. Resisting stoutly, they sank the German cruiser *Blücher*, causing heavy casualties. The Norwegian royal family escaped and made their way to Britain. From April 18 to 23, British, French, and Free Polish troops, some 12,000 in all, landed near Trondheim. Irresolutely led, they did poorly against the German forces. So did the Allied air units. An RAF fighter squadron, 263, set off for Norway to support the ground forces. The squadron's equipment, obsolete Gloster Gladiator biplanes, were considered the only fighters capable of taking off from the aircraft carrier *Glorious*, which transported them to Norwegian waters.

Ploughing through a snowstorm, 180 miles out at sea, *Glorious* prepared to fly off the eighteen Gladiators. None of the pilots had previously taken off from a carrier. The aircraft carried no radios, and the pilots had only the barest of information about their destination. Two Canadian pilots were among their number: Phillip Purdy, from St. Stephen, New Brunswick, and Alvin Williams, from Toronto. An FAA Skua, with a navigator in the back seat, took off into the mist and low cloud hugging the sea. Remarkably, the Gladiators succeeded in taking to the air without incident. They followed the Skua to a rudimentary base carved out of a frozen lake. Their new home had no refuelling facilities, only stacks of four-gallon fuel cans, all filled to the brim with the wrong grade of fuel. Similarly, the only oil on hand was the thin summer type, which promptly froze in the frigid conditions.

The next day, after breaking the aircrafts' wheels free of ice and getting their frigid Mercury engines to turn over, a patrol shot down a Heinkel 115 seaplane. It was a good start. But the Luftwaffe quickly retaliated. Gaggles of Heinkel 111s came roaring overhead, bombing, strafing, wrecking the Gladiators, and heavily damaging the tiny strip.

Serving with 228 Squadron of RAF Coastal Command at that time were Flying Officer Lawrence Skey of London, Ontario, and Pilot Officer Lawrence Jones of Saskatoon. (Another Canadian in the unit – and another Lawrence – was Lawrence Ellis of Sioux Lookout, Ontario.) Skey and Jones were the two pilots of a Sunderland that on April 15 had flown from Invergordon, Scotland, to Norway. Aboard the big flying boat was Major General Carton de Wiart, who had had the unenviable task of taking command of the British troops sent to capture Trondheim from the Germans.

The journey had been uneventful. Skey and Jones had landed at Namsen Fjord north of Trondheim and begun to taxi the big, four-engined flying boat toward an RN destroyer waiting to take on the general. Before the transfer could be made, four Ju 88s and two He 111s came roaring in over the hills. For nearly ninety minutes the German bombers had attacked the destroyer and the Sunderland, dropping bombs and strafing. Although they wounded one man aboard the flying boat, the Germans failed to prevent de Wiart from boarding the destroyer. The big Sunderland flying boat, engines roaring, had lumbered about the fjord, ponderously avoiding the bombs and bullets. When at last the enemy aircraft made off, Skey and Jones had taken to the air and headed home to Scotland.

Although Skey had no more involvement with the Norwegian débâcle, Jones was soon flying with an RAF pilot, Bob Craven, on supply trips to Norway. On April 27, they took off, taking several mechanics on the first leg of their journey to the airstrip on Lake Lesjaskog, where the outnumbered Gladiators of 263 Squadron still fought the Germans. Although the weather was atrocious, the big flying boat arrived safely at its destination, Molde Fjord. Almost predictably, a gaggle of Ju 88s put in an appearance and did their best to destroy the Sunderland. For Jones, it was an unwelcome repeat of the events of the 15th. Craven, the skipper, kept the Sunderland moving, neatly evading stick after stick of bombs.

Eventually, Craven decided to accompany the air force person-nel ashore to see if the Sunderland was needed further. While he was gone, Jones continued to taxi on the water, presenting a moving target to the predatory Junkers. Inevitably, the Sunderland's engine began to overheat. Jones decided to take off. No sooner had he become airborne than an Me 110 attacked. The Sunderland's rear gunner with his four Brownings and the hatch gunners with their hand-held weapons quickly disposed of the intruder. It crashed near a sizable group of British soldiers, who applauded the Sunderland crew for their efforts.

Jones put the Sunderland back on the water, intending to pick up Craven and get away. But the tender used to transport passengers to and from the shore had been sunk. Not until the early hours of the following morning could Craven board the Sunderland. It got away safely and returned to Scotland. Jones and Craven both received DFCs.[2]

By late April, 263 Squadron had been evacuated from Norway. The squadron's personnel abandoned their landing strip without regret and returned to England by sea, the Canadians Phillip Purdy and Alvin Williams among them. Later, a second base was established at Bardufoss with more Gladiators. It was little better than the first; another poor excuse for a landing ground hacked out of the ice and snow that still blanketed the earth. Although the unit scored a number of successes, losing only two aircraft in combat, the uneven struggle was short-lived. By the latter part of May, 263 Squadron was covering the British Army's evacuation from Bodo. On June 6, the squadron embarked on the carrier *Glorious*. Two days later, she was sunk by the German navy. Most of the aircrew went down with her, including Purdy and Williams. The Royal Navy had done well against the Germans in Norway, but its achievements paled into insignificance beside the disaster of the campaign itself. Far worse was to come.

A sad little story took place at about this time. A Canadian airman, twenty-one-year-old James Lewis, of Morden, Manitoba, had joined the RAF before the war. Although he had a private pilot's licence, he wasn't accepted as aircrew. The recruiting officer advised him to join up as ground crew, with a view to transferring to aircrew later. Lewis did so, only to discover that since the declaration of war, all trades had been frozen. Despairing of becoming a pilot by legitimate methods, he took a Blenheim bomber and flew it solo from Wyton, England, to Norway to demonstrate his ability. He didn't return.

III

In France, the first hesitant signs of spring began to be seen. Pellucid sunshine played on snowbound airfields and tarpaulin-wrapped aircraft. Slowly, almost reluctantly, temperatures inched upward. Soon the snow gave way to floods. Roads became lakes; power lines washed away. The conditions precluded much combat flying, but airmen still died. On March 12, Lloyd Bishop, of Castleton, Ontario, a Hurricane pilot with 73 Squadron based at Rouvres, suffered an oxygen failure and dived to his death two miles from St-Privot la Montaine. Albertan Sergeant George Stiles, an observer in a Blenheim of 107 Squadron, died when his aircraft was shot down during a reconnaissance over Sylt Island, off the west coast of Northern Germany, on March 27. On March 29, Patrick Nettleton of Calgary, a Gladiator pilot, failed to return from a patrol and was later reported killed. Peter Aldous of Victoria was lost while flying an Anson of 269 Squadron.

As the weather improved, it became clear that Hitler would soon strike. Many on the Allied side could hardly wait. The uncertainty was almost over. Hitler had blustered and bamboozled too many millions for far too long. Now the lines were finally drawn. The little moustachio'd corporal was in for the fight of his life.

On the Allied side, hopes were high. The Scandinavian débâcle had simply been a case of poor planning and unfortunate timing. The publicity mills kept grinding out propaganda about the magnificent Maginot Line and the unbeatable Royal Navy, the marvellous air forces of both Britain and France and, of course, the incomparable Tommies and the *poilus* of France, all of whom couldn't wait to get to grips with the Hun. Uncounted millions comforted themselves with the thought that Britain and France had walloped the Germans the last time and so could do it again. The inspiringly named General Edmund Ironside, Chief of the Imperial General Staff, had explained it all to reporters from America. "The German army is a wonderful machine but it lacks commanding officers," he pointed out. None of the present crop of German commanders had risen beyond the rank of captain in the Great War, whereas "Britain and France have many more experienced commanders, colonels and generals galore."[3] One has to wonder how many times he rued that statement.

The Allies would have been less complacent had they known with what audacity and ingenuity the enemy planned to take the war to the west. In the early hours of May 10, the long-anticipated German offensive began. With almost surgical precision, the Germans eliminated several key elements of the elaborate defensive system. They took the supposedly impregnable Belgian fortress of Eben Emael by the simple expedient of bringing in an assault team by gliders and landing on the fortress roof, the one approach that hadn't been considered by the fort's designers. The small force of attackers did the job at the cost of six dead and twenty wounded. More paratroops captured the long bridges at Moerdijk, south of Rotterdam. A flight of twelve Heinkel 59 float biplanes landed on the water in the heart of the city. One hundred and fifty combat engineers and infantry jumped into rubber dinghies and captured the Willems bridge in a matter of minutes. Paratroops took over city streetcars and transported themselves into the centre of the city. Simultaneously, two panzer divisions sliced through the narrow strip of Holland that separates Germany and Belgium, heading for the Dutch town of Maastricht.

The Germans had employed almost their entire force of airborne troops in these operations. It was a calculated gamble, and it paid off handsomely. Less than two hundred of the troops became casualties.

This was Blitzkrieg (lightning war) in action: screaming dive-bombers and fighters strafing at ground level; rapid-fire thrusts by armour; subversive warfare, with the seizing of lines of communications and broadcasting facilities. The combined French–British–Belgian–Dutch forces, with their top-heavy command structure, lacklustre leadership, and generally inferior equipment, found themselves outmanoeuvred from the start.

As the Germans had anticipated, British and French units moved rapidly into Belgium. But the Germans' main thrust came through the supposedly impassable Ardennes, the heavily wooded plateau in southwest Belgium east of the Meuse river. A powerful force of tanks and armoured vehicles smashed their way through to the flat country beyond. Tossing aside conventional strategy, the German forces didn't pause to regroup or wait for additional forces to protect their flanks. With dive-bombers and strafing fighters clearing the way ahead, they thrust into the heart of France, tanks and armoured vehicles suddenly appearing in villages whose occupants thought themselves reassuringly distant from the front.

Most people thought of "the front" as something static, like the miles of trenches from the last war. But there was nothing static about this war. It was all about movement: thundering lines of tanks and armoured vehicles, wailing dive-bombers and terrified refugees clogging roads as they desperately tried to escape from the battle.

According to newspaper stories, British troops were singing jolly marching songs as they moved in to meet the enemy, with grateful Belgians strewing flowers in their path. It was all very heart-warming, but totally irrelevant in the light of the Germans' advance through the Ardennes. The much-vaunted Maginot Line, that concrete-and-steel symbol of France's flabby will, played no part in the equation. The Germans outflanked it. Then they headed for the coast.

At this critical juncture, a new French commander in chief of Allied ground forces took over. The diminutive seventy-three-year-old General Maxime Weygand seems to have been an extraordinary choice for the job of leading the multinational force, for he made no attempt to conceal his dislike and distrust of the British – or, apparently, of any politician, no matter what nationality.

By the time the self-important Weygand had seen for himself how desperate the situation was, there was little he could do to save it. The unthinkable seemed to be coming to pass: France teetered on the brink of defeat. The only positive item of news came from London when it was announced that Winston Churchill had taken over from the ailing and increasingly ineffectual Neville Chamberlain.

On the first day of the invasion, a Canadian Hurricane pilot, Allan Angus of 85 Squadron RAF, flew on patrol over elements of the British Expeditionary Force (BEF) as they advanced into Belgium. Everything looked tranquil below. No sign of the Germans. No flak in sight. Angus kept circling, watching. Then his heart leapt. An aircraft! The twenty-two-year-old from McCreary, Manitoba, quickly identified it as one of the Luftwaffe's speedy Junkers 88 bombers. There it was, just a few hundred yards away, looking as unconcerned as if it were going for a Sunday afternoon flip. Remembering to check for other aircraft in the vicinity, Angus gave chase, diving to intercept the Jerry. The moments became strangely extended. The 88 looked exactly like the photographs and aircraft recognition drawings: black crosses on mottled wings ... prominent "glasshouse" housing the huddled crew ... and, yes, the rear gunner manhandling his machine-gun, turning it in *his* direction!

Angus pressed the button. He saw his tracers smacking into the lean, good-looking bomber, some bouncing off armour plate, some seemingly swallowed by the structure. And he saw return fire from the gunner. Rounds curved through the air, then whipped past his head at furious pace.

Bull's-eye! Smoke, followed by flickers of flame from the Jerry's port engine. Angus kept firing. Moments later the twin-engined bomber turned steeply, then more steeply still, until it fell away out of control. It dived vertically into the ground, leaving a dirty trail of oily smoke. An explosion among the trees marked its final resting place.

Elated, Angus turned for home. But his delight turned to dismay when he discovered that the enemy gunner had scored hits on his Hurricane's Merlin engine. Disconsolate puffs of white emerged from the cowling. Angus shook his head. It was becoming a misty stream. No question: Glycol. In a moment the engine would lose all its coolant. The temperature gauge's needle climbed into the red. The engine was going to blow up or burst into flames or seize up solid. Or all three. Should he abandon the aircraft? Or try to get it onto the ground? There were no other choices. Angus opted for a forced landing, plonking the smoking Hurricane down in a Belgian field. Uninjured, he made his way back to his squadron and was flying again the next day.

It was a time of utter confusion. On the same day that Angus made his forced landing, the RAF strafed a Dutch airfield that had been captured by the Germans. They came across a score of burned-out Ju 52 transports. Spotting one that was still undamaged, they immediately set upon it and soon had it burning merrily. Some time later they discovered that the Dutch had recaptured the field from the Germans and had set fire to the Ju 52s, leaving one in which to escape to England. That was the one the RAF destroyed.[4]

The morning after the invasion, the Belgians asked the British to bomb the bridges on the Albert Canal near Maastricht. In the pleasant, but misty, dawn, 114 Squadron at Conde-Vraux loaded their Blenheims with bombs and prepared for a 6:00 A.M. take-off. It didn't happen. As crews warmed up their engines, a force of Dornier bombers streaked in at treetop level: four units of Lieutenant-Colonel Paul Weitkus's II/KG2. Waiting in serried ranks for the signal to take off, the Blenheims presented textbook targets for the Dorniers' 200-kilogram bombs. In a matter of minutes, the squadron had been wiped out. One of the Dorniers carried a newsreel photographer. His footage showed the lines of Blenheims blazing away, emitting great billowing clouds of black smoke.

Some elements of the French air force seemed strangely disinterested in what was happening. Peter Brothers, an RAF fighter pilot, landed at a French airfield to refuel. While waiting for the job to be done, he watched appreciatively as a French fighter performed aerobatics overhead. A German bomber appeared. The Frenchman made no attempt to intercept. When Brothers pointed this out to a French officer, he was told: "Oh, today he is authorized for aerobatics, not combat."[5]

The RAF were quick to criticize their French allies – just as British troops on the beaches of Dunkirk would criticize British fighter pilots. The fact that friendly aircraft weren't overhead, shooting at the enemy, didn't necessarily mean that they were all inactive. There is plenty of evidence of fierce and heroic fighting by French pilots. Unfortunately, despite the overheated prewar propaganda, the French air force possessed only a few hundred Morane-Saulnier MS 406 fighters.* The best French fighters, the Dewoitine D.520s, saw virtually no service in the battle. Few reached the front in time to take part.

Among the many unpleasant surprises in store for the Allied air forces were the devastatingly efficient German flak batteries gathered around every target. With their 20-mm and 37-mm light flak and 88-mm heavy flak guns, they filled the sky with almost solid curtains of fire into which hapless Allied formations flew. German fighters, too, took a heavy toll of Allied aircraft. The hard-pressed Hurricane squadrons of the Air Component tried to provide escorts for the bombers, but the flak batteries and the Messerschmitts were too numerous and too efficient. The Luftwaffe had taken complete control of the air above the battlefield. RAF casualties mounted at an alarming rate. Furthermore, as if the harried aircrews didn't have

---

*   After the war, French General L. M. Chassin said that 600 French fighters and 100 bombers had faced the Luftwaffe in May 1940. He claimed that 919 German aircraft had been shot down for the loss of some 400 French aircraft.[6]

enough problems, they seldom knew precisely where many of their targets were located. Harried squadron commanders provided their pilots with lists of roads on which their targets *might* be found. A Fairey Battle squadron, No. 12, was ordered to attack two bridges over the Albert Canal, believed to be approximately one mile west of Wilre. The order added helpfully that for more information on the exact location of the target the Michelin Guide for Belgium should be consulted.7

On May 12, two days after the invasion started, the Canadian Allan Angus shot down two more enemy aircraft. A few days later, he had another pair to his credit. He had destroyed five enemy aircraft, becoming the first Canadian ace of World War II. The accomplishment had taken him precisely one week.

If one believed the papers, everything was going splendidly in France. "British gain upper hand," chortled the headlines, adding that over four hundred enemy aircraft had already been destroyed, a loss rate that would surely drive German airmen from the skies of France in a matter of days.8 The Germans were losing aircraft four times faster than the Allies, according to one totally fallacious report. "Heinie's nose bloody each time in clashes with British Tommies," crowed the papers at home. "The situation of the Allies is improving faster and better than anyone had anticipated," the story continued with specious confidence and chaotic syntax.9

About a quarter of Britain's combat aircraft was based in France. Complicating an already top-heavy administrative structure, they were spread among two forces: the Advanced Air Striking Force (AASF: eight squadrons of the hopeless Battles, two squadrons of Blenheims, and three of Hurricanes) and the Air Component of the BEF (four squadrons of Blenheims, five of Lysanders, and four of Hurricanes).

At dawn on May 12, nine 139 Squadron Blenheims took off to attack enemy troops. Seven were shot down in a matter of minutes by enemy fighters. Five Battles from 12 Squadron attempted to bomb bridges at Vreonhoven and Veldwezelt, near Maastricht, Belgium. Four went down at once; the fifth had to make a forced landing on the way back to base. The plan had been for Hurricanes from 1 Squadron to escort the Battles to and from the target area, but German fighters prevented the two groups of aircraft joining up. The Battles went on anyway, ploughing into curtains of flak from the devastatingly efficient batteries below. How could anyone survive such almost-solid fusillades? How long before all the Allied aircraft had become twisted, blackened piles of scrap metal?

A young Canadian wireless operator/air gunner, Gordon Patterson, from Woodrow, Saskatchewan, was flying that day in Battle P5241 of 12 Squadron. British Pilot Officer T. D. H. Davey was his skipper. Renowned in his unit as a deadly shot, Patterson operated a single Vickers gas-operated machine-gun with ring and bead sight, a ludicrously inadequate weapon with which to face the 20-mm cannons of the Messerschmitts:

> Our pans held 100 rounds each, and if the pans – which were spring loaded – were wound to 4 ½ turns, they gave the gun a speed [rate of fire] of about 750 rpm, but we used to wind them up to six turns and get them nearly a 1,000 rpm. Pans were loaded so the first ten shots were tracer for warning purposes in case it was one of our own planes. Thereafter we used a mixture of tracer, ball, armour piercing, and incendiary bullets.[10]

As Davey commenced his dive, three enemy fighters attacked. Displaying remarkable skill and gallantry, Patterson took on all three enemy aircraft and may have shot down one, and possibly two, with damage to a third before his Battle plummeted, riddled and burning. Davey ordered the crew to bale out. All three airmen survived, although Patterson was injured when he hit the Battle's tail and smashed his right forearm when he jumped. On landing, he broke his left foot. Fortuitously, he came down in a hospital courtyard in Liège, Belgium. Awarded the DFM (Distinguished Flying Medal), the first of the war for a Canadian airman, Patterson spent the next five years as a prisoner.

The following day, May 13, the RAF's first Victoria Crosses were won – posthumously – by Flying Officer Donald Garland and his observer, Sergeant Tom Gray, for their gallant attack on a bridge across the Albert Canal. (Inexplicably, their air gunner, Leading Aircraftman L. R. Reynolds, received no recognition.) In the furious dogfighting, RAF fighter pilots claimed eleven of the enemy, but lost several of their number. Hilly Brown, the Manitoban who had been the first Canadian pilot to go to France in World War II, limped back to base after taking a number of hits from enemy cannon shells. Although his Hurricane was in bad shape, the irrepressible Brown was uninjured. Even at that early stage of the war, fellow airmen regarded him as a brilliant fighter pilot, one of the RAF's best. Now a flight lieutenant and second in command of his squadron, he seemed totally unconcerned by the daunting odds that he and his comrades faced daily. He hurled himself into battle like "an enraged hornet, eager to open fire on any terms and from just about any position."[11]

Reports on the ground battles became increasingly confused. Bases moved repeatedly. Pilots often took off without knowing where they would be landing. Numbing fatigue was as dangerous an enemy as the Germans.

The devastating losses continued. Ten of 24 Blenheims sent to attack the bridges over the Meuse were lost. Gordon Gratton, of Sault Ste. Marie, Ontario, a Blenheim pilot with 110 Squadron, was killed during the futile attacks on the Maastricht bridges. The operation cost eight of the eleven Blenheims dispatched. Fifteen Battles attacked targets near Bouillon; six went down to the guns of enemy fighters. By the evening of May 12, the AASF bomber force had been reduced to a mere 72 aircraft, having lost almost three-quarters of its strength in two catastrophic days. A young Canadian pilot, Flying Officer James Alex Campbell, of Nelson, British Columbia, was killed when his Hurricane went down in flames near Maastricht. Campbell, a member of 87 Squadron RAF, had four victories to his credit. On the same day, another Canadian Hurricane pilot, Raymond Lewis, of Fort Qu'Appelle, Saskatchewan, was shot down into the Channel. Flying Officer Lewis survived this incident only to lose his life in action a few months later. He had four victories to his credit. Flying Officer Albert Ball, of Montreal, survived the crash of his Hurricane after a dogfight but died a few days later of his injuries. Other Canadians who died that day were an air gunner, Vancouver's Charles Child, lost when his 139 Squadron Blenheim disappeared without trace, and George Morgan-Dean, who had journeyed from Kaleden, British Columbia, to join the RAF, and who died in the crash of his 103 Squadron Battle, L5512, near Sedan.

On May 13, the Germans crossed the Meuse. Nothing, it seemed, could stop them.

Early on the 14th, the French air force mounted an attack on the Germans' Sedan bridgehead, some 120 miles northeast of Paris. The formation met such ferocious opposition from flak and fighters that it scattered and withdrew, participating in no more actions that day. In the late afternoon, more than seventy RAF bombers – virtually the entire remaining AASF bomber force – were sent in to attack. The Germans shot down forty. Squadron commanders wondered numbly how long their units would continue to exist. No one in their worst nightmares had imagined such ghastly losses. And even if some prescient soul had done so, who would have believed him? At this rate, the RAF in France would soon cease to exist.

The survivors retreated to the Troyes area.

The Germans were astounded. They had expected good results from their Blitzkrieg tactics, but *this*? The more cautious souls in the German camp wondered whether their armies were falling into a monstrous trap. Few on the Allied side entertained such thoughts. The confusion and panic were too real, too frightening.

For home consumption, any news about aerial activities was meticulously expurgated. Photographs in the press depicted beaming, confident airmen, thumbs resolutely raised. But the smiles were only for the cameras. Many airmen recall seeing their comrades, nerves in tatters, vomiting before clambering into their aircraft for yet more hopeless operations. On May 17, No. 82 Squadron sent twelve Blenheims to attack an armoured column near Gembloux, Belgium. One came back, so badly damaged that it had to be scrapped. Among the fatalities was twenty-year-old Pilot Officer James Grierson of Toronto. His squadron had ceased to exist.

The same horrific day saw the death of that talented Canadian Allan Angus, whose Hurricane went down in flames near Dunkirk. Just seven days earlier he had achieved every fighter pilot's ambition by becoming an ace. Now he was dead.

In England, the pilots of 242 Squadron waited. They had been expecting to fly to France for several days. Orders were issued. Orders were cancelled. The pilots continued to wait.

The unit had been formed in October 1939, its ranks filled with Canadians in the RAF. The commanding officer, Squadron Leader Fowler Morgan Gobeil, was a member of the RCAF. Political considerations had shaped the unit from the start. The idea of having a Canadian fighter squadron had emerged during the convoluted discussions that led to the creation of the British Commonwealth Air Training Plan. Mackenzie King wanted Canadian airmen to serve in Canadian units, not fill the ranks of RAF squadrons. Unfortunately, no matter how vociferously King demanded, the country didn't have the modern aircraft or trained personnel to equip such units. The British, eager to impress both allies and enemies with the solidarity of the Commonwealth, undertook to form a fighter squadron manned by Canadian pilots in the RAF. But it was not until December that the unit received operational aircraft – Blenheims and Battles at first, then Hurricanes. Now, in May 1940, 242 finally saw action, although not initially as a unit. Two groups of its pilots went to France to bolster 607 and 615 squadrons, which had suffered severe losses in the furious fighting. It was a sensible move; the Canadian fliers desperately needed operational experience. In the course of the first patrol flown by the 607 Squadron contingent, four Hurricanes went down. One Canadian pilot was killed: John Lewis Sullivan, from Smiths Falls, Ontario. He was the first 242 Squadron member to die in action.

Incredibly, the French ended up the calamitous Blitzkrieg with more aircraft than they possessed at the beginning. Hundreds of factory-fresh fighters sat on French airfields, lacking guns. The aircraft industry's failures – and the antediluvian thinking of the French High Command – negated every effort by French aircrew, no matter how valiant. General François d'Astier de la Vigerie, head of the French air force at the front, later complained that he telephoned the army commanders daily, asking what missions were required. Invariably, he claimed, the offers of air support were turned down.

During this period, the RAF's strategic bombing campaign had its beginnings. Raids on Hamburg, Bremen, and Cologne took place, although they seemed to have little or no effect on the catastrophe taking place in France. The RAF's losses there were reaching critical proportions. Churchill sent additional squadrons from England, but it was far too little and far too late.

Canadians continued to die: Robert Weatherill, twenty-four, from Vernon, British Columbia, an ace with five victories to his credit; Henry Anderson, twenty, from Winnipeg, Manitoba, a Hurricane pilot with 253 Squadron; Ken Lucas, nineteen, from St. Thomas, Ontario, a Hurricane pilot with 145 Squadron. Two of the slow and suicidally vulnerable Lysander army cooperation aircraft of the BEF's Air Component were lost on May 19. One carried a 4 Squadron air gunner, thirty-eight-year-old Clarence Butterill of Toronto, to his death. Another air gunner from Canada, Matthew Whelan of Saskatoon, was killed when his 88 Squadron Battle was shot down. The same day, a twenty-two-year-old fighter pilot, Garfield Madore, also of Saskatoon, died in the crash of his Hurricane. He had been one of the original members of 242 Squadron.

Roland Dibnah of Winnipeg had joined 1 Squadron just before the battle began; he shared a 109 with Hilly Brown, after which he destroyed a Dornier 17. On May 26, he was hit. As he began to lose blood and the earth raced up to meet him, he experienced a strange euphoria. A moment later came the shuddering shock as his Hurricane hit the ground, and an overwhelming feeling of relief overcame him. At last, he recounted in his memoirs, after weeks of frenetic activity, he could sleep as long as he wanted. He heard the hissing and crackling of the engine, but he hadn't the strength to pull himself out of the cockpit.

Someone must have done so, however, for the next thing he remembered was a French doctor urging him to "breeze deep" as an oxygen mask was pressed over his nose and mouth. Dibnah was flown back to Britain and recuperated at a hospital near Hatfield, near London, site of the de Havilland plant. If the Germans invaded, Dibnah was told, he would be expected to go to the airfield and fly a Tiger Moth in action. Twenty of the diminutive trainers had been fitted with bomb racks. Bombs were released by pulling a string in the cockpit.

IV

By May 26, the BEF had fallen back on a pocket only little more than a hundred miles in circumference around the town of Dunkirk, on France's northern coast. The extraordinary success of the German advance had Hitler worried. Like every other German veteran of the Great War, he remembered all too vividly the brilliant attack of

March 1918, sometimes known as the Kaiser's Battle, that had come so heartbreakingly close to winning victory for Germany. The German advance had been too rapid for its own good. Badly extended, the Germans became increasingly vulnerable to attacks on the flank. In a few months, in a shattering, unbelievable reversal of fortunes, the war had been lost. Germans still found it hard to accept. The same thing happening in 1940 was the stuff of Hitler's nightmares. He flabbergasted his generals by ordering the advance on Dunkirk halted until forces could be brought up to protect the Panzer corridor to the coast. For two days the armour waited for orders – and gave the British and French precious time to begin the all-important evacuation from Dunkirk.

The British government had already ordered the Admiralty to draw up plans for the evacuation of the BEF from France. The five regular divisions, five territorial divisions, and three so-called "labour" divisions of semi-trained recruits, would become the nucleus of the force that would eventually meet the enemy again. Had the German advance continued, had the British army been destroyed, it is hard indeed to predict the course history might have taken.

The Admiralty calculated that, with luck, as many as 100,000 British and French troops might be rescued from France. In fact, some 338,000 men (including 112,000 French and Belgians) were plucked from the deadly beaches – and evacuations from other ports raised the total to well over half a million. By any standards, it was an extraordinary accomplishment, intensely satisfying to the British, perhaps the supreme example of "muddling through" in their history. Making the very best of a humiliating defeat, London's *Daily Mirror* ringingly proclaimed it "the greatest feat of arms in history."

While most of the credit went, quite properly, to the fleet of vessels of all shapes and sizes that braved the fury of the Luftwaffe to reach the beaches, none of it would have been possible without the air force. The Luftwaffe was doing everything in its power to halt the evacuation, and the British army and the RN demanded nonstop air cover over the beaches. Given the distances and the numbers of squadrons available, it was an impossible request. The troops on the beaches seldom saw any RAF aircraft in action. Bitterly they told each other that the "Brylcreem Boys" had let them down. They hadn't. The RAF fighters were doing battle out of sight of the beleaguered troops, trying to keep the Luftwaffe away from the beaches. The RAF fighters were also experiencing the same problem that a few months later would beset their Luftwaffe opponents: limited range. Once they had flown across the Channel, the Spitfires and Hurricanes could operate for only a few minutes at full throttle before they had to return to Britain to refuel.

During the evacuation, the notable New Zealander Al Deere was shot down during an air battle inland. He made his way to the beaches by hitching a ride and stealing a bicycle. But when he attempted to board a British destroyer, an army major stopped him. Deere declared himself to be an RAF officer and said he was trying to get back to his squadron. The major refused to let him on board, saying that, for all the good they were doing, the air force might as well stay on the ground.

Evading the intransigent major, Deere managed to get on the destroyer. He made his way to the wardroom, to be greeted by stony silence from a throng of army officers.

"Why so friendly?" asked Deere. "What have the RAF done?"

"That's just it," said one of the "brown jobs." "What have they done?"[12]

One of Canada's greatest contributions to victory in the air began to gain his reputation during the evacuation from Dunkirk. Stocky, powerfully built, blunt of manner and impatient with small talk, Stan Turner of Toronto hardly fitted the popular image of the dashing fighter pilot. With his pipe seemingly cemented in his mouth, he regarded the world in the stolid manner of a man who is ready for anything or anyone that fate might send his way. He had seen the chaos of the Battle of France. In his methodical way he had used the experience to hone his skills as a fighter pilot, becoming increasingly self-confident. He was a natural, an excellent shot, who combined determination with intelligence. One of the original members of the Canadian 242 Squadron, he had been temporarily posted to 615 Squadron, then based in France. Involved in a succession of patrols over the retreating Allied armies, Turner hadn't scored any victories over the Luftwaffe, but he had begun to handle his plane instinctively, becoming one with his aircraft.

Now back in England with 242 Squadron, Turner flew daily patrols over Dunkirk, finding his way there by pointing his nose at the huge columns of smoke rising high above the place. (Some pilots claimed it wasn't necessary to look for the smoke; all they had to do was follow the stink of burning oil.)

Göring, the overweening chief of the Luftwaffe, had assured Hitler that he would put a stop to the evacuation. The German airmen did everything in their power to prove him right. The battles lasted over a week. They became Stan Turner's finishing school. All the lessons suddenly paid off. On May 25, he shot down two Messerschmitt 109s, and probably a third. On the 28th, he dispatched a 109, with a "probable" and one "damaged" on the 29th. Two days later his gunfire sent a 109 spinning into the sea off Dunkirk. The first day of June saw Turner shooting down yet another 109 and claiming a probable.

Another Canadian pilot who had his first successes in the Dunkirk operations was Willie McKnight of Edmonton. A good-looking young man, short of stature but imbued with the nervous energy and bubbling confidence of all good fighter pilots, he was destined to become one of the stars of the squadron. Like the majority of fighter aces, he possessed remarkably sharp eyesight. He had joined the RAF early in 1939 and had completed most of his pilot training when the Germans invaded Poland. In November, he became a member of 242 Squadron and a close friend of Stan Turner's. During the final chaotic days of the evacuation from Dunkirk, his victory tally rose in spectacular fashion. Near Ostend on May 28, he shot down a Messerschmitt 109. Two days later, he scored an impressive hat trick, shooting down two 109s and a Dornier 17. On the 31st, McKnight found himself surrounded by about twenty-five Messerschmitt 110s. The twin-engined fighters got in each other's way as they tried to destroy his solitary Hurricane. Two collided and went tumbling away, shedding bits of themselves as they plummeted, streaming fire. McKnight slipped away unscathed.

On June 1, he added two dive-bombers to his list of victories. The famous crank-winged Ju 87, the very symbol of Hitler's Blitzkrieg, had proved itself a devastating weapon against the Poles and in the French campaign. Nevertheless, it was easy meat for the RAF's best fighters, and severe casualties would soon force its withdrawal from combat in the West. McKnight used up all his ammunition shooting down the two Ju 87s, but he continued to make feint attacks. His aggressive tactics appeared to unnerve the Luftwaffe pilots; they soon broke off and headed for home.

Although the German raiders succeeded in sinking four destroyers and ten other vessels that day, at the same time an amazing total of 64,400 Allied troops got away from the deadly beaches.

Among the Canadian airmen who died over Dunkirk was a comparative veteran, thirty-five-year-old Capel Adye, of Fort William, Ontario, who had joined the RAF in the late 1920s. A flight lieutenant with 17 Squadron, he died in the wreckage of his Hurricane.

Albertan Pilot Officer Horace Scott, an air gunner with 264 Squadron, was shot down in one of the new Defiant two-seat fighters. The Defiant was a dismally unsuccessful attempt to combine the manoeuvrability of a single-engined fighter with the hitting power of a four-gun turret. Only a few days after the Blitzkrieg began, the clumsy Defiant had been introduced to the general public as a brilliant innovation: "New Aerial Weapon Employed by Britain in Fighter Planes," declared the press, the "weapon" being a bulky hydraulic gun turret loaded onto a slender airframe immediately behind the pilot's cockpit.[13] The Defiant proved to be totally inadequate in dogfights and not much better when it was later employed as a night-fighter. It lacked forward-firing guns and became unstable when the turret was swung to the full-beam position. The aircraft was "thoroughly bad," according to Air Chief Marshal Sir Basil Embry. The Defiants' few successes came when German fighter pilots mistook them for Hurricanes and attacked them from the rear, only to find themselves looking down the barrels of four Brownings.

Mistakes in aircraft identification would cost lives throughout the war. Over Dunkirk, Fleet Air Arm Skua two-seat fighters patrolled the beach area. On May 27, a flight of Spitfires attacked the unfamiliar Skuas, shooting down two and seriously damaging a third. Other Canadian casualties included Pilot Officer John Shepherd of Victoria, British Columbia, a member of 1 Squadron, Hilly Brown's unit, and Dale Jones of 242 Squadron, who had strummed the ukulele with George Formby a few months before. Jones had joined the RAF in February 1939. His last letters home to his family in Dinsmore, Saskatchewan, talked of his being "extremely busy and quite tired." When Jones was shot down into the Channel, his mother convinced herself that her son, a powerful swimmer, would be able to swim to safety. But after six months, the family received word from the American Red Cross that Jones had been buried in the Oostdunkerke Cemetery, near Ostend.

Jack Hatfield of Yarmouth, Nova Scotia, a twenty-year-old pilot of a 264 Squadron Defiant, was killed when his aircraft was shot down on May 25. George Ayre of St. John's, Newfoundland, flying a Spitfire with 609 Squadron, died attempting to land in England after being wounded over Dunkirk. Two died ironic deaths, having just escaped the hell of the Dunkirk beaches. LAC Harold Smith, of Westmount, Quebec, and Sergeant George Hills, of Port Arthur, Ontario, both ground crewmen, scrambled aboard the 16,000-ton liner *Lancastria*. Four bombs from Stukas sank the ship and some three thousand went down with her, including Smith and Hills.

The ferocious air battles over Dunkirk cost 229 RAF fighters. From the beginning of the invasion on May 10, the RAF had lost an alarming total of close to a thousand aircraft of various types, about half of them the precious fighters needed to protect England from the air assaults that everyone knew must come if Hitler was to invade the British Isles.

V

After Dunkirk, 242 Squadron went back into France with 17 Squadron, landing at Le Mans, southwest of Paris. The battle still raged, although the majority of French citizens seemed to feel that it was all over. Not all the British forces had been evacuated at Dunkirk; two divisions and various smaller units remained in France. Stan Turner recalled: "The battle by then was so confused, it was often difficult to tell friend from foe."[14]

Soon after their arrival in France, Turner and his wingman had to make a forced landing due to lack of fuel. They managed to put the Hurricanes down in a wheat field. But when the two Canadian pilots climbed out of their cockpits, an angry rabble of French farm workers sprang from the hedges and rushed across the field, wielding lethal-looking scythes and clubs. Only after frantic exhortations and gesticulations were the pilots able to convince the Frenchmen that they were RAF, not Germans. Not that being an RAF airman was any guarantee of a warm welcome by the French. Much of the population resented the continued presence of the British "warmongers," who, it was felt, wanted the war to continue.

Turner soon added to his tally of victories. On June 9, he destroyed two more 109s. On that occasion, 242 Squadron-mate Donald MacQueen, of Drumheller, Alberta, who had three enemy aircraft to his credit, was attacked by two 109s coming from different directions. Turner tried to get to MacQueen in time to assist him, but the twenty-year-old Albertan went down in flames. Turner shot down both of MacQueen's assailants. He was rapidly becoming an expert at his trade.

On June 14, the Germans entered Paris. The swastika broke over the Arc de Triomphe and General von Koch-Erpach's 8th Infantry Division marched along the Champs Élysées, watched by silent Parisians. Elsewhere in France, the fight continued, although it was clear that the end could not be far off. 242 Squadron flew to Nantes in company with two other units. The squadron had done well in the battle, accounting for about thirty enemy aircraft, but it had suffered serious losses: seven pilots killed, two wounded, one grounded with a nervous breakdown. And no one seemed to know where the CO was. "Most of the patrols were now being led by myself or Willie McKnight, who had just won a DFC," Stan Turner recalled.[15] The ground crews had already returned to England; the pilots had to refuel and arm their own aircraft and look after minor servicing chores. At night they slept under their Hurricanes' wings, taking turns at standing guard.

As Turner would recall, the RAF men soon found how unpopular they had become among their former allies:

One night we went into Nantes, and soon wished we hadn't. As we came out of a bar, we were sniped at – probably by another Fifth Columnist. We beat it back to the airfield and found the canteen tent abandoned. It was loaded with liquor, so we had a party. Willie McKnight, I remember, refused to drink from a glass. Whenever he needed a drink, he reached for a bottle, smashed the neck, and took it straight.

The day France surrendered [June 25], French soldiers set up machine-guns along our runway. "All aircraft are grounded," an officer told us. "There's to be no more fighting from French soil." We saw red. A brawl was threatening when I felt a tap on my shoulder. Behind me was a British army officer, who had come out of the blue. "Go ahead and take off," he said. "I'll look after these chaps." He pointed to his platoon which had set up a machine-gun covering the French weapons. The French officer shrugged and left.

Time was running out. The Germans were over the Loire River and heading toward us. On June 18 we flew a last patrol over Brest and made a couple of sorties inland.

Later that day, 242 Squadron was ordered to evacuate. The pilots had to destroy several abandoned Hurricanes, after which they sadly demolished the canteen, a necessity rued by Turner:

All that booze – it was heartbreaking. We armed and fuelled our aircraft and climbed in. We were a wild-looking bunch, unshaven, scruffily dressed, exhausted, grimed with dirt and smoke. We were also in a pretty Bolshie mood. After weeks of fighting we were all keyed up. Now that the whole shebang was over, there was a tremendous let-down feeling. As we headed for England we felt not so much relief as anger. We wanted to hit something, and there was nothing to hit. The skies were empty – not a German in sight – and the ground below looked deserted too. It was all very sunny and peaceful, and quite unreal. As if the war didn't exist. But we knew the real war had only just begun.[16]

Southwest of Paris, a burly Canadian fighter pilot squeezed his ample frame into the cockpit of a Tiger Moth trainer. He hadn't flown one of these little crates since his training days, and he took a minute to check its controls. While he was so engaged, an "erk" (aircraftman) ran up to the aircraft and asked if he could come along. Cowboy Blatchford nodded. "Hop in," he said. Between them, the two airmen got the Tiger started. Blatchford glanced at the windsock and opened the throttle. There was no time to waste. The

Germans were reported to be only a few miles away, and the rest of Blatchford's unit had already departed, leaving great columns of oily smoke rising from the burning aircraft and supplies. The Tiger Moth scurried across the field and rose uncertainly into the air.

Blatchford headed west, landing at Poitiers, a flight of about an hour. "We had no kit, no shaving gear, no food, no anything," he later recalled. The two airmen spent an uneasy night in a service station, with reports of the imminent arrival of Germans regularly interrupting their sleep. They spent the second night with some French soldiers in an abandoned house. "The third day," Blatchford said, "along came another 'evacuee Moth' piloted by a New Zealander ... so we joined forces and flew to a place called Fauntney le Compte. From there we planned to take off for the Channel Islands on the way home. We each lashed a twenty-gallon spare drum of petrol in our Moth and set off."

The tiny trainer reached Nantes, in western France, a few miles from St. Nazaire. The airmen had heard reports that the town had been occupied, but Blatchford saw Hurricanes circling the airfield. He landed. "There we found an amazing accumulation of damaged and half-serviceable aircraft of all makes and types," Blatchford later recounted. "I managed to swap my Moth for a Fairey Battle bomber."[17]

He had never flown a Battle, but Blatchford seldom let minor technicalities deter him. He succeeded in taking off and landed at Heston, near London.

VI

An almost unnerving calm settled upon the scene after Dunkirk. France had surrendered. Good riddance, many Britons told one another – including King George VI, who should have known better. "Personally I feel happier now that we have no allies to be polite to and to pamper," he wrote his mother, Queen Mary.[18] The British were of the opinion that the French had been a liability, unreliable and unhelpful. Interestingly, the French had much the same opinion of the British; the evacuation from Dunkirk had left a major part of the French army in the lurch. Blithely indifferent to such details, the British somehow convinced themselves that they were better off now that the French were out of it; the country could concentrate on fighting the war without having those irritating French distracting everyone.

The air force had been cruelly battered, as historian John Terraine points out:

> Fighter Command, by the end of the Battle of France, was in a seriously weakened condition in relation to what Dowding [AOC Fighter Command, 1936 to 1940] never ceased to consider its prime purpose – the defence of Britain against the "knock-out blow." Unreal for most of the time that it haunted British imaginations, that threat was real enough now, and against all the ill consequences of the knock-out blow theory in the prewar years one has to set in balance the fact that, thanks to it, detailed preparations to deal with the contingency of 1940 had been in hand since 1937. What had not been foreseen was a heavy battle over the Continent in the course of which every squadron in Fighter Command except three in Scotland would be engaged (12 of them twice), and suffer more or less heavy losses.[19]

In July, Hitler made his so-called peace offer during a speech in the Reichstag. Later, copies of the Führer's words were dropped from German aircraft, only to be auctioned off in Britain, the proceeds going to the war effort.

It was as well that so few citizens realized just how desperate the situation was. The British army had lost most of its armour and artillery in France; in fact, at that time, General Andrew McNaughton's First Canadian Division was probably the best-equipped division in England. In all, about two hundred tanks were available to meet the invaders, few of them a match for the powerful German Panzers, which had battered their way through France. Rumours quickly filled the information vacuum. Tens of thousands of paratroops disguised as nuns would soon be landing in Britain. Hundreds of English-speaking Germans had sneaked aboard the ships at Dunkirk in British army uniforms and were now awaiting the right moment to rise up, like modern-day Trojans. The Jerries had already tried to invade; their bodies were lying on the beaches at Brighton and Bexhill-on-Sea, heaven knows how many of them, all charred beyond recognition because the seas had been set alight. Everyone knew someone who knew someone else who had seen them with his or her own eyes.

VII

The remnants of 242 Squadron assembled at Coltishall, near Norwich. They were a demoralized and unkempt group, frustrated at having been ejected from France, and angry at the authorities for their apparent lack of interest. They had a new CO. And, according to rumours from the Orderly Room, he was an unusual bod: regular RAF, but minus his undercart. He had lost his legs in a crash before the war, the know-it-alls declared, but in spite of that, he had somehow managed to wangle his way back into the force. It was said he had done well over Dunkirk, but the members of 242 weren't impressed. After what they had been through, it seemed sourly appropriate that they should get a lame-duck CO.

When Douglas Robert Steuart Bader came stumping, stiff-legged, into A Flight's hut accompanied by Peter Macdonald, his new adjutant, he got a frosty reception. His Canadian pilots were slumped in easy chairs or sprawled full length on bunk beds. None of them stood up. It was the beginning of a confrontation that has become part of air force lore.

In crisp, patrician tones, Bader demanded to know who was in charge. The pilots looked at one another and shrugged. No one seemed to know, or care. Eventually, a firm-jawed young man with a powerful frame unwound himself from a bunk. Unhurriedly, he said he guessed he was the senior pilot. Bader noticed that on the man's sleeve was the single ring of a flying officer.

"What's your name?"

"Turner . . ." the young pilot paused, "sir."

Bader informed Turner and the others that they were a disgrace to their uniforms and their service and that he intended to knock them into shape. What did they think of that?

"Horseshit," said Turner. Another pause. "Sir."

With that, Turner turned the tables. Bader found himself on the defensive. He had the sense to realize that these untidy young pilots had had the stuffing knocked out of them in France. They had been ordered here and there, enduring one catastrophe after another. They were beyond caring. They needed a large injection of pride, in themselves, their unit – and their commanding officer. Bader was just the man for the job.

He promptly turned and went striding, in his peculiar lopsided way, out to the flight line. He summoned a fitter, heaved himself into a Hurricane, took off, and gave the squadron a half-hour air display of remarkable skill and verve. The fact that he had never before flown a Hurricane mattered not a whit. Whatever else Bader lacked, it was never self-confidence. A Hurricane was just another airplane; therefore, he could fly it superbly. After a flawless demonstration of his prowess, he landed, taxied up to the dispersal, pulled himself out of the cockpit, and slid off the wing to the ground – an everyday job for most pilots, but no easy matter for a man with two artificial legs. Bader didn't even glance at his pilots, now clustered around the flight-hut door. He knew they had watched it all. The immaculate rolls, spins, and stall turns were far more eloquent than anything he could say. So he said nothing. He stomped across the tarmac, clambered into his car, and drove off.

His Canadians were impressed. This guy could *fly*, legs or no legs. At that moment a warm and mutually beneficial relationship was born. As far as the Canadians were concerned, Bader tended to care a little too much about dress regulations (a perennial problem with Brit regulars, they told themselves) and formation flying. Yet it didn't seem to matter, and neither did the fact that Bader was a teetotaller. With his overwhelming personality, his boundless energy, and his keen personal interest in every airman on the unit, he quickly forged an excellent team. The Canadians no longer cared that their CO had no legs; in fact, they delighted in the fact. He was different; *they* were different.

At about this time, No. 1 Squadron was re-forming at Northolt, near London. Hilly Brown wrote to his sister, telling her that he was "darned annoyed about the French packing up."[20] He had been recommended for the Croix de Guerre; now he would never get it. *Bad show.* The ebullient Brown had already acquired an assortment of Briticisms since joining the RAF. His letters were spiced with frequent "jolly goods" and "wizard prangs." He seemed to be having the time of his life. When Roly Dibnah returned to the squadron, Brown called him "Gimpy" because he walked with a limp after his crash. Dibnah soon had his revenge.

VIII

On the afternoon of Wednesday, July 10, a cluster of German bombers and fighters, more than a hundred in all, attacked a convoy of coasters steaming west from Dover to Dungeness. It was the opening act in one of history's most famous battles. German strategy was straightforward. The RAF's fighter force had to be destroyed before the invasion of Britain could take place. Therefore, attack targets that the RAF had no choice but to defend. Draw them into battle. Shoot them down.

For his part, Hitler hoped the mere threat of invasion would be enough to bring the British to their senses, and so to the conference table; he had no wish to embark on such a risky venture as an invasion of Britain. He wanted to settle the situation in the west before embarking on the march east, which now occupied his thoughts. Besides, as he repeatedly declared, he had never wanted to fight the British; he saw the British empire as a sort of policeman to the world, a curb on the ambitions of the United States and Japan.

When the Luftwaffe came across the Channel in force that bright July day, the British were ready for them. Top-secret radio-location equipment (later known as radar) had spotted the units assembling over the Pas de Calais. A sizable dogfight ensued. Fighter Command claimed eight victories and admitted to one loss. A 242 Squadron pilot, John Latta of Victoria, British Columbia, shared in the destruction of a Heinkel 111, what most historians regard as the first British "kill" in the Battle of Britain.

From then on, the British (and Canadian) public believed the battle to be a totally one-sided victory over the Luftwaffe. Wildly inflated claims of victories appeared in newspapers, and even the BBC radio announcers, usually so icily correct, couldn't squelch the occasional spark of excitement entering their voices. The hour by hour tally of enemy aircraft was updated on newsvendors' spreadsheets like the prewar cricket scores: "18 for 1." No one questioned the numbers. To do so would have been tantamount to treason. Anything that boosted public morale was acceptable. So the David-and-Goliath stories proliferated ("Twenty RAF fighters rout Hun formation of 200"), making the best reading since war was declared. Göring kept sending vast armadas of Luftwaffe aircraft across the

Channel, and the jaunty RAF pilots with their polka-dot scarves and outrageous moustaches kept shooting them down. Newspapers printed pictures of workmen munching lunchtime sandwiches as they relaxed in the bent and battered remains of German bombers. Captured Luftwaffe aircrew were shown being marched off to captivity – in Canada, in most cases – looking suitably humbled and bewildered. "Our" chaps grinned infectiously from scores of photographs, relaxing between sorties, in shirtsleeves and flying boots, apparently quite unconcerned about the battles to come. Picture by picture, the illusion was created of a nation cheerfully indifferent to the best efforts of the Luftwaffe. In fact, Fighter Command was soon reeling from the Germans' attacks on radar installations and fighter airfields in the southern counties. The coastal airfields of Lympne and Manston, near Dover, had already been badly damaged. If the Luftwaffe had concentrated on the fighter airfields, heaven knows what the result might have been.

It is one of the myths of the battle that radar was a British invention, and that its existence came as a shock to the Germans. In fact, the Germans had done a great deal of work on radar themselves and were, at the time of the battle, further ahead in some aspects of its development than was Britain. Indeed, a British radar set captured during the retreat in France had been rated as "rather primitive" by the Germans.[21] Where the British had outpaced the Germans was in their method of integrating radar into a central communications network, an air-raid warning and ground-to-air control system that had no equal in the world at that time. Its foundation was a network of long-range radar stations, twenty-one of them on Britain's south and east coasts. They could detect approaching aircraft nearly 150 miles away at altitudes up to 30,000 feet. Aircraft attempting to slip beneath this electronic screen could be detected by short-range, low-level stations. Civilian spotters, members of the Observer Corps, tracked enemy aircraft once they had crossed into British territory. The first reports of approaching aircraft went first to the filter room at Fighter Command HQ. There, plotters – principally

Waafs, members of the Women's Auxiliary Air Force – kept track of enemy and RAF aircraft, maintaining a minute-by-minute "picture" of the situation on a huge map of Britain by moving markers representing RAF and enemy aircraft to various locations. Controllers could watch the proceedings from a balcony and advise the appropriate Fighter Command Groups of developments.

It was a brilliantly successful concept. Luftwaffe General Adolf Galland later wrote: "From the very beginning the British had an extraordinary advantage which we could never overcome throughout the entire war: radar and fighter control. For us and for our command this was a surprise, and a very bitter one. . . . The British fighter was guided all the way from take-off to his correct position for attack on the German formations. . . . In battle we had to rely on our human eyes. The British fighter pilots could depend on the radar eye, which was far more reliable and had a longer range."[22]

The Early Warning System enabled controllers to make the most effective use of the fighters at their disposal, eliminating the need for standing patrols. In most instances throughout the battle, the defenders were ready and waiting for the German formations when they arrived. The controllers liked to send the Hurricanes after the bombers while the faster Spitfires tackled the fighters, although the exigencies of combat didn't always permit such tidy allocations of forces. Many encounters became whirligigs of diving, turning, skidding aircraft, very much a case of every man for himself.

The ranks of "The Few" contained several outstanding Canadian pilots. Stan Turner and Willie McKnight, those two stalwarts of Bader's 242 Squadron, fought throughout the battle. Johnny Kent of Winnipeg was another Canuck who made his mark. Kent had learned to fly in Manitoba, earning the distinction of being the youngest licensed pilot in Canada. He had joined the RAF in 1935 and, after serving with 19 Squadron flying Gauntlet biplane fighters, he joined the Royal Aircraft Establishment, the RAF's technical division, at Farnborough. Life in the RAE was never dull. Kent had tested aircraft and equipment, including a hair-raising series of investigations into the effects of hitting barrage balloon cables. In a two-year period, Kent deliberately collided with about three hundred balloon cables. On one occasion he had had the job of testing the efficiency of a new idea to make Britain's skies safe from enemy aircraft. The inventor had suggested barring the way to London or other major areas with "curtains" of balloons. From each balloon a bomb hung on piano wire. When an aircraft hit the wire, the bomb would spin around its wing like a chestnut on the end of a string. That was the theory. Kent's unappealing job had been to find out whether the notion had any merit.

In his memoirs, he recalls flying a Battle single-engined bomber straight into the wire. Things had happened with astonishing rapidity: "I saw the aileron shatter and, at the same time, felt a jerk on the control column, but at no time did I see any sign of the cable actually on the wing or any sign of the bomb attached to it. On return to Farnborough, however, the film was run through and I was amazed to see that the cable and bomb had gone right round the wing two and a half times, the bomb striking the underside of the wing before the cable unwound itself."[23] Surprisingly, Kent had survived these experiments without a scratch, and received a well-deserved Air Force Cross (AFC) for his efforts.

In the early days of the war, he had become a pilot with the RAF's Photographic Development Unit, flying unarmed Spitfires. Curiously, he scored his first victory during this period. A predatory 109 dived at him and went straight into the ground.[24]

When Kent became a fighter pilot with 303 (Polish) Squadron, he had gone out one day to test his guns on a target range in the Dee Estuary, southwest of Liverpool. Enthusiastically, he blazed away, but after a few seconds, the brisk chatter of Brownings gave way to an impotent hiss of compressed air. Kent returned to base and complained that all eight guns had jammed simultaneously. His flight commander shook his head. The guns had stopped because they had run out of ammunition. Only miserly quantities of rounds could be spared for target practice.

Kent had then become a flight commander in the Polish squadron. Intensely aggressive and operationally experienced though the Poles were, their English was, with few exceptions, appalling, and they had much to learn about RAF tactics and procedures. Not the least of Kent's problems had been the fact that the Poles were accustomed to flying fixed-undercarriage fighters. They kept forgetting that they had landing gear that had to be lowered before returning to terra firma. They wrote off several Hurricanes in wheels-up landings. Fortunately none of the pilots suffered injuries in the mishaps, and replacing aircraft was infinitely easier than replacing skilled pilots.

Kent's airmen had soon developed an intense affection for their flight leader. "Kentowski," as he was known to them, flew with the unit throughout the Battle of Britain, and 303 Squadron became the top-scoring unit of the RAF. Its first casualties were Flying Officer Cebrzynski and Sergeant Wojtowicz. Kent wrote: ". . . Cebrzynski knew he would be killed and he told me quite dispassionately only two days before that he would not survive long enough to see the end of the month. He was not morbid about it, he was just stating a fact which he accepted and merely wondered vaguely when it might be."[25]

Kent shot down four German aircraft during the Battle of Britain. In mid-October, he became CO of 303 and received a DFC.

Cowboy Blatchford spent most of the battle flying with 212 Squadron, a photo reconnaissance unit, transferring to 257 in late September. He shot down a Dornier 217 the day after arriving at 257's base, North Weald, a few miles northeast of London. The following month, Blatchford had just taken off when a formation of bomb-carrying Me 109s and twin-engined 110s raided the field. Blatchford's Hurricane was riddled; a cannon shell passed between his knees. He baled out and landed safely. A month later he led the squadron to attack a formation of Italian aircraft attempting a daylight bombing raid on Harwich. He shot down one and shared in the destruction of another. During the encounter, he nearly collided with a Fiat biplane. When he returned to base, however, he found blood on his propeller blades, suggesting that he had come closer to the enemy than even he had realized.

Other Canadian pilots also made their mark in the Battle of Britain. The colourful, outspoken Lionel Gaunce, of Derwent, Alberta, destroyed four and probably destroyed a fifth enemy aircraft during the battle, but was killed in action the following year. John Latta, of Victoria, British Columbia, shot down four German aircraft and shared in the destruction of a fifth. Hugh Tamblyn came from Watrous, Saskatchewan, to join the RAF in 1937. He became a member of 141 Squadron, flying the indifferent Defiant, later transferring to 242 Squadron and converting to Hurricanes. Tamblyn was credited with 4 ½ victories during the Battle of Britain. Roly Dibnah shot down a Ju 87 off Dover. The dive-bomber exploded, yet both crew members escaped with their lives, tumbling out of the debris that had been their aircraft and managing to deploy their parachutes before they hit the sea.

The record of Canadians flying in the Battle of Britain is a proud one, but the cost in young, promising lives was dreadful. On the second day of the battle, twenty-year-old Duncan Hewitt of Saint John, New Brunswick, was shot down during a convoy patrol near Portland, not far from the Isle of Wight, and was killed. A few days later, Richard Howley, a member of 141 Squadron flying a Defiant, became the victim of a Messerschmitt 109 near Dover. Twenty-one-year-old Bill Nelson of Montreal had joined the RAF in March 1937, becoming a bomber pilot on the lumbering Whitleys. He won a DFC as a bomber pilot, then transferred to fighters and won a Bar. On July 23, he joined 74 Squadron, the famous unit in which Edward "Mick" Mannock, VC, DSO, the greatest British ace of the Great War, had served (he outscored Billy Bishop by one). Nelson, a young man of exceptional courage and determination, had the right instincts. He invariably got in close to his enemy before opening fire. One of his combat reports from late in the Battle of

Britain recounts how he shot down a 109, giving his opponent "a three-second burst at 150 yards, another at 100 yards, and finally a two-second burst at 50 yards."[26] The fight began at 25,000 feet and ended almost at ground level when the Messerschmitt crashed close to East Grinstead Hospital, where many of the air force's worst burn cases were being treated. Sadly, it was Nelson's last victory. On November 1, he was shot down and killed over Dover. John Boyle of Ottawa scored five victories before being killed on September 28. Norris Hart of Dugald, Manitoba, had four victories to his credit when he was killed on November 5, flying with 242 Squadron. Twenty-year-old Joe Larichelière of Montreal destroyed six German aircraft in two action-packed days during the battle, but lost his life on August 16.

Just before the start of the Battle of Britain, the first Royal Canadian Air Force fighter squadron had arrived in Britain. No. 1 (RCAF) Squadron had been formed at Trenton, Ontario, in 1937, flying Siskin biplanes. Re-equipped with Hurricanes in September 1939, its ranks augmented by several pilots from 115 Squadron (an Auxiliary squadron from Montreal), the unit had travelled to Britain, arriving at its first base, Middle Wallop, near Salisbury, in June 1940. There, its Hurricanes had to be replaced because they were early Mark Is with fixed-pitch, two-bladed propellers. In command of the squadron was Squadron Leader Ernie McNab. At thirty-five, McNab was elderly by Fighter Command standards; he had joined the RCAF in 1926.

The unit was soon ordered into the battle.

"This was the lowest point in my life," McNab later recalled. "I didn't think my men were ready for combat. They had fired at a moving target only once. Their aircraft recognition training had consisted of an instructor hastily shuffling a pile of silhouettes."

In August the unit went into action. Responding to a report that German bombers were heading north across the Isle of Wight, the Canadians swarmed in to attack. Three enemy bombers – Ju 88s, everyone thought – were flying line astern. McNab ordered his Hurricanes, "Echelon starboard . . . go!"

It had all the makings of a textbook attack. But it wasn't. As McNab neared his prey, he saw something that chilled his blood. The nearest bomber had a gun turret amidships. The Ju 88 had no such gun turret. And as the distance telescoped at a crazy pace, McNab saw something else: red-white-and-blue roundels and fin flashes. They were Blenheims!

McNab yelled, "Break, break! Don't attack!"[27]

His section reacted instantly, swinging away to port. At the same instant the Blenheims fired Very flares, identifying themselves as friendly. The pilots behind McNab, every one of them flying his first operational sortie, took the yellow dots of light to be tracers. They opened fire. One Blenheim lurched into a spin, trailing flame, breaking up before it hit the water. The three-man crew died. The other two Blenheims managed to crash-land, severely damaged.

The usual things were said. Such tragedies were inevitable in the heat of battle. No one blamed the Canadians. It had happened before and would happen again. Everyone understood. In the next few days, the unit made a successful attack on a formation of Dorniers. The tally came to three Dorniers downed, four damaged. But it came at a cost. Robert Edwards from Cobourg, Ontario, was killed, the first RCAF pilot to die in action in World War II. There was a bitterly ironic footnote: A few days earlier, Edwards had jotted down in his diary some comments about England. He observed that Woking, Surrey, was "the prettiest, most peaceful place. . . ." His body was laid to rest in Woking's cemetery.

Paul Pitcher from Montreal, one of the squadron's pilots, remembers an incident that seemed to typify the taut-nerved times:

In the first Wing take-off at Northolt, the three squadrons stationed there – 303 Polish [John Kent's unit], 1 RAF, and 1 Canadian – were lined up for take-off at their respective dispersal areas in three different parts of the field. Due to a confusion in take-off orders, all three squadrons opened throttle simultaneously and headed towards the centre of the field, where the thirty-six aircraft met!

By some miracle, no aircraft collided with another or with the ground, although the turbulence from slipstreams was unbelievable. The station commander, who was witness to the scene, had to be helped into the officers' mess for alcoholic resuscitation. I seem to recall that part of the confusion arose from the fact that two No. 1 Squadrons were involved. In any event, all Canadian squadrons overseas were renumbered thereafter and given "400" numbers, 1 becoming 401.[28]

Their early errors notwithstanding, the RCAF pilots soon accumulated an impressive tally of victories. By early October, when the unit was withdrawn from battle for a rest, the total stood at thirty, for a loss of three pilots killed and ten wounded.

Two of the unit's pilots became aces during the battle – and both were numbered among the squadron's senior citizens. Ernie McNab shot down five Germans, as did Roy "Gordie" McGregor, who at thirty-nine was the oldest Canadian fighter pilot to see action in the war.*

Legend has portrayed the Battle of Britain as a sort of sporting event, with the ever-so-unconcerned RAF pilots quaffing jugs of lukewarm beer and, between sorties, winning the hearts of crisp-tongued English beauties while the sun shone ceaselessly. It didn't. July was uncommonly wet, with a good deal of mist and light fog. Conditions improved in August, although thunderstorms pre-

---

* His fifth victory was confirmed thirty-seven years after the event, when the Sussex and Surrey Aviation Historical Society recovered the remains of a Ju 88. An investigation revealed that it was the Ju 88 McGregor had claimed as a probable on September 27, 1940. The oldest Canadian pilot in the Battle of Britain was an ace at last![29]

cluded flying on many days. September was the best month of the period, and October provided the typical mixture of fine and poor conditions, with repeated showers and frequent mist.

British morale was generally good. And if in some quarters it wasn't, it always *looked* as if it was. Photographs of the period depict everyone taking all the beastliness the Jerries were handing out and laughing it off, with forests of thumbs resolutely raised. The photographers insisted on such signs of confidence, knowing all too well that their work wouldn't get past the censor if marred by any hints of gloom. So big smiles were *de rigueur*, from harassed ground crews working on engines or patching bullet holes, to the pilots, groggy with fatigue, their insides churning from the effects of the latest combat, nerves already jangling as they contemplated the next. Scenes beloved of the cameramen included groups of pilots lolling on the grass in front of their Spitfires and Hurricanes, officers and NCOs clustered in democratic good fellowship, sharing side-splitting jokes with one another, apparently giving not a thought to the dangers of the battles to come. They invariably wore flying boots, with unfastened Mae Wests draped over their shoulders. Battledress had not yet been introduced, so the pilots were in shirtsleeves or unbuttoned dress uniforms.

Civilians, too, were in holiday mood throughout the conflict, if the photographs were to be believed. One widely published shot showed a family laughing uproariously as Mum and Dad carried a few pathetic belongings from the remains of their house, which had just been blown to bits by the Luftwaffe. The photographer made them look as if they were leaving for a vacation at Brighton. Much of this joviality was for overseas consumption, particularly America's. It was essential that Britain be shown as unbowed by Hitler's attacks, since the country was becoming increasingly dependent upon the United States for essential supplies.

The aerial battles had a peculiarly remote quality for the citizens watching from below. The fighting went on at great heights, and if the fighters were visible at all, they were tiny dots gyrating to the accompaniment of the dry rattling of machine-guns and the heavier thumping of cannons. The noise of the firing carried a surprising distance.

For the fighter pilots, the strain was devastating. Despite the jolly pictures in the papers, most pilots suffered nervous and digestive troubles. Numbing fatigue affected nearly all who took part in the daily battles. There just wasn't enough time to recuperate between sorties. Some pilots fell asleep in their cockpits after landing, some while taxiing to dispersal. Many dozed off during meals and could be awakened only with difficulty. Yet, in the contrary way of the human mechanism, uncounted numbers of pilots who could barely keep their eyes open on touching down were unable to sleep when at last they had the opportunity to do so. The medical officer of No. 1 (Canadian) Squadron reported: "There is a definite air of constant tension and they [the pilots] are unable to relax as they are practically on constant call. The pilots go to work with forced enthusiasm and appear to be suffering from strain and general tiredness."[30] A British pilot, Colin Gray, of 54 Squadron, commented that the battle "was no picnic despite what anyone might say later. . . . Most of us were pretty scared all the bloody time; you only felt happy when the battle was over and you were on your way home, then were safe, for a bit, anyway."[31] Harold Bird-Wilson, who survived the Battle to rise to the rank of air vice-marshal, remembers the terrible toll of "witnessing the execution in mortal combat of your friends. A fighter pilot was apt to place an invisible shield about himself, which may have given the air of callousness, but in reality it was a necessary protection against mental and physical strain."[32]

Hilly Brown was active throughout this period. "During the enemy attacks on southeastern England," he noted, "the fighter squadrons there were in the air most of the time. They came down to reload and refuel and were up again within the hour, chasing Germans. They had one meal a day, and a few cups of tea. Somehow they got about five hours' sleep a night, and were up again before dawn."[33]

In mid-August, Brown nearly lost his life. Shot down over the Channel, he managed to bale out, landing in the sea with only minor leg injuries and facial burns (which cost him his moustache, of which he was inordinately fond). Like most of his fellow fighter pilots, he had shoved his goggles up on his forehead for better visibility; his eyebrows were singed but his eyes were undamaged. (Roly Dibnah took this as an opportunity to lecture him on fighter tactics.) Brown was fortunate enough to be picked up soon after landing in the sea. After a day or two, he was back in action.

At that period of the war, German pilots who "ditched" had a rather better chance of survival than their RAF counterparts. Their planes carried inflatable dinghies, which were far more efficient life-saving devices than the Mae Wests worn by Allied pilots. Luftwaffe aircrew's life-saving equipment included a chemical that stained the water a yellow-green, vastly increasing their chances of being spotted from the air. Furthermore, the Germans had organized an air-sea rescue service with about thirty aircraft and high-speed launches. The British service would not be in action for several months.

Fledgling fighter pilots learned their trade rapidly. Or they died. The job of fighter pilot demanded great flying skill combined with the courage and nerve of a racing car driver. The best fighter pilots never hesitated to attack their enemies at terrifyingly close quarters. Most of them were indifferent shots. The countless thousands of hours spent by the prewar RAF in practising formation flying would have been better spent teaching pilots to shoot. Dozens of young men went into battle having fired no more than a few hundred rounds, and with little instruction on how to improve their aim. Peter O'Brian, of Toronto, who joined the RAF in 1937 and won the Sword of Honour as the outstanding Cranwell cadet of the year, sought assistance from a squadron colleague in the difficult art of deflection shooting; specifically, how to hit an enemy aircraft passing across one's flight path. "Aim to miss the bugger in front," was the advice, "and add a few feet for luck." O'Brian found it good counsel and soon shot down a Heinkel.

At that point in the war, in spite of the experience gained in France, most RAF squadrons still flew in the outdated "vic" or V formations. Some would continue to do so until mid-1942, more from habit than for any tactical reason. It took time for new ideas to take hold. Pilots learned to fire short bursts of one or two seconds (novices tended to push the "tit" until the guns were empty, a matter of about a dozen seconds). They quickly discarded all that the training schools had taught them about smooth flying. It had no place in the world of combat. They learned to change direction with sudden, violent movements of the stick, using every inch of its play as they jammed it into the corners of the cockpit with the throttle lever thrust forward to its maximum. Every day provided further evidence that it was fatal to fly straight and level for more than a few seconds in a combat area, and that it was equally perilous not to keep glancing in every direction, searching for the enemy. They all knew that height is the supreme advantage in air warfare, but all too many forgot to leave some of their number at higher altitudes to cover them when they dived to attack. They found out the dangers of following a stricken enemy down to watch it crash. They fought their instincts and made themselves turn *into* tracer passing on the left or right from an enemy at the rear, because the enemy would correct his aim, and a movement in the opposite direction stood a better-than-even chance of surprising and distracting him.

British fighter aircraft were equipped with Browning machine-guns of .303-inch calibre, both the Hurricane and Spitfire carrying eight wing-mounted guns, although early in the battle some had only four because the guns were in short supply. The Browning was a recoil-operated gun weighing 26 ½ pounds. Its muzzle velocity was 2,440 feet per second, and it fired 1,200 rounds per minute. Originally harmonized to converge at about 400 yards' range, the guns were soon modified on most units to converge at about 250 yards, which was found to be the best, most destructive range.

It soon became distressingly obvious, however, that the Brownings didn't have the destructive power of the 20-mm cannons carried by German fighters. During the Battle of Britain, RAF pilots expended thousands of rounds of .303 ammunition on German bombers, only to have them fly away home, apparently none the worse for the encounter. The Canadians, for their part, found the Dornier bombers particularly troublesome: "These babies seem pretty tough as every time we run into them we fill them full of lead but cannot claim anything much more than damaged," complained the operational diary of the No. 1 (Canadian) Squadron.34 Some Spitfires were experimentally fitted with 20-mm cannons in the summer of 1940, but they performed poorly, repeatedly jamming and freezing in the frigid temperatures of 20,000 feet or more at which most of the dogfights were fought. Freezing could also be a problem with the Browning machine-gun if fighters had to climb through cloud to meet the enemy. The condensation often froze at high altitudes, rendering the guns useless. A temporary solution was the sealing of gun-muzzle ports with pieces of fabric, but eventually the problem was solved when engine heat was fed to the guns. Not until the Battle of Britain was over did efficient cannons equip RAF fighters.

An important element in the RAF's arsenal was the De Wilde incendiary bullet, a Belgian invention purchased a few months before the declaration of war and modified for use by the RAF. Many pilots had four of their guns loaded with regular ammunition, two with armour-piercing bullets, and two with De Wildes. Pilots thought highly of the De Wilde, since it exploded with a bright flash when it hit home, providing a most useful aid to aiming. Fograve "Hiram" Smith, of Edmonton, shot down a Heinkel 111 on August 15, and wrote, "I could see the incendiary bullets flash as they ricocheted on contact. I was close astern when the aircraft blew up with a tremendous explosion and disintegrated in a ball of fire . . ."35

For more than half a century, arguments have raged about whether the Spitfire or the Hurricane contributed more to victory in the

Battle of Britain. Although the Spitfire was faster than the Hurricane, the latter provided a stable and manoeuvrable gun platform, capable of absorbing a great deal of damage without falling out of the sky. The Hurricane's guns were grouped in two clusters of four just outside the propeller arc; the Spitfire's guns were more widely spaced, resulting, some pilots said, in greater vibration and difficulty in holding the aircraft steady when firing, although other pilots were loud in their praise of the Spitfire's steadiness while the guns were being fired. It all depended on what you were used to.

Peter O'Brian of Toronto flew both the Hurricane and Spitfire during the battle and remembers each type with affection. "It always seemed to me that physically the rugged Hurricane was essentially male in character and the very graceful Spitfire essentially female," he comments. Jeffrey Quill, who was much involved in the test flying of the Spitfire, remarked:

> After many years of reflection I take the view that it took both of them to win the Battle of Britain and neither would have achieved it on its own. The Hurricane achieved the greater damage to the enemy (as has often been pointed out), but without the Spitfire squadrons to fight the 109s their casualties might well have led to the losing of the battle. As a man intimately involved with the Spitfire from its early stage in our own flight trials, the above is the most objective view I can take. I would not like to have been a Hurricane pilot in 1940 and greatly respect the courage and achievements of those who were.[36]

Test pilots flying Spitfires from Supermarine's Castle Bromwich plant, near Birmingham, often encountered Hurricanes manufactured by the Austin factory a few miles away. Renowned British test pilot Alex Henshaw says:

The more experienced Spitfire pilots could deal easily with the Hurricane. . . . In the case of the less-experienced, there were times when one would report that he had a Hurricane on his tail and could not shake it off. To some extent I was thus able to judge the calibre of their airmanship by the manner in which they dealt with such situations. In the end, I came to the conclusion that, given two aircraft of comparable performance, the more skilful and resourceful pilot would choose his own battleground and win the contest every time.[37]

Hilly Brown had flown the Hurricane since joining No. 1 Squadron. He was intensely loyal: "The Spitfire is a very nice machine, and a better match for the Me 109 in speed, but just the same, nobody on Hurricanes wants to change. Our big advantages are a steadier gun platform, better manoeuvrability, and easier servicing. Also we can operate under much worse conditions re size and surface of landing fields."[38]

Perhaps the only really important point is that both fighters were available when needed. Moreover, their performance was given a significant boost when constant-speed propellers were installed and the more powerful 100 octane fuel began to be used in Fighter Command. Fortunately, these changes were implemented shortly before the Battle of Britain began. Jeffrey Quill points out that the introduction of 100 octane fuel

> had the effect of increasing the combat rating of the Merlin. . . . This, of course, had a significant effect upon the rate of climb, particularly as the constant speed propellers (also introduced just before the battle) ensured that 3,000 rpm was obtainable from the ground upward whereas previously it had been restricted by the two-pitch propellers. It also had an effect upon the maximum speed, but this was not so significant as the effect upon the rate of climb.[39]

It is interesting to note that of the approximately one hundred Canadian pilots active during the Battle of Britain, only five (Nelson, Larichelière, McGregor, McKnight, and McNab) became aces, having scored five or more kills. Rather more than half of the Canadian pilots in action during the Battle of Britain claimed victories. The big scores went to the few who found that they possessed the all-important combination of nerve and flying talent to succeed in this extraordinarily demanding profession. And it is worth noting that in spite of the legends, no sensible pilot indulged in the so-called "Victory Roll" when returning from successful sorties. The manoeuvre was a creation of newspaper writers, and a thoroughly unsafe one it was. No pilot could know what damage had been done to his aircraft during combat, and a graceful Victory Roll over the airfield was all too likely to end up in a shower of spare parts as a battle-damaged Spitfire or Hurricane disintegrated in mid-air.

Canadian fighter pilots made an important contribution to victory in the Battle of Britain, but a Canadian civilian also played a major role. Max Aitken, Lord Beaverbrook, took on the role of Minister of Aircraft Production just before the Battle of Britain. Beaverbrook, an aggressive, hard-driving workaholic, ruffled many bureaucratic feathers and made his share of mistakes, but he did much to speed the production of aircraft of many types – although in some cases the wrong ones. Beaverbrook, like many highly successful individuals, was remarkably lucky. He took over the job just at the right time, when production was already on the rise. Beaverbrook's son, another Max, was a fighter pilot with an auxiliary squadron, 601, known as "The Millionaires' Mob" because its members included a disproportionate number of well-to-do young men. Max Aitken, Jr., scored an impressive 16 ½ victories as a fighter pilot. He cultivated the image of the devil-may-care man about town, but in fact, Aitken, his father's son, was highly disciplined and an effective squadron commander who could be a hard taskmaster. He rose to the rank of group captain, survived the war, and was knighted in the 1960s.

Although Beaverbrook and his ministry kept the new fighters streaming from the factories, the supply of pilots was a more difficult proposition. No matter how talented a fledgling pilot might be, he was a liability to his squadron until he had acquired experience. Most didn't live long enough. It took time for a pilot to learn to act instinctively, no longer having to think about controlling his high-spirited, self-willed fighter. Every time a fledgling managed to survive a sortie, he had acquired a precious morsel of experience. Gradually, the morsels accumulated, and like pennies in a child's bank, they began to add up to something significant. If a fledgling survived long enough, he at last became a useful member of his squadron. Thus, in the callous accounting of wartime, the loss of an ace was a far greater tragedy than the loss of a fledgling. Fledglings were expected to die. They were aerial cannon fodder.

In the fall of 1940, although Britain was still undefeated, many Germans felt it was just a matter of time. Hitler even demobilized some divisions of the Wehrmacht – a move that may have been designed to calm Russian suspicions concerning his next moves. In Britain, despite a striking aerial victory, everyone knew that the war had just begun.

IX

They made a brave show as they thundered across the airfield, bumping heavily on the uneven grass surface, labouring to take to the air with their twin engines bellowing away at full power. Navigation lights flashing like electric banners of battle, they headed away into the darkening night. After the last of them had vanished from sight, even the sharpest of ears could not detect their din, which a few minutes earlier had echoed about the airfield.

In those days, citizens watched – or merely heard – the bombers passing overhead on their way to bomb the enemy. Countless thumbs were raised in encouragement; unnumbered prayers were whispered, asking that the young airmen might all return safely from the hostile skies. Most imagined a sort of Armageddon when the Hampdens, Wellingtons, and Whitleys arrived at their destinations. That generation of citizens had for years been hearing of the frightful effects of bombs and seeing awe-inspiring special-effects in umpteen films: factories disappearing in enormous explosions, smokestacks toppling like felled redwoods, heavy vehicles spinning into the air like toys tossed out of a cradle, canals breaking their banks, clouds of poison gas, citizens dying... panic in the streets... utter collapse of a nation's morale. The bomber seemed to threaten civilization itself.

"Serves 'em right," commented most Brits. "They shouldn't have started it."

Despite what postwar historians might say, that was the general feeling of the British population in the early forties. The more bombs on Germany and Italy the better. The Jerries and Eyeties were getting a taste of their own medicine.

It would have dismayed those spirited patriots to know how little the efforts of Bomber Command had affected the enemy so far. Neutral observers saw few bombed buildings in Germany's major cities. All those hundreds of photogenic bombs with the saucy messages to Adolf and Hermann chalked on them might well have been tossed into the North Sea for all the good they seemed to be doing. At that stage of the war, it was perhaps enough that the people at home *thought* a lot of damage was being done. The stories did wonders for morale. The newspapers printed pictures of cheerful young airmen clambering up rickety metal ladders into Wellingtons and Whitleys. Invariably they turned and grinned for the camera. If you believed the propaganda, it was just as much fun flying bombers over Germany and being fired at by ten thousand guns as it had been fighting hordes of Luftwaffe aircraft in the Battle of Britain – or being "dehoused" by bombs. In the never-never land of the Ministry of Information, every British bomb found its target. And every target was a military objective, you could be sure of that. No indiscriminate bombing marred the record of the clean-cut young heroes of the RAF.

It couldn't be denied that RAF Bomber Command had gone to the war with the best of intentions. Operations against the enemy were to be precise, deadly accurate, and utterly devastating. The bombers would pick off specific targets at will: docks one day, power stations the next. This factory, that railway marshalling yard. One by one, the key components in German's industrial structure would disappear in a shattering series of explosions, until the whole rotten mess collapsed.

With the hindsight of more than half a century, it is easy to scoff at the naïvety – and sheer ignorance – of those who expected so much of a few dozen medium bombers of questionable efficiency manned by crews barely capable of finding their targets, let alone destroying them. But at the time, belief in the power of the bomber reached incredible levels. A year before war broke out, a Bomber Command report claimed that by bombing nineteen power plants and twenty-six coking plants, German war-making capacity could be brought to a standstill in two weeks. Major-General J. F. C. Fuller, one of Britain's foremost military experts of the time, predicted that, after a single hypothetical raid, "London for several days will be one vast raving Bedlam, traffic will cease, the homeless will shriek for help, the city will be a pandemonium." The general confidently declared that the government would be "swept away by an avalanche of terror."[40] When such things failed to happen, the pundits claimed that the superiority of the British character had made the all-important difference.

Prewar, the Air Ministry had done a highly efficient job of politicking to ensure its independent status; it had done a far less effective job of preparing its airmen for war. After the fall of France, Bomber Command found itself in an embarrassing position. For years, the "bomber barons" from Trenchard down had been saying that bombers could win the next war. Now Churchill demanded that they do precisely that. The RAF's bombers were the only means of hitting and, everyone hoped, *hurting* the enemy.

At that early period, the public relations efforts of Bomber Command were considerably more effective than the bombs. The films and the books created new heroes of modest young men in ungainly flying garb, draped in Mae Wests and parachute harnesses, leather helmets framing their perpetually smiling faces. Even if the enemy seemed to be largely unaffected by their nightly incursion, the general public in Britain and the Commonwealth was hugely impressed. The more bombs dropped on Hitler and his cronies the better.

Commonwealth volunteers were well represented in the ranks of Bomber Command, as they would be throughout the war. Many of the Canadians in the bomber crews had tried to get into the RCAF before the war, only to be discouraged by that service's lofty educational requirements and limited opportunities. Typical of the breed were Nelles Timmerman, of Kingston, Ontario, and Pitt Clayton from Vancouver. Timmerman learned to fly at a local club, then worked his way across to England on a cattle boat to join the RAF. In 1937 he joined 49 Squadron. The unit flew Hawker Hinds, two-seat, open-cockpit biplanes derived from the famous Hart, which dated back to the twenties. The RAF was using such outdated types in large numbers to give its crews something to fly while they waited for new bombers – the Hampdens, Battles, Wellingtons, and Whitleys – then beginning to emerge from the factories. One of Timmerman's classmates was Jack Challes, of St. Catharines, Ontario, who would die two years later, shot down during the disastrous daylight raid on Wilhelmshaven on December 18, 1939.

In the fall of 1938, 49 Squadron replaced its biplane Hinds with the RAF's latest bomber, the Hampden. Other squadrons soon followed suit, including 83 Squadron, which had among its members Pitt Clayton and a supremely confident young English-man named Guy Gibson, who couldn't wait to get to grips with the Jerries.

The new Hampdens were a revelation. Twin-engined bombers with attractive lines, they seemed to be the epitome of modernity and efficiency, a far cry from the multi-wing relics that Bomber Command had been flying for so many decades. Although some pilots initially had misgivings about these sleek, rakish aircraft with their singular profiles, they found them surprisingly agile and, although more complex than the Hind, they posed no serious handling problems. Lack of room to move about in the exception-ally narrow fuselage and feeble defensive armament were the type's most serious deficiencies.

The proportions of the Hampden also complicated instruction, for there was no room for side-by-side seating. Pitt Clayton recalls having to learn to fly the Hampden by doing circuits standing behind the pilot's seat and looking over his instructor's shoulder. Once that stage of the initiation had been completed, the positions were reversed. The system had its shortcomings. On his first approach to land the Hampden, just as he was nearing touch-down, Clayton heard the instructor telling him, "Pull back, pull back!" Puzzled, Clayton obeyed, although the approach appeared perfectly satisfactory to him. The Hampden stalled and came thumping back to terra firma with an almighty jolt to the airframe. Clayton's instructor walloped his head on the roof, and promptly lost interest in the proceedings, telling his pupil to carry on alone.

When war came, fledgling bomber skippers flew on the first few operations as navigator/bomb aimers.

Both Timmerman and Clayton rapidly established themselves as excellent bomber pilots with more than their share of initiative. On May 1, 1940, Timmerman went out to drop sea mines (an activity known officially as "Gardening"). On the way home, he noted a suspicious light on the water in the region of the Frisian Islands. His eyes narrowed. A flare path? It seemed highly probable. He throttled back, deciding to investigate. Sure enough, an Arado 196 appeared, its landing lights on. Timmerman slipped behind the floatplane and fired his fixed .303 machine-gun. The Arado crashed. Timmerman sped for home.

An oddly similar incident took place on one of Pitt Clayton's early operations. In those days, it was not uncommon for solitary bombers to go ranging over hostile territory – a virtually suicidal practice later in the war. Clayton glimpsed a flight of heavy aircraft with landing lights on. Without further ado, he switched on his own landing lights and joined the enemy aircraft, although maintaining a discreet distance. Unwittingly, the German bombers led the Canadian to their base. He bombed it, then headed for home.

It was the age of innocence for Bomber Command. Although most of the newspaper and magazine illustrations of the time depicted swarms of bombers over a given target, the reality was that the Wellingtons, Whitleys, and Hampdens usually wandered to the targets in two and threes. There was no attempt to create a "stream" of bombers; indeed, there was a general feeling that by sending small clusters of aircraft at irregular hours, the enemy population suffered the greatest inconvenience and loss of sleep. Routes and bombing altitudes were usually decided at the airfield before take-off. Individual skippers plotted their routes, with the aid of "Dim" (the intelligence officer) and "Windy" (the met man). And when the op had been completed, the aircraft headed for home, taking due note of the flak and the searchlights for Dim's benefit.

In the latter days of the Battle of Britain, raids on concentrations of landing barges became common. Pitt Clayton recalls flying over Ostend one night and noting with surprise that the German landing barges that had been gathered there had disappeared. The long-awaited invasion must have begun! He passed on the information to base, causing a red alert in Britain. Then he went down low to look things over at close quarters. Roaring over the sea at an altitude of about fifty feet, he gave his rear gunner an opportunity to shoot up a lighthouse, after which he turned and sped in the direction of home. He hadn't gone far when, to his astonishment, he saw masses of barges moored together in the open sea. The Germans had dispersed them in the hope that the predatory RAF bombers wouldn't spot them. Clayton remembers seeing quite clearly a man standing on the stern of one barge, firing a rifle at the Hampden. "My gunner took care of him," he remarks. Clayton bombed the barges, then headed home without taking a hit. He told his story, and the red alert was cancelled.*

On September 15, 83 Squadron won a Victoria Cross. A Torontonian in the RAF, twenty-one-year-old Clare Connor, was skipper of a Hampden attacking landing barges in the Antwerp docks. Intense flak greeted the bomber, and it took several hits in the wings. Hayhurst, the observer/bomb aimer, released the bombs, and almost at the same instant, an incendiary shell scored a direct hit in the gaping maw of the bomb bay. Shrapnel lacerated the wing tanks. The narrow crew compartment quickly become a furnace. George James, the rear gunner, baled out – or rather fell out, when the fire burned away the fuselage beneath him. Fortunately, he had donned his parachute; he survived, becoming a prisoner for the rest of the war. Hayhurst very reasonably thought the entire crew was baling out. He followed suit. The wireless operator, eighteen-year-old John Hannah, a Scot from Paisley, saw the floor beneath him dissolve into molten alloy. Around him, electrical wiring burned, showering sparks like some fireworks display gone mad, while rounds of ammunition fired off in all directions as flames licked at the stacked drums.

---

* At about this time, Clayton survived a dead-stick landing (i.e., without power) on a minefield on the east coast. He and his crew had to sit for hours in their Hampden until a coastguard could be found who knew a safe passage through the area.

When Hannah informed his skipper that the aircraft was on fire, Connor asked, "Is it very bad?"

"Bad, but not too bad," Hannah replied.

Connor ordered him to get ready to jump if the situation worsened. The flames – fanned into a furious blowtorch by the wind screaming through the holes in the fuselage – enveloped the wireless compartment. Hannah managed to grab two fire extinguishers. With these he fought the fire for several minutes. When the first extinguisher was empty, he beat the flames with his logbook, while his parachute pack smouldered beside him. The smoke began to affect him, and he felt his consciousness ebbing away. He struggled into the upper cupola and threw open the Perspex cover. Leaning out into the frigid slipstream, he gulped in fresh air. Revived, he went back to the fire, emptying the second extinguisher, after which he attacked the flames with his still-smouldering parachute pack and his gloved hand. Rounds in the ammunition pans kept going off in bursts, like crackers at a Christmas party.

In the pilot's seat, Clare Connor stared ahead as he tried to wend his perilous way through the flak. In the windscreen the reflection of the fire amidships looked like a malevolent presence lurking behind him, ready to pounce. He felt the heat on the back of his neck and winced as the ammunition exploded, rounds striking the armour-plating behind his seat. How long before the aircraft simply fell apart in the air? Unaware that half the crew had already baled out, he still hoped to wend his way through the murderous flak and reach his base at Scampton, Lincolnshire. Only Hannah remained, single-handedly fighting to save the aircraft.

Hannah came forward. When he saw him, Connor was horrified. The boy's face was a black mask; his eyes were swollen almost shut, brows burned off, flying suit charred and brittle. But Hannah grinned, exuding confidence. The fire was out, he told Connor. The others? Gone, Hannah reported, making his way back to the remains of the wireless compartment. He attempted to get a location fix. No chance; the set had become a blackened, distorted pile

of junk, fit only for the scrap heap. He threw the remaining ammunition pans overboard.

Making his way forward again, Hannah found Hayhurst's map
and spent the rest of the journey home helping Connor to navigate.
The Hampden landed at Scampton shortly after 3:00 A.M.

Hannah recovered from his wounds, but his health was permanently affected. He never flew operationally again. On October 1,
it was announced that Hannah had been awarded the Victoria
Cross for his "courage, coolness, and devotion to duty."[41] Clare
Connor received the DFC. A little over a month later, the Canadian
was killed when his Hampden crashed into the sea while returning
from a sortie.

X

Long after victory had been won, Churchill was to admit that "the
only thing that really frightened me during the war was the U-boat
peril. . . . It did not take the form of flaring battles and glittering
achievements, it manifested itself through statistics, diagrams and
curves unknown to the nation, incomprehensible to the public."[42]

The U-boat menace began to assume truly frightening proportions when the Germans took over the French Atlantic ports of
Brest, Saint-Nazaire, La Rochelle, and Lorient in mid-1940. Hitler
immediately ordered the construction of immensely thick concrete
pens. Now the *Unterseeboot* fleet would have a safe haven on the
threshold of Britain's most important trade routes. Little wonder
that Churchill fretted. Without huge imports of non-ferrous metals,
many types of machine tools, oil, and – most significant of all –
about 50 per cent of her foodstuffs, Britain would go down to
defeat. It was inevitable. Britain's sea lanes were her lifeline. And her
Achilles' heel. Concerted attacks by U-boats and surface raiders

could win the war for Germany. It had almost happened in 1917. Between the wars, Grand Admiral Karl Dönitz, a former U-boat skipper, had lobbied for the construction of a fleet of three hundred submarines instead of the vast and costly battleships so beloved of navies the world over. Operating in well-organized "packs," such a force of U-boats, forming a barrier across the Atlantic, would guarantee victory, Dönitz declared. He might well have been proved right; however, he did not get his armada of U-boats until it was too late. When war broke out, he had under his command only twenty-seven oceangoing U-boats.

RAF Coastal Command had been created to protect Britain's vital trade routes. But when war came, it was incapable of doing the job. It didn't have the right aircraft in sufficient numbers. The all-important anti-submarine patrols required long-range aircraft such as the excellent four-engined Sunderland flying boat, but in September 1939 Coastal had only three squadrons of Sunderlands. The Air Staff had discontinued production of the plane in favour of the Stirling heavy bomber, a product of the same manufacturer, Shorts. The Sunderland's replacement was a new flying boat, the twin-engined Lerwick. It was hopeless, viciously unstable both on the water and in the air. Thus several Coastal squadrons had to go to war flying Saro Londons, Short Singapores, and Stranraers, heavily braced and bestrutted biplane flying boats that wouldn't have looked out of place in 1916 at the battle of Jutland. One airman was heard to remark of the Stranraer and its maze of wire bracing, "It's hard to know whether to fly it or play it."

Much was expected of a new torpedo bomber, the Blackburn Botha. A high-wing, twin-engined torpedo-bomber designed to supersede the ancient biplane Vildebeestes and Vincents, the Botha, when it finally emerged from the factory in 1940, turned out to be another dud. It consistently failed to deliver its promised performance and had the unpleasant habit of shedding ailerons at inconvenient moments. In addition, its engines often cut out if take-off power was held too long. Wartime test pilot H. A. Taylor noted that the Botha could "*of course* carry a torpedo, but only with near-empty fuel tanks, and that it could *of course* go an awfully long way if it was not expected to carry anything."[43]

Coastal Command had ten squadrons of the good-natured but innocuous Avro Anson, a civil design from the early thirties adapted for military use – and widely used as a trainer at many Canadian flying schools. Powered by two 295-horsepower Cheetah engines, the Anson could take to the air – just – carrying a bomb load of five hundred pounds and a crew of four.

The most modern aircraft in Coastal's inventory was another conversion of a civil design, but more successful than the Anson. The Hudson evolved from the American Lockheed 14 airliner – a fact that raised the hackles of the British aircraft industry. Despite this, there can be little doubt that the purchase of the Hudsons was a lifesaver for Coastal Command in the early days of the war. At first, the aircraft alarmed Coastal's pilots. Accustomed to handling genteel old biplanes, they regarded it as dangerous, a handful to land with its high-wing loading and unusually powerful flaps. Besides, they viewed with suspicion its unfamiliar modern features, the Sperry Gyropilot, propeller and wing de-icers, and a fuel-jettison-ing system. Familiarity soon bred intense affection. It was a Hudson of 224 Squadron that shot down a Dornier Do 18 flying boat in early October 1939, the first German aircraft to fall to the RAF in World War II.

Another new aircraft for Coastal Command was the Beaufort, a British design, similar in layout to the Blenheim (already in use by Coastal Command) and made by the same builder, Bristol. It made a bad initial impression on Coastal Command crews, exhibiting a dangerous tendency to swing on take-off, as well as proving to be an "exceptionally poor bombing platform," at an altitude of 10,000 feet "being subject to an excessive and continuous roll which made determination of drift particularly difficult."[44] Worse, the aircraft was powered by the unreliable Taurus engines. In the spring of

1940, the CO of 22 Squadron, Wing Commander Mack, was killed when he suffered an engine failure. The unit had just been re-equipped with Beauforts. A few days later, a Canadian on the unit, John Berryman of Toronto, also suffered a failure of one of his Beaufort's Taurus engines. He crashed, killing himself and his crew.

XI

Italy played an "ignominious, Johnny-come-lately part"[45] in the defeat of France, waiting to attack until June 1940, when their allies the Germans were within days of victory. The four French divisions that faced the Italians fought doggedly and gallantly. Nowhere did the outnumbered French yield more than a kilometre or two. The struggle cost the Italians nearly five thousand men; the French lost only eight. Benito Mussolini had to be satisfied with symbolic victories. German transport aircraft landed a battalion of Italian troops behind the French lines, so that they might be publicly championed as triumphant conquerors. The Germans themselves weren't impressed. "The whole thing is the usual kind of fraud," scoffed German General Franz Halder, chief of the general staff; "I have made it clear I won't have my name mixed up in this business."[46] After France had fallen, the armistice terms permitted Italy to occupy the Franco-Italian border country to a depth of fifty kilometres on the French side. Although hardly the sort of glorious victory that Mussolini had envisioned, it was better than nothing, and it whetted his appetite.

For years Mussolini had eyed French and British possessions in North and East Africa. If Italy were to control Egypt, the Suez Canal and the Sudan would create a land link with the Italian colonies of Eritrea, Ethiopia, and Somaliland; moreover, possession of French and British Somaliland would give Italy control of the

Red Sea. The Mediterranean would become "an Italian lake," Mussolini boasted, providing all manner of strategic advantages in the Balkans. Italian forces had already occupied Albania; Yugoslavia and Greece would be next. Mussolini calculated that Britain would go the way of France. And soon. So the time to act was now, in the spring of 1940, if any of the spoils of victory were to come Italy's way. Mussolini saw an opportunity when the British destroyed most of the French fleet at Mers-el-Kébir, the naval base near Oran, when its admirals refused to sail out of the control of the fascist Pétain government. He calculated that the French, bitter at the loss of more than a thousand sailors, would refuse to come to the aid of the British should they come under attack. On July 4, he sent units from the Italian garrison in Ethiopia to occupy frontier towns in the Sudan, which was controlled jointly by Britain and Egypt. On July 15, the Italians swept into the British colony of Kenya, and a few weeks later occupied British Somaliland on the Gulf of Aden. Mussolini had already dispatched over 200,000 soldiers to the Italian colony of Libya. Now Italian forces began assembling on Libya's eastern frontier, a few short miles from the British protectorate of Egypt.

The British faced the Italians with a mere 60,000 troops and about three hundred aircraft, half of them in Egypt and the rest scattered around a command encompassing an enormous area that included Sudan, Palestine, Trans-Jordan, East Africa, Aden, Somaliland, Iraq, and even extended to the Balkans. The RAF's aircraft in the region were sadly outdated, but for a few squadrons of Blenheims. Most of the fighters were Gauntlets and Gladiators, radial-engined biplanes, long since discarded by front-line squadrons in England. A handful of Wellesleys and Bombays, plus some antediluvian biplane Valentia transports, made up what was optimistically known as the bomber force.

An RAF squadron, 33, was in the process of replacing its obsolete Audax two-seaters with equally obsolete Gloster Gladiator biplane fighters.

One of the unit's pilots was a soft-spoken Canadian from Victoria, British Columbia, by name Vernon Woodward. Like many young men of his generation, Woodward had long been passionately devoted to flying. Turned down by the RCAF for pilot training because he lacked a college degree, he had approached the Air Ministry in London with a view to joining the RAF. He lodged with an uncle, a farmer in Gloucestershire, during the summer of 1938 while the RAF considered his application. To his delight he was accepted for a short-service commission, and had entered flying training with all the enthusiasm of one finally realizing a lifelong ambition. In 1939, he graduated as a pilot officer – and had been promptly posted to Egypt to join 33 Squadron.

In those last few months of peace, Woodward had found himself in a sanctuary of privilege. As an officer in the RAF he became a member of what many ex-air force men remember as "the finest flying club in the world." He lived in comfort, with all the mundane details of daily life taken care of by servants, and with most days blessed by unbroken blue skies and delightful weather. He had little to do but fly Gladiators. It was nirvana for the young man from Victoria. But the good times were destined to be short-lived.

On the day the Nazis invaded Poland, 33 Squadron had moved to a coastal airfield named Mersa Matruh. A bleak spot with few amenities, Mersa Matruh lay midway between Alexandria and the Libyan border in an ocean of sand, punctuated by outcroppings of rock, with bits of foliage defiantly sucking some kind of nourishment from the barrenness. Only lizards and flies seemed to flourish here. Only they could cope with merciless weather, the sudden sandstorms that blinded everyone in their path, that filled engine intakes, "turning lubricating oil into an abrasive paste. . . . Guns became jammed, Perspex cockpit canopies scored and scratched, and food was ruined by the invasion of this menace, which also filled eyes, ears, noses and fingernails, making life at times a gritty nightmare."[47] It was a world of blazing daytime heat and bitter overnight cold, a world of canned food and strictly rationed water.

You never threw away the water you had used for washing or shaving; you kept it to fill the radiators of motor vehicles.

Training had been intensified. The Italians were expected to cause trouble soon. But when? The months had drifted by and the pilots of 33 Squadron became impatient, stuck here in this inhospitable land while earth-shaking events took place in Europe. They expected to be sent to Norway. Then France. Instead, they waited.

They had waited until June. With France defeated, the opportunistic Mussolini declared war on Britain and France. On that day, Vernon Woodward and the rest of 33 Squadron had moved to Sidi Barrani, on the border of Egypt and Libya. Four days later, a flight of Gladiators from 33 Squadron encountered a formation consisting of a Caproni 310 twin-engined bomber and its escort of three Fiat CR-32 fighters. The Fiats were biplanes, roughly equivalent in performance to the Gladiators. Woodward soon shot down the Caproni and claimed a Fiat as probably destroyed. The first aerial victories of the Desert War had been recorded. Although Woodward was impressed by the airmanship of the Italian pilots, he rated them as poor shots.

It was a promising beginning both for Woodward and for 202 Group, the British air component facing the Italians. The Group had at its head a remarkable Canadian airman, Air Commodore Raymond Collishaw, CB, OBE, DSO, DFC. A native of Nanaimo, British Columbia, the forty-seven-year-old "Collie" combined an adventurous spirit with a boisterous sense of humour. Back in 1910, as a teenager he had joined the merchant marine and had sailed with Scott's ill-fated expedition to the South Pole. During World War I, he became a member of the Royal Naval Air Service (RNAS), shooting down an amazing total of sixty enemy aircraft. He ranked third among British and Commonwealth aces, after Edward "Mick" Mannock and Billy Bishop. When Italy declared war in 1940, Collishaw was given command of 202 Group, consisting of three fighter squadrons, 33, 80, and 112, all equipped with Gladiators – plus a solitary Hurricane on 80 Squadron's strength. The gung-ho

Collishaw sent this aircraft, the only modern fighter in the region, from airfield to airfield in an effort to make the Italians think he had lots of Hurricanes at his disposal. Often he flew it himself. Collishaw called his solitary Hurricane "The Battleship" because of its multitude of machine-guns. Collishaw's Group also had four squadrons of Blenheim I bombers – 30, 45, 55, and 211 – and 113 Squadron flew the newer Blenheim IVs. Some of the Blenheims were fitted with packs of four Brownings under the fuselage.

The Italians had the advantage in numbers: more than two to one by most estimates. Their principal fighters were Fiat biplanes – CR-32s and 42s – the former as manoeuvrable as the Gladiator, the latter speedier but rather less agile. The Fiats' armament consisted of two 12.7-mm machine-guns (approximately half-inch calibre). At this time, the Italians began to introduce two monoplane fighters, the Fiat G50 and the Macchi C200, although initially they were seldom seen. Italian bombers were in general rather more modern than their fighters. The Savoia-Marchetti SM-79, the Cant Z1007, and Fiat's BR-20 were among the best bombers of their day, although their performance suffered because of Italy's lack of high-performance engines. Hence the number of three-engined aircraft in the Regia Aeronautica.

The battleground known as the Western Desert consisted of the northern coastline of Egypt and Libya, extending up to one hundred miles inland. Collishaw knew North Africa well. And he had little respect for the Italians' fighting qualities. "He believed that, instead of attacking obvious targets, it was better to be unconventional and bombard something different every day," wrote George Houghton, an RAF squadron leader who served under him. "He wanted the vast Italian air armada to burn itself out with exhaustion."[48]

Collishaw revelled in sessions with war correspondents such as Matthew Halton of the Toronto *Star* and Godfrey Anderson of Associated Press. Dining with such visitors, he would regale them for hours with his views of the war and his enemies. He was also enormously popular with his pilots; "a terrific chap," according to Tony Dudgeon, who flew Blenheims under the Canadian's command. "The only problem I had was that he rather worked on the basis that, if you were sent out on a raid, it was like going over the top in World War I. You went out and either succeeded and came back – or got yourself killed."[49]

Collishaw had "hunches," according to Houghton. "He would stand before a map and say: 'Now, the enemy knows we have our fighters here' (he would point), 'so we will bomb them from there. Well, we've got to fox 'em. See? We'll bomb him first, so that he's too busy to have a go at us. Then if his troops are withdrawing from here, he'll think we will bomb this road. So he won't use it. He'll run south, along this track. That's where we've got to hit.'"[50]

Clashes between the RAF and the Italian units became more frequent. In general, the RAF pilots did well against the Italians. Vernon Woodward rapidly acquired a reputation as a first-class fighter pilot – and a thoroughly cool customer who took the stresses and strains of combat with aplomb. No wonder his comrades were soon calling him "Imperturbable Woody." His tally of victories mounted as rapidly as his reputation. Patrols, escort duties, and ground-strafing made up most of 33 Squadron's days. Raids on enemy airfields were commonplace, with both sides often surprising the other and leaving dozens of wrecked aircraft in their wake.

In July, 33 Squadron handed in the Gladiators that had served so well, receiving Hurricanes in their place. The "tropicalized" version of the Hurricane incorporated a large air filter to protect the engine against the murderously abrasive sand, which made short work of unprotected engines. The tropical Hurricane was slower than its European counterpart, with a poor rate of climb; nevertheless, in the Western Desert at that time, it was the best fighter available.

The ground war in the desert had been dormant for many weeks. It was eerily reminiscent of the calm on the Western Front in the spring. Everyone knew it couldn't last, and it didn't. Early in

September, the commander of the forces, Italian General Rodolfo Graziani, invaded Egypt. His army made good progress until it was about sixty miles inside the Egyptian border. Then, concerned about overextending his lines of supply, Graziani halted and began building accommodations and fortifications. For three months there was little ground action in the desert, although air operations continued apace. By mid-October, 33 Squadron had sixteen operational Hurricanes, with four reserve aircraft. Late that month the unit put its new Hurricanes to good effect in an encounter with a force of SM-79 bombers escorted by twelve CR-42 fighters. Three bombers and one fighter went down to the Hurricanes' guns, with two more SM-79s claimed as probables. One 33 Squadron pilot was lost, a Canadian, twenty-year-old Edmond Leveille of Winnipeg. He crashed near Mersa Matruh and was killed instantly.

General Graziani had a reputation as a capable but ruthless commander, who had made a practice of tossing uncommunicative Arab prisoners out of aircraft. But he met his match in British General Archibald Wavell, Commander in Chief, Middle East. The fifty-seven-year-old Wavell, who had lost an eye on the Western Front, was a veteran of desert warfare, having served under General Sir Edward Allenby, commander of the Allied Expeditionary Force in Palestine. He ordered his aircraft to attack the Italians' communications and supply lines and to prevent the enemy snooping behind the lines. Wavell was preparing a surprise, and he didn't want the Italians to find out about it.

At dawn on December 9, 1940, Wavell struck. Matilda tanks swarmed into Graziani's encampment, taking the Italians completely by surprise and knocking out twenty-five tanks before their sleepy crews were fully awake. Simultaneously, two battalions of British infantry charged with fixed bayonets, hurling grenades, routing the bewildered Italians. More assaults followed, while the Royal Navy bombarded Sidi Barrani, 250 miles west of Alexandria. Cut off by an armoured advance by the British as audacious as that of the Panzers in France six months before, nearly 40,000 Italian troops surrendered. Later in the month, the 6th Australian Division advanced rapidly along the coast while the British 7th Armoured again sped across the desert, outflanking the rapidly retreating Italians. In a matter of weeks, Wavell's forces, under the command of Major-General Richard O'Connor, had thrust the Italians back some five hundred miles, defeated ten Italian divisions, and taken some 130,000 prisoners, all at a cost of less than 2,000 casualties. It was a dazzling performance. The air force could take a great deal of credit for the success. Fighters and bombers had been harassing and strafing the enemy, pioneering many of the ground-attack techniques that later led to victory in Europe.

Vernon Woodward, now a flight lieutenant, shot down at least five CR-42s during this period. One of his comrades in 33 Squadron, an RAF pilot known as "Deadstick" Dyson, achieved the extraordinary feat of destroying seven enemy aircraft in one sortie. It happened on December 11. The squadron encountered a sizeable formation of Italian fighters and bombers and claimed four victories. One Hurricane didn't come back: Dyson's. Almost a week went by before Dyson returned at the head of a column of eight hundred Italian prisoners. He reported that during the dogfight on the 11th, he had popped out of a cloud bank to find himself directly behind six CR-42 fighters escorting an SM-79 bomber. Dyson opened fire on the two vics of fighters, succeeding in hitting them all. One collided with the bomber, bringing it down. In a matter of minutes, the entire formation had become bonfires on the desert. More Italian aircraft arrived on the scene, forcing Dyson down. He made contact with British troops and eventually returned to his base.

Although Dyson's claim was met with polite scepticism at first, reports from army units soon confirmed everything. Dyson received a Bar to the DFC he had won in 1938 during the Arab revolt in Palestine.

At this early stage in the Desert campaign, Woodward was the second highest-scoring fighter pilot in the Western Desert, nudged out of the top spot by a British pilot, Flying Officer Lapsley of 274 Squadron. On the 18th, both Lapsley and Woodward shot down CR-42s. The following month, Pilot Officer "Imshi" Mason of 274 Squadron overtook them as the leading fighter pilot in the Desert.

It was a heady time for the Allied forces; they had taken on a numerically superior enemy and had acquitted themselves magnificently. Sustaining astonishingly low casualties, they had almost pushed the Italian forces out of Africa. Now they began formulating plans to capitalize on this success and finish the job off by conquering Tripolitania. Fate had other plans.

PART THREE
1941

The Lonely Fight

CONSOLIDATED CATALINA

*"We are so outnumbered there's only one thing to do.
We must attack." – Sir Andrew Browne Cunningham*

I

Benito Mussolini, the son of a blacksmith, the former teacher and journalist, ached to emulate Hitler's military triumphs, to become a modern-day Caesar. In October 1940, he had ordered an invasion of Greece from Italian-occupied Albania. He misjudged his opponents. The invasion quickly turned into a disaster. The Greeks had beaten off the Italian attacks, inflicting heavy casualties. Winter brought fresh miseries for the ill-prepared Italians, and soon they were in full retreat. The stalwart Greeks occupied about 25 per cent of Albania.

Mussolini was humiliated, Hitler furious. The German dictator, totally preoccupied by his forthcoming attack on Russia, had little interest in this Balkan "sideshow," but he had to come to his Italian ally's aid. In April he dispatched his Twelfth Army, under Field Marshal Siegmund List, to invade Greece and southern Yugoslavia.

Churchill demanded reinforcements for the Greeks. The order could hardly have come at a worse time. Wavell had been readying his forces to run the Italians out of North Africa, but now political pressure took precedence over military strategy. Most of the British land and air forces in the Western Desert set off for Greece. Unfortunately, they were too few to influence the campaign. It was yet another of the hopeless situations in which the Allies kept finding themselves.

Vernon Woodward had gone to Greece with 33 Squadron in February, before the Germans invaded. The unit established itself at Paramithia, where the airfield was "a flat, grassy field with no control tower or permanent buildings. The only running water was an icy-cold brook. Mountains shielded the area from winds but presented their own hazards – 8,000-foot peaks wrapped in mist, unpredictable wind currents that could shake airplanes as roughly as an angry child shakes a doll."[1] The locals greeted the RAF airmen as saviours, carrying them on their shoulders in triumph through village streets.

Escorting the RAF's Blenheim bombers became 33 Squadron's principal occupation. On February 27, Blenheims attacked the airfield at Valona, on Greece's west coast. Fifteen CR-42 fighters appeared on the scene. The RAF fighter escort promptly shot down seven – and two more wrote themselves off in a collision. The next day an even larger dogfight ensued. About thirty RAF aircraft – Hurricanes and Gladiators from 33, 80, and 112 squadrons – ran into about fifty Italian fighters and bombers. Accounts differ, but it seems likely that about twenty of the enemy were shot down without a single loss to the RAF units. Such brilliant successes would soon be ancient history, however; the Luftwaffe was on its way.

At 33 Squadron, a new commanding officer took over: Squadron Leader Marmaduke St. J. Pattle – "Pat" to his contemporaries – a South African with a superb record in the air.

Early in April, 33 Squadron had its first encounter with the Luftwaffe. The Germans lost five aircraft, the RAF none. On the same day, Woodward and two other pilots scrambled to intercept five Italian Z1007 bombers heading toward Vólos, on the east coast some 120 miles northeast of Athens. Woodward took off late, because his aircraft was being rearmed; an inexperienced armourer had installed several belts incorrectly, and Woodward eventually got away with only four of his eight machine-guns functioning.

By the time Woodward caught up with the Italian bombers, there was no sign of his squadron-mates, so he attacked alone. He aimed for a Z1007's wing roots, where, according to intelligence reports, the aircraft's fuel tanks were located. The initial burst seemed to have little effect. Woodward dived, quickly zooming up again and firing more bursts into the bomber's wing roots. At last, results! A spectacular plume of smoke and fire streamed from the bomber. Woodward now turned his attention to a second Z1007. He aimed for the same spot. Again he was rewarded. With the Italian aircrew hastily taking to their parachutes, the two bombers went spiralling into the ground, trailing smoke and flames. He fired at a third bomber and saw it going down in flames. Ground observers reported that it crash-landed. Woodward touched down at Lárisa with dry tanks.

But while the RAF had its successes, so did the Luftwaffe. British bombers in particular suffered heavy losses. On one notably grim day, April 12, six Blenheims set off to attack German columns. None returned. The next day, Woodward set off on a reconnaissance trip over Monastir, Yugoslavia. He was intercepted by three Me 109s. Woodward shot down one and drove the others off, after which the ever-imperturbable Canadian "was able to finish his reconnaissance before returning," according to squadron records.[2] The day after that, he shot down two Ju 87 dive-bombers. His score was mounting rapidly.

On April 15, German aircraft mounted ferocious attacks on RAF airfields in northern Greece. More than thirty Hurricanes and Blenheims were destroyed, most of them on the ground. 113 Squadron had been wiped out. A Canadian in 33 Squadron, John Mackie, from Regina, Saskatchewan, was shot down and killed attempting to take off during one of the raids. An ace, Mackie had seven enemy aircraft to his credit. Other successful Canadian pilots involved in the battle were Bob Davidson, from Vancouver, a member of 30 Squadron, flying twin-engined Blenheim fighters, and Homer Cochrane, from Vernon, B.C., flying old Gladiator biplanes with 112 Squadron.

The Luftwaffe kept up the pressure, strafing and bombing airfields with the same ruthless efficiency it had demonstrated in France and Poland. Day after day, the modest RAF force kept shrinking as its aircraft fell victim to the Germans, in the air and on the ground. The ground crews did their best, but the numbers of serviceable aircraft kept slipping.

By mid-April, little more than a dozen Hurricanes remained to defend the Athens area. To add to Allied woes, the rudimentary early warning system – observer outposts in the hills to watch for approaching aircraft – had been bombed and strafed out of existence. Now the RAF had no advance warning of raids. When at 1800 hours on April 20, the remaining Hurricanes and Gladiators assembled to take off on an offensive sweep, a massive onslaught by about one hundred German fighters and bombers caught them by surprise. Woodward shot down an Me 110 and damaged three more, but the RAF was completely outnumbered, probably by about ten to one. The battle could have only one outcome. During the slaughter, 33 Squadron's fine commander, Pat Pattle, lost his life. (The best evidence suggests that despite his premature demise, Pattle was the Commonwealth's leading ace of World War II, with well over forty victories.)

For the troops and airmen involved, the Greek campaign was an unmitigated disaster. Once again, the Allies had been outnumbered, outgunned, and outmanoeuvred. The unpalatable truth couldn't be denied: the Germans were better armed and better led. The dismal Greek campaign ended in an evacuation as humiliating as that from Dunkirk.

By the time the withdrawal was complete, the Italians had regrouped in Tripolitania – and had been reinforced by a small force of German troops under the command of a German general, Erwin Johannes Eugen Rommel, whose name would soon become better known to the average Allied soldier than that of his own commander.

33 Squadron left Greece in haste, flying 150 miles to the small and mountainous land of Crete and setting up a rudimentary base near Maleme. German Ju 88s lost no time in attacking the island's three airfields and landing strips. Defending RAF fighters claimed a handful of victories, including five bombers shot down while bombing shipping at Suda Bay. It was a brief moment of triumph in a catastrophic episode. Once again the RAF airmen faced overwhelming numbers, fewer than forty fighters and bombers against some six hundred Axis aircraft, most of them German.

The situation was just as grim for the ground forces. About 30,000 ill-equipped troops, having just escaped from Greece, had to defend an island 170 miles long and 40 miles wide with little artillery and only rudimentary communications. Their commander, the able New Zealander General Bernard Freyberg, VC, anticipated an airborne attack on the island. "Ultra," the system of interception and decryption of enemy ciphers, had told him so, even down to a last-minute change in the date of the attack. It was the sort of knowledge that would have been of inestimable value, had Freyberg the men and the equipment to take advantage of it. He hadn't. Most of the aerial action had come to an end by this point. The Luftwaffe attacks had wrecked the airfields and most of the RAF aircraft, and German fighters and bombers maintained standing patrols over every airfield, strafing and bombing whenever they saw any movement. On May 19, the Allies' last fighters on the island – four Hurricanes and three Gladiators – managed to take off without being spotted by the enemy. They flew to Egypt. Vernon Woodward remained behind to help defend the airfield.

Hitler was anxious to get the operation completed as rapidly as possible. The Balkan campaign had already put the launching of the Russian invasion back some four weeks, from May to June (which possibly made it one of the most important conflicts in the war). Field Marshal Wilhelm Keitel, the German chief of staff, wanted to conquer Malta with the airborne troops used in Crete. He correctly saw the island as far more important than Crete. Hitler didn't agree. As usual, Hitler prevailed.

On the morning of May 20, troops defending Crete looked skyward. Dozens of Junkers 52 transports soon appeared in loose formation, many towing gliders, all protected by scores of fighters. The invasion had begun.

Vernon Woodward was having breakfast at the time. He jumped into a slit trench as fighters dived down, guns blazing. The din was mind-numbing. Woodward later recalled eloquently: "Cut the sound track from the film of memory, and those few minutes become a magnificent scene in an aerial ballet. Big three-engined Junkers move steadily in serried ranks across the blue sky. Beneath them the first canopies appear, white, green, and red. Some hundreds of figures are drifting down. About them, fighters and dive bombers wheel in the last stages of their macabre dance."[3]

The paratroops of General Kurt Student's Fliegerkorps XI suffered frightful casualties as they drifted down beneath their parachutes. One company lost 112 killed out of 126. Three-quarters of one battalion were dead by the end of the day. But German reinforcements kept arriving.

For two days, Woodward operated as a member of the ground forces, manning a captured German tommy-gun and going out on patrols. Strafing by German aircraft had now become almost nonstop, while Ju 52s by the dozen kept droning overhead, bringing reinforcements. The defenders' ammunition had begun to run dangerously low.

A senior New Zealand officer urged Woodward to get himself and the few remaining RAF airmen off the island as rapidly as possible. The situation was hopeless, he said. Joining up with a party of Royal Marines, the RAF airmen succeeded in marching by night east to Canea, where they were picked up by an Australian ship and taken to Alexandria.

Vernon Woodward was awarded the DFC, having displayed "gallantry and devotion to duty in the execution of air operations." The London Gazette made no mention of the fact that his aerial victories now topped twenty, with many more damaged. Perhaps it wasn't so surprising. Dominion airmen serving in one of the "outposts of the Empire" usually regarded themselves as largely forgotten when it came to publicity, promotions, and decorations.

The catastrophic campaign was over, yet another in the unhappy series of defeats administered by the highly professional Germans. Arthur Longmore, the head of the Middle East Air Command, became the scapegoat. He was relieved of his command and replaced by a former deputy, Arthur Tedder, who, in a later, happier time would become General Eisenhower's deputy commander in Europe.

After the Greek and Crete fiascos, the army criticized the RAF as bitterly as they had during the evacuation from Dunkirk. Tedder responded that both campaigns had been lost because the army had failed to secure adequate air bases. Indeed, it was Tedder's contention that the whole war was becoming a battle for airfields.

Despite the humiliations of the retreat from Crete, a victory of sorts had been won, because the assault on the island had torn the German paratroop force to pieces. It ceased to be a significant military weapon, and its loss undoubtedly influenced the German decision not to attempt an invasion of Malta.

II

The situation in the Western Desert became volatile with the arrival of Erwin Rommel and the Afrika Korps. Wavell had been unable to follow up on his triumphs against the Italians in late 1940 and early 1941; his forces had been squandered in the hopeless campaigns in Greece and Crete. Now, only forty days after arriving in Africa, Rommel attacked. Quickly the Axis forces dislodged the British from their positions at Beda Fomm. Benghazi fell. A week later Rommel had arrived at the line from which Wavell's highly successful offensive had been launched four months earlier. Tobruk, in Libya, with its priceless deep-water harbour, was surrounded. Despite Rommel's best efforts, however, the port didn't fall. It was a serious setback to the capable German commander, the first he had suffered in the desert.

Canadian Pilot Officer Don Lush of 33 Squadron met Rommel at about this time. Shot down over Sidi Omar in Libya, he was picked up by a German patrol and taken to Bardia, where a German hospital team removed fragments of flak from his leg. During his recuperation, he found that he was the subject of much interest among the Germans. They couldn't understand why a Canadian would be fighting in the desert. Then the German commander "just dropped in on one of his flying trips, and he heard they had a Canadian air force guy in hospital. And he came in and shook hands and wanted to know how I was, how I was being treated. Spoke great English. And of course he was looked on as God by the Germans. And I was very impressed with him."[4]

Churchill had fired Wavell, replacing him with Sir Claude Auchinleck, who launched Operation Crusader in driving rain. Designed to relieve Tobruk and to recapture Cyrenaica, the campaign saw some of the heaviest air battles to date. A young Canadian pilot, Joseph Jean Paul Sabourin, of St. Isidore, Quebec, joined 112 Squadron, which was equipped with the indifferent Curtiss P-40 Tomahawk fighter. At the time, the Germans had recently introduced the Messerschmitt 109F to the desert. With its uprated DB 601 engine and its aerodynamic refinements, armed with a Mauser MG-151 20-mm cannon firing through the hollow propeller shaft and a pair of fuselage-mounted 7.9-mm machine-guns, the latest version of the famous fighter came as a shock to the Allied air force in the desert. Nevertheless, Sabourin did well in his first major encounter with the enemy. Some twenty Tomahawks ran into about forty Ju 87s escorted by thirty German and Italian fighters. Sabourin shot down a 109, an Italian G50, and a Ju 87, and damaged three other Axis aircraft.

After some of the fiercest fighting of the desert war to date, Tobruk was relieved. It was a signal triumph for the British. They pushed Rommel back to Al Agheila, about 250 miles to the west, and the Germans found themselves in a difficult position, desper-ately short of fuel and equipment. The insatiable demands of the Russian front were partly responsible, but equally significant were the relentless attacks by the Royal Navy and the RAF on Axis shipping in the Mediterranean, using bases on Malta and the mainland. Since the beginning of November, sixteen ships had been sunk, every one packed with vital supplies for Rommel. For the Germans and Italians, the all-important trip from Sicily to Tripoli had become a nightmare.

The lines now became established, hinging on the coastal village of Gazala, about forty miles west of Tobruk. The opposing forces dug in while they caught their collective breaths and prepared for the next round.

III

Early in May 1941, personnel and aircraft began to arrive at Driffield, Yorkshire, and a new unit began to take shape. By mid-month, the unit's CO, Wing Commander Peter Alexander Gilchrist, DFC, of Weyburn, Saskatchewan, was installed. Two flight commanders followed: Robert Bisset, from Edmonton, Alberta, and Walter Keddy, from Burnside, Nova Scotia. They were all RAF "types" and highly experienced. No. 405, the first RCAF bomber squadron formed overseas – and the forerunner of many more – would soon be ready to take its place as part of 4 Group RAF.

No doubt Mackenzie King congratulated himself on having insisted on the formation of Canadian bomber squadrons. They would be symbols of the new Canada, a forceful expression of the country's determination to go to war in its own way. It is questionable, however, whether King ever realized how long it would take for them to become operational. The reasons weren't hard to find. Canada had no bomber aircraft to bring to the battle, and it had no trained bomber crews. The RAF had to supply almost everything. 405 Squadron went to war with the usual Commonwealth mix of airmen. Ottawa wanted 405 to be all-Canadian as rapidly as possible, and confidently expected Canadian airmen to be lining up to transfer from RAF units to the new squadron. It didn't happen. Peter Gilchrist recalls: "The AOC of 4 Group gave me permission to call any pilot, navigator, or flight engineer in the Group and invite him to join the squadron. I called a number of them without success. All replied, 'We're happy with the RAF squadrons and don't wish to join you.'"5

King would not have been pleased.

405 squadron experienced the usual teething troubles: ground staff's inexperience with the Merlin engines that equipped the unit's Wellingtons, most of the ground personnel having come from squadrons equipped with Mercury-powered Blenheims; and dissatisfaction with the Spartan accommodations and mediocre heating, the miserable weather, the frightful food (porridge with the consistency of glue, powdered eggs tasting like mashed-up cardboard, the incessant Brussels sprouts, the endless – and, for aircrews, highly inappropriate – baked beans).

The squadron undertook its first operation on the night of June 12, 1941, four Wellingtons taking off from the grass field at Driffield and heading for Schwerte, near Dortmund. It was in the heart of the Ruhr, "Happy Valley" to the aircrews. One of the bombers developed engine trouble and had to return to Driffield. The others pushed on and, with eighty RAF Whitleys, pressed home their attack. All 405 Squadron aircraft returned safely, and their crews reported a successful op. In fact, it's doubtful whether any of them hit their intended target. The air-raid sirens certainly woke up the citizens of Schwerte and sent them scurrying to their shelters, but according to local sources, no bombs fell on the city that night. It's probable, however, that the 405 crews dropped their bombs on some part of the Ruhr; it was almost impossible to miss the hodgepodge of factories and foundries, cloaked, as usual, in a thick industrial haze.

The first aircraft of 405 Squadron to be lost was a Wellington II shot down by flak over Hannover in July. Like so many 405

Squadron aircraft of the period, it was manned by a crew consisting almost entirely of RAF airmen. The solitary exception was Sergeant Jim Kirk of Hamiota, Manitoba, the front gunner.[6]

The crew experienced little trouble in finding their target, a rubber factory. They dropped their bombs and prepared to turn for home. Then the Wellington staggered, hit by flak. The starboard engine had to be shut down. Sergeant Thrower, the RAF pilot, found that he could no longer maintain height. He ordered the crew to bale out.

Jim Kirk was the first to leave the crippled aircraft. He got away without difficulty, landing in an open field. He could see clearly in bright moonlight. He was in Germany, according to the navigator, who had done a quick calculation moments before the crew jumped, some thirty miles on the wrong side of the German–Dutch border. Kirk lost no time in burying his parachute in the muddy bank of a stream, after which he located the North Star and began the long walk westward to freedom, a path followed by so many of his compatriots in the months and years ahead.

Kirk kept to the fields and woods, walking during the short summer nights and sleeping as best he could during the days. The trek continued for three days and nights. "Two small chocolate bars and an orange were all I ate the first night, and after that I became hungrier and hungrier," he recalls. At night he had to keep moving; the farmers began work at daybreak and he daren't let one of them see him. He found a scarecrow sporting an ancient and very ragged coat. Kirk put it on over his tunic. Soon afterwards, he came across a broad, water-filled ditch with barbed wire on either side. The Dutch border? It had to be. He pushed his way through the wire. Now he was sure he had reached friendly territory. Hunger gnawed at him. After a sleep in a nearby wood, he was awakened by rain. He saw houses. And teenage girls entering one – attractive girls, Kirk noted, despite his hunger.

Kirk made up his mind. He had to get help from someone, and

why not someone attractive? Cautiously, he approached the house and knocked. A middle-aged woman answered the door. Kirk tugged the scarecrow coat off one shoulder to reveal his Canada flash.

Without a word, the woman pulled him into the house. Her father, Peter Dekker, whom Kirk describes as "a spirited gentleman of seventy," arrived and promptly announced that he had a small motorboat on the North Sea coast. He would, he said, take Kirk back to England.

He seemed disappointed when Kirk shook his head. Having survived the shooting-down of his Wimpy, Kirk could generate little enthusiasm for taking on the North Sea and German naval and air patrols. He spent the night at the Dekker farmhouse. The next day, a policeman arrived with two bicycles and a spare uniform. He told Kirk that his aircraft had crashed at Zwolle and that four of the crew had been picked up by the Germans. Another member of the crew was still at large.

No one paid any attention when two uniformed Dutch policemen – one of them Kirk – cycled to a small general store and bakery a short distance away. There, Kirk was introduced to Fritz Prenger and his two sisters. They were to be his hosts for the next ten days. The Prengers gave Kirk a room directly over the store, where there was little to do but sit and listen to customers – who included many German soldiers.

Across the road Kirk could see a prominent sign warning local citizens that the price of harbouring Allied soldiers or airmen was death. It was a constant reminder of the extraordinary courage of the Dutch people who without question assisted him and other Allied aircrew. They had everything to lose and nothing to gain, but few hesitated.

The days passed slowly. In the evenings Kirk would listen to the BBC on the Prengers' radio at a barely audible level; often he helped Prenger in the bakery.

He came down with the flu. The Prengers called Dr. Post from the village of Bergentheim. Not only did the good doctor treat

Kirk's flu, he also promised to put him in touch with the Resistance. Boldly, he drove the Canadian to a photographer at a nearby town to have his picture taken for false documents. (Later in the war, such photographs were taken in Britain, and aircrew carried them on ops to give to Resistance workers if needed.) Soon Kirk had identity papers declaring him to be a deaf mute. Three months after being shot down, Kirk left by train, escorted by the same young policeman with whom he had cycled to the Prengers' shop. The train took them to Voorschoten, north of the Hague, where Kirk stayed three weeks with Teunis and Marie Rijnsburger. They cut out a section of flooring in the entrance hall of their house, preparing an emergency hiding place for use if the Germans searched the premises. And make use of it they did. On one occasion, Kirk had to remain there for more than twenty-four hours.

Eventually, the time came for the trip back to England. Two members of the Dutch Resistance took him to nearby Hengelo. A surprise awaited him there: Sergeant Bill Dossitter, rear gunner on Kirk's crew. He, too, was awaiting his turn to escape. Kirk was able to inform him that none of the crew had been lost in the crash.

Six weeks later, they went to Utrecht by train, in company with a member of the Resistance. At Utrecht they joined two Dutch Jews and a corporal from a Highland regiment who had been on the run since Dunkirk. Soon, they told themselves, they would be in friendly territory. It wasn't to be. Just outside Utrecht they ran into a roadblock manned by SS troops. The game was finally up. For Kirk, the rest of the war was a series of prison camps in Germany and Poland until he was liberated in April 1945.*

---

* The gallant Dr. Post was shot by the Germans for his clandestine activities. Kirk lost touch with the two Dutch Jews and the soldier from the Highland regiment, but he has maintained contact with the Dutch families who aided him so unstintingly. The Prengers hid a Jewish couple for more than two years in the room that Jim Kirk had formerly occupied. The Rijnsburgers had five children, one of whom was named Jim, in Kirk's honour. Peter Dekker lived well into his nineties, helped along by a daily cigar

At the time of Kirk's misadventures, Bomber Command provided its aircrews with little or no advice on what to do if shot down. When Canadian Flight Lieutenant Tony Pengelly of 102 Squadron was shot down in November 1940, he found himself being expertly disarmed during his interrogation by

> an absolutely charming German officer. . . . He looked like he'd just stepped out of a tailor's shop. Terribly polite. Called me by name. Asked me, "How's life in 102 Squadron?" Of course I hadn't told him the squadron. And then he started to tell me little stories about different people on the station to show that he knew everything, and therefore he didn't really need to know anything. Very smooth. And he had English cigarettes which they had captured at Dunkirk. This chap had been a history professor in Austria. His major was English history, and he'd travelled extensively in England. And he knew everything about 4 Group and 102 Squadron. We'd had no training in this at all. . . . Every time he got to what I considered to be security-conscious material, I told him I didn't have to tell him that. No problem. He said, "That's all right, I'll find out some way or other . . ."[7]

For some time, Churchill's scientific adviser, Lord Cherwell (Professor Frederick Lindemann), had been wondering how effective the much-publicized bombing campaign really was. He ordered D. M. Butt of the War Cabinet Secretariat to study the accuracy of Bomber Command's bombing by night, using crews' target photographs and logbooks. The results sent shock waves through Bomber Command. Butt pulled no punches. He made it clear that

---

and a glass of gin. George Gussenhoven, one of the students who led Kirk on his escape attempt, is now a retired heart specialist; he and his wife, Lise, have twice visited Kirk in Victoria. Recalling those days, Kirk downplays his own role in the drama: "I did nothing but hide. It was the courageous Dutch who deserve all the credit."

his investigation had dealt only with those crews who claimed to have bombed their primary targets (usually about two aircraft out of three). According to Butt's findings, only one in three of those supposedly successful aircraft came within five miles of the aiming point on "average" targets. When Ruhr targets were involved, only one in *ten* of the bombers got that close. Aghast, senior air force officers protested that the tests had been carried out in bad weather, that equipment had been faulty and all manner of other factors had to be considered. Nevertheless, Butt's findings couldn't be ignored. A comfortable myth of awesome proportions had been exploded. Had they leaked out, the findings of the Butt Report might well have toppled the government; Bomber Command itself might have been broken up, just another weapon that had been tried and found wanting. The news would have been welcomed by the Royal Navy; Harris's long-range bombers were just the thing the admirals needed for U-boat hunting.

What saved Bomber Command was that Britain at that stage simply didn't have any other way of attacking the enemy. Churchill had always seen the bomber force as the one glimmer of hope in an almost unrelievedly dark vista. Although he seems to have maintained a healthy scepticism when listening to the air marshals' rasher promises – for example, their claim that Germany would be in danger of collapse in 1941 largely because of the effects of the RAF's bombing – he still nurtured high hopes for Bomber Command. Nothing would have pleased him more than to deliver absolutely pulverizing blows against every German city. No matter what, the technical problems of night-bombing had to be solved.

The air and ground crews of Bomber Command knew nothing of these problems. For them, it was business as usual. They were hitting the enemy night after night, struggling through vile weather and braving the searchlights, flak, and fighters. They did their best to find their targets, and each time they could only hope the built-up area below was the town they were looking for. They could seldom be sure.

A Canadian observer, Jack Watts of Hamilton, Ontario, flew on an operation in September 1941 that typified the difficulties of night-bombing at that period. The target was a synthetic rubber factory in a town called Hüls, deep within Germany and by no means an easy place to bomb. "Hüls was a very small community," Watts remembers, "and the plant was not within the town itself but in a nearby rural location. . . . This would be a severe test of the Bomber Command crews and their observers, who would have to navigate perfectly." Watts worked hard and steadily as the Wellington headed for its target. "The weather co-operated and I was able to incorporate some astro observations in my navigation. As we came off the North Sea into Germany, I felt confident that we were right on track for Hüls. There was little of an identifiable nature to be seen on the dark earth beneath us. Ten minutes before our estimated time over target, I crawled forward to the bombing panel in the nose to set up the bomb sight and, letting my eyes adjust to the darkness and night vision, I began studying the ground for any recognizable feature."[8]

There wasn't much to see at Hüls.

The area seemed to be wooded, but the indistinct shape gave no clue to its location. I was able to pick up, dimly, what appeared to be a railway line and follow it to a small marshalling yard not far away. This correlated reasonably well with the target map, on which a similar line served the factory we were looking for. I was convinced we were in the target area, so we carried out a square search using the railway for our point of reference. We wanted so badly to see that factory. But no matter how hard we looked, no matter how long we stared down into the blackness, we could see nothing else. . . . I agonized over our inability to identify the target visually, but we had to break off the search if we were to preserve enough fuel for the return flight. We flew back to the railway line as I reset the bomb sight and made our attack on the marshalling yard . . .

We were a worried crew all the way home and not at all happy with our failure to attack the primary target. My navigation home helped to reassure me that we had been in the target area. This raised my spirits somewhat, until we reached the debriefing room later that night. We could not help but overhear some of the reports of earlier crews, which reflected a far more successful and more colourful operation than we had to report. It was even worse when we awakened later in the day to hear news reports of a highly effective air attack on the Hüls factory.[9]

Some hours later, all crews were ordered to report to the station theatre. There they learned that Photo Reconnaissance Unit (PRU) aircraft had been out at first light to take photographs of the remains of the Hüls plant. The photographs were shown to the crews. "They showed the factory clearly. No damage at all had been done to it. In fact, not a single bomb crater could be seen in any of the photos. Eighty-six aircraft had attacked that night, seven had been lost, and all to no purpose."

It was a less-than-impressive performance by the RAF, a force whose principal *raison d'être* was strategic bombing.

Bob Dale of Toronto also flew a tour of bomber operations at about the same time and experienced similar problems with the primitive navigational techniques of the period. "Our only navigational aids were radio beacons, astro navigation, and occasional visual identification of cities or towns to supplement our dead-reckoning plots," he says.

Dale was a member of 150 Squadron, a unit that had been virtually wiped out flying Battles with the Advanced Air Striking Force in France. Now equipped with Wellingtons, the squadron was part of Bomber Command's 1 Group. "In retrospect," Dale notes, "Bomber Command tactics at that time were amazingly bad. As there were not many aircraft available, the attack on any particular target was spread over several hours, with each squadron being allocated a specific time over the target. The stated object was to damage German civilian morale, but it meant that each of our aircraft had the undivided attention of the searchlight and anti-aircraft batteries and provided the night-fighters with a better chance at interception."

Luck played a major part in any crew's survival. On Dale's sixth operation, to Duisburg, his Wellington was "coned" by searchlights for a seemingly endless ten minutes. The flak batteries on the ground did their best to destroy the bomber, trapped like some hapless moth by the blinding lights. While taking violent evasive action, the Wellington came down to 5,000 feet and was full of smoke from innumerable hits. "All of a sudden," Dale says, "the firing stopped, and a Ju 88 night-fighter flashed over the top of our aircraft and we were out of the searchlights. Somehow the fighter had failed to finish us off, although he had riddled the aircraft and wounded our rear gunner. We limped away in the darkness."

No one will ever know how many Bomber Command aircrew were lost because of the lack of essential navigational aids. Dale's crew nearly became one. During an attack on Mannheim, they took flak hits, losing their radio as they began the long trip home. They had no choice but to depend on dead reckoning, "supplemented by two star shots, which were questionable at best." At the time of the aircraft's estimated landfall, Dale altered course for base, gradually losing altitude in heavy cloud, a thoroughly unsafe practice when there is some doubt about one's whereabouts. "Finally the clouds began to dissipate, and we were able to break through – only to find that we were still over water." According to Dale's calculations, the Wellington should have been over the middle of England:

I could only assume that we were so badly off course that we were either south of England or that we had overshot and were moving out over the Atlantic. . . . We had by this time been in the air over seven hours, were low on fuel, and had no communication of any kind since leaving the target. I instructed the pilot to steer due north, figuring that we would hit England somewhere, or perhaps Ireland if we had overshot. We finally located an airfield beacon and, after firing off our emergency colours of the day, the flare path was turned on. We started our approach, but unfortunately the fuel ran out and we had to crash-land, after eight hours, fifteen minutes in the air.[10]

Afterwards, Dale found that his navigation had been commendably accurate. The aircraft had emerged from cloud over The Wash, "but we had absolutely no way of checking our position."

He recalls that the strain on aircrews was unrelenting. "In one period during July 1941, our crew carried out five attacks against heavily defended targets on five consecutive nights, with a total flying time over enemy territory of thirty-six hours."

In addition to all these troubles, even if Bomber Command aircraft succeeded in finding the targets and hitting them, the tonnage was insufficient to cause really serious damage. In short, the bombers of the day couldn't carry enough bombs.

Fortunately, new bombers were on their way. The first was the Short S.31, later called the Stirling. It emerged from the factory four months before war broke out. Soon, two more new bombers joined the Stirling: the four-engined Handley Page Halifax and the twin-engined Avro Manchester. The first was a disappointment, the other a catastrophe. The Halifax first operated with 35 Squadron at Linton-on-Ouse, Yorkshire, in November 1940. It quickly acquired an unenviable reputation among aircrew, who found it dangerously underpowered. Bill Swetman, of Kapuskasing, Ontario, flew the early Halifax and recalls that "when you were fully loaded, there was only about twenty knots between cruise and stall speeds." Worse, it was found that the bomber on which so many hopes were pinned had a fatally flawed tail unit, causing "rudder overbalance," which killed dozens of crews. The other new bomber, the Manchester, built by Avro, had an excellent airframe saddled with two atrocious Rolls-Royce Vulture engines, 24-cylinder monsters that consistently failed to deliver their rated power and acquired an alarming reputation for bursting into flames without warning. Both the Halifax and the Manchester would be subject to drastic modifications, and eventually they would re-emerge from the factories as excellent operational aircraft, the Halifax having its forward gun turret removed, engines changed, and tail redesigned, the Manchester having its two treacherous Vultures replaced by four Merlins and, with various structural modifications, being redesignated the Lancaster. But this took time. For well over three years, Bomber Command was a mighty weapon in name only.

IV

He was aggressive and impatient, often brusque, sometimes downright rude, yet he could display considerable charm when it suited him. He flew an airplane superbly. And he got things done. Not for him the lighthearted approach of so many airmen, the breezy downplaying of danger, the casual assumption of risk. John Emilius Fauquier, destined to become Canada's leading bomber pilot, was under no delusions about the dangers of his profession, but he had total confidence in his skill and experience. Born in Ottawa of well-to-do parents, he learned to fly early in the thirties, becoming a successful bush pilot. On the outbreak of war, he volunteered. The air force welcomed him into its ranks – as an instructor. The huge Commonwealth Air Training Plan was being planned, and men with Fauquier's expertise were in demand. Although impatient to get into combat, Fauquier bowed to the inevitable. He did a good job as an instructor and turned out pilots efficiently, although he could muster little enthusiasm for the job.

At last, in June 1941, Fauquier got his wish: a posting overseas.

It was a time of mounting casualties among the bomber squadrons. (Bob Dale, who graduated as an observer in December 1940, recalled that of his group of 42 novice navigators who reported to the RAF depot at Uxbridge, near London, only four survived their first tours.) Fauquier joined 405 Squadron at Driffield, Yorkshire, flying his first operation, to Emden, on Germany's northwest coast, in October 1941. Resourceful, totally dedicated to the task of getting the bombs on the target, he seemed to have been born for the job. Like Guy Gibson, he derived intense satisfaction from taking on the formidable odds of ops, and beating them time and again. His unique qualities brought him rapid promotion. In January 1942, he became a flight commander on 405; a month later he became CO, replacing Wing Commander Fenwick-Wilson, of Rock Creek, British Columbia, who had been in command since the previous August. It was a meteoric rise. Soon the name Fauquier was becoming well known in Bomber Command circles.

To his squadron-mates, Fauquier appeared to be a totally fearless individual who flew into danger without hesitation, never concerning himself about the risks – "dapper, cool-faced, steely-eyed as a swordsman," the *Star Weekly* called him.[11] Fauquier must have squirmed. He himself always maintained that a man without fear was a man without imagination. The trick was to keep fear under control, and this Fauquier did supremely well. The complete professional, he saw survival in his dangerous profession as a matter of percentages: crew teamwork counted for so much, constant vigilance for so much, intercom discipline for so much, and so on. He knew there was nothing absolute about it: a lucky 88-mm flak shell could make it all count for nothing. Perhaps that was the spice, the flavour that proved irresistible to a man of his nature.

Like many individuals of powerful character, Fauquier was usually referred to by his surname only. There was only one Fauquier. Some hated him because he seemed unaffected by casualties – "Tough break" was all he would say when an aircraft failed to return. Realist that he was, he knew there would be casualties, so what was to be gained by overreacting? When things went wrong, Fauquier's gaze froze, "and it looked as if it could penetrate solid steel," according to Lucien Thomas, an air gunner in 405 Squadron during the Fauquier era. Every op was a maximum effort as far as he was concerned, and no allowances were made. A totally inexperienced crew arrived on the base and the next day went off to Schweinfurt, fifty miles northwest of Nuremberg, on Fauquier's orders. The navigator of the crew, Allan Turton of Ottawa, recalls being shot down because, "typical of sprog crews, we were flying straight and level at 22,000 feet in an avenue of fighter flares." A German night-fighter fired his cannon into the Halifax's belly and, says Turton, "blew the middle out of the aircraft." Five of the crew escaped, two died.

There is no doubt that Fauquier drove his crews hard, invariably dissatisfied with their performance. They could always have done better, in his opinion. Edith Kup, a WAAF intelligence officer at Pocklington, East Yorkshire, one of the squadron's bases, remembers a harried – and inebriated – aircrew officer threatening to shoot Fauquier. He wasn't going to put up with any more of the CO's brow-beating, he declared, producing a service revolver in an unsteady hand. Fortunately for the war effort, he didn't carry out his threat.

There is no doubt that Fauquier was one of the toughest of commanders. He saw his job as getting every available aircraft on the target on every night of operations and had no patience with any incompetence or inefficiency that might compromise that goal. Although well read, he was no sophisticate. Edith Kup remembers him eating the flowers on his table at dinner at the Royal Station Hotel after a few drinks. Many of his airmen found his language salty, his manner crudely abrasive. The ground crews thought the world of him, because he thought the world of them and never took them for granted, always remembering to take them bottles of beer or other treats if they had worked particularly hard. Many considered him Canada's greatest bomber pilot.

Mark "Hilly" Brown of Glenboro, Man, joined the RAF in 1936. He fought throughout the battles of France and Britain, scoring 8 1/2 victories. He was killed in action late in 1941 over the Mediterranean. (Imperial War Museum)

Pitt Clayton of Vancouver during flying training in Britain, 1939. Clayton, one of about 400 Canadian pilots in the prewar RAF, flew two tours of operations and commanded two RCAF bomber squadrons: 405 and 408. (Pitt Clayton collection)

A Canadian pilot, Omer Levesque of 401 Squadron, was the first Allied pilot to produce an accurate sketch (*inset*) of the Focke Wulf 190 and the first to shoot down one of the formidable new German fighters. (Omer Levesque collection)

The Gloster Gladiator was a first-line fighter when war broke out, but was soon replaced by Hurricanes and Spitfires. This patched-up Gladiator was photographed at Kasfareet, Egypt, in 1943. Note sandbag revetment. (David Howe collection)

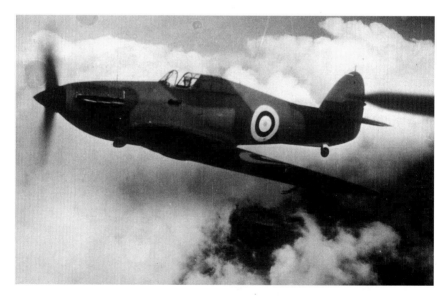

One of the few modern military aircraft on the outbreak of war: a Hurricane of No. 1 (RCAF) Squadron, photographed in 1939. No. 1 Squadron served in the Battle of Britain, later becoming designated 401 Squadron, RCAF. (Canadian Warplane Heritage Museum)

James "Stocky" Edwards, of Battleford, Sask, one of the outstanding Canadian fighter pilots of the Western Desert. This shot was taken in March 1942, when Edwards, age 20, had just arrived in the desert. (James Edwards collection)

Beaufighter night-fighter ace pilot Carl "Moose" Fumerton of Fort Coulogne, Que, and his observer/radar operator, Pat Bing of Regina, Sask, examine the remains of a Ju 88 they shot down near Alexandria. (DND, PMR 77-552)

417 (RCAF) Squadron pilots at Marcianise, Italy, are briefed for an operation. In the truck (*l to r*): Jack Evans, Intelligence officer; Bert Houle, squadron commander; Hedley Everard, flight commander. (Bert Houle collection)

Leading British and Commonwealth fighter pilot, with 38 victories, "Johnnie" Johnson of the RAF had high regard for Canadian pilots and spent much of his wartime career in their company. He commanded 126 and 144 (RCAF) wings. (DND, PL-30459)

The backbone of RAF Bomber Command in the early war years, the Vickers Wellington was one of the most successful British designs. This Mark III model, photographed in 1942, served with 419 (RCAF) Squadron. (Canadian Warplane Heritage Museum)

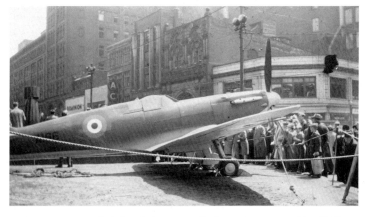

Torontonians gape at a Spitfire fighter on display at Toronto City Hall in 1942 during a War Bond drive. (Canadian Warplane Heritage Museum)

Allied experts had little respect for Japanese aircraft or airmen before Pearl Harbor. Inferior fighters, such as this Curtiss Mowhawk IV, were considered adequate for the Far Eastern theatre. (Gerry Beauchamp collection)

Harold Siefert of Winnipeg survived nearly two years on Mowhawks with No. 5 (RAF) Squadron. In November 1943, after converting to Hurricanes, Siefert lost his life when his aircraft broke up in the air. (Gerry Beauchamp collection)

Ken Boomer was the only Canadian to score an aerial victory in the Aleutians campaign. He shot down a Zero floatplane and won the DFC, but was killed two years later in a Mosquito of 418 (RCAF) Squadron. (DND, 76-596)

Low-level attacks on enemy shipping were hazardous. This 407 (RCAF) Squadron Hudson suffered hydraulic damage in such an attack, the subsequent landing being described as "unconventional" by the pilot, Cameron Taylor of Winnipeg. (Cameron Taylor collection)

An unusual view of the cockpit of an old Stranraer biplane flying boat, March 1941. Photo taken by the skipper, Jack Holmes, from the forward hatch. Copilot Hugh Hirst (r) is at the controls; at left, Canadian navigator John Iverach. (John Iverach collection)

The gunner of a Fleet Air Arm Swordfish lets fly at a target drogue (r). An early Thirties design, the Swordfish served throughout the war in a variety of roles, with remarkable success. (Frank Harley collection)

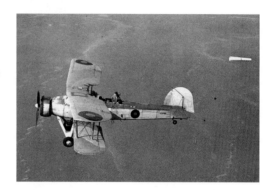

Like a Roc: One of the many mediocre aircraft with which the Fleet Air Arm went to war was the Blackburn Roc. Sluggish and slow, it was soon relegated to training duties. (Frank Harley collection)

The elderly Valentia bomber/ transport saw action at the beginning of the Western Desert campaign. An RCAF fighter pilot, David Howe, photographed this Valentia at Kasfareet, Egypt, April 1943. (David Howe collection)

British and Commonwealth airmen carried Russian-language identification when flying over or near Soviet territory. When confronted by unfamiliar servicemen, Soviet troops tended to shoot first and ask questions much later. (Gordon Gray collection)

The three Turnbull brothers of Govan, Sask, were operational airmen with Bomber Command. In December 1943, near London, they had their picture taken with a friend, Peggy Brown. *From l*, Bob, Walter, John. (John Turnbull collection)

V

When John Iverach of Winnipeg arrived in Stranraer, on Scotland's
west coast, in the early spring of 1941, he was informed that the
town, with a population of 17,000, had the country's highest rate of
venereal disease and pregnancy among unmarried females. Iverach,
a young man of twenty-three with a lively curiosity, was intrigued.
Stranraer certainly didn't look very sinful. Nestled in the hilly shore
of Wig Bay, it was the main departure point for ferries to Northern
Ireland, and one of the RAF's principal flying-boat bases. The Flying
Boat Training School (FBTS) and two operational flying boat
squadrons, 209 and 240, were based there. Iverach recalled:

> To those of us who had never before seen a flying boat, the
> motley variety of them scattered around the harbour,
> snubbed up to their mooring buoys, was a thrilling sight: the
> FBTS's fleet of operationally obsolete Singapores, relics of a
> bygone era; 240 Squadron's Supermarine Stranraers, the
> pride of the RAF when first introduced in 1936, but now just
> one short hop from the museum; and 209 Squadron's
> Saunders-Roe Lerwicks, looking like miniature, twin-
> engined versions of the mighty four-engined Sunderlands.
> The Sunderlands, bristling with four-gun turrets, were
> respectfully called by the Germans "flying porcupines"; the
> Lerwicks, in contrast, because of their tricky handling capa-
> bilities, were called by those who flew them, "flying pigs."
> Only about fifty Lerwicks had been built, and 209 Squadron,
> the only one equipped with them, was rapidly using them up,
> much to the relief of the flight crews and the maintenance
> staff. But to us newcomers, they were all objects of great
> beauty, our passports to high adventure.[12]

The following morning, Iverach and three other new Canadian arrivals met the "Chiefie" (flight sergeant) in charge of aircraft maintenance. His greeting was less than effusive: "What in hell do you colonials think you can possibly contribute here? . . . We don't need the likes of *you*; what we need is some buggers with a little experience!" It was the sort of heart-warming greeting that many Canadians received in those early days of the war.

Iverach became a member of 240 Squadron. The unit's pilots were all experienced air force regulars, products of an age when RAF flying-boat captains considered themselves the élite, almost on a par with the skippers of the Queens. Iverach noted,

> Only the top "Cranwell Boys" were selected for flying boats, and before joining squadrons they had to complete a gruelling and very thorough training in a wide variety of subjects not required by bomber and fighter pilots. . . . The Cranwell Boys generally looked down their noses at the VRs [Volunteer Reservists] as inferior upstarts. They considered all "colonial" volunteers, such as us, just about the lowest form of aircrew life. However, our stature rose, in their eyes, grudgingly, but noticeably, when they learned that we were astro-trained navigators. We avoided any discussion of the actual extent of our training and experience.[13]

Iverach's first skipper was Flight Lieutenant (later Air Commodore) Jack Holmes. To the gregarious Iverach, he seemed frosty and distant. But competent. He handled his cumbersome biplane Stranraer flying boat superbly. Soon Iverach came to realize that the somewhat strained relations on the flight deck were the product of shyness between young men of totally different backgrounds rather than of any ill feelings. Jack Holmes recalls that "whatever John thought of me, I liked him from the word go. The fact that he was a Canadian – of whom we'd seen very few at that time – was a source of much interest to me." Holmes had been an aircraft apprentice at the RAF Electrical and Wireless School at Cranwell for three years before being awarded a flight cadetship, after which he spent a further two years training to be a pilot. "Both the RAF College," he says, "and more especially the Electrical and Wireless School, instilled a firm discipline, and five years of regimentation inhibited all but the most extroverted personalities. By contrast, John Iverach, broadly educated in the wide open spaces of Manitoba, was a free spirit embarking on a great adventure. He was a jaunty, ebullient character with a great sense of humour. He had a light touch, which I lacked; his ability to crack a joke at difficult times helped to bolster morale and keep the crew together as a team." From the start, Holmes respected Iverach's skills: "John had been well trained in Canada. He was an adept navigator who could assimilate evidence from a variety of instruments and calculate positions and course without forgetting to look out of the window occasionally to check on conditions outside. Some navigators become so immersed in charts and tables that a major error escapes notice."

On their first night trip together, Holmes and Iverach flew the Stranraer out to search for a group of disabled ships that had become separated from a convoy. Iverach stared into the inky darkness but could see nothing. Holmes suddenly yelled, "There they are!" Iverach still couldn't see the ships. Holmes explained that he was making the mistake of trying to look straight at the vessels. "You can't see them because you're looking right at them. You have a blind spot in the centre. Try looking a bit to the side and you'll see their outline in your peripheral."[14] He was right.

During those early war years, there existed a vast gulf between commissioned and non-commissioned ranks in the RAF, particularly in the flying-boat squadrons. It affected every aspect of life. "In hotels and bars there was quite strict segregation," Holmes recalls. "It was 'not done' for NCOs and airmen to drink with officers, so the former stuck to the public bars and the officers to the saloon bars and lounges. As many of the RCAF aircrew sergeants were well-educated college graduates, such discrimination must have seemed bizarre to them." The discrimination reached lunatic levels when the squadron moved to Lough Erne, in Northern Ireland. The station was still under construction when Iverach arrived there late in February. "But when our single aircraft arrived, no provision had been made for a Sergeants' Mess, or even for a dining room for anyone except the officers. We ate our dinner standing outside in freshly falling snow while the officers dined in a private dining room."[15]

Soon afterwards, Iverach was commissioned and was thus spared such inequities. At about this time, the squadron began trading the antediluvian Stranraers for American-built Catalinas. The Catalina was ideal for long-range patrols, possessing the ability to stay aloft for more than twenty-five hours – thirty-five with overload tanks.

Late in May, the crew was involved in the hunt for the German battleship *Bismarck*.* Near Iceland, they saw "an unmistakable outline on the horizon, probably fifty miles away to the north: the flagship of the British fleet, the mighty HMS *Hood*."[16] Another vessel could be seen nearby. Puffs of smoke and flashes of fire could be seen coming from both, even at that distance. To Iverach and the crew it looked as if the *Hood* was busy with target practice.

"Not long after we landed," Iverach recalled, "we heard the tragic news: the *Hood* had been sunk in a brief battle with the *Bismarck*, by one freakish bit of bad luck, when a single shell landed smack in the *Hood*'s magazine. There were only three survivors out of a total complement of about fifteen hundred men, we were told. We were stunned in disbelief. The 'gunnery practice' we had witnessed undoubtedly was part of the *Hood*'s final battle."[17]

The following day, the squadron's Catalinas took off to shadow the German battleship.

---

* Displacing some 50,000 tons, the *Bismarck* was the most formidable battleship in the world, with a top speed of over thirty knots and an alarmingly potent armament of eight 15-inch guns. The British ships capable of sinking her couldn't catch her; those that could catch her couldn't sink her.

By then, the bright sunshine of the previous day was long gone. Low stratus cloud hung over the sea, and the visibility steadily deteriorated as we moved further south. We tried to get close enough to take some photographs with our long-range camera, but it was hopeless. Whenever we attempted to move in, the giant ship almost blew us out of the sky, so accurate was her gunnery. It was almost amusing to recall that the armament people had been so naïve as to equip us with two 500-pound armour-piercing bombs to "drop on her if you get the chance." Even if we had been stupid enough to try, and lucky enough to succeed, such tiny missiles would have bounced off her mighty deck, whose upper armour was 50-mm thick and lower armour 80- to 120-mm thick. Looking down at the massive bulk crashing through the heavy sea, sending great clouds of spray into the air with each impact, I found it hard to realize that I was seeing the mightiest battleship ever built.[18]

Earlier in the year, the two formidable German battle cruisers *Scharnhorst* and *Gneisenau* were berthed in Brest harbour. British bomber crews had done their utmost to destroy them, flying some two hundred sorties, most of them in daylight. Of all the hundreds of bombs dropped, not one had scored a direct hit. One, however, had landed on the dry dock directly beside the *Gneisenau*, but like so many British bombs of the period, it had failed to detonate.

Had the bomb exploded, it would probably not have done much damage to the heavily armoured ship. Ironically, as a "dud," it had posed a more serious threat to the enemy. It lay only a matter of feet from the great ship. Would it explode? Could it cause critical damage? There was no doubt about it: the bomb had to be disposed of.

The Germans had not dared tackle the job with the *Gneisenau* so close. So they had run the ship out into the harbour and secured her. In a matter of hours, the bomb would be disarmed and the ship could be returned to the safety of the dry dock.

Such was the situation on April 5, 1941, when a PRU Spitfire photographed the harbour. The sight of the *Gneisenau* in mid-harbour set pulses racing at Coastal Command HQ. Might it be possible to sink the battleship with torpedoes? In theory the answer was yes, but the sortie would have to be classified as suicidal. Only the most incredible luck would enable an aircraft to deliver a torpedo and get away intact. At another time, in different circum-stances, that would undoubtedly have been the end of it. But in the spring of 1941, the air force had been taking a great deal of criticism for its apparent inability to sink the two German battleships. So, although it meant almost certain death for the crew, perhaps there was an outside chance of a lucky hit on the battleship. In the merci-less profit-and-loss of war, it became a venture worth undertaking.

Brest harbour was one of the most heavily defended targets on earth, with batteries of guns covering every approach. An aircraft would face about a thousand guns, a quarter of them of heavy calibre. What was more, a stone mole (a protective wall) had been built to protect the inner harbour. If, by some miracle, an aircraft managed to penetrate the harbour, the torpedo would have to be dropped just beyond the mole. The ground rose sharply behind the harbour, necessitating a climbing turn for the attacking aircraft, virtually guaranteeing an early demise for the crew.

They gave the job to a detachment of six Beauforts of 22 Squadron, temporarily based at St. Eval, Cornwall. Three were to bomb the torpedo nets, three to attack the ship with torpedoes.

The airfield at St. Eval was large, but it lacked paved runways. That alone nearly doomed the operation, for after recent heavy rains the field had become a quagmire. As the three bomb-carrying Beauforts taxied out over the sopping grass to take off, two of them became bogged down, their main wheels sinking up to their axles in the morass. Frenzied revving of their engines helped only to embed the heavy aircraft more securely.

Just four Beauforts got away, the last taking off shortly after 0500. The one remaining bomb-carrying Beaufort soon got lost in the murk, as did one of the torpedo aircraft. Now the strike force had shrunk to two.

A heavy veil of mist hung over the sea, and rain showers did their best to eliminate what little visibility remained. In one of the two Beauforts, Ken Campbell, a twenty-four-year-old pilot from Ayrshire, Scotland, was finding the going tough. The windshield of his plane was streaked with rain that kept distorting his vision; hardly a satisfactory state of affairs at low level. Campbell's observer, Jim Scott of Toronto, had been a fellow trainee with John Iverach in Canada, "one of the most voluble of students," according to Iverach, and an engaging character, who once appeared on parade in polka-dot neckwear because he had mislaid his standard-issue black tie.

Approaching Brest, Campbell's crew glimpsed the other Beaufort. Jimmy Hyde, the Australian. He, too, seemed to be uncertain about what to do. Where were the others? What had happened to the bomb-carrying Beauforts? Had they already bombed the torpedo nets? If they had, the harbour looked remarkably tranquil. The orders were straightforward: Do not attack until the torpedo nets have been destroyed. And yet . . .

Now the first glimmers of dawn began to peep under the heavy clouds. It would be daylight in a few short minutes. Then there'd be not the slightest possibility of getting away with this . . . But what difference did it make? The operation had been suicidal from the start, hadn't it? Campbell peered out across the rainy, misty waters. No sign of activity, hostile or otherwise. What had happened? He didn't know that two of the bomb-carrying Beauforts were still trying to extricate themselves from the mud of St. Eval, and that the third had got lost en route to the target. Neither did the Canadian, Scott. The entire plan had come apart at the seams.

They made up their minds. It was absurd to have come all this way only to go around in indecisive circles. The *Gneisenau* had to be sunk. The briefing officer had explained it all: the danger to Atlantic convoys; the potential loss of merchant ships and precious cargoes. It could mean the difference between victory and defeat!

Crouched on his seat in the nose of the Beaufort, the powerfully built Jim Scott watched the target growing as it neared. Suddenly, the harbour's defences came to life. Multicoloured flak streaked across the water, rising, falling, curving, seeming to pick up speed as it flew. The surface of the sea tilted, streaming away a few feet below. It steadied as Campbell lined up for his all-important approach, the water a blurring carpet a few feet below the bouncing, vibrating aircraft. Bullets and shrapnel hit the aircraft with flat metallic thuds. A flak ship materialized out of the mist. More flashing gun barrels. More streaking dots of light. More smacks on the hull. It was like flying into a metallic hailstorm. The sharp stench of explosive filled the trembling hull of the aircraft. Ahead, taking form in the fog like some ghostly apparition, the vast bulk of the *Gneisenau* . . .

Fifty feet above the water, the Beaufort sped for the huge vessel, taking hits, yet somehow continuing to fly. Over the mole . . . It wasn't possible, yet it was happening . . . Her metal flanks lacerated by shrapnel, the Beaufort flew on, engines still functioning, crew still alive and alert.

The torpedo dropped away. A perfect launch. Campbell and his crew had achieved the impossible; they had taken on the toughest defences in the world and had defied them, bursting through the fire to drop their torpedo at point-blank range.

What happened next is debatable. It is almost certain that Campbell was hit at some point in the approach. He may have cried out to Scott. He may have been unable to say a word. In any event, it seems that during the suicidal run-in to the target, the Canadian scrambled out of his compartment and went to Campbell's aid. Possessing a rudimentary knowledge of flying, he was probably able to take control. But the occupants of the stricken bomber had only moments left. The defensive fire, an almost solid barrage of steel, had ripped their Beaufort to pieces. The inevitable happened. The aircraft went out of control, twisting as if in pain, smashing into the water, dissolving into a million fragments. Those crew members still alive died at the instant of impact.

But their sacrifice had not been in vain. Campbell's torpedo found its mark, bursting against the side of the battle cruiser. The great ship heaved, like some primeval monster disturbed from its slumber. Had she been on the open sea, there can be little doubt that she would have gone straight to the bottom, a total loss. Because *Gneisenau* was in the harbour, the Germans were able to save her. While she lay helpless, they brought in a dozen or more ships to support her while they pumped out the sea water. They got her back into dry dock and began repairs. The work took many months – precious months. In fact, the ship did not emerge from Brest until the famous Channel dash of February 1942, almost a year later. Although Campbell and Scott and their crew didn't succeed in sinking the *Gneisenau*, their extraordinarily gallant attack put the great ship out of action long enough to save the strategic position on the Atlantic. Hitler had been planning a massive assault on Britain's trade with America. The *Scharnhorst* and *Gneisenau* were to have joined forces with the *Bismarck* to create a naval force that, he calculated, could savage Atlantic traffic to such a degree that the war might well be won in two or three months. It was by no means a fantastic concept.

According to Resistance sources, when the shattered hulk of Beaufort N1016 was dragged from the harbour, Jim Scott's body occupied the pilot's seat.

Campbell won the Victoria Cross for his exploits; Scott received the DFM. The contributions of the other two members of the crew, Sergeants Mullins and Hillman, went unrecognized.

RAF fighters went on the offensive in 1941, attacking the Germans in occupied France almost daily – "leaning into Europe," as Sholto Douglas, the new chief of Fighter Command, put it.

Offensive sweeps were dangerous, and cost the lives of hundreds of pilots, but they were necessary, according to the Air Staff. As in the Great War, the RAF chose to take the offensive no matter what the cost. Loosely known as "sweeps," the offensive patrols over occupied territory came in various shapes and sizes. A "Circus" was an attack by one or more heavily escorted bombers on a short-range target with the purpose of enticing the Luftwaffe fighters to come up and fight. A "Ramrod" was an operation in which the destruction of the target was the prime purpose. A "Rhubarb" was a low-level attack by fighters and fighter-bombers attacking targets of opportunity, usually with plenty of cloud cover. A "Ranger" was a strong fighter sweep in search of German fighters, usually passing close to enemy airfields. A "Roadstead" was an attack on enemy shipping, at sea or in harbour.

At first the sweeps were fought with the Germans on more-or-less-equal terms. The RAF flew the Spitfire V, powered by the Merlin 45 engine, and the Hurricane, although the latter was rapidly becoming obsolescent. The Germans flew the Me 109F. There was little to choose between the aircraft of either side. But the Luftwaffe had a surprise in store. At first the reports were inconclusive. Some pilots thought the Luftwaffe was using Curtiss Mohawks, since some of these mediocre American fighters had been ordered by the French air force; they might have been taken over by the Luftwaffe for use in combat. But the pilots who encountered the new fighter rated it far superior to the Mohawk – and in a number of important ways superior to the Spitfire V. A Canadian pilot with 401 Squadron, Omer Levesque, of Mont-Joli, Quebec, was the first to describe the new aircraft accurately to intelligence officers – and the first to shoot one down. The new fighter was soon identified as the Focke-Wulf 190. Levesque had been involved in a battle with 190s during a sweep over France in the fall of 1941. The radial-engined German fighters were impressive performers. Levesque didn't recognize them, but he took note of their features, and sparkling performance. Returning to base, he sketched the formidable new aircraft, and soon copies of Levesque's sketch had been distributed throughout Fighter Command. On November 22, Levesque succeeded in shooting a 190 down in flames:

> All of a sudden, somebody got on the tail of the Spit in front of me. We were in a sharp turn, and the next thing I knew, my leader got shot down. . . . I could see they were a new type of enemy fighter. . . . I made a steep turn and got on one's tail and got him right in his wing tanks. I stuck with him, and it's a good thing, because the sealant in the fuel tanks went to work, and I could see the gas that was streaming out got less and less. . . . I could see the German pilot looking at me so clearly in the turn-abouts. . . . He went down in a straight dive in flames. The pilot didn't get out. . . . After the fight we found popped-out rivets on my wings, and the plane never did fly straight again.[19]

Tales of the Focke-Wulf's remarkable performance sped around the officers' and NCOs' messes of Fighter Command like a particularly virulent plague. Hugh Godefroy of Toronto, who had recently joined 401 Squadron, heard of one pilot who spotted a 190 streaking into a formation of Spitfires escorting Blenheims:

> He had half-rolled and gone straight down on the bombers, shooting one down at 90 degrees deflection, pulled out of the dive below the bombers and had gone straight up through them again shooting down another. He had enough speed to

climb five thousand feet for a victory roll before diving back into France. The escorting fighters couldn't get anywhere near him. . . . From the point of view of speed, flying our Spitfire Mark V against FW 190s was like flying Hurricanes against 109s. There was only one consolation. At least we could still turn inside them.[20]

Sweeps appealed to some pilots – Douglas Bader, for one – but most detested them. Johnnie Johnson, the RAF's leading ace, admitted to "a deep, dark hatred" of them.[21] The trouble with sweeps was that the enemy usually held all the advantages. It was the Battle of Britain all over again, only in reverse. This time, Allied pilots who parachuted to safety after being shot down were in enemy territory, just as the Luftwaffe pilots had been the previous year. Once again it was the Allied pilots' turn to worry about having enough fuel to get home after combat.

Of the various forms of incursion practised by Fighter Command at this period, the most effective was undoubtedly the "Circus." Usually four bombers – Halifaxes, Stirlings, or Blenheims – would head for France surrounded by a wing of some thirty-six or more Spitfires. The formations looked like huge beehives droning across the sky; indeed, the term was sometimes used in official reports. Support wings would "sweep" the way to the target, engaging any fighters that might rise to attack the beehive. A target-withdrawal wing met the fighters and bombers as they turned for home. The sweeps seem to have caused the enemy only minor casualties. If the results were unimpressive, at least they were a way of "blooding" the dozens of new pilots now streaming across the Atlantic, graduates of the British Commonwealth Air Training Plan in Canada.

Circuses became larger and more frequent after the German invasion of Russia, in June 1941. The idea was to alarm the Germans to such an extent that they would keep sizable fighter forces in Europe, or even bring units back from the Soviet Union. It seems doubtful, however, that the sweeps caused even one Luftwaffe fighter unit to be withdrawn from the Eastern Front.

Hugh Godefroy's first "circus" was led by the notable Battle of Britain ace Robert Stanford Tuck, DSO, DFC. Godefroy appreciated Tuck's "spotlessly clean" Hurricane at dispersal; it bore a wing commander's pennant and twenty-five swastikas painted on its immaculate flank. Godefroy recalled: "We climbed slowly in good order into a cloudless sky over the sparkling ultra-marine blue of the English Channel flecked with white caps. With butterflies in my stomach, I saw for the first time the pointed bill of Cap Gris-Nez, and to the west of it, the curved jetty sticking out into the Channel from Boulogne Harbour. We levelled off at twenty thousand feet and for the first time R/T [radio/telephone] silence was broken by Bob Tuck: 'Okay, chaps, keep your eyes open.'"

Godefroy was amazed by the number of aircraft in the formation: a squadron of Spitfires at every thousand feet up to 27,000. "Below us, like a mother hen with its brood, was a single four-engined Stirling bomber surrounded by squadrons of Hurricanes."

When enemy aircraft were reported, Godefroy was so busy looking for them that, like countless fledgling fighter pilots before him, he lost touch with the rest of his formation. "In an instant, I was miles from my squadron, now on their way home. With my throttle wide, I gave chase, kicking my tail out of the way from time to time to check the blind spot beneath it. Excited reports of diving 109s buzzed in my ear, and I felt sure that everyone was warning me. From high above, an aircraft slowly spun down on fire, leaving a long black snaking trail behind it. Around me on all sides were black puffs from exploding heavy ack-ack shells. They looked so completely harmless in the brilliant sky."[22]

Godefroy caught up with his unit over Dover and returned to base, only to be told off for not staying in formation.

By this time, increasing numbers of officers were questioning the wisdom of continuing the attacks that achieved so little but cost so much. John Kent, the Canadian who had led the Poles during the

Battle of Britain, caused a stir at an 11 Group conference by asking what was the purpose of the sweeps:

> If it was to destroy the industrial potential of the various targets and so reduce the contribution of industry in the occupied countries to Germany's war effort, I maintained that it would require a far greater bomber force than we had so far escorted. If, I continued, the bombers were merely there as bait to bring up the fighters, we should restrict our radius of activity to that which would permit us to fight without the nagging fear of running out of fuel. This mental obstacle seriously interfered with a pilot's fighting spirit, and it was my opinion that we had lost far too many first-class men because these factors were not receiving sufficient attention."[23]

The sweeps went on.

Between mid-June and the end of December 1941, Fighter Command lost (killed, wounded, or missing) 395 pilots. Claims for Luftwaffe aircraft shot down totalled 731. The Battle of Britain "numbers game" was in full swing again, with similar results. Postwar investigations reveal that the Germans lost only 154, "of which fifty-one were not even attributable to RAF/RCAF action; probably at least half the Germans who were shot down survived to fight another day."[24]

Promotion came quickly to the pilots who kept coming back. Hilly Brown, one of the earliest Canadian aces, now wore the three stripes of a wing commander. The young man from Glenboro, Manitoba, was twenty-nine. In October he was posted to Malta. From RAF headquarters in Valletta, he wrote to his sister, announcing his safe arrival and hoping that his letter would reach her by Christmas. It did, but it was the last she would receive. Ten days later, Hilly Brown was hit by flak during a sweep over Sicily. His Hurricane was seen gliding earthward, after which his comrades lost sight of him. A few days later, an unidentified aircraft dropped a note saying that "Lieutenant-Colonel" Brown had been killed in action and had been buried with full military honours. Canada's first great fighter pilot of the war was dead.

Precisely one week after Hilly Brown's death, Lionel Gaunce from Derwent, Alberta, died when his Spitfire plunged into the sea off the French coast. Gaunce had flown with 615 Squadron during the Battle of France. At the time of his death, he was the CO of 41 Squadron.

Four stalwarts of the Canadian 242 Squadron lost their lives during 1941: Willie McKnight of Calgary, twenty-three; Lawrence Cryderman of Toronto, twenty-one; John Latta of Victoria, British Columbia, twenty-seven, who had shared in the very first RAF victory in the Battle of Britain; and Hugh Tamblyn of Yorkton, Saskatchewan, twenty-three.

VII

By late 1941, Japan was growing increasingly bellicose. It was becoming vital to bolster Allied defences in the Far East. Many aircrew were ordered to fly operational aircraft out to their new units. Only a few years earlier, such long-distance flights had been the stuff of panegyrics in the newspapers. Now sending inexperienced crews to fly halfway around the world smacked of desperation, but it had to be attempted.

In November 1941, John Wilson, of Blairmore, Alberta, set off in a reconditioned Beaufort to fly to Ceylon (now Sri Lanka). He carried a three-man crew, all RAF. The crew had just undertaken operational training in Devon. The first leg of the trip, to Gibraltar, took over seven hours and was the longest flight that any of them had completed. After a few days in Gibraltar, Wilson was ordered to leave for Malta, the first step on the journey east. He was to take off in daylight in order to land at Malta two hours after dark to avoid enemy fighters.

Shortly after take-off, Wilson encountered a low-lying fog. Now none of the crew could see any sign of land, or indeed of anything. The mist was a smothering, blinding blanket. The navigator calculated that they had overshot Malta. "We had been using our radio – an old crystal set – in an effort to get some sort of assistance from Malta, as we did not have a loop for direction finding," Wilson recalls. Malta didn't respond to the crew's appeals for assistance, apparently not having been told that the Beaufort was coming. Typical. The radio operators there probably thought the frantic calls were some trick of the Germans. The wireless operator continued to transmit, without success. Wilson glanced anxiously at his fuel gauges. No more than an hour's flying time left; after that . . . goodness knows.

Now Wilson turned west, blindly groping his way through the darkness, keeping down to an altitude of about fifty feet, where the fog was less dense. He occasionally glimpsed the leaden sea below.

Then, in a magic moment, the crew saw land! It had to be the east coast of Sicily, they decided. Thankful to have a "fix" to work from, Wilson turned south, seeking the southeast of the island, little more than fifty miles from Malta.

It was a lonely trip; the only sign of life was a flame-float, which must have been dropped by another aircraft. But the Beaufort crew saw no sign of the plane. They pushed on, until they arrived at what Wilson took to be the southeast point of Sicily. The navigator provided a course to Malta. Its accuracy was questionable because, as Wilson points out, "We had had no gen on winds for hours."

The trip to Malta should have been completed in a matter of minutes, but the minutes kept ticking away without a glimpse of anything in the murk. Wilson began another square search, feeling like a man groping his way about a darkened, totally unfamiliar house.

"We flew around in ever-widening circles for what seemed

hours, finding only water and still more water." The tension in the confined space of the Beaufort's cabin became almost palpable. "Finally, around midnight, I headed north again, looking for Sicily," Wilson recalls. To the crew's relief, they found land about half an hour later, although they couldn't identify it. "At this point, we had been flying for over ten hours, and the fuel tanks, including the spare in the bomb bay, were nearly empty." Wilson knew he had no choice. He had to ditch while he still had power. There was land within sight. It was now or, in all probability, never. He warned the crew to prepare themselves, turned his wing lights on, lowered flaps, and cut the throttles. He glanced at his altimeter as the Beaufort lost height. Minus eighty feet, it told him, as aircraft and sea made noisy, destructive contact. One propeller parted company with its engine, and the Beaufort's front compartment shattered, instantly filling with water. But everyone was all right, and the aircraft stayed afloat long enough for the crew to scramble into the dinghy, which soon ran ashore. The crew became prisoners of the Italians. The next day they met Luftwaffe airmen at Comiso. The Germans spoke excellent English. All were surprised that the Beaufort was aloft on such an unpleasant night; Luftwaffe aircraft had been grounded because of the weather, they explained. Wilson later heard that some thirty Beauforts were lost attempting to fly east through the Mediterranean at that period. Wilson and his crew spent the rest of the war as prisoners.

The Luck of the Game (1): Eric Cameron, of Trois-Rivières, Quebec, joined the RCAF in 1940 and trained as a wireless operator/air gunner. A year later he was undergoing OTU training in England. One winter evening he missed the last bus back to camp and had to spend the night in an empty, and unheated, air-raid shelter. When at last the first bus of the day arrived, it broke down before reaching Cameron's destination. The shivering passengers had to wait for a relief bus. By the time Cameron got to the field, his aircraft was warming up, about to take off. He hurried out onto the field, hoping to catch the pilot's eye. He didn't. The Whitley's engines roared, and the slipstream knocked Cameron flat. Disconsolate, aware that by being absent for take off he had committed one of the most heinous of aircrew crimes, Cameron watched the Whitley depart without him. It vanished without a trace. The next day three Whitleys were dispatched to search the area where it had gone missing. One crew was short a WAG, so Cameron and another man volunteered for the trip. They tossed a coin to see who should go. Cameron lost the toss and stayed behind. That Whitley also vanished without a trace.

PART FOUR
1942

Nadir

CURTISS KITTYHAWK

*"We have forty million reasons for failure but not a
single excuse." – Rudyard Kipling*

I

The Japanese invaded Burma in January 1942. The agonizing struggle in the jungle had begun, with the vital 680-mile Burma Road, connecting Burma with China, at stake. Rangoon fell on March 8, another stinging humiliation for the British and her allies. The Japanese aimed to cut off China's last links with the outside world and to establish a springboard for taking India. Allied scaremongers even postulated that, after India, the Japanese would advance west, eventually to meet their German allies in the Middle East, but it is doubtful whether even the most sanguine of the Japanese planners ever seriously considered such an ambitious strategy. Nevertheless, Churchill had good reason to call this the most critical phase of the war, even more perilous than that facing Britain after the fall of France.

Allied fortunes had hit rock bottom. Hong Kong had fallen. So had Manila. And Bataan. The humiliating loss of Singapore was preceded by the sinking of the British battleship *Prince of Wales* and the battle-cruiser *Renown*, in bizarre circumstances. Vice-Admiral Sir Tom Phillips, the man in charge, was a gallant old salt but myopic on the subject of air power; he "resolutely and violently rejected the idea that an aeroplane could be any real threat to a man-of-war," according to Sir John Slessor, later marshal of the RAF.[1] Phillips learned his lesson the hard way when his flagship was sunk beneath him, the victim of Japanese bombers.

The conflict between East and West had been many years in the making. Although Japan had fought on the Allied side against Germany in the Great War, relations soon deteriorated. In the inter-war years, a spirit of "intense racialist nationalism," as historian John Keegan calls it, pervaded the island nation of sixty million. Japan's industrial power depended upon the importation of massive quantities of food and raw materials, particularly oil. Japanese nationalists proposed a solution to the problem: imperial conquest. They looked to China, seeing it as a contemptible hotbed of incompetence and corruption ripe for the picking. In 1931, Japan took over Manchuria, in northeast China. It was the beginning of a succession of "incidents" which made so many headlines in the thirties.

By September 1940, Japan had been committed to the Tripartite Pact with Germany and Italy. The lines had been drawn. For more than a year, the fragile peace held. On December 7, 1941, it was irrevocably shattered at Pearl Harbor.

The Japanese, like most of the belligerents, went to war burdened by an appalling lack of knowledge about their enemies. In retrospect, it seems almost beyond belief that the Japanese could so misjudge the strength and will of the United States and Britain. But in many ways, the Allies were just as misinformed about Japan. British officers made no secret of their scorn of the "short-sighted little men in baggy uniforms" who constituted the Japanese army. Japanese aircraft and other weapons were dismissed as inferior copies of outdated Western designs.

II

At the beginning of April 1942, a twin-engined Catalina flying boat took off from Kegalla, Ceylon, about fifty miles south of the capital, Colombo, and set out on patrol east across the tranquil Indian Ocean. The warmth of the tropics was a pleasant change for the pilot, Squadron Leader Leonard J. Birchall, of St. Catharines, Ontario, and his mixed RCAF/RAF crew. Until a few days before they had been operating in the unrelenting gales and bone-chilling temperatures of the Shetland Islands. The order to go to Ceylon had been received with wide grins. A trip to the tropics! Just the job! They flew the Catalina to Ceylon via Gibraltar, Cairo, Abu Qir, Basra, and Karachi. Birchall and his crew had had little time to settle in and look around their new home. They had to go on patrol.

It was a tense time in that part of the world. The Japanese, then at the peak of their campaign of conquest of Southeast Asia, were expected to attack Ceylon any day. And if they came, the Allies were not at all sure they could fight them off. No one had done it so far; the British, the Americans, or the Australians.

By the time of Birchall's patrol that day, the reputation of the Japanese military, naval, and air forces had assumed Olympian proportions in some quarters. No longer considered "funny little short-sighted men in ill-fitting uniforms," they had acquired the qualities of supermen, before whom all of Asia might fall.

For Len Birchall and his crew of 413 Squadron, the day passed quietly. High above the sun-drenched ocean, they cruised, revelling in the warmth and clear skies. The navigator, Bart Onyette, had his work cut out. He had no landmarks and had to rely totally on his dead-reckoning calculations. Now the day was almost over. Onyette wanted to remain in the area until he obtained a fix from sun and moon shots. Birchall agreed. It would take only a minute or two.

On such seemingly unimportant decisions does history some-times revolve. While Onyette was working on a course back to base, Birchall spotted dots on the distant horizon. He presumed them to be ships of the British Eastern Fleet. He turned. At an altitude of two thousand feet, he approached the fleet. Drawing nearer, he shook his head in surprise. Four battleships, five aircraft carriers, plus cruisers, destroyers, and support vessels . . . a formidable armada.

A fighter approached, the pilot waving cheerfully. More fighters came in behind the first, gently rising and falling as if bouncing on the tropical air. Birchall started to return the greeting, then stopped, eyes opening wide in dismay. The fighters bore the red rising-sun symbol on their camouflaged flanks. Japanese Zeros, for Pete's sake! That wasn't the British fleet, it was the Japs!

As he heaved the heavy flying boat into a steep turn to the north, Birchall called to his RAF wireless operator, Sergeant F. C. Phillips, ordering him to break radio silence and get the news through to Ceylon. At once! Phillips went to work as the speedy Zeros angled in to attack. The Catalina's gunners swung out their weapons in preparation for combat. Birchall poured on every ounce of power at his disposal. He looked about the sky. Not a cloud to be seen. Nowhere to hide. He resigned himself to his fate. It wouldn't take long, he was convinced of that. A few bursts from the Zeros' guns and the stately Catalina would be torn to shreds.

It was during Phillips's third transmission (orders were that every message must be repeated twice) that the Zeros struck. Bullets snapped through the light-gauge aluminum skin like angry insects. Cannon shells tore great chunks out of the airplane. One shell blew the radio equipment to bits, wounding the wireless operator.

More shells set fire to the fuel tanks. Crew members managed to get the fire out, but another started at once. Bullets stitched lines of holes in the hull. An explosive shell tore the leg off one member of the crew, and black, acrid smoke filled the trembling hull. Birchall dived in a frantic effort to get the aircraft down before it fell apart.

He knew he had only moments to live. That didn't matter. What did matter was that the message about the Japanese fleet got through to Colombo. "A few seconds after the bombardment started," says Birchall, "we knew it was all over for us. We had no self-sealing tanks, so when the one we had was ruptured, the gas poured down through the tunnel between the wing and the hull. The explosive shells started the fire."[2]

Birchall slapped the Catalina down on the sea. The tail broke away and the riddled hulk began to sink at once. Most of the crew managed to scramble out, but the air gunner who had lost a leg went down with the aircraft; the others couldn't save him. The Japanese fighters swarmed in for the kill, strafing the sinking Catalina, their shots kicking up spurts of water around the airmen struggling in the water.

"The poor buggers could not escape the bullets, and they never had a chance. The six of us who were still alive were able to dive under the surface, and doing so saved us. You could see the splashes of the bullets on the water. Three of the guys were wounded and bleeding so we knew the sharks would soon be around. Finally, the strafing stopped."3

A Japanese destroyer lowered a small boat, picked up the survivors, and took them back to the ship. "They hauled us up on the deck and started to question us, pound us around, and question us some more. The wounded guys were in bad shape. One had collected a whole burst of shells right up one leg; another's arm was torn open and a third had been shot in the hip. We might have been a sorry-looking bunch," Birchall adds, "but we weren't saying much."4

An English-speaking Japanese officer ordered the senior officer to identify himself. Birchall spoke up. The officer began to hit him while demanding to know whether a signal had been sent back to Ceylon. Birchall denied it, as did the other surviving crew members.

It almost worked. So vehement were the crew's denials that the Japanese seemed to be on the point of believing them. But fate intervened. The ship's radio picked up a signal from Ceylon asking the Catalina's crew to repeat their message. Birchall and the others could do nothing but shrug and await their fate. The Japanese tossed them into a tiny paint locker. There was room for one man to lie down while two sat and one stood. The crew remained in the locker for three days without medical treatment, their only food a cup of soup every twenty-four hours.

Birchall and the remains of his crew were later transferred to the aircraft carrier *Akagi*, which put in at Yokohama. The timing was unfortunate; Jimmy Doolittle's famous raid on Tokyo and other targets on the Japanese mainland had taken place the day before.*

---

* Sixteen B-25s had taken off from the aircraft carrier *Hornet* to carry out the raids, which caught the Japanese completely by surprise. The raid caused only minor damage, but was a shattering blow to Japanese belief in the inviolability of the homeland.

Birchall and the others were paraded before the population, who seethed with anger at the "Europeans" who had the temerity to invade the sacred territory of Japan.

At dawn on Easter Sunday, the Japanese launched a strike force against Colombo. Vice-Admiral Chuichi Nagumo had hoped to destroy the British fleet at Colombo, duplicating the triumph of Pearl Harbor. He was to be disappointed. The Japanese found no British naval units of significant size at Colombo. Birchall's message had arrived in the nick of time, enabling the British fleet to seek refuge at Addu Atoll in the Maldives, southwest of Ceylon.

About forty RAF Hurricanes and Fleet Air Arm Fulmars waded into the fleet of 120 Japanese aircraft. The Fulmars were no match for the agile Zeros, and the Hurricanes were weary veterans of the Desert War. They claimed seventeen victories over the Japanese aircraft, but lost more than thirty. (Two Canadians were among the pilots: Flight Lieutenant Robert Davidson, and Flying Officer James Henry Whalen, both from Vancouver. Davidson, who had downed two Italian aircraft in the Western Desert, shot down a Zero and a Val – the Aichi D3A1 type 99 carrier-borne bomber – over Colombo; Whalen shot down three Vals.) In addition, the British fleet lost two cruisers, one aircraft carrier, two destroyers, a corvette, a merchant cruiser, and twenty-three merchant ships.

The encounter seemed yet another victory for the Japanese. But in fact it spelled the end of Japanese ambitions in that part of the world. Vice-Admiral Nagumo, apparently alarmed by the ferocity of the defence, lost his stomach for the fight in the Indian Ocean. The most dangerous moment had passed. Ceylon, one of the few remaining sources of natural rubber available to the Allies, was safe.

For Len Birchall, the rest of the war became a dreary and danger-ous endurance test, which would make his name illustrious. For more than three terrible years, he endured as a prisoner of the Japanese in a variety of camps, each more disgusting than the last.

He was the senior officer in a POW camp near Yokohama and gained the admiration and respect of all his fellow prisoners by his conduct. "We had no medicines or medical treatment; we were on a starvation diet, with no proper clothes or footwear, only wooden clogs. We got one bath a month and a tiny piece of soap a week to do all our washing and laundry. Infested by body lice, fleas, and bedbugs, about a third of the POWs in Japan died during the first winter. All POWs went on working parties. If any were too sick to work, the guards beat them with clubs and rifle butts until they went off to work, or died."

On one occasion, Birchall could not stand the brutality any more; he stepped forward and attacked the Japanese sergeant in charge. In return, Birchall was punished for more than a month, until fellow prisoners staged a sit-down strike to protest. Reluctantly, the Japanese permitted the sick prisoners to return to their bunks. It was a tiny victory in a callous, merciless war. Birchall found himself in a special disciplinary camp in Tokyo Harbour, a dangerous place, flanked by a flak battery on one side and a search-light battery on the other. Nearby was a fighter base. When single B-29s flew overhead, probably on photographic missions, the prisoners ran onto the parade ground and formed the letters POW, hoping they would be seen by the U.S. aircrews.

Fire-bombing raids destroyed the area around the camp, so the prisoners were loaded on trains, jammed into boxcars without food, heat, or any sanitary facilities. After being shunted around various railway lines, the train ended up in the mountains north-west of Tokyo. Again, Birchall found himself the senior officer of nearly three hundred POWs: American, Dutch, British, Australian, and Canadian. Some were blind from lack of vitamin A; some had lost feet or hands because of beri-beri or gangrene. Still they had to work in the nearby mine, digging out ore. The men were slowly starving to death, so Birchall and three other officers organized stealing teams, finding vegetables, soya beans, chickens, and rabbits. Most of the prisoners managed to survive until the atom bombs were dropped on Hiroshima and Nagasaki, resulting in the Japanese surrender.

The gallant Canadian with the unquenchable spirit received the OBE – and the lifelong gratitude of hundreds of prisoners of the Rising Sun.

Half a world away, in the strategically important but bleak and fog-enshrouded Aleutians, the Japanese occupied two of the most westerly islands, Kiska and Attu. It happened in June, shortly after the Japanese defeat at Midway. 115 (RCAF) Squadron had moved to Annette, Alaska, to assist in the defence of the Aleutians – thereby becoming the first Canadian squadron based in U.S. territory to assist directly in American defence. Two more squadrons, 111 (with Kittyhawk fighters) and 8 (with Bolingbroke bombers) had arrived later. Early in June, the Japanese attacked the Aleutians, bombing Dutch Harbor and seizing the islands of Kiska and Attu. The Japanese defeat at Midway made the Aleutian adventure virtually irrelevant; nevertheless, perhaps for face-saving rather than strictly strategic reasons, they elected to remain with an estimated 15,000 to 18,000 troops. Although the Canadians spent much of their time dive-bombing the Japanese, they seldom saw the enemy in the flesh.

In September, a combined Canadian–U.S. force of Liberators, P-39s, and Kittyhawks attacked Kiska, strafing gun positions. Swinging around for a second pass, the fighters encountered two A6M2-N Rufes – Zero fighters on floats – rising to challenge the interlopers. Squadron Leader Ken Boomer of Vancouver, the CO of 111, attacked one of the Rufes from below and sent it down in flames. The Japanese pilot jumped just before his aircraft hit the sea. U.S. Major John S. Chennault, son of the famous leader of the American volunteer group in China, shot down the other Rufe. Boomer's was the only aerial victory by a member of Canada's Home War Establishment, the network of RCAF squadrons based in Canada for home defence.

III

On the damp and cloudy afternoon of February 12, 1942, rows of youthful aircrew listened in uneasy silence as the briefing officers told them the bad news. The powerful German battle cruisers *Scharnhorst* and *Gneisenau*, and the cruiser *Prinz Eugen*, had slipped out of their harbour at Brest. At this very moment they were steaming at top speed through the Straits of Dover. They had to be sunk, no matter what the cost in aircraft or men.

For almost a year, the RAF had been trying to do just that. No less than 3,413 tons of bombs had been dropped on Brest harbour. In the process, a dreadful total of 127 bombers and crews had been lost. By now the damage inflicted by Ken Campbell and Jim Scott and their crew almost a year earlier had been repaired, and the Germans wanted to get the ships away from Brest to the greater safety of a German port, where they would be readied for attacks on Allied shipping in the Atlantic. Failure to sink the German ships now could literally alter the course of the war, the briefing officers told the aircrews.

No one could ever say that the British didn't try their best to eliminate the German warships; there was no shortage of courage. Unfortunately the same couldn't be said of leadership and organization. The break-out from Brest could have come as no surprise to anyone of senior rank in the RAF or the RN. It had been expected for months. Detailed contingency plans had been drawn up by RAF Coastal, Bomber, and Fighter commands. Coastal's plan was the key:

> A striking force of a squadron of torpedo-bombers will be maintained at [St. Eval, Cornwall]; a second, small striking force of torpedo-bombers will be at [Thorney Island, Hampshire]. These two forces will be responsible for night work in the Channel. If there is no moon, the reconnaissance aircraft,

when they have located the enemy, will be responsible for illuminating the enemy force with flares during the period of the torpedo attack. Cooperation between the torpedo striking forces and the reconnaissance aircraft will be arranged by Nos. 19 and 16 Groups. A daylight attack on the enemy force, if it passes successfully through the Straits of Dover, will be carried out by a striking force of torpedo-bombers at present based on Leuchars [near Dundee, Scotland].[5]

But, as Air Marshal Sir Edward Chilton, former Commander-in-Chief of Coastal Command, points out: "the mere issuing of a directive does not get things done when no overall coordinating commander is in charge of the planning."[6] It was bad enough that the RAF Commands were virtually autonomous, but to make matters worse, Coastal Command was controlled by the Navy. "Each command issued its orders, but all were unrelated to each other, and were certainly not on an integrated basis. For example, the vital Channel patrols of Coastal and Fighter Commands were not meshed into one foolproof net to prevent the ships from slipping through unobserved. All this was further complicated by the very high degree of secrecy maintained, especially by No. 11 Group, which was to play a key role in the operation."[7]

On some stations, security considerations outweighed common sense, many aircrew on the operation being "unaware of what they were to look for and what they had to attack," according to Chilton. "Perhaps the worst unnoticed error was in No. 11 Group's operation order of 5 October 1941, which stated that R/T silence was to be maintained, except in an emergency, until the enemy had been engaged! This unfortunate phrase had been copied from an earlier order which was quite unrelated to the needs of an operation against enemy shipping, when early reporting is vital."[8]

For months, photo-reconnaissance flights had been keeping a day-by-day record of the happenings in Brest harbour, supplemented by morsels of information from "Ultra," the secret decrypting-system. By the beginning of February 1942, there could no longer be any doubt. Destroyers, motor-torpedo boats, and minesweepers had joined the battleships in the harbour. Supply vessels fussed about them like infants around their mothers. It could be any day. But what day? And at what time of day?

The British had convinced themselves that the Germans would make the dash through the Straits of Dover by night. They were wrong. Cleverly anticipating British thinking, the Germans decided to head through the straits in daylight, relying on surprise, poor weather, and a heavy escort of fighters. Little did they know how much they would be assisted by the outright bungling of their enemies.

The British picked up radar signals on the morning of February 12 indicating intense aerial activity. The filter room at RAF Fighter Command correctly interpreted the data and advised 11 Group. So far so good.

After that, very little went right.

At about 10:00 A.M., two Spitfires took off from Hawkinge, near Folkstone, Kent, to investigate. Since Hawkinge had not received 11 Group's message concerning R/T silence, the big news nearly slipped through the bureaucratic net. Squadron Leader Oxspring, the pilot of the leading Spitfire, spotted the German ships protected by an umbrella of fighters. He called base and passed on the intelligence, after which he turned for home. For reasons still to be explained, Oxspring's message got no further than Hawkinge. The German fleet sailed on. About an hour later, a Spitfire landed at Kenley. Its pilot was Group Captain Victor Beamish, the very officer who had issued the fateful 11 Group order concerning R/T silence some months before. He too had seen the German ships but, obeying his own instructions, he had kept the information to himself until he returned to base.

Now the scrambler lines hummed. At this critical stage of the proceedings, the commanders of 11 and 16 groups wasted precious time arguing about details of the attack. In effect, a highly complex operation involving air force and naval units was being cobbled together on the spur of the moment. It was almost funny, an aerial Keystone Cops comedy, but for the fact that men's lives were at risk. 42 Squadron didn't have enough torpedoes to arm all its Beauforts. The crews took off anyway, intending to pick up torpedoes at another base. They found the base snowbound. They diverted to Coltishall and landed in good order. But Coltishall had no torpedoes. And so the sorry story continued.

No airman underestimated the perils of tackling the German battle cruisers. Fighter escorts were supposed to accompany the bombers, but a rendezvous in this weather would be difficult. Low cloud, drizzle, snow showers, mist . . . even the birds would be inclined to stay on the ground today.

At North Coates, Lincolnshire, members of the Canadian 407 Squadron, known as the Demon Squadron, wondered what use their 250-pound general-purpose bombs would be against the heavily armoured battleships. A sergeant muttered, "To sink the buggers we will have to put the bloody bombs down the smoke-stacks."[9]

Kim Abbott, one of the unit's pilots scheduled to take part in the operation, suggested to his CO, Wing Commander Alan Brown, that bombs aboard the unit's Hudsons be replaced with semi-armour-piercing bombs. Brown shook his head. There wasn't time, he explained. Besides, the Hudsons weren't expected to sink the battleships; their job was to attack ahead of 42 Squadron's Beauforts, to draw the flak.[10]

Leading the attack would be six Fleet Air Arm Fairey Swordfish torpedo-bombers, the same outdated biplanes that had scored the impressive victory over the Italians at Taranto. Since everyone expected the Germans to sail through the Channel at night, a similar operational plan had been developed whereby the open-cockpit Swordfish would glide down, engines throttled right back, drop their torpedoes in the darkness, and slip away unobserved. But now the Swordfish had to drop their torpedoes in full view of the enemy, with his fearsome flak defences and hordes of fighters. Five RAF fighter squadrons had been assigned to escort the Swordfish during their attack. In the murky weather, the fighters and their charges failed to rendezvous. The Swordfish went on alone, led by Lieutenant Commander Eugene Esmonde, the stocky, aggressive Fleet Air Arm officer who had made a name for himself by leading the successful attack against the *Bismarck* the previous year. Undoubtedly he was aware that he had little chance of getting back from this trip.

The 407 Squadron Hudsons took off and, as instructed, flew to Manston, Kent. There they found dozens of aircraft circling the airfield in a wide left-hand circuit waiting for the Beauforts and fighter escorts to arrive.

They waited in vain. Earlier in the day, Air Vice-Marshal Leigh-Mallory, AOC of 11 Group, had decided that fighter protection during bomber and torpedo attacks would consist of "cover support over the targets, rather than close support for individual strikes." It was, comments Kim Abbott, "a surprising last-minute adjustment that stripped away the essential ingredients needed for a well-coordinated shipping strike, and eliminated any real possibility of success. All afternoon we sent out aircraft in a haphazard manner resulting in needless losses without compensating results."[11] Leigh-Mallory's action seems incomprehensible in the circumstances.

Meanwhile, the Swordfish approached the target, huge vessels dimly visible through the mist and sheets of rain. The promised fighter escorts had not materialized. Lieutenant Commander Esmonde attacked anyway. It was hopeless, another of the suicidal Charge-of-the-Light-Brigade attacks that had all too often been the lot of Allied airmen in this war.

No doubt in many a senior officer's mind there was the glimmer of a hope that the gallantry of the Fleet Air Arm crews might carry the day. A lucky hit or two would make it all worthwhile. It was not to be. Ploughing on through the mist at their ludicrous speed, the Swordfish crashed into the sea one by one, picked off by Germans like moving targets at a carnival.

"Not one of the Swordfish escaped," wrote Adolf Galland, who commanded the Luftwaffe's fighters during the "dash." "Thus the first British attack, performed with death-defying courage, was repulsed."[12]

Other sorties were equally hopeless, and a few minutes after leaving Manston, Kim Abbott received instructions to return to base. He obeyed with alacrity, "as there was little we could do with our 250-pound general-purpose bombs."[13] But to cap a truly awful day, British naval units opened fire on the 407 Squadron Hudsons as they made their way home. One crash-landed back at base due to damage to its landing gear, and Abbott himself took hits in the rear fuselage and tail, fortunately without injury to any of the crew.

Four 407 aircraft didn't receive the recall instructions and pressed on to the target, attacking escort vessels. Two of the unit's most experienced pilots died in the hopeless venture, both having completed thirty operations with 407: Lonsdale Cowperthwaite, of Brantford, Ontario, and Andy Anderson, DFC, of Winnipeg. According to Kim Abbott, "Of all the Canadian captains who flew with the Demons, the most outstanding was Andy Anderson.... He was quiet, reserved, and very brave. He was not the type who was likely to survive a war, but he was the kind of man who made sure we won it."[14]

Of the four Hudsons that pressed on, two survived and returned to base. Sadly, neither of their crews had long to live. One of the skippers, Jim Creedon, of Paris, Ontario, won a DFM for his part in the "dash," but his luck ran out three months later, when he crash-landed in England after a sortie to the Frisian Islands. On touch-down, the aircraft burst into flames. All the crew died. By curious coincidence, Creedon was on his thirty-first operation, just as Cowperthwaite and Anderson had been. The captain of the remaining Hudson, Chuck Race from Edmonton, lost his life on

May 29, shot down near the Dutch coast. His Hudson dived into the water and exploded. None of the crew survived.

Another Canadian casualty of the futile operation was Omer Levesque, the first Allied pilot to shoot down an FW 190. Levesque took a hit in his Spitfire's radiator as he patrolled the area. Flak? Or fighter? Levesque never knew. He ditched in the frigid Channel, his Spitfire plunging into the depths. Levesque walloped his head when the aircraft hit the water. Semi-conscious, he began to accept the reality of death; it really wasn't so bad, quite peaceful, really . . . Somehow he came free of the aircraft and he snapped back to full consciousness as he fought his way to the surface. Gasping in great lungfuls of air, he watched the battle overhead. A German air-sea rescue launch picked him up, and he spent the rest of the war as a prisoner.

IV

By the time John Iverach arrived at Calshot in February 1942, he felt twinges of uneasiness. He had broken one of the cardinal rules of service life: he had *volunteered*. Worse, he had no idea what he had volunteered *for*. It all started when the call went out for an experienced navigator willing to undertake "a special job." At the time, Iverach had little to do. He had recently completed his first tour of operations and had been appointed squadron navigation officer. The job bored him. The signal from Group seemed the answer to his prayers.

At Calshot, across the Solent from the Isle of Wight, he made the acquaintance of a pilot, Sam Morrison, had also volunteered for this "special" work and who was equally ill-informed. Morrison had been flying Walrus amphibians on air-sea rescue work. Joining Iverach and Morrison was a WAG (wireless operator/air gunner) named Frank Gilbert, who had just completed a tour on Hudsons. Like the others, he had no idea what he was getting into.

At last, after more than a week, the three airmen received orders to report to the station commander's office. They met two middle-aged officers, both from Air Ministry Intelligence, who took them to a nearby maintenance hangar. There, a large twin-engined seaplane stood on wheeled dollies. The astonished airmen recognized it as German, a Heinkel 115. They were told that the Heinkel would be their aircraft for the next few weeks. It was one of four that had been "liberated" by Norwegian pilots and flown to Britain. It had been equipped for a special assignment, they were informed.

The three airmen looked at one another. Sam Morrison lost no time in proclaiming himself quite incapable of flying the big Heinkel. He had never flown a twin-engined aircraft, he said, and he hadn't landed on water for months. Never mind, was the impassive response, a highly experienced Norwegian pilot would soon be available to provide the necessary training. One of the officers turned to Frank Gilbert and informed him that in addition to his duties as wireless operator/air gunner, he would be required to act as the rigger, responsible for mooring the aircraft to buoys. Had he ever performed such duties? Gilbert shook his head. He had recently returned from Gibraltar and declared that he didn't know anything about seaplanes or mooring buoys, and he couldn't swim a stroke. "I hate everything about water," he concluded, "especially salt water."[15]

The officer nodded understandingly, then showed the airmen the eight Browning machine-guns installed in the Heinkel's wing: four in the leading edge, four in the trailing edge, operated by the pilot by means of a reflector sight. Each of the aircraft's massive floats contained a seat and intercom connections, plus a pair of lights trained downward. "You will be flying very low," he explained, "about fifty or even twenty-five feet. Since your altimeter can't give you exact enough readings, we installed these spotlights in the wings to guide you. When the two spots converge on the water, you will be at precisely fifty feet, unless they are set for twenty-five."[16] It was,

of course, similar to the system that would be used on the famous
Dambuster raid the following year.

Sam Morrison didn't remain long with the unit. During training
he ran one of the four Heinkels into a Sunderland, wrote off both
aircraft, and was soon back with his Walrus unit. His replacement
was an outstanding Norwegian naval lieutenant named Knut
Skavhaugen, who had many hours on Heinkel 115s in Norway.
Iverach describes him eloquently: "Knut was not really a handsome
man – just average height, blond, lean and sinewy. But he had a face
one never forgot. Even to this day I can still see it: the plain, square
features; the jutting chin, split down the middle; the blue Nordic
eyes, whose hardness seemed to be in conflict with the laughter-
lines that stood like grave markers of happy times long dead; the
penetrating gaze that warned against trifling or deception, yet at the
same time seemed to invite a good joke."[17]

A few days later, Iverach and the others signed forms quoting
forbidding-looking extracts from the Official Secrets Act and took
delivery of .32 Colt automatic pistols and various other items,
including matchboxes with false bottoms containing tiny compasses
and suicide pills. They received confirmation of what they had been
uneasily suspecting for some time: they had volunteered themselves
into the espionage business. They would be transporting agents in
and out of enemy territory. Although the big Heinkel wore RAF
markings, it was unmistakably alien, a wolf in sheep's clothing.

The first trip was easy. The Heinkel and its crew delivered two
men who were picked up by a sailing boat off the French coast. The
second involved a delivery in the Bay of Biscay. On this occasion, a
Hampden torpedo-bomber was supposed to meet the Heinkel on
its return to the British Isles. Five miles from the Isle of Wight,
everything went wrong. Two fighters suddenly attacked. A large
bullet hole appeared in the chart in front of Iverach.

At the same time something kind of spidery whirled out in
front of our nose; it was our starboard propeller! Our starboard

wing became a sheet of flame as a hail of bullets riddled it and the fuselage between Knut and Frank. Miraculously, none of us was hit.

An aircraft hurtled past us, and Knut screamed into the intercom, "It's a Spitfire! Fire a recco signal, Yonny!"

I grabbed the Very pistol, slid back the canopy over my head and fired. But that only compounded the problem, for I had grabbed the wrong pistol, the one with the German signals in it!

Meanwhile, our brave escort, the Hampden, opened its throttles and took off like a scalded cat.

Knut shoved his control column forward in a steep dive. The force of the wind, luckily, extinguished most of the flame, and, minus one engine, Knut skilfully set the Heinkel down on the calm sea. We quickly put out the rest of the fire.[18]

A launch towed the bedraggled seaplane back to Calshot. Later, a court of enquiry established that Fighter Command had been tardy in informing local squadrons of the Heinkel's movements. The Polish fighter squadron, 303, had had two aircraft on patrol. When they saw the Heinkel and what they took to be a Dornier 215 (the Hampden bore a passing resemblance to the Dornier), they had attacked, fortunately without killing anyone. The Heinkel was a write-off, however, and had to be replaced by one of the two remaining aircraft.

The crew completed several deliveries and pick-ups – never learning the names of the individuals concerned. Once, returning from the Bay of Biscay in the half-light just after dawn, they encountered two Ju 88s. Quickly, Knut grabbed the Aldis lamp and flashed a message to the German bombers. They made off. Iverach asked what message Knut had flashed. "Heil Hitler," he replied.

In the late summer, now based at Woodhaven, on the Firth of Tay, they received orders to fly to a small fjord in Norway to rescue some agents being closely pursued by the Germans. On this trip, uncertainty overshadowed everything. No one knew how many agents were involved, and it was even suspected that the Germans might have captured the real agents and substituted their own people for the rendezvous.

Iverach recalled: "We followed our usual procedure of making a landfall a considerable distance from our ultimate destination and positively identifying our position. We then flew as low as possible, using our special wing lights as our altimeter, until we reached the fjord, where we skimmed in to a landing. Knut then quickly taxied around to where we would have a maximum take-off run into wind, shut off the engines, and waited for some sign of our passengers, who were to come out in a small boat to meet us."

He would remember every detail of the nail-biting trip.

The great black Heinkel rocked gently with the wavelets that lapped her pontoons. Her menacing shadow seemed grotesquely out of character with the serenity of the September moon shimmering across the quiet fjord. The night sounds were lost in the thunder of my heart pounding out its frantic warning as the three of us strained our eyes toward the shoreline, dark in the distance. The seconds ticked by in funereal cadence.

And then I saw it.

At first it was just a speck, with no perceptible movement. But, gradually, it transmuted to a shape, growing bigger, closer – a strange night creature crawling relentlessly across the water. And now its legs had become tiny oars, stroking their slow rhythm at the sides of the little boat, and its antennae became three human heads, outlined against the sheen.

"They're coming, Knut!" I whispered hoarsely into the intercom. Knut's calm voice came back. "Okay, Yonny – Frank – be ready!"

Quickly, I shoved my small navigator's table forward on its

runners, slid open the transparent hatch above my head, reached for my tommy gun, and stood up.

Torso protruding into the chill night air and tommy-gun at the ready, I peered tensely into the night, searching for the signal light that would distinguish friend from foe.

Back in the rear cockpit, Frank stood likewise, a ludicrous Martian silhouette in his wireless operator's headphones. I wondered if his palms, like mine, were slippery with the cold sweat of fear, and if his temples, too, were ready to burst from the pounding within.

Iverach glanced at Knut, the pilot, sitting impassively in his seat. The Norwegian seemed to love every moment of these nerve-knotting ops. Iverach didn't. He forced himself to concentrate. The boat kept approaching, but no one aboard the Heinkel knew yet if its occupants were friendlies or Germans.

"Now the little boat was only about two hundred feet away, closing fast, and still no signal," Iverach recalled.

"Come on – come on – flash your bloody signal, for God's sake!" I prayed to myself.

To Knut I said, "Christ, Knut, they're getting too damned close!" I strained to keep from screaming it into the intercom. "What'll we do?"

The brief moment of silence seemed like an agonizing hour. And then, calmly, unemotionally, but with a controlled tenseness that betrayed the terrible burden of his decision, came Knut's clear reply: "Let 'em have it – and let's get outa here, fast!"

The port propeller was starting to turn as I aimed at the dark forms, now close enough to have faces.

"Jesus! Two years of war without shooting anyone I could actually see, and now I have to kill some poor buggers who may really be on our side – maybe even members of Knut's own family!" I thought.

In a few seconds they'd all be dead, and I'd never know whose side they were on. Sofiano and Shaw [the two Intelligence officers] would know, you could bet, but they'd never tell us. They only told us what was necessary for the job: where, when, how many, and the code. Never who. Never why.

The sight was full on now, and I knew I couldn't miss. I daren't, for there would be no second chance. Them or us. Six feet under was the same distance down for all of us, but I really wasn't ready to go just yet. Tears blurred my eyes as I squeezed the trigger.

But nothing happened! I squeezed again – and again – and again – desperately, frantically. I wouldn't move. And then I remembered.

"The safety catch! You dumb, stupid bastard! The safety catch!"

As I fumbled in a panic for the release, I wondered why Frank wasn't firing either. I took one wild glance in his direction, and was shocked to see him standing still as before, watching and waiting, as if part of another scene.

By now, the BMWs [the Heinkel's engines] were roaring and the Heinkel was starting to move. But even the deafening noise couldn't cover the desperation in Knut's voice as he sensed something was wrong.

"*Shoot!* For Christ's sake, vy don't you *shoot!*"

I whirled my tommy-gun back on target, praying that I would get it before it got us.

But just as my finger found the trigger again, Knut's scream almost tore off my ear.

"Vait, Yonny – Frank! Yesus, hold your fire! Dere it is!" And he shut down the engines.

It was only a pinprick of light, a faint glimmer that I had
not noticed in my panic, but still enough to flash the code
that told us these were indeed our passengers, not our execu-
tioners.[19]

Shortly after this episode, the last Heinkel was wrecked in a collision with a ship. The undercover operations had ended. Iverach,
Frank Gilbert, and their splendid skipper, Knut Skavhaugen, went
their separate ways.*

V

Although the merchant shipping losses by U-boats had reached catastrophic proportions (in June 1942, 141 ships were sunk), glimmers
of hope had begun to relieve the gloom. ASV (Air to Surface Vessel)
radar had been introduced in 1940, a variant of the AI (Airborne
Interception) used in night-fighters. It proved to be of limited value
initially, largely because of the size and weight of the equipment and
the amount of confusing "clutter" it picked up, mostly from the sea.
The Mark II ASV, with a more powerful transmitter, was a significant
improvement, but reception was still less than ideal. A third version,
incorporating the magnetron oscillator, promised even better
performance, but no one knew when it would become available.

At this point in the war, U-boats usually remained submerged

---

*   Later in the war, Knut Skavhaugen was killed in the crash of a Mosquito on
operations. John Iverach had a distinguished war record, flying to the Soviet
Union, the Middle East (sitting on 2,000 two-pounder shells destined for the battle
against Rommel), and the Far East. He became the first member of the RCAF to
complete three tours of operations; and indeed came within a handful of ops of
completing four.

during the day, making their attacks on shipping by night. This strategy presented a problem familiar to both Bomber Command, in its attempts to hit targets at night, and Fighter Command, in its efforts to shoot down enemy night-bombers: what Arthur Coningham called "the never-ending struggle to circumvent the law that we cannot see in the dark." In 1941, Squadron Leader H. de V. Leigh, a personnel officer, had succeeded in fitting a twenty-four-inch naval searchlight into the "dustbin" (ventral) turret of a Wellington. Directed by ASV, the Leigh Light did well in tests, but it was many months before it could be proved in action. Even when they were eventually introduced, the Leigh Light Wellingtons did not help to sink many U-boats; but they did force the submarines to stay submerged in critical areas such as the Bay of Biscay, reducing their effectiveness.

The Hudsons of Canadian 407 Squadron were engaged principally in shipping strikes in the spring of 1942. These operations were, with few exceptions, carried out at extremely low level – and the squadron suffered heavy casualties, usually about one in every four aircraft. The unit's war diary states: "Since this squadron became operational again on 1st April we have lost twelve crews, in all fifty persons either missing or killed. During the past month six crews have been designated missing or killed on operations with the loss of twenty-seven lives. This does not take into consideration the fact that after every major operation of this nature at least two or three aircraft are so very badly damaged that they are of no use to this, or any other squadron."[20]

Something had to give. The low-level strikes sank some ships, but the aircraft losses were out of all proportion, about six aircraft per vessel from April 1940 to March 1943. One of the squadron's most successful pilots, Cam Taylor of Winnipeg, recalls several wheels-up landings after flak damage to his Hudson's hydraulics suffered during low-level attacks. But the memory of one incident in particular has stayed with him. Departing the coast of Norfolk en route to the Dutch coast, he gave his gunner permission to test the guns. A moment later came a report: "Left lower gun inoperative." Taylor responded, "Well, get the damned thing operative! And smartly!"

Silence for a minute, then: "Gun will remain inoperative."

Demanding to know why, Taylor was told that the gunner had swallowed part of the gun. It transpired that the weapon had jammed and the air gunner had attempted to free it, popping the rear sear keeper and pin into his mouth while he worked. When the Hudson hit rough air, the parts slipped down his throat. "On our return to base," says Taylor, "after a rather successful attack off the Frisian Islands, I delivered the gunner (who shall remain nameless) to the MO with a request that he be given a couple of gallons of castor oil. The following morning at breakfast, the MO delivered to me the missing parts neatly wrapped in an RAF burn dressing."

VI

Artillery opened up as the elderly Bombay transport touched down at Antelat, eighty miles south of Benghazi, in Libya. A handful of young airmen scrambled out of the aircraft and dived for cover. It was just as well they did, for a pair of Ju 88s suddenly appeared and dropped bombs on the airstrip, sending up great eruptions of sand and dust. It was one of the many minor skirmishes of the period, in which the British advance to the west ended and Rommel's own offensive began.

One of the new arrivals trying to burrow into the sand was a pilot from Battleford, Saskatchewan. He was twenty years old and looked even younger than his years, a compact individual with an unruly mop of hair and a ready smile. His name was James F. Edwards, soon to be known throughout the RCAF as Stocky.

As he got to his feet and dusted himself off after the Ju 88s' departure, Stocky Edwards wondered why none of the Hurricanes parked about the strip had set off in pursuit. He soon found out. The Hurricanes couldn't take off; they couldn't even move. Their wheels were embedded in mud. The fact seemed to trouble no one; it was just the latest in a series of "cock-ups" that had been besetting 94 Squadron for weeks. It had suffered heavy casualties, losing six pilots in the last few days. Morale had plummeted. The squadron was about to be withdrawn from front-line duty to be re-equipped with American-built Curtiss Kittyhawks. The news thrilled no one. Rumours had been circulating for weeks about the big Curtiss fighters, about their sluggishness and poor rate of climb, about their mediocre performance at altitude. It was said that seasoned RAF fighter pilots had refused to fly them. Edwards listened to the stories and mentally shrugged. He would wait and see for himself.

He did, and found that more than a few of the complaints were justified. The newly arrived Curtiss was no nimble Spitfire; its controls were heavy, it had a nasty yaw, and its performance dropped off quickly above 20,000 feet. But the Kittyhawk had its merits as well. It was a tough customer, capable of absorbing terrific punishment and remaining in one piece. And it was manoeuvrable enough to turn inside (that is, more tightly than) a Me 109. Moreover, it packed an impressive wallop with its six .50-inch machine-guns.

An outstanding RAF officer commanded the newly equipped unit. Squadron Leader Ernest "Imshi" Mason was one of the early aces of the Desert War, with seventeen victories in Libya and Malta. In mid-February, Mason led six Curtiss Kittyhawks from 94 Squadron plus twelve from 112 Squadron in a low-level attack on the German airfield at Martuba, near Tobruk, Libya. The Luftwaffe was unquestionably in the ascendency, with better aircraft and more experienced pilots. Mason's plan depended on catching the German fighters on the ground, but when the RAF fighters appeared, a single 109 was already airborne, high over the airfield. Displaying remarkable courage and marksmanship, the German pilot attacked the formation of Kittyhawks single-handed. In a matter of minutes, he had shot down five of the 94 Squadron aircraft and had severely damaged one 112 Squadron aircraft. Mason was killed. The pilot responsible was Otto Schulz, an ace with thirty-seven victories to his credit. "Such was the prowess of the 109 in the hands of an experienced desert pilot," says Edwards, who was fortunate enough to have missed that operation. Lack of operational experience and unfamiliarity with the Kittyhawk was unquestionably a big factor in the catastrophe. "I don't believe anyone had a dozen hours on the aircraft at the time," he remarks.[21]

Again withdrawn from operations, 94 Squadron relocated at the aptly named Gasr El Arid, near Gambut, east of Tobruk. The new CO was Squadron Leader I. N. MacDougall. He was a rarity: a Defiant pilot who had survived the Battle of Britain. For the next three weeks, he took his unit through a period of intensive training.

On March 21, 1942, the squadron was operational once more. Two days later, twelve Bostons from 24 (South African) Squadron took off from their base to bomb Martuba, a front-line landing ground. One of the Kittyhawks flying as escort to the Bostons had Edwards at the controls. It was his first operational sortie. As the formation approached Martuba at about 10,000 feet, Edwards could see the plumes of dust rising from the desert below: enemy aircraft taking off to deal with the intruders.

In the ensuing combat, Edwards shot down an Me 109 that strayed in front of his Kittyhawk. A quick squeeze of the trigger blew the enemy fighter to pieces. Elated, Edwards attempted to reform with his squadron-mates, but where were they? Where in fact were any aircraft? The sky, which a few moments before had been a free-for-all of diving, turning fighters, was now empty. Feeling more than a little conspicuous, Edwards set course for home. But finding one's way around the desert was seldom easy: "Seen from above, [the desert] offered no evidence of habitation or life. There were shades of sand, brown and darker spots or lines were intermixed. . . . There was nothing of note for miles in the vastness below. Some pilots had more trouble than others finding their way around; novices could be right over an airfield and not recognize anything at first glance. Then, the sun would glitter off an aircraft Perspex or something else on the ground, and the entire camp would come into focus."[22]

During the spring of 1942, screaming, blinding sandstorms prevented any flying for days at a time. Indeed, they prevented normal life of any variety, as they blew sand and dust into food, into eyes and mouths, into the barrels of guns, scratching cockpit canopies into opacity, wrecking engines, obliterating landing strips. There was no escaping the stuff. It dominated every moment, every aspect of life. Then, abruptly, sudden downpours turned landing strips into quagmires. Desert life was hard, but its basic quality appealed to Edwards. No parades. No uniform code. No military claptrap. Flying and fighting were all that mattered.

Operating from new landing strips graded out of the desert twenty or thirty miles inland, the pilots lived in tents erected over deep gravelike pits to offer some protection against artillery. The Operations Room might be the back of a truck; the Mess could consists of several tents joined together. The only thing to be said for this inland area was that it was spared the clouds of voracious flies that tormented most of North Africa.

Early in May, Edwards was transferred to 260 Squadron, another Kittyhawk unit. He continued to hone his skills, learning to get the most out of the big Curtiss fighter. The Kittyhawks operated by 260 Squadron were Mark Is, a faster, better-armed version of the original P-40, called the Tomahawk in the RAF. The aircraft had an impressive rate of dive and was powerfully armed, but its tendency to yaw made it a tricky gun platform. Another of its faults, Edwards discovered, was that the turn-and-bank indicator had been installed in one corner of the instrument panel. Edwards had already begun to think like a professional; he realized that it was vital to fly absolutely accurately when firing the guns. Any hint of a skid would send your shots spraying all over the sky. He had the ground staff move his turn-and-bank indicator to directly beneath the gunsights. Now he could look through the sights and see the indicator at the same time.

"I found that one had to have a very strong right arm to control the Kittyhawk I during most manoeuvres," he says.

> In dive-bombing, the aircraft would pick up speed very quickly in the dive, but it had a great tendency to roll to the right. One could trim this out reasonably well with the left hand, but even then, when one pulled up, it wanted to roll to the left quite violently. So I learned to trim out about halfway in a dive and hold the control stick central by bracing my arm against my leg and the cockpit wall. I found out I had more control this way and didn't have to take off so much trim when pulling out, and the speed was reduced. It was also distracting to have one's left hand on the trim all the time, when it should be on the throttle.[23]

In a dogfight, with attitude and speed changing constantly and violently, it was all one could do to fly the aircraft, he recalls. Thus the Kittyhawk was hardly the ideal aircraft in which to take on the nimble, heavily armed Me 109Fs, which had replaced most of the 109Es in the area.

Another potentially catastrophic shortcoming was the jamming of the P-40's guns during violent manoeuvres. "All the Kittyhawks I flew had six .50 guns, excellent for strafing or blowing up a target. . . . In ground strafing one could count on firing all the ammo without problems, but when it came to dogfighting and excessive G-forces came into play, the guns often packed up after a few bursts, leaving the fighter in a most perilous position."[24] Edwards adds that the German aircraft never seemed to experience any problems with their 20-mm cannons firing through the propeller boss. When he flew a captured 109, Edwards found it superior to the Kittyhawk in most respects – even its cockpit canopy was better. Being made of glass rather than Perspex, it was far less prone to scratching in the viciously abrasive desert environment, where aero engines seldom clocked more than forty hours of operation before they became scrap metal.

Losses were heavy, Edwards recalls, with flight commanders coming and going constantly: "No sooner would one be promoted and take over, than he would be shot down." He also criticizes the unit's tactics: "260 still flew the stupid old Hurricane formation with six aircraft in a flight. There were three section leaders and three weavers flying behind. Everyone looked after their own tails and no one coordinated anything when the 109s showed up.... The weaver had a hell of a time trying to keep up with their leader while weaving and watching behind."[25]* The formation was "a confused glob of aircraft that could be turned into a confused shambles by a small number of 109s attacking from above, out of the sun."[27] He knew he could improve the squadron's performance in combat, but he was a new boy; for the time being, he had to leave it to others to lead the unit.

In May 1942, 260 Squadron faced its greatest challenge. For several months the opposing armies had been re-equipping and reinforcing themselves. The front line ran south from the coastal village of Gazala and consisted of a maze of minefields, barbed wire entanglements, and half a dozen strongly fortified "boxes," each about two miles square. The British had the advantage in armour: 850 tanks, including 167 new American Grants armed with 75-mm guns. The Germans and Italians had about 600 tanks.

Churchill, impatient for action and desperate for a victory in the

---

* Interestingly, Rudolph Sinner, an engineering officer of the Luftwaffe, had much the same opinion of RAF tactics at this period: "The British units always flew very low and always in senseless combat formations.... From one mission to the next I was afraid the British *must* recognize the cause of their helplessness, and change their formation to a looser one. But, God be praised! My fears were groundless!"[26]

desert, urged General Auchinleck to attack. Rommel moved first.
The battle that followed was "among the most reckless and costly
fought during the desert war."[28] The air forces were busy throughout, bombing and strafing, as the situation on the ground changed
hour by hour. The opposition was fierce, and casualties mounted at
an alarming rate. Between May 29 and 31, nearly forty Allied fighters
were lost. In many instances, the chronic jamming of the
Kittyhawks' guns was responsible for these dismal results; in others,
it was the superiority of the enemy's aircraft and the experience of
their pilots that gave them the advantage. More and more frequently,
the Kittyhawks carried 500-pound bombs beneath their bellies. The
usual pattern was to dive-bomb, then strafe the target after the
cumbersome bomb had gone. The weather played a part in the
drama, with huge Khamsins – warm winds carrying dust and sand,
rising as high as 10,000 feet over the desert – obliterating landing
grounds and roads and making life miserable for friend and foe.

On June 8, a large force of Kittyhawks and Tomahawks set out
on an offensive sweep over Bir Hacheim, southwest of Tobruk.
Messerschmitts and Macchis soon made an appearance, diving to
attack the Allied aircraft from above, their preferred tactic. Edwards
caught a 109 with an accurate burst of fire in the propeller spinner
and engine. Feldwebel (Sergeant) Johann Walchhofer spun to his
death. It was Edwards's first victory with 260 Squadron.

On the ground, the battle was going Rommel's way. Under his
efficient leadership, German and Italian forces drove eastward, the
Commonwealth forces falling back, mile after weary mile, giving
up all the territory won at such cost a few months before.

During this anxious period, Edwards shot down two 109s in one
day. It was June 17, and the Canadian was on his thirty-third operational sortie. The 260 Squadron Kittyhawks had been escorting
Boston bombers operating near Tobruk. Shortly after the Bostons
went home, the Kittyhawks came across a mêlée involving 109s and
Hurricanes. Diving to the RAF fighters' aid, the 260 Squadron
aircraft rapidly found themselves in a tough fight. Although

Edwards was all too conscious of the Germans' superiority, he used his Kittyhawk's manoeuvrability to advantage. A 109 overshot him. For a fleeting instant, the German became a target. Edwards fired a brief burst. He saw a flash in the Messerschmitt's engine. Down went the 109. The temptation to dive after his victim and make sure of his destruction was almost irresistible, but Edwards had already learned some of the hard truths of aerial combat. Too many pilots had "bought it" by following victims down to make sure they crashed. Edwards headed east. The dogfight had ended as suddenly as it began. The air, moments earlier full of diving, turning, climbing fighters, was now empty. Feeling as conspicuous and alone as he had several weeks before, Edwards flew at ground level, hurtling over the barren terrain, the shadow of his aircraft bounding effortlessly from hillock to hillock. Then he saw them: a cluster of 109s wheeling at low level, firing at something on the ground, stinging the sand and dirt into a mad dance. As Edwards approached, one of the German fighters came near in a diving turn. Edwards banked and opened fire from about sixty degrees at close range. His skill at deflection shooting paid off. The 109 lurched, twisted like an animal in pain, and dived into the ground, disappearing in a ball of fire.

Edwards jammed his throttle wide open, every fibre of his being concentrated on getting as far away as possible while the other 109s were sorting themselves out after this unexpected interruption in their sport. Once he was clear, he heaved a heartfelt sigh of relief. He had been fantastically lucky, attacking such a bevy of 109s and getting away with it.

It turned out Edwards had shot down Otto Schulz, the Luftwaffe pilot who had decimated 94 Squadron on February 15. He had also saved the life of another Canadian ace, Wally Conrad, of Melrose, Ontario, a Hurricane pilot with 274 Squadron. Conrad had had more than half a dozen victories to his credit when he was shot down by Schulz. He had made a successful crash-landing in the desert, and when Edwards came on the scene, the German was attempting to set fire to Conrad's downed Hurricane to ensure its destruction. Conrad survived the incident and returned safely to his unit – to learn some years later that it was Stocky Edwards who had shot down Schulz.

Like most Allied pilots, Edwards knew none of the German aces by name. There's little doubt, however, that every Allied soldier and airman knew the name Rommel. The German general commanded a blend of respect and fear. Although he appears to have been an ardent supporter of Hitler for most of his career, he was always considered by Allied troops and airmen to be a "square-shooter," a simple soldier who had little interest in politics.

The fall of Tobruk on June 21 was another humiliation for the British, one to match the surrender of Singapore and Hong Kong. Many secretly wondered if the Allies could ever win; the enemy seemed to be so damnably *capable*. Panic began to infect Cairo. How long before Rommel occupied the city? Faces were long at the Gezira Sporting Club and the Continental Roof Gardens. The staff of the British Embassy and the Middle East High Command burned acres of documents in preparation for evacuation.

It was a time of dispiriting retreat for the RAF: packing up, moving to another base, packing up again. The air force units became adept at it. Yet every day they kept up the attacks on the advancing Axis armies, zero-altitude, flat-out screamings across the gaunt battlefield, into the storms of flak, the darting tracer, the thudding 88s. Still Rommel, now promoted field marshal, kept advancing. German newspapers called him invincible. So did many on the Allied side. Defeat seemed an almost foregone conclusion. On June 29, the vainglorious Mussolini clambered aboard a white charger and rehearsed his part in the triumphal parade through the streets of Cairo that would surely take place in a matter of days.

RAF headquarters in Cairo ordered all ranks to be ready to evacuate at twelve hours' notice. Staff officers wore sidearms; radio broadcasts assured Egyptian civilians that the city would not fall, which only served to convince everyone that it would. On July 1, the German 90th Light Division attacked. The battle for Egypt had begun. And, although few in either camp realized it, the tide had begun to turn.

The Desert Air Force was now becoming an increasingly important part of the Allied battle against the Afrika Korps. Air attacks on Rommel's supply lines were proving particularly useful. Rommel began to find himself in a position similar to that of the British forces at Dunkirk. He complained of "incessant" attacks by Allied bombers and fighters – with little evidence of the Luftwaffe to put heart into his embattled troops. The Germans were learning the cost of spreading their forces too thinly.

Early in July, Stocky Edwards led a flight of 260 Squadron into battle for the first time. Already recognized as a highly capable desert fighter pilot, he still wore the stripes and crown of a flight sergeant and had received no awards for his prowess in the air. He soldiered on as an NCO month after month, probably the most "desert-wise" pilot on the squadron, and certainly its most successful. By now he had some forty operational sorties to his credit. He was a veteran with a wealth of irreplaceable experience. He could size up an opponent in moments simply by observing how he handled his aircraft. He knew the vagaries of the desert, its weather, its dangers. He knew how to use the sun, the only reliable navigational aid in the desert. In short, he had become the complete professional.

But, like so many Canadian airmen in the Middle East and Far East, Stocky Edwards appeared to have been forgotten by the authorities, overlooked again and again for promotion and decorations. He was one of the many victims of "Canadianization," the avowed policy of Mackenzie King to avoid the Great War tradition of Canadians simply filling the ranks of British units, indistinguishable from any other troops. King wanted the Canadian airmen to be distinctively Canadian. Hence the "Canada" shoulder flashes and the emphasis on the exploits of Canucks in the war news – at least, the war news publicized in Canada. The trouble was, most Canadian airmen (some 60 per cent) served not in RCAF units but with the RAF. Thus they tended to be of less than immediate concern to both the RAF and the RCAF – and those in Africa particularly so, since the RCAF had no senior representatives there.

Rommel's advance ran into unexpectedly fierce opposition just inside the Egyptian border. The artillery of the South African brigades took a terrible toll of troops and armour. Seriously overextended, the Germans were starting to run short of ammunition and fuel. The once-invincible Rommel had gone as far as he was going to get. The German 90th Light Division came to a complete halt and had to dig in. They reported heavy air attacks "every twenty or thirty minutes" by strong forces of bombers and fighters.[29] Again the plea went out for support from the Luftwaffe. But the German fighters were grounded by fuel shortages and bad weather.

On some operations, the Kittyhawks of 260 Squadron became part of the bomber force while they performed their escort duties. Carrying 500-pound bombs, they flew alongside the Bostons and Baltimores, releasing their bombs as the bombers dropped theirs. After their bombs had gone, the fighters became full-time escorts again.

A new weapon to appear about this time was the "Tank Buster" Hurricane. The famous Battle of Britain fighter had been modified to carry two massive 40-mm Vickers cannons. No. 6 Squadron was the first to receive the new Hurricanes. Allan Simpson of Ottawa, a flight commander in the unit, recalls that the missile "had a slug of soft metal in the base which plunged forward on impact, into the hollow conical core, to force a sort of mechanical, rather than chemical, explosion, or to give it another thump to make good its entry into the target. . . . The projectile was able to penetrate the 20-mm armour-plating on a German Mark III tank, and to weld itself into the metal on the far side." But tank-busting was hazardous. On run-of-the-mill ops, of every three Hurricane IIDs going out tank-busting, the loss could be expected to be: one shot down, one damaged, and only one returning unscathed. "As we neared the target," Simpson says, "we dove to pick up speed and attacked from about 1,000 yards at ten feet off the deck. The book said twenty-five, but that was based on a flying speed of 250 knots, which our aircraft couldn't quite attain and maintain in the desert. A lower altitude seemed to compensate, although some of the boys took off their tail wheels by hitting tank turrets, and one pilot came home with his prop bent."[30] Although they did a useful job, the tank-buster Hurricanes were soon outdated, the 40-mm cannons giving way to rocket projectiles.

On July 3, the Desert Air Force flew an unprecedented 770 sorties. All that day, 260 Squadron's Kittyhawks roared over the desert, bombing and strafing enemy vehicles, tanks, and armoured cars. It was dangerous, exacting work, but highly productive. Rommel waited in vain for fuel and equipment. Air power had neutralized his supply routes.

The front became uncharacteristically quiet. "Enemy air activity appeared to drop off considerably," Edwards recalls. "Attacks on our aircraft by small numbers of 109s were almost half-hearted."[31]

VII

On August 4, Winston Churchill arrived in the desert. Bitterly disappointed by the failure of his armies to produce a decisive victory, he fired General Auchinleck, replacing him with Harold Alexander. Bernard Montgomery took over the Eighth Army, and a gigantic build-up of men and *matériel* began. The biggest battle of the campaign would soon be fought; a new spirit of confidence and enthusiasm permeated the ranks of the Allied armies.

The air force also trained for the coming battle. No. 260 Squadron now had a new base on the Alexander–Cairo road, and, in the

temporary calm, industriously trained the unit's new pilots. The aim
was to enable the new men to survive their first few sorties, so that
the all-important process of acquiring experience might begin. For
too long, fledglings had arrived on the squadron knowing how to fly
their aircraft but not much more. They had little training in combat
manoeuvres, practically none in deflection shooting. Such airmen
were usually easy meat for the experienced German fighter pilots.
Ron Cundy, an Australian friend of Edwards, said years later: "I
can't understand why arrangements weren't made for experienced
fighter pilots to lecture us at OTUs [Operational Training Units] on
fighter tactics – particularly how to react to attacks by enemy aircraft
and how to manoeuvre to place ourselves in an advantageous position to attack them. Flying inferior aircraft did detract from our
ability to attack but we were not taught how to take full advantage
of those occasions when we were in a superior strategical position.
Hence too many valuable opportunities and pilots were lost."[32]

Edwards concurs, pointing out that, since the squadron spent so
much of its time in bomber-escort duties, it was necessary to train
new pilots in defensive tactics: "In the Kittyhawk, the only
manoeuvre that truly thwarted the 109 attack was the steep turn."
Of crucial importance, however, was the precise moment when the
pilot began the turn and how steep he made it. Generally, the 109s
attacked from above and behind.

It was when the 109 started its dive that the steep turn was
carried out – always into the attacker. In the four formation
[the "finger-four" formation, developed by the Germans in
Spain and eventually adopted by the Allied air forces], the
leader would call the turnabout over the R/T or by dipping
one wing two times, turning on the second dip. The leader
would gauge his turn to meet the circumstances and the
others would turn to maintain formation. The formation
turned as a viable unit and carried out cross-over turns in the

same manoeuvre when necessary. We taught the pilots the turns and had them carry them out in pairs and alone, right on the deck. But there were very few pilots who could do a really steep turn properly at deck level while watching behind and above.

Edwards feels that new pilots seldom received enough training before going on operations. "Every flight, even on operations, was a training flight, and eventually this method began to improve the squadron combat strength."[33]

During August, 260 Squadron scored four confirmed kills, two probables, and two more damaged. Seven Kittyhawks were lost, but only one pilot was killed. The balance was definitely shifting. The Germans were losing their control of the desert sky.

Rommel chose this moment to attack. He had no choice. He had to beat Montgomery to the punch. But Montgomery was ready for him and had prepared a trap. The Germans found themselves in a vast minefield, where aircraft attacked them ceaselessly. Rommel ordered a retreat to a line at Bab el Qattara, some twenty miles to the west. The fortunes of the desert war had now changed irrevocably.

On September 3, Montgomery sent a message to Air Marshal Arthur Coningham, declaring that the success of the Allied armies "could not have been achieved unless the RAF had put forth so great and sustained an effort." Rommel himself talked of the great superiority of the Desert Air Force.

But the Luftwaffe could still be a formidable foe. On September 6, a force of Ju 87s escorted by 109s approached the front line near El Alamein. Kittyhawks and Tomahawks quickly tangled with them. Edwards witnessed the death of a Canadian member of 260, Dick Dunbar, from Woodstock, New Brunswick, whose aircraft plunged in flames and crashed in the desert.

Moments later, Edwards led his section 180 degrees to face their attackers. It was one of the manoeuvres he had drilled into them.

The training paid off. When more 109s attacked, the Kittyhawks repeated their "turnabouts," maintaining their finger-four formation, diligently following Edwards's lead. Then the 109s began to attack in pairs, from both ends of the formation. Repeatedly turning, Edwards and his section forced the 109s to break off their attacks and pull up to rejoin their formation above. Although outnumbered and several hundred feet below the enemy formation, Edwards flew directly under the enemy so that they had to dip their wings in order to spot their prey, frustrating their attempts to attack out of the sun. Edwards hit a 109 and saw smoke streaming from its engine as it headed for home. It had been a tense and uncommonly lengthy battle, lasting some twenty minutes. Edwards says that when the section returned to base, the pilots walked slowly to the Ops tent, none of them saying a word. All of them were completely wrung out and exhausted. One man broke down in tears as he recovered.

The fighters now spent most of their time on sweeps. On September 14, Edwards led 260 Squadron on a sweep over enemy airfields. Six USAAF pilots flew with 260 Squadron that day, including Lieutenant-Colonel Salisbury, commander of the 57th U.S. Fighter Group. He was flying as number two to Edwards, still a flight sergeant; such was the absurd imbalance of rank and responsibility in the desert.

The next day, Edwards shot down a 109. Burning furiously, it turned on its back and spun in – but the victory was never confirmed; no one saw it crash. When Edwards returned to base, Air Vice-Marshal Arthur Coningham, head of the Desert Air Force, was standing on the flight line. He was incredulous to learn that Edwards, a flight sergeant, had led the squadron. Before long, the young Canadian was interviewed for a commission.

The Desert Air Force continued to consolidate its superiority over the Luftwaffe and the Regia Aeronautica, bringing overwhelming numbers and better aircraft and pilots to the fray. By mid-1942

Spitfires were frequently seen in the desert. And not a day too soon, in Allied pilots' opinion. They had read of immense numbers of Spitfires employed in fighter operations over Europe, and it infuriated them that for many hard months the air force wouldn't send any of the superb fighters to the desert. Now, at last, they were arriving, Mark Vs in the main, with the big air filter beneath the nose to protect the engine from sand and dust. They weren't the latest models, but they were far better than anything that had been available to date. Had the Spitfires arrived on the scene earlier, they might have prevented some of the Allies' cruel losses.

The Desert Air Force now comprised about 1,500 aircraft, 600 of them fighters. They faced some 350 Axis aircraft. The decisive battle was about to begin, and the Desert Air Force underwent considerable reorganization to prepare it for the task. Fighter squadrons were to have thirty pilots each, with every unit carrying its own spare parts, rations, water, and other supplies so that they could move rapidly as the anticipated advance began.

On October 21, Edwards was involved in a fracas with 109s and Macchi 202s. Firing from two hundred yards at thirty degrees, he shot down a 202. The pilot baled out successfully, but he died from loss of blood shortly after landing. The next day, Edwards shot down a 109. But the day's victories came with a price. Killed was twenty-one-year-old Eric Keith Tomlinson of Toronto, who had recently joined the squadron.

That night, the Battle of El Alamein began.

For the Desert Air Force, the days brought virtually nonstop action, escorting bombers and strafing Rommel's ground forces. On October 28, Edwards was engaged in three operations. In mid-afternoon eleven Kittyhawks went out to strafe enemy tanks, diving through clouds of blinding dust churned up by the heavy vehicles. As Edwards completed his run, he glimpsed an unusual sight through the murk: a cluster of 109s at ground level! For once, 260 Squadron had the opportunity of taking on the Luftwaffe fighters on advantageous terms. At 150 yards he opened fire. The Messer-schmitt went straight into the ground, exploding in a great fireball. Seconds later he opened fire again. Another 109 staggered under the impact of his fire. Edwards couldn't spare a glance to see what happened to it. Later, he learned that the pilot had been killed instantly, his aircraft crashing among the thundering tanks below.

A number of outstanding Canadian fliers were now making their mark in the desert. Carl "Moose" Fumerton, of Fort Coulonge, Quebec, the first RCAF fighter pilot to shoot down an enemy aircraft at night, was now with 89 Squadron, flying Beau-fighters. George Keefer, a Canadian born in New York City, was flying Spitfires with 274 Squadron. Joseph Jean Paul Sabourin, from St. Isidore, Quebec, flew successfully with 112 and 145 squadrons before being shot down and killed in September.

Among these fliers was Bert Houle, from Massey, Ontario. The short and aggressive Canadian looked like a boxer or wrestler, and in fact he had been both. On September 1, Houle was part of a patrol from 213 Squadron that encountered a flight of Ju 88s. He fired about fifty rounds of 20-mm cannon shells at one. His guns then jammed. Furious, he had little choice but to make for base – where, to his surprise, he received congratulations from fellow pilots; they had seen the Junkers crash.

Shortly after the El Alamein battle began, Houle became part of an elaborate trick on the Luftwaffe. It was common knowledge that German operators spent much time listening in to RAF radio trans-missions. So, in the late afternoon of October 26, two Hurricanes took off, their pilots chattering away on the R/T, complaining about being low on fuel and having to head for home. To their German listeners, it sounded like a large number of pilots, an entire wing possibly. Meanwhile, as a formation of Ju 87 dive-bombers was heading back to base – no doubt relieved to hear that the enemy fighters were out of the picture – two squadrons of Hurricanes sped for the lines, Houle among them. By then it was almost dark.

When I hit the coast, I turned west just out to sea and about eight hundred feet above the water. For ten or fifteen minutes, nothing showed up. Then I saw a Stuka at eleven o'clock above and reported it to Carrick, who came back excitedly with, "I see it!" Roy Marples called up to ask where I was and, as I didn't know exactly and was just closing in, I replied, "Down here." Carrick and I were down in the comparative darkness near the sea. The whole skyline, a brilliant red from the setting sun, seemed to come alive with dots that were heading for home, probably elated over the ease of their victory. I closed in on the first one to within fifty yards, stayed slightly below, and gave it both cannons up the jacksie. Large pieces blew off; it belched smoke, turned on its back, and went straight down. I didn't bother to follow it but veered slightly to starboard where there was another Stuka, all unsuspecting, and poured cannon fire into it from close range. Its nose dipped slowly and it started down in a gentle dive. I followed, giving it the odd burst for good measure until it hit the sea. Pulling up behind another, I was able to give it a short squirt, knocking pieces off it before it went over and down. Just over the coast, I saw a few bursts of Breda (Italian flak) and a Stuka put on its navigation lights to show that it was friendly.

I wasn't, and pulled right in behind. I was so close that the bullets from my cannons, mounted in the wings, were going to each side of the Stuka's fuselage without hitting it. Then a high-explosive incendiary bullet hit a wing tank and it became a blazing inferno. I pulled sharply to one side to avoid hitting it, and I saw the pilot and gunner shrinking to one side away from the flames. The aircraft made a slow spiral and hit the deck, lighting up the whole countryside. In the light of the flames from the burning Stuka, I was spotted by another Stuka which got on my tail. The first thing I knew, four machine-guns were tracing their patterns towards me. I immediately banked and applied sharp rudder to get below its level. It swung on inland, leaving me alone. I attacked another Stuka ahead of me and blew a few pieces off it. It started in a gentle dive for the sea. Fearing I might be short of ammunition and fuel, I turned for home. I was pretty jubilant as I taxied in and parked the aircraft.[34]

Subsequently, Houle learned that the pilot of one of the Stukas he shot down was a much-decorated Luftwaffe pilot, Kurt Walter, a Knight's Cross winner and squadron commander. Walter baled out of his stricken aircraft, but he was too low. His parachute didn't open.

Strafing became the principal job of the fighter squadrons. It was effective, but costly. "We had it pretty rough, and the losses were heavy," says Houle. "When 20 to 50 per cent don't come back from a sweep, it doesn't take much of a mathematician to calculate that your number must come up soon. Many pilots built up their courage with a philosophy that went something like this: There is only a 25 per cent chance that I'll get shot at, and if I am, there is only a 25 per cent chance that my aircraft will be hit. If the aircraft is hit, there is only a 25 per cent chance that the hit will be serious. If it hits a vulnerable spot, there is only a 25 per cent chance it will be fatal. With odds like that, why should I worry?"[35]

He soon found out. No. 243 Wing, consisting of thirty-six Hurricanes of 213 and 238 squadrons, was selected for a "big show." Houle recalls that at the briefing the pilots were told "not to bank too much on coming back, as we were to land well over one hundred miles behind the enemy lines to operate, strafing enemy transport on the roads between Benghazi and El Agheila." With lofty disregard for any superstitions among the pilots, the planners had scheduled the "show" for Friday, November 13. For Houle, the date had special significance: he had joined the RCAF on that date two years before. He wondered uneasily whether Friday 13 would soon acquire even more significance for his family.

The pilots took their bedrolls and stowed them in their aircraft. At dawn, Hudsons landed to pick up the groundcrew and equipment, and the fighters escorted the transports to Sidi Hineish, thence to LG125, an abandoned airstrip with rough runways marked by empty fuel cans. The Hudsons landed first, followed by the fighters, all without the use of R/T. "One ground crew man was assigned to each aircraft," says Houle.

The pilot assisted him with refuelling from four-gallon tins which had been unloaded from the transport. It took a long time to put more than one hundred gallons through a funnel into an aircraft. By the time this chore was completed, lunch was ready, and we hit it with gusto. Immediately after lunch, Wingco [Wing Commander] Darwen gathered us around him for a briefing for the first show. He told us that sections were going out on divergent sectors to hit the road at seven points from El Agheila to Benghazi. We marked out our positions on the map and drew vectors and distances to various points on this road. These had to be memorized, as we were not allowed to carry maps.[36]

No R/T was to be used, "even if it was a case of life or death," the pilots were told. After strafing, the aircraft were to stay at ground level to make it impossible for the Germans to tell where the RAF fighters might have come from.

The Hurricanes flew at zero feet for more than an hour, then the German transport vehicles swept into view, "bags of them," says Houle, "in the distance, rolling for safety behind the El Agheila line. We hit the road and turned north, weaving across from side to side, taking shots at any target that presented itself." He describes it as "a field day." "We attacked big six-wheelers absolutely jammed with troops, packed so tight that only a few could extricate themselves and jump clear.... There was no return fire, so we had little to worry about. When all our guns were empty, we turned for home and found it without much trouble.

"The other sections came back one by one with exactly the same story. The venture was a howling success, although we lost Bart Campbell and Gordie Waite. They had hit the telegraph line stretched close to the road. Both ended up prisoners of war. The CO hit the same telegraph line, but it merely tore the long-range tank off and he was in the clear."[37]

For the next two days, the fighters roared over the desert at ground level, blazing away at armoured cars and trucks, leaving about a hundred of them burning by the roadside. At the airfield at Gialo, the Hurricanes caught the occupants completely by surprise. About a dozen German and Italian aircraft went up in flames, including a three-engined Cant Z1007, which Houle shot up. He recalls one British pilot remarking disbelievingly, "When I fired, there was a bloke still wiping the windscreen."

The flak on these ops was fearsome. Houle took so many hits on one sortie that when he landed, his Hurricane had to be written off. Eventually, the Germans sent an armoured column to deal with the intruders stationed at LG125. By the time the column reached the dusty airstrip, the fighters had departed, their job done. It had been, as Houle says, a howling success. "The very audacity and element of surprise were the factors that contributed most to its success.... In retrospect," he adds, "I wonder if we were sent on this mission as expendable. The aircraft were almost in that class."[38]

On November 1, Stocky Edwards shot down another 109, its pilot surviving the crash. Edwards had destroyed five enemy aircraft in two weeks, a record. He now had ten enemy aircraft to his credit. Ron Cundy, his Australian squadron-mate, later observed: "That Eddie was a first-class shot goes without saying. I recall one occasion when he was flying top cover to my section on a bomber escort when we were attacked by 109s. Eddie's section was the first to be jumped and I remember seeing him calmly evade the enemy attack and then quickly position himself for a wide, climbing deflection shot which was successful. I doubt if the German pilot knew what hit him or how it happened."[39]

Rommel's forces were reeling. The Desert Air Force kept up the pressure, working in close contact with the Eighth Army. Early in November, Squadron Leader "Pedro" Hanbury returned to lead 260 Squadron.

Every op seemed to involve strafing. "Strafing missions were flown right on the deck," Edwards says, "where surprise and accuracy in locating targets depended solely upon the leadership of the experienced desert pilots."[40] It was a hazardous, nerve-racking business that inevitably resulted in high casualties. Most of the tactics developed in the desert were later to be used to great effect in Northwest Europe.

Rommel was in serious trouble. Not only had the Eighth Army's attack at El Alamein thrown his Afrika Korps into confusion, the wily German field marshal was running out of fuel. Without it, he couldn't counterattack. He told Hitler the bad news, insisting that the precious fuel be sent directly to Tobruk, the fastest route but the most vulnerable to air and sea attacks. Hitler agreed.

The British spotted the 5,000-ton German tanker *Proserpina* in a major convoy nearing the Libyan coast. From Gianaclis, near Alexandria, a strike force set out consisting of Beauforts, Beaufighters, and Bisleys (also known as the Blenheim V, a notably unsuccessful variant of the well-known design). A Canadian, Ralph Manning of Vancouver, was one of the 47 Squadron Beaufort pilots, whose job it was to torpedo the tanker while the other aircraft kept the flak gunners busy by bombing and strafing.

By the time the strike force made contact with the Germans, the convoy had broken up, no doubt in the hope that the RAF aircraft would concentrate on the freighters and destroyers, leaving the all-important tanker to slip along the coast unobserved. Initially, that is just what happened, but Manning and two other pilots saw through the German strategy. They continued up the coast, and soon came across the tanker, accompanied by a destroyer.

Manning was an experienced and highly capable torpedo-bomber pilot. Earlier in the year, he had been part of a four-aircraft section of Beauforts attacking the German heavy cruiser *Prinz Eugen*. The flak, a screen of darting balls of light, had seemed impenetrable. Manning's aircraft was the only one to get back to base, although it was beyond repair. Now, as he lined up to attack the *Proserpina*, Manning saw the big ship turning to present a more difficult head-on target. Every instinct screamed at him to drop the torpedo and hope for the best. Instead, he abandoned the approach and manoeuvred through the merciless storm of flak to make a second attack. This time, he came at his target from the landward side. At 700 yards, with anti-aircraft fire coming at him like a multi-coloured snow storm, he jabbed the torpedo-release button. As he did so, a Bisley streaked across his path – immediately losing a wing as it failed to clear the ship's mast. The hapless plane cartwheeled into the sea.

Manning didn't see the effect of his torpedo. But one of his gunners, "Nimmy" Niverovsky, did. The missile hit the tanker a glancing blow on the port bow. For a heart-stopping moment, it looked as if all the effort and courage had been in vain. The torpedo didn't explode, but ran along the hull. Then, with a great eruption of spray, it detonated near the stern. The tanker burst into flames and began to sink.

When the Eighth Army attacked Rommel's troops again a few days later, the Germans and Italians could do little but retreat, their fuel tanks dry.

Manning was another of the Canadians serving with RAF squadrons who fared poorly when decorations were handed out. The gallant action in which the *Proserpina* was destroyed earned four decorations for the aircrew involved; but Ralph Manning, the man who dropped the torpedo that sank the vital tanker, wasn't one of them.

On November 5, another Canadian member of the squadron, George Harttung, of Kitchener, Ontario, died, shot down by flak near Sidi Hineish. On the 11th, Edwards destroyed two Ju 88s on an airfield by dropping one bomb between them. By mid-November, the Germans began their evacuation of Tobruk, the port that had seen such bitter fighting for so many months. Day after day, 260 Squadron strafed enemy airfields and transport. At one airfield, Edwards spotted three 109s being serviced. Hurtling along only a few feet above the ground, he opened fire at the parked aircraft and, he recalls, "all three collapsed in a heap of flames."[41]

The Germans and Italians had fallen back some 450 miles. The Desert Air Force advanced with the army, bombing and strafing a field one day, flying operations from it the next. Wrecked enemy aircraft lay scattered about like dead birds, wings bent and broken, pathetic skeletons blackened by fire. Sad little mementoes of individual hubris could be seen in the mottoes and mascots painted on crumpled fuselages.

"My brushes with the 109s certainly seemed different from that time on," says Edwards. "I really didn't see them that often, and when I did, they were, in most instances, some distance away."[42] Once all-powerful, the Luftwaffe in the desert had become a spent force.

On Derna airfield, west of Tobruk, 260 Squadron personnel found a Heinkel 111 in mint condition. They painted RAF roundels on the Luftwaffe bomber, and Ron Cundy of the RAAF was appointed chief pilot. The German plane was far more capacious than the squadron's fighters. He flew it to Alexandria several times to buy beer, turkeys, and fresh vegetables for the squadron. During such trips, an escort of Kittyhawks protected the Heinkel from attacks by "friendlies."

The unit enjoyed a good feast at Christmas, courtesy of the Heinkel: "Without this aircraft, it would have been plain bully beef," says Edwards. (Also preparing for Christmas, Bert Houle, by this time a flight commander in 145 Squadron, crammed two cases of liquor and several thousand cigarettes into his Spitfire V in Cairo and flew them back to base.) For Stocky Edwards, now a warrant officer, the festive season was brightened by a promotion to flight lieutenant, an impressive if long-delayed jump of three ranks. "I was made pilot officer one day, flying officer the next, and flight lieutenant three days later." Now he was the commander of "B" Flight, a highly experienced desert pilot with more than 120 operational sorties to his credit. On December 30, Edwards flew his first sortie as a commissioned flight commander, leading eight Kittyhawks over the front lines. They came across a gaggle of 109s strafing Allied troops and shot down six of them without loss.

Later, the squadron received orders to attack a contingent of newly arrived 109Gs at their airfield. Squadron Leader Hanbury was in command, Edwards leading the top cover. The squadron approached at ground level, then climbed to a few hundred feet in preparation for their attack. Over the field, Edwards's section ran into Luftwaffe fighters. A full-scale dogfight ensued. Edwards led his flight into the standard defensive circle. He saw the German fighters diving and attacking from different angles. He fired a short burst and damaged a 109, then set another on fire. He got on the tail of a third 109 and – as had happened so many times before – his guns jammed. Equally familiar was the way the sky emptied. Edwards headed for home, but a 109 spotted him and attacked. For several heart-thumping minutes, Edwards turned and turned, preventing the German from getting a clean shot at him. His guns still wouldn't fire. At last, his ammunition gone, the 109 pilot broke off. He had hit Edwards's Kittyhawk several times, but had done no serious damage.

Edwards's engine cut out moments before he touched down. He thumped the Kittyhawk down and rolled to a stop outside the operations tent. It had been a tough fight and, to Edwards's sorrow, he had lost his wing man, the only such instance during the war. It was also the only time his aircraft was ever damaged during combat.

Now at last the awards came Edwards's way. He received the

DFM, followed four days later by the DFC. In addition to his score of victories in the air, he had destroyed about two hundred vehicles in ground attacks.

By now, the Luftwaffe was hopelessly outnumbered, but it continued to put up spirited resistance. As the Allied advance swept into Libya and Tunisia, Stocky Edwards continued to notch up aerial victories. One was a huge, six-engined Me 323 transport, which he destroyed near Zembra Island, Tunisia. "At approximately 250 yards, I fired a long burst and the Me 323 folded up like a stack of cards and fell into the sea."[43]*

VIII

About 250 miles north of Tripoli, like a sentry on guard over the western entrance to the Mediterranean, lies the island of Malta. The Phoenicians had battled for the island, as had the Greeks, the Carthaginians, the Romans, the Saracens, the Turks, the French, and the British. Now the Italians wanted it. Back in 1940, on the evening of June 11, a force of thirty-five Savoia-Marchetti 79 bombers approached, escorted by eighteen fighters. They bombed the island towns of Valletta, Hal Far, and Kalafrana. Two biplane Sea Gladiator fighters rose and shot down one of the escorts. The air battles over Malta had begun. For some weeks, the air defence of the

---

* Soon after this victory, Edwards was "screened" from operations and sent as an instructor to the Middle East Central Gunnery School in El Ballah. Thus ended Stocky Edwards's contribution to the desert war. He had flown 195 sorties and had destroyed 15 ½ enemy aircraft. Later, in Italy, he joined 417 Squadron, then under the leadership of Bert Houle. The unit was part of 244 Wing, commanded by that resolute Canadian Stan Turner. Edwards would score half a dozen more victories in Italy, then, in the closing days of the war, two more, including a jet Me 262 damaged south of Hamburg.

island consisted of three Sea Gladiators, named Faith, Hope, and Charity (although, contrary to popular belief, the names were never painted on the Gladiators' fuselages). The diminutive force put up such a spirited performance that the Italians reckoned the RAF had at least twenty-five Gladiators in action. Their pilots quickly became local heroes; stores displayed their photographs in their windows. After two weeks of attacks, the Italians announced that they had wiped out the British defences and naval base of Malta. They sent a photo-reconnaissance aircraft to take pictures of the devastation. The Gladiators shot it down.

A few weeks later, in early August 1940, a dozen Hurricanes arrived on the island, having successfully flown off the venerable aircraft carrier *Argus*. By this time, the remaining Sea Gladiators were in sorry shape, having been cannibalized for parts. The Hurricanes, although small in number, took over at the right moment.

The battle for Malta was one of the great sieges of history. For three years, the Italians and Germans were to attack the tiny, ninety-square-mile island almost without pause, making it the most-bombed place on earth, according to many historians. The strategic importance of Malta could hardly be overstated. It was an unsinkable aircraft carrier permanently anchored at just the right spot in the Mediterranean to plague the Axis powers. Had Malta fallen, the Battle of El Alamein would probably never have taken place, and the war would undoubtedly have taken a different course. It might even have ended in victory for the Axis powers.

During the worst years of siege, the RAF defenders always operated at an appalling disadvantage in numbers. Ten to one was considered normal. For many months, the aircraft that attacked Malta were Italian. Early in 1941, the Luftwaffe appeared on the scene, bombing and strafing the island from their bases in Sicily. Then the campaigns in Greece and Crete occupied their attention, followed by the invasion of the Soviet Union. Not until late in 1941 did the attacks on Malta resume at full strength. How long, everyone wondered, before the Germans attempted an invasion? It could only be a matter of time. But Hitler, always uneasy about leaving dry land, decided to let the Luftwaffe take care of Malta. Hermann Göring had promised to bomb the island into surrender.

The Maltese remember this grim time as "The Black Winter," a period of ceaseless air raids, of starvation rations for civilians and service personnel alike (stealing food was a capital offence), of critical shortages of power and water. The end, surely, was not far off.

During this period, a Canadian radar officer, Al Glazer of Toronto, arrived on the island. Glazer was a ground-radar man, who had graduated to aircrew duties in an unusual way. He had taken an Air to Surface Vessel (ASV) radar course in Prestwick, Scotland, becoming an expert at handling the somewhat cranky radar equipment. He often acted as a radar operator in the air. Then Glazer heard that the Air Ministry had promulgated a new aircrew badge for radar observers. Since he had qualified for such a badge with his many flights, he applied. To his delight, he was granted the badge, effective May 17, 1941. It was one of the first to be issued.

In October, Glazer and three radar mechanics – Corporal Fred Few and LACs Tom Rogers and Les Card – flew to Malta to establish the first British radar unit outside Britain. The top-secret Special Duties Flight (SDF) had three Wellington VIIIs equipped with the new 10-cm ASV Mark II radar. (Interestingly, on his departure for Malta, Glazer had been approached by an engineering officer by the name of Lloyd. He said he had a brother on Malta and would Glazer give him a letter? Glazer asked how he would find the man's brother. "Everyone out there knows him," was the reply. He was right: the engineering officer's brother turned out to be the redoubtable Air Vice-Marshal Hugh Pughe Lloyd, the AOC of the Mediterranean area, who was destined to become an invaluable ally of Glazer's.)

For months, Axis ships had been sailing from the Sicilian towns of Palermo and Messina in daylight, timing their journeys to North Africa so that they steamed past Malta during the night. Most got through, simply because there was no way for the Malta defences to intercept them in the darkness. Radar changed all that. The ASV-equipped Wellingtons could detect shipping at a range of nearly one hundred miles. Once the enemy had been spotted, an attack force could now strike from Malta. The force consisted of a Fleet Air Arm unit, No. 830, with its venerable Swordfish torpedo-bombers flying in formation in the darkness, since only the lead aircraft carried radar, plus Bomber Command Wellingtons, and Force "K," the RN light cruiser HMS *Aurora* and several smaller vessels. Chief pilot of the SDF was an RAF officer, Tony Spooner, whose innovative mind and flying skill won him the DSO and DFC. Spooner devised a simple code, using familiar first names, in order to exchange information with the attack force and bring the hunters within shooting distance of the hunted.

The Wellingtons, with their distinctive "stickleback" ASV antennae mounted on the fuselage, were out on patrol almost every night. That the SDF flights were never logged, and that their aircraft had to be back on Malta before daylight, gives some idea of the degree of secrecy involved. It proved to be a remarkably successful system. In the fall of 1941, SDF and the attack force sank more than twenty enemy ships – and Al Glazer's contribution was recognized with a DFC, one of the few flying decorations ever bestowed on an RCAF "ground staffer."

Out of the semi-experimental operations of the SDF grew a Malta-based strike force that eventually did much to frustrate the Axis powers in the Mediterranean. The ASV radar helped to spot enemy ships in plenty of time for attacks to be organized from Malta. It was the beginning of the campaign that would eventually cripple Rommel the following year, robbing him of the fuel to continue his advance. But in the grim winter of 1941/42, mere survival on Malta seemed questionable. The Germans and Italians seemed certain to invade. How would they be stopped? Ammunition was already in critically short supply. Bofors gun crews were limited to five clips per day. To the defenders of Malta, it seemed that everyone from Churchill down had abandoned them.

Now, in February 1942, only a handful of serviceable Hurricane fighters remained to defend the island – and they were aged Mark IIs, no match for the 109Fs that the Luftwaffe kept sending across the fifty miles of sea from Sicily. The character of the air-fighting over Malta had changed. No longer were the defenders gleefully taking on the attackers and punishing them. Now the worn-out Hurricanes were hopelessly outclassed, their pilots weary and demoralized. In January, twenty-two Hurricanes had been scrambled to intercept a formation of enemy aircraft. Three had to turn back with mechanical troubles just after take-off. The remainder had still been struggling to gain height when a force of 109s "bounced" them. Seven Hurricanes went down in a matter of minutes. Not one 109 was even damaged. It was the lowest point in the defence of Malta.

Soon after this incident, a Canadian squadron leader arrived on the island. Just as direct and brusque as ever, "granite-faced, pipe-sucking" Stan Turner had come to take over 249 Squadron and prepare the Malta defences for the arrival of long-awaited Spitfires. Turner had been ordered by the Air Ministry to find out what had to be done to make the defences of Malta more effective, and do it. He was an inspired choice. He swept through the battered Hurricane units, telling them about the Spitfires they would soon be receiving, mercilessly criticizing outdated practices, patiently explaining the advantages of *his* way of doing things. Turner was just the tonic the island's defenders needed. He noted that there were more pilots than aircraft; some units could field only a pair of Hurricanes each. Turner formed a pool of every serviceable fighter on the island, to be made available to all squadrons. It might help to get the most out of the aircraft until reinforcements arrived, he reasoned. But Malta's troubles went deeper. Most of the units on the island still flew into battle using the air force's old-fashioned "vic" formations, with some unfortunate pilot weaving at the rear to warn the others of attacks from behind. Turner was aghast. Such antiquated, and downright dangerous, practices had to stop immediately.

When Turner took over 249 Squadron, one of his flight commanders was an urbane ex-journalist and golfer, Laddie Lucas. Lucas remembers Turner announcing: "'I want you to learn this line-abreast stuff with me. And quickly.' He then removed the empty pipe from his mouth and with it started marking out on the dusty floor of the verandah [in the Officers' Mess at Mdina] all the line-abreast manoeuvres, emphasizing the need to get the cross-overs in the turns, as he put it, 'spot on.' 'This way,' he said, 'a couple of guys will never get bounced; attacked maybe, yes, but never surprised.'"44 After this lesson, Turner and Lucas went flying. Turner demonstrated the basics of the finger-four formation. He never wasted words, yet he invariably got his message across. And, like all good teachers, with a curt nod or a pithy word, he managed to impart his opinion of a pupil. Lucas said, "I felt as if I had moved up into Division I of the Flying League. When he wanted to – and only when he wanted to – Stan Turner had the capacity for making a follower stand taller than he was."45

In March, fifteen Spitfire Vs arrived in Malta, having flown off the aircraft carrier *Eagle*. In April nearly fifty more Spitfires took off from the U.S. carrier *Wasp*. Thirty of them were blown to bits by German and Italian bombs before the sweating ground crews could refuel them.

Early in May some sixty more Spitfires took off from *Wasp* bound for Malta. John Sherlock of Calgary was one of the pilots involved:

I think we were all a little apprehensive about the take-off. Our Spits were loaded with 90-gallon belly tanks, four 20-mm cannon instead of the customary two, including extra ammo, and the planes had been modified with tropical air scoops, all of which cut down the performance. In addition, spare parts had been stowed in the aircraft wherever possible. Mine had a tire and wheel attached to the armour plate at the rear of the seat. The planes were equipped with de Havilland metal airscrews, which I found to be not as good as the wooden Rotols for take-off and rate of climb. However, with the poor landing strips like we had at Halfar, undoubtedly the metal airscrews were the best in the long run.

The Spitfires were hardly ideal aircraft for carrier take-offs, since their flaps were not adjustable: fully up or fully down were the only available positions normally. To obtain maximum lift for take-off, blocks of wood had to be jammed under the flaps, creating a 15-degree setting.

Take-off was controlled by an experienced deck officer; his instructions had to be obeyed without question. Sherlock and his fellow landlubber pilots found the view from the deck alarming:

At one moment you would see only the sky, and the next moment you would see the ocean and the sky. Also, the plane in front of you would be reaching the bow of the carrier and would momentarily disappear, which was distracting. As the flagman dropped his flag, the chocks were yanked away, the pilot released the brakes, gave full throttle, corrected for the strong torque, and was away. Before he was halfway down the deck, the next plane was being spotted for take-off. Timing was all-important. The flagman's signals ensured that each Spitfire was actually going down a slight incline as it began its take-off run; by the time it reached the end, the deck was level with the horizon. The plane dropped down after take-off, but because of the height of the carrier, this was no problem. As soon as the plane was airborne, the pilot whipped up the wheels, climbed to 500 feet or so, adjusted the pitch and throttle, and turned to join his group. Around 1,000 feet we dropped the flaps for a second to release the blocks of wood, then changed over to our overload tanks.

There were always a few seconds before the engine picked up again, during which time you held your breath and your heart stopped beating.

In one remarkable incident, Jerry Smith of Regina got away from the carrier only to find that his overload tank wouldn't work. He couldn't reach Malta. So he turned about and landed back on the carrier, the first time a Spitfire *sans* tailhook had accomplished the feat. The U.S. Navy pilots were so impressed, they presented Smith with naval wings.

On Malta, the latest batch of Spitfires were welcome indeed. Now the defenders of the tiny island could at last meet the enemy on more-or-less-equal terms. But why had the authorities waited so long to supply the desperately needed Spitfires? In the first three months of 1942, the island had received the attentions of more than 17,000 sorties by the Germans and Italians. In the same period, the Luftwaffe had flown precisely 151 daylight sorties over England, where thousands of Spitfires sat in their dispersals.

Living conditions on the island were still poor – and were deteriorating day by day. Everything was in short supply. Bully beef and canned stew became the pilots' daily fare, and even the servings of *that* dwindled rapidly. Hard biscuits accompanied most meals, with smearings of an unappetizing spread known as gharry grease, so called because it was said to taste like axle lubricant.

In June, another batch of Spitfires arrived, having flown off the British carrier *Eagle*. One of the pilots was a tousled-haired young man with the eyes of a veteran and the insouciance of a schoolboy. He flew a brand new Spitfire V, its belly made chubby by a ninety-gallon long-range fuel tank. On landing, he had been taken in hand by a gang of wild-looking characters. Some wore shorts, many sported steel helmets, others opted for bush hats or other headgear. None bore much resemblance to serving members of His Majesty's armed forces. They gestured to him like impatient traffic policemen to taxi *that way*, then *turn there* and pull in *there*, and *fast!* He found himself in a rudimentary blast pen, a chaotic erection of sandbags and bricks, bits of corrugated iron, and barbed wire.

The Spitfire's engine had no sooner gasped to a halt than another gang of unshaven, unkempt toughs swarmed over the fighter. They looked like bandits from the hills sent down to rob him. But they had no interest in his money, only his aircraft. They seemed angry, their gestures impatient. Get out of the bloody plane! We need it! *Faster!* Jerry's on his way! He scrambled out of the narrow cockpit. Heat enfolded him, moist and clammy. Flies buzzed about his head. An officer in shorts and flying gear hurried to the Spitfire, sweat streaming down his tanned face. With barely a nod to acknowledge the presence of the man who had flown the precious fighter in, he clambered onto the wing, while soldiers sloshed fuel into wing tanks from jerrycans. Armourers, with belts of ammunition over their shoulders, unfastened the gun ports and thrust in hundreds of big 20-mm rounds. The Spitfire's engine burst into renewed life and, propelled by angry bursts of power, the aircraft went trundling out of its blast pen, leaving the pilot standing watching, slightly bewildered.

Twenty-year-old George Beurling, of Verdun, Quebec, had arrived in Malta. In the next hour, he witnessed in bewilderingly rapid succession an air raid, a low-level strafing by Messerschmitts, a dive-bombing attack by a gaggle of Ju 88s, several aircraft going down in flames, a handful of aircrew swinging beneath their parachute canopies like loose-limbed puppets. And judging from the resigned expressions of the ground crew, the rapid-fire air show was nothing out of the ordinary. This Malta, he decided, was his kind of place!

Before his departure from England, Beurling had served briefly with 403 and 41 squadrons. He had shot down an FW 190 during an offensive sweep over France in the spring. In getting his kill, he had committed a cardinal sin: he had abandoned his formation. It wouldn't be the last time.

Beurling, a lanky, untidy individual, wearing the stripes of a sergeant pilot, had a lean, appealing face dominated by penetrating blue eyes. A slightly cryptic smile played on his full lips. He came from an intensely religious family; Bible study was a daily ritual, alcohol and tobacco were forbidden, even the acquisition of a radio was condoned only because of the need to follow the war news.

Aviation had fascinated Beurling for as long as he could remember. He had learned to fly at nearby Cartierville, doing odd jobs to pay for lessons. A quick and intensely enthusiastic pupil, he soloed at sixteen. At eighteen, he found a job in Gravenhurst, Ontario, as copilot to a man named Langley who flew freight to the goldfields in northern Quebec. The job helped fill Beurling's logbook, but it involved far more labouring than flying. Beurling quit in late August 1939 when he heard that the Chinese needed pilots.

That adventure ended when U.S. immigration authorities arrested him in Seattle, charging him with illegal entry. Although he explained that he was on his way to China, Beurling was packed into a train and sent back to Montreal. World War II began while he was en route. Now he was convinced that the RCAF would take him immediately – after all, he was a trained pilot, wasn't he? The RCAF turned him down. Prewar restrictions still applied: you had to have a university degree to become a pilot in Canada's air force. When the Soviet Union invaded Finland, the ever-persistent Beurling contacted the Finnish consulate in Montreal. The interview went well, until the official said that, in view of Beurling's age of nineteen, he would have to get his father's approval. Not surprisingly, his father refused to sign the form. Frustrated, Beurling had to wait until the spring of 1940, when he saw a story in a newspaper about the RAF accepting applications from experienced pilots. He crossed the Atlantic working as a deckhand on a Swedish ship, *Valparaiso*, carrying explosives.

In Scotland, Beurling presented himself at the nearest RAF recruiting office. To his delight he found that here at last was an air force that wanted him! But now he ran into another snag: he had neglected to bring his birth certificate. The RAF insisted on proof of age. Beurling told the recruiting officer that he would be right back. He was, too, after working his way back to Montreal to get the precious document, and working yet another passage to return to Scotland. He reported to the recruiting office and was signed on.

When Beurling joined 249 Squadron, the unit had been on Malta for a year. Stan Turner had just relinquished command, having been promoted wing commander. The squadron's weary Hurricanes had been replaced by the new Spitfire Vs. The squadron was ready for the toughest battles in the history of the beleaguered island.

Beurling's sojourn on Malta nearly came to an early end. Robert "Buck" McNair, from Springfield, Nova Scotia, was "B" flight commander, and an ace with five victories (described by Laddie Lucas as "a critic of anything and anyone he thought to be substandard."[46]) McNair spotted Beurling's name on the list of recently arrived pilots. He knew of Beurling, and he didn't want him in his flight. Fortunately, Laddie Lucas, "A" flight commander, had a certain affection for eccentrics. He decided to take a chance on the ill-disciplined young Canadian, but he told Beurling that if he didn't toe the line, he would be sent home immediately.

"George Beurling, by any test, was exceptional," Lucas later wrote. "He was exceptionally untidy, exceptionally imprecise in his discipline and exceptionally individualistic. He possessed a penchant for calling everything and everyone – the Maltese, the 109s, the flies – 'those goddam screwballs.' The name stuck."[47]

With that half-respectful, half-mocking smile on his lips, Beurling assured Lucas that he would behave. He wanted to stay on Malta. He liked it, its rawness, its frontier quality, its total lack of spit and polish. He had found a sort of spiritual home.

Beurling quickly made his mark, almost certainly destroying an Me 109 within three days of his arrival (although Beurling received only a "damaged," he shot most of the fighter's tail away, which meant it probably crashed). Early in July, he damaged a Z1007 bomber and destroyed two MC202 fighters. Later that same day, he shot down an Me 109.

It was the beginning of a phenomenal career. Almost daily, Beurling added to his tally of victories, demonstrating an amazing gift for deflection shooting, the trickiest of shooting for pilots of that era, who had to rely on basic gunsights. In essence, deflection shooting meant aiming ahead of the target so that bullets and target met in the same bit of sky. With aircraft constantly turning, quickly and violently, the art called for marksmanship and judgement of an almost-magical order. Most fighter pilots sprayed thousands of rounds about the sky when deflection shooting was involved. Only with the arrival later in the war of gyro (gyroscopic) sights, which automatically adjusted for speed, distance, span, and other factors, did the average fighter pilot stand much of a chance of hitting anything, except by luck, in a deflection shot. Beurling always claimed that he had honed his skills shooting rabbits and birds in the fields near Verdun. But there was more to it than that. Despite his casual, almost slapdash, manner, Beurling had an analytical mind; he approached the business of air-fighting as a mathematical problem, an exercise in lightning-quick estimates of angles, speeds, and distances. In his spare time, he would shoot at the ubiquitous Maltese lizards with his service revolver, using the same theories. After every combat, he jotted down diagrams and columns of figures, spending hours studying his data on angles, speeds, heights, every aspect of every combat; cumulatively, they provided him with all he needed to know when faced with a situation in the air.

He was awarded the DFM, a medal more highly regarded by most fliers than the DFC, simply because far fewer DFMs were handed out. Offered a commission, he turned it down. He equated rank with responsibility, and he wanted none of it. He became friendly with another Canadian, Joseph Paradis, whom he called Jean, from Shawinigan Falls, Quebec. In free hours they would escape from the sweltering summer heat by going to the beach to swim. The two young Québécois became friends, briefly. On July 22, the twenty-five-year-old Paradis crashed into the Mediterranean, shot down in a dogfight. He died instantly. After that, Beurling avoided friendships with members of the squadron; losses were easier to take when fellow fliers were just names and faces, and the lists got longer day by day. In one week, half of 249's pilots became casualties. Usually they were fledglings, pilots on their first or second operational flights. Replacements kept arriving, pale-faced youngsters fresh from England, tyros who had to be initiated into the singular ways of Malta. Most of them quickly became statistics, forgotten names buried in squadron records, unremembered faces on fading snapshots.

Laddie Lucas, Beurling's flight commander, watched the progress of his protégé with interest. "I had a feeling about George Beurling the moment I met him and as soon as I had seen enough of his work as a fighter pilot. Something told me that he was made for this rarefied form of island warfare, whereas he was unlikely to be suitable for the large, set-piece wing operations with which we were so familiar at home. In the event, he proved to be, in this environment, a genius."[48]

His flying was meticulous, his shooting superlative. Where most pilots simply blazed away and hoped for the best, Beurling made every bullet, every cannon shell, count. During one encounter with a mixed force of Italian and German fighters, Beurling shot down a 109 and a Macchi 202. Nearby ack-ack personnel confirmed both claims. At debriefing, Beurling told the intelligence officer, almost as an afterthought, that as he had been breaking away, he had spotted another Macchi near the island of Gozo. He saw his shots hitting the Italian's fighter's flanks and engine, but he had to break off when a gaggle of 109s came to the Italian's aid. He wasn't sure whether to claim the Macchi as damaged. Later, Beurling was told that his Macchi had crashed on Gozo. Though pleased with his victory, Beurling was dismayed to learn that none of his shots had hit the Macchi's engine. In his own odd way, he regarded the Macchi as something less than a complete victory, because his shots had not gone precisely where he thought they had gone.

By early August, Beurling had become the leading fighter pilot on Malta. He had destroyed sixteen enemy aircraft and become a celebrity on the island. That didn't protect him from "Malta Dog," a notably virulent and unsavoury form of dysentery endemic to the island. Beurling's attack cost him thirty-five pounds and left him so weak that he could barely get to his feet. It was while he was incapacitated, flat out on his bunk, that a signal arrived from London. Sergeant George Beurling was *ordered* to accept a commission. Belatedly, the authorities had realized what calibre of hero they had in the singular young man. He *had* to be an officer and a gentleman. Convention demanded it.

The Canadian newspapers were breathless with excitement. Here at last was a golden youth to make citizens forget about the litany of defeats that had plagued the Allies for months. Here was a hero who could take on the best of the Axis and win. Not only that, he was good-looking and photogenic, a press agent's dream. An article headlined "Untidy, but what a flier!" introduced him colourfully if not very accurately to Canadian readers. He was described as French-Canadian, the bearer of the nicknames "Skewball" and "Buzzy." The reporter gushed, "George is the most untidy RAF pilot I have ever seen. His hair looks as if it was never brushed and he is careless about his clothes. In fact, he is careless about everything except his flying."[49]

Recovering from "The Dog," Beurling returned to duty. His tally of victories mounted at a remarkable rate. He became a celebrity among fellow fighter pilots. Everyone acknowledged that he was the master. He kept "training" his eyes, often sitting for hours, staring into space, then suddenly turning and peering at a nearby wall. Success in the air, he claimed, depended on how rapidly you could adjust your focus to spot tiny objects aloft.

In mid-October Beurling became a casualty. In a huge dogfight he downed three German aircraft, but then he felt his Spitfire taking hits. Cannon shells and bullets burst through the thin metal skin, wounding him in the chest and the left heel and leg. Flames streamed from his engine and were whipped by the fierce slipstream into an aerial blowtorch. Wounded, dazed, Beurling could do little but await his fate. The sea revolved in his windshield, rushing toward him at an alarming rate as the burning fighter plummeted. In a few seconds it would be all over. An instant of shattering impact. Then nothing. Blackness. But maybe not . . . At 2,000 feet, he felt his consciousness returning. He managed to drag himself out of the narrow cockpit and tumble into the rushing, bellowing air. In the nick of time, at a mere five hundred feet, he tugged at his ripcord and his parachute snapped open. He hit the water and lost consciousness.

In hospital near Takali, surgeons worked on his wounds. Beurling watched the battle from his hospital bed, frustrated because he was missing some of the most furious action in the siege of Malta. On October 25, the AOC Malta, Air Vice-Marshal Keith Park, of Battle of Britain fame, came to visit Beurling. He had news: Beurling had been awarded the DSO (he already wore the ribbons of the DFC and the DFM and Bar, befitting the man who had shot down twenty-seven enemy aircraft since his arrival in Malta). Park had more news: Beurling was going home; he was needed in Canada for recruiting and bond drives. Aghast at the prospect, Beurling shook his head. But Park was adamant. Besides, it would take more than a mere air vice-marshal to have this order rescinded. It had come from the loftiest of levels on Parliament Hill. Park told Beurling to start packing.

On November 1, 1942, the latest Canadian hero boarded a Liberator bound for Gibraltar. Again Beurling's luck was tested. Running into a violent thunderstorm during his approach to "Gib," the Liberator pilot, Warrant Officer Rupert Davey, of Fort William, Ontario, attempted to go around for a second attempt. The Liberator stalled and crashed into the sea, killing everyone aboard except Beurling and another RAF fighter pilot, A. H. Donaldson, both of whom jumped just before the crash. The fabulous Beurling luck was holding. (One of the victims of the crash was John Williams, DFC, of Chilliwack, B.C., an ace with nine victories, all won over Malta.)

Recuperating in a British hospital, Beurling held court for a bevy of excited reporters who peppered him with questions, hanging on every word as if they were interviewing Churchill himself. Nothing in his background had prepared Beurling to be a celebrity. For a day or two he was tongue-tied by every question. He wished the reporters would leave him alone. But then, as if a switch had been flicked, Beurling found it was kind of fun. The reporters were nice guys, anxious to make him famous. Soon he was chatting away as if he had been giving interviews all his life. He found it amusing to watch these excitable guys with their notepads and pencils. They were like puppies at feeding time, gobbling up anything he said, scribbling it all down. As Beurling described his "science of killing" for Scott Young, the celebrity was fingering cannon shells lying on the coverlet and "looking at his interviewer with big, extremely pale eyes. 'The Huns are yellow, unless they have all the advantages of height, speed and power, they won't attack.'"[50] The next day, he saw everything he had said, column after column of it, complete with pictures of him in his hospital bed. Being *somebody* had its advantages. It was as if shooting down a few Huns had changed him, made him into some sort of revered teacher. He never really recovered from the experience.

A certain arrogance and impatience began to take over the ever-so-casual persona. People jumped when he spoke. He liked that. He journeyed back to Canada, still weak from his wounds, and endured endless receptions with the likes of Mackenzie King and Charles Gavan Power, the air minister. Banalities suffused every exchange with King:

"'What is the secret of your achievement?' asked the Prime Minister.

"'Well, I was given a good upbringing by my parents,' replied the flier.

"'That is an answer that will be greatly appreciated by the people of Canada,' said the Prime Minister."[51]

Beurling generally conducted himself well during the ordeal of press conferences and personal appearances, but at times he could barely conceal his irritation and impatience. The famous blue eyes lost their warmth and became icy. He took his revenge on the air force hierarchy by appearing at important functions with an "operational" peaked cap from which the wire stiffener had been removed and wearing a battledress blouse instead of a tunic – and compounding the sin by turning up the collar in defiance of regulations.

Beurling travelled across Canada, visiting army camps, factories, air training schools, and recruiting offices. It was tedious, but there were compensations. Beurling was a glamorous figure in a handsome uniform with pilot's wings and an impressive row of medal ribbons ("gongs" in air force parlance). He was recognized wherever he went. There were autographs and congratulations aplenty. Women adored him, lined up to meet him, shamelessly inviting him on dates, hinting at heaven knows what delights in store. No more prepared for this than he had been for the attentions of the press and politicians, Beurling found himself in a wonderful new world, a sensual, perfumed world in which he was a star. He lapped it up, revelled in it. Soon the legends of his conquests in the bedroom were as numerous as those of his conquests in the air.

IX

When Air Marshal Arthur T. Harris took over Bomber Command, many felt that the right man had at last got the job – and just in time. Autocratic, single-minded, and seldom troubled by self-doubt, Harris was going to make a difference, everyone thought.

Harris took over when the bomber force was at a crossroads. The general public in Britain, Canada, and the other Allied countries fondly believed that Germany had already been brought to the brink of collapse by the night-bombers. The air force and the government knew better. The strategic bombing campaign, of which so much had been expected – and promised – had been a virtual failure so far, partly because of inadequate equipment, partly because of poor tactics. Harris set out to recreate the bomber force. He quickly imposed his singular personality on the entire organization, from group commanders to the humblest of aircraftmen second class. And, incredibly, he did it from his HQ at High Wycombe. Not for Harris the matey standing on ammunition boxes and delivering pep talks à la Montgomery. He seldom visited his hard-pressed squadrons, but they all knew him and called him "Bomber" or "Butch." In the hard months to come, some airmen would rate Harris as a callous commander who cared not a whit how many aircrew he lost as long as he achieved his aims. Most, however, admired their crusty AOC, seeing him as a man capable of winning the war.

Although the early part of 1942 was a grim time for Bomber Command, it was a good time for Harris to take over. Several of the key problems that had hindered the bomber assault to date had been solved. The "Gee" navigational aid became operational early that year. The first practical trials with "Oboe" took place a little later, after which "H_2S" appeared (getting the name H_2S, because, according to legend, when Harris was told about it, he remarked in his acerbic way, "Here's another stinker!"). H_2S developed from the ASV equipment used at sea for detecting U-boats and other vessels. Contained within the aircraft, and operating independently of any ground stations, the new device enabled operators to scan the ground through the thickest cloud cover. Although it had its limitations, particularly in its earliest forms, H_2S was a remarkable advance, with exciting promise.

When he assumed command, Harris found to his dismay that his force was little larger than it had been at the beginning of the war. He had fewer than four hundred front-line bombers and crews ready for battle. He estimated that it would take four *thousand* heavy bombers to destroy Germany's industrial infrastructure and bring her to defeat. The prospects of getting such a gigantic force in the foreseeable future seemed remote indeed. The Admiralty was currently demanding that every long-range aircraft in the air force be employed on anti-submarine patrols rather than on strategic bombing. The voracious U-boats and surface raiders of the German navy and the aircraft of the Luftwaffe were sinking Allied shipping at a terrifying rate. One convoy to Russia had lost fifteen of its twenty-three vessels.

Doggedly (sometimes unwisely), Harris argued that strategic bombing of the enemy's centres of production was the most effective way of defeating the U-boats and, in fact, every other enemy. But Churchill seemed to be wavering on the side of the Admiralty. Harris knew that he had to do something without delay.

Despite his forbidding demeanour and acid tongue, Harris possessed a sure instinct for the dramatic. He decided that the time for rhetoric was past; the way to sell the government and the country on Bomber Command was to mount the biggest air assault in history and wipe a well-known city off the map. Such an attack would capture the imagination of everyone from Churchill down and would silence the critics of Bomber Command. A force of a thousand bombers could do it. Never in history had such a huge attack been mounted, not even by the Germans. The potential of Bomber Command would be demonstrated in the most dramatic way imaginable. No one would dare disband the force after such a raid; it would be like demolishing Downing Street.

Only someone with the damn-the-torpedoes mentality of Harris could have pulled it off. The thousand-bomber raid was a confidence trick. Harris didn't have a thousand bombers. He didn't have five hundred. He had to call on Coastal Command and the training commands to make up the numbers. The Admiralty came close to scuttling the whole project, refusing to permit the use of any Coastal Command aircraft for the gigantic air show. Harris refused to be deterred. He ordered his squadrons to round up every airman capable of filling an aircrew seat. The rest of the force would come from the training units. Harris preferred not to contemplate the very real danger, if they suffered heavy casualties, of losing both his entire force *and* his reserves in one awful stroke.

Originally, the target was Hamburg. Bad weather over the North German city prompted a last-minute change to Cologne.

In the early evening of May 30, in scores of briefing rooms, young blue-clad figures sat open-mouthed as intelligence officers described the night's operation. A *thousand* bombers! It was fantastic! The biggest air raid *ever*! And they were all going to be part of it. The briefing officers told them something that raised their eyebrows another notch: the thousand bombers would bomb Cologne in a mere ninety minutes, swamping the defences with sheer numbers.

Twenty-year-old Albin Lucki, of Komarno, Manitoba, a student navigator in the final stages of his training, wasn't sure what to make of it. Lucki, still attached to No. 12 OTU, was one of hundreds of airmen who found that they had become members of the hastily assembled crews; any and every aircrew "bod" was being roped in to make up Harris's magic thousand. Lucki joined a crew of strangers. The pilot and wireless operator, Bob Ferrer and Ron Grundy, were English, the others, like Lucki himself, were Canadians: nineteen-year-old Ken Buck, of Owen Sound, Ontario, was the bomb aimer and front gunner; and John McKenzie, of Trois-Rivières, Quebec, was the rear gunner.

Lucki liked what the briefing officer said about pushing through massive numbers of bombers, rendering the enemy's elaborate radar system impotent because it would be unable to concentrate on more than a tiny fraction of the attackers. On the other hand, what of the danger of mid-air collisions? Wasn't there every likelihood of dozens of bombers running into one another in the darkness? As if he had been privy to Lucki's thoughts, the briefing officer said that no one should worry about the danger of collisions. The statisticians had worked it all out mathematically. According to their calculations, only two aircraft would be involved in a collision over the target. ("But which two?" was the query at one briefing.) Two out of a thousand wasn't much to worry about, was it? You had a better chance of being run over by a bus at Hyde Park Corner.

Dr. Basil Dickins, chief of the operational research section at Bomber Command HQ, had approached the subject with the objective eye of the statistician: "We had to reduce it all to mathematics, and work out the actual chance of a collision. And it became quite obvious to us at ORS that while a collision was a half per cent risk, the chance of being shot down by flak or fighters was a three or four per cent risk. So we could allow the collision risk to mount quite a bit, provided that in doing so we would bring down the losses from other causes."[52]

To the airmen, night-bombing was a matter of probing lights and searing flame and constant, nagging dangers; to the statistician it was all numbers. Privately, Harris was prepared to accept a loss of sixty bombers. Churchill thought the propaganda benefit would be worth a hundred. Operation Millennium was on.

Lucki's aircraft was an elderly Wellington, a battered veteran of many a sortie, now put out to pasture at an OTU, spending its last days dragging target-drogues about the sky. Its Pegasus engines weary and delivering far less than full power, its battered metalwork showing through ancient paint, its fabric covering threadbare in spots, Wellington Ic, X9874, was typical of the OTU aircraft pressed into action for the great raid. Most were well past their prime, but if they seemed capable of getting into the air carrying a crew and a bomb load, they went.

Further north, at Middleton St. George, County Durham, all sixteen Wellingtons of the recently formed Canadian bomber squadron, 419, were fully manned. The unit's immensely popular CO, the pink-cheeked, cherubic Wing Commander John Fulton, of Kamloops, British Columbia, had no crew of his own. But

"Moose" Fulton, as he was known to everyone, had not the slightest intention of being left behind. He laid claim to an old Mark IC Wellington used for the training of "sprog" (fledgling) crews, and assembled a crew made up of any available aircrew.

At Pocklington, East Yorkshire, a dozen miles from York, 405 Squadron had just converted from Wellingtons to four-engined Halifaxes. The thousand-bomber raid would be the unit's first opportunity to fly their new aircraft on ops. Since mid-February, the squadron had been under the command of the hard-driving Johnny Fauquier, who had, in a few months, earned a reputation as one of the best COs in Bomber Command. In spite of his presence, things had not been going well of late. Shortly before Operation Millennium, the capable and experienced commander of "B" Flight, twenty-one-year-old John McCormack of Toronto, had taken off in a small two-seater Magister with a passenger, William Fetherston, from Arnprior, Ontario. McCormack threw the Magister into a series of aerobatics near the airfield. Eyewitnesses said the little trainer stalled during a slow roll, dived vertically into the ground, and blew up. McCormack and his passenger had died instantly.

The squadron's new Halifaxes were a problem. Hydraulic and radiator troubles tormented the ground crews; lack of power and uncertainty about the Halifax's airworthiness did much the same for the aircrews. All in all, it was a far from encouraging situation. To make matters worse, the big Halifaxes could carry twice the bomb load of the old Wimpies, but the squadron's ground handling equipment had not been modified accordingly. "We could not get the bombs out of our dump fast enough. Every vehicle was hauling bomb carts, even Fauquier's car."53

With the immeasurable advantage of hindsight, it is easy to scoff at the extravagant expectations of Bomber Command for the big raid. Some senior officers held that it might even end the war. A thousand bombers should wipe Cologne off the face of the earth, and what a devastating message that would send to Hitler and his gang, indeed to the whole German nation. If the British could do this to Cologne, it would be only a matter of time until they did the same thing to Essen and Berlin and every other city. One by one, the German centres of production would vanish, blown to bits and burned to a crisp. Such were the comforting fantasies of the time. Few in Britain grasped just how large and resilient the German industrial machine really was.

As the light faded on that May Saturday, the first bombers began their take-off runs. Operation Millennium had begun. In all, 1,047 bombers took off for Cologne. Four RCAF squadrons were involved, contributing 71 aircraft. The Gee-equipped Wellingtons of 419 Squadron attacked in the first wave. Their job was to start the fires, lighting up the target for the other bombers. It was hardly necessary; the city could be seen in remarkable detail in the bright moonlight. Moose Fulton observed that the "ground defences seemed very ineffective."[54]

The first bombs fell shortly before 1:00 A.M. The incendiaries took hold immediately, particularly in the old part of the city, where wooden buildings predominated. Aircrews watched dozens of fires springing up, merging, flaring, dying, being reborn, as if the conflagration had a life of its own. In a few minutes, the entire city seemed to be ablaze. Ralph Wood, of Woodstock, Ontario, an observer with 76 Squadron, was vastly impressed. The target looked to him like "the red-hot embers of a huge bonfire." The entire city was being cremated. God only knows how the inhabitants were managing. Poor devils, they must be dying in their thousands. The scene looked overwhelmingly Biblical: fire and brimstone . . . God's punishment for the evil Third Reich. Still the bombers came, still the bombs fell, as the searchlights probed, great columns of light swaying ponderously, searching the dark corners of the sky. Bombers caught by the searchlights looked from the ground like tiny metallic insects, turning, diving, frantically trying to escape. For the bomber crews, being trapped in the searchlights was a frightening experience. A flood of light burst into the aircraft, shocking and disorienting the crews. Many later said that they felt they couldn't breathe in the intense light. One of the bombers caught by searchlights that night was flown by Johnny Fauquier, the CO of 405 Squadron. Coolly, efficiently, he corkscrewed out of the dazzling beams and returned to Pocklington in good order.

Forty-one Bomber Command aircraft weren't so lucky. One was the Wellington piloted by Bob Ferrer, on which Albin Lucki was the navigator. A Messerschmitt 110 attacked the elderly Wimpy as it left the target area. Ron Grundy, the RAF wireless operator, saw bullets striking the fuselage and bouncing off the electrical panel on the starboard side of the aircraft. John McKenzie, the Canadian rear gunner, was hit and cried out for help over the intercom. After shaking off the night-fighter, Ferrer sent Grundy and Lucki back to assist him. They got him out of his turret and on to the rest bunk. By that time the old Wimpy was well out to sea, and one of its two engines had begun to lose power.

Thirty miles from the English coast, the second engine began to falter. Although Ferrer, the pilot, kept the old Wimpy flying as long as he could, eventually, still miles from land, he had to ditch. It was a difficult business at the best of times, but infinitely more challenging in the dark over a motionless sea. The young pilot couldn't see the surface clearly; he had no means of estimating his height with any accuracy. He miscalculated. With a shattering crack, the Wimpy hit the water, breaking up instantly. Only Ron Grundy and Ken Buck escaped alive.[*]

Forty-one bombers did not return from Cologne, an "acceptable" loss rate of 3.93 per cent of the aircraft dispatched. However, as historian John Terraine points out, nine more aircraft crashed in accidents over Britain. Bomber Command made a practice of omitting such losses from raid statistics, categorizing them as

---

[*]   Buck died almost exactly a year later while serving on 102 Squadron.

accidents, but if they are included in the totals, the loss rate rises to 4.79 per cent:

In addition, 116 aircraft were damaged to a greater or lesser extent, of which 12 had to be written off, so that the final count of aircraft completely lost as a result of Millennium was 62 – 5.94 per cent. And since a further 33 aircraft were seriously damaged – which meant that they would certainly not be available for the next operation, only two days later – it is not unfair to say that the full count for Millennium was 95, or 9.1 per cent.[55]

It might be added that such statistics could reasonably be applied to most of Bomber Command's operations; the publicized losses invariably fell far short of the actual casualties suffered by the hard-pressed squadrons.*

For Harris, the thousand-bomber raid was a triumph. It made headlines around the world, with newspapers outdoing one another as they lavished praise on the gallant bomber crews. *The Vancouver Daily Province* declared: "Today the proud city of Cologne is a burnt-out ruin, shattered, smouldering and useless.... 'I'd estimate nearly seven-eighths of Cologne was in flames,' [Wing Commander Johnny] Fauquier said. 'When we got there I almost felt like leaving to find another target. It didn't seem possible we could do any more damage than had already been done.'"[56]

Initial estimates of casualties among Cologne's population ran to tens of thousands, with most of the city's industry destroyed. Air power had demonstrated awesome impact, succeeding in eliminating a major city, just as the pundits said it could. A few more such

---

* Dr. Dickins' predictions about the dangers of collision (quoted on p. 205) proved remarkably accurate. Two bombers collided over Cologne.

raids, Harris told himself, and the job would be done. Germany would collapse.

There could be no doubt that the raid was a tremendous blow to Cologne and its citizens. As Sunday morning dawned, a vast pall of smoke hung over the still-burning city. The city's principal paper reported: "The sun was dimmed and all we could see of it was a purple disc behind the writhing smoke, a circle which at its edges broke up into the colours of the rainbow, then into deepest black. . . . For many hours the glare of the flames was brighter than daylight." The paper bade a sad farewell to the city everyone had known, "because the integral part of the character, and even the traditions, of the city, is gone forever."[57]

But the *Kölnische Zeitung* had written off the city too quickly. So had Harris and his colleagues at High Wycombe. The Commander-in-Chief's euphoria cooled as the facts became known. The raid, spectacular though it was, had killed fewer than five hundred citizens of Cologne. And although a great deal of damage had been done – more than 3,000 buildings destroyed, 2,000 badly damaged, and 45,000 people made homeless – the city rebounded with astonishing energy. Within two weeks, life in Cologne had returned to something approaching normal. Workers found places to live; companies discovered that much of the machinery buried under rubble had not been seriously damaged. In countless cases it took no more than a clean-up and minor repairs to put equipment back to work; utilizing basements or tents until new facilities could be built, factories were soon in operation again. The investigators found that the ingenuity and resilience of the German people was astounding, just as admirable as that of the inhabitants of London. It would bedevil Harris for the rest of the war: again and again it seemed that this or that city had been demolished, yet in a matter of weeks it would be producing war products again.

Not unnaturally, the public in Britain and Canada expected a string of thousand-bomber raids, believing that Bomber Command had quietly built itself up to a force of war-winning strength. Now a series of sledgehammer blows could be expected to destroy the evil Nazi empire and bring peace to the world. Hadn't the press already hinted at such triumphs? The *Vancouver Province* had declared on June 1: "Well-informed experts agreed a succession of such raids, increasing in scale as United States Air Forces become available, might bring Germany to her knees by autumn . . ." It was a heart-warming thought.

But the raids didn't happen. They couldn't. Although Harris sent his massive force to strike two more targets, Essen and Bremen, weather conditions were disappointing on both occasions. So were results. Essen was hit on the night of June 1, but with eleven houses destroyed and little more than a hundred casualties, the town's authorities thought they were receiving the "strays" from a raid on another city. (Although Harris was less than enthusiastic about the Essen raid, it impressed Ralph Wood, the Canadian navigator, who considered it "spectacular"; the view from his Halifax reminded him of one of the paintings of the Great Fire of London. It seems probable that Wood was looking at fires in Essen's suburbs; on that occasion the city centre was not seriously damaged.)

The third raid, on Bremen, during the night of June 25/26, was more successful than the attack on Essen but couldn't be compared with Cologne. Heavy cloud and vigorous anti-aircraft fire combined to blunt the attack. "It was a hot one," says Ralph Wood, "and they were ready for us. The damn' flak was like lightning flashing in daylight all about us as the searchlights grabbed us over the target. The shell bursts made a squeaky, gritty noise. The smell of cordite was strong and you had the feeling that someone was underneath, kicking your undercarriage, keeping time with the bursts." Curiously, the losses suffered by the OTU crews were high (11.6 per cent) on this raid, whereas they had recorded the lowest loss rate (3.3 per cent) over Cologne.

On the raid on Bremen, the Admiralty relented and permitted Harris to use 20 Wellingtons and 82 Hudsons of Coastal Command. Eleven crews from the Canadian 407 Squadron joined the force, although the distance involved was at the extreme limit of the Hudson's range. Cameron Taylor of Winnipeg, a 407 Squadron skipper, spotted a large fire and dropped his bomb load on it. He turned for home and just made it before his fuel ran out. Several 407 Squadron aircraft had to turn back before bombing with fuel running too low for comfort. Heavy cloud obscured the city, and many crews never even saw the target and had to bomb blindly.

The last of the thousand-bomber raids achieved little. German Civil defence authorities estimated the size of the attacking force at less than a hundred aircraft. It was a thoroughly discouraging follow-up to what the *Province* had called "the most devastating air raid in history," and it revealed how desperately slender the margin between success and failure could be on operations. The meticulously wrought plans of Bomber Command counted for little when the weather failed to cooperate.

A curious backlash followed the "thousand-bomber euphoria." Raids of two or three hundred bombers now seemed a trifle puny, vaguely half-hearted, as if Harris and his crews weren't really trying. Harris had whetted a dangerous appetite without the means to satisfy it. And his slender resources were being stretched to breaking point by the continuing demands of the navy. The First Sea Lord wanted more and more Bomber Command squadrons for anti-submarine duties; Harris's "heavies" were ideal for the task. Sympathetic though Churchill was to Harris's complaints, he knew all too well of the pressing need to protect Britain's shipping lanes. The war could well be lost on the Atlantic. He permitted more of the "heavies" to go to Coastal Command. And so, when the whole world thought Harris had at least a thousand operational bombers at his disposal, the fact was, he could barely maintain the strength of his command. The United States had been expected to supply vast numbers of heavy bombers to the RAF, but this source of supply proved a disappointment. After Pearl Harbor, the Americans dedicated most of their heavy bomber production to supplying their own air forces.

In Germany, the uproar that followed the thousand-bomber raids soon dissipated. For many months to come, no more huge armadas of bombers penetrated the Fatherland and overwhelmed the defences.

One thing was obvious: too many sorties ended up with bombs falling on open fields, or in the sea, or on decoy fires. On too many nights, conditions were simply beyond the capabilities of the average crew, young men with ample courage but inadequate experience or knowledge. Perhaps the answer was to create an élite corps in Bomber Command, crews who had the skill to find the targets in the worst conditions and "mark" them for the other crews. Several Group commanders had experimented with various ideas for illuminating targets; in fact, the concept had been used in the thousand-bomber raid on Cologne. The Gee-equipped bombers had the responsibility of starting fires on which the others could bomb. Now it was suggested that a special group be formed to do this on every raid. Churchill enthusiastically embraced the idea. Harris did not. All his instincts rebelled against the creation of a *corps d'élite* in Bomber Command.* Despite Harris's objections, the Path Finder Force (PFF) came into being in July 1942. An Australian airman, thirty-two-year-old Donald Bennett, was selected to head the new force. One of the world's finest navigators and a pilot of great skill and courage, Bennett proved to be an excellent choice for the difficult post. Undoubtedly his youth irked many of his fellow Group commanders who had spent their entire careers achieving their lofty perches in the air force hierarchy. And Bennett did little to endear himself to his colleagues. He had an impatient, often

---

* In effect, however, that was precisely what he had in 5 Group. Harris himself had commanded the group early in the war. So deeply ingrained was the notion of 5 Group's "special status" among bomber crews that when a discussion was going on about the young Princess Elizabeth and whom she might eventually marry, a voice piped up resignedly, "It's bound to be someone from 5 Group."

sarcastic manner and a barely concealed contempt for anyone unable to match him intellectually. But it couldn't be denied that the man was brilliant.

At first, PFF consisted of only four squadrons: 7, flying Stirlings; 35, with Halifaxes; 83, with Lancasters; and 156, operating Wellingtons. In addition, 109 Squadron, flying Mosquitoes, was attached to the new group to test the new "Oboe" radar equipment. One of the PFF's biggest problems in the early days was to develop efficient markers; that is, bombs that would burn brightly and distinctly so that they would be visible to the Main Force crews far above.

One member of 35 Squadron was an outstanding Canadian pilot, Reg Lane, of Victoria, British Columbia. At twenty-two, the fair-haired young man with the ready smile and friendly manner was a veteran. He had joined 35 Squadron just after the unit converted to the four-engined Halifax. Lane's first tour of operations was horrendous. The squadron suffered crippling casualties, and Lane himself had been extraordinarily fortunate to come through unscathed. The worst op of the lot was probably a nine-hour trip to bomb the *Tirpitz* at Trondheim, Norway. Flak had smashed into the Halifax's main spar, narrowly missing a fuel tank. The flight home became a nerve-jangling endurance test, with the crew waiting to see if the spar would fail and send the aircraft spinning into the North Sea. Lane landed safely; the Hally was a write-off. It had been a near thing, but it was just one of many. On one trip, he had come back with 120 holes in the fuselage and wings.

Reg Lane was unusual among his contemporaries in that he had had little interest in aviation before joining the air force. Airplanes simply hadn't had any part to play in his life. Besides, as he recalls, there was very little flying going on in Victoria in those days. He had decided to enlist in 1940, and in a spur-of-the-moment decision, he walked into the air force recruiting office. He had chosen well; he was a natural flier and graduated first in his class during training.

Many crews had been lost in the months since Lane arrived on 35. But the amiable, soft-spoken Canadian kept coming back. He seemed able to handle the nervous strain of operational flying better than most other airmen. Like Johnny Fauquier, he had total confidence in his skill as a pilot and had hand-picked every member of his seven-man crew. But before the advent of the PFF Lane had been contemplating, without much enthusiasm, the inevitable posting to instructing duties at an OTU. It was the "rest" period given to those who completed their tours. Although the completion of his tour had once seemed an almost impossible dream, it had been realized. And Lane wasn't at all sure that he wanted it. He cringed at the prospect of instructing at an OTU, with its ham-fisted students and ropey old kites. Like most of the experienced aircrew in Bomber Command, Lane found life in an operational squadron greatly to his liking. The sense of importance of every day was almost palpable. The comradeship of every member of the aircrew team simply couldn't be equalled. And there was intense satisfaction in doing something that few others could do. A tour of ops was the ultimate exercise in skill, in vigilance, in taking on appalling odds and beating them again and again. In comparison, a spell at an OTU held all the appeal of a sentence to POW camp.

Lane had, however, resigned himself to a training job when word came that 35 Squadron was to be 4 Group's contribution to the newly formed PFF. It was, everyone supposed, a compliment. Only the best went to PFF. Forty-five sorties was the minimum tour. To his delight, Lane found that if he stayed with 35 Squadron and became a member of the PFF, he would be allowed to continue his tour without interruption.

Morale in 35 Squadron was so good that almost all of the unit's crews felt as Lane did, preferring to go to the PFF rather than instruct. Lane says it was entirely due to the outstanding leadership of the commanding officer, Wing Commander Jimmy Marks, DSO, DFC. "He was the finest leader I encountered in the air force," he says.

Lane went off to enjoy his end-of-tour leave. On his return, he got shattering news: Marks had been killed on an op. It seemed scarcely credible. "I went into the mess," Lane says, "and it was like a funeral parlour, hushed and strained. Everyone felt Marks's death deeply, such was his impact on the squadron." The airmen shook their heads in bewilderment, trying to grapple with the fact that Marks had gone; he had seemed indestructible.*

But the war went on. The personnel of 35 Squadron grew intensely proud of being part of 8 Group, the "élite." They liked to wear their PFF badge, a tiny hovering eagle, on their tunic pockets immediately below their wings. (But they weren't allowed to wear them on ops in case they became prisoners; there was always the danger of Path Finder techniques becoming known to the enemy. Similarly the PFF eagles were never worn on battledress blouses, since, even if the badges were left behind, the pin holes in the material could lead astute German interrogators to identify PFF personnel.) They knew that the success or failure of almost every major operation depended upon how well they did their job.

In fact, the first operations flown by the fledgling PFF were by no means triumphs. It could hardly have been otherwise, for Harris insisted that the PFF squadrons were to become operational immediately, with no time given to training. Flensburg, a submarine base in the very north of Germany, near Kiel, became the first PFF target. Weather confounded their best efforts, and the raid failed. Wryly, Don Bennett remarked in his memoirs, "The Flensburg raid, of course, had the great advantage that it gave the cynics throughout the Command the opportunity to say, 'There you are. I told you so; the Path Finder Force won't work!'"[58]

---

* At about the same time, the personnel of 419 Squadron received similarly unbelievable news. Moose Fulton, their ebullient CO, went on an op to Hamburg and didn't return. A message was received from his aircraft near the Frisian Islands; it was under attack and several of the crew had been wounded. Then silence.

X

Pitt Clayton took over command of 405 Squadron, the RCAF's longest-established bomber unit, in the fall of 1942. Johnny Fauquier had commanded the squadron until August, and shortly after his departure, 405 had become one of the bomber squadrons transferred – to Harris's ill-concealed fury – to Coastal Command. Instead of going through the nerve-grinding dangers of flak and fighters to bomb Germany, the aircrew of 405 were now spending their time cruising over the ocean for hours at a time, searching for U-boats and other hostile vessels that might attack the troop-ships headed for North Africa.

When Clayton arrived, he found a squadron in disarray. Aircraft serviceability had plummeted. Aircrews had acquired a chronic reluctance to take to the air. The intangibles of pride and enthusiasm, the backbone of any military unit, had dissolved. Now the reasons why things *couldn't* be done were invariably more convincing than the reasons why they *should*. It is a not-unfamiliar story in the annals of military history. The best units can quickly be ruined when their foundations are taken away. And in such conditions, every problem becomes magnified. Certainly 405 had its problems. 405 had recently moved to Beaulieu, in the heart of the New Forest. It was hardly a model of modern accommodations. The huts were draughty and cold; many had no lights, and the washrooms and toilets, such as they were, seemed to have been situated as far from the living quarters as possible. The famous wild ponies that roam the New Forest took great interest in the activities on the airfield, frequently wandering onto the field when aircraft were landing and taking off. Again and again, personnel had to rush to chase them off active runways.

These problems had been compounded by a commanding officer with a drinking problem. He had taken over after Fauquier.

Rapidly, the finely wrought unit deteriorated, becoming a sorry reflection of its former self. And on top of everything else, dysentery soon affected many members of the squadron.

The rigid British class system only exacerbated a difficult situation. The local hostelries took a jaundiced view of the Canadian ground crew personnel, apparently considering them dangerous characters, uncertain of temper and probably carrying concealed knives, knuckledusters, and other weapons indigenous to North America. It didn't help that many of the airmen had only battledress to wear, since they had been detached from their former base at short notice. Most had left their dress blues behind. The non-commissioned Canadians were infuriated when local publicans refused to serve them in lounges, haughtily directing them instead to the public bars. Beaulieu seemed to many of the squadron's airmen the most snobbish and unfriendly of places. Moreover, one 405 airman remembers: "We were always in dutch with the service police, because our ID cards had our squadron number blacked out, as the squadron was on special duty and we were not to identify the squadron as such."[59]

Clayton discovered to his dismay that the CO had been off the base for two weeks and no one knew where he was. Clearly, there could be no delay in shaking everyone up. Clayton started off by interviewing all the aircrew, several of whom had become expert at the fine art of finding things wrong with their aircraft. "You will fly," he told them, "or you will be reduced to the ranks." They got the message. He made the acquaintance of a sergeant pilot who liked to dress in squadron leader's uniform and spend his time in Bournemouth bars telling tall tales to admiring young ladies. Clayton had the man arrested and held for court martial. (A year or more later, when Clayton had returned to Canada, he was having dinner in a hotel in Hull, Quebec, when an aircraftman walked across to him and asked him if he was Wing Commander Clayton. By this time, Clayton had reached the rank of group captain, but he nodded. The man then took a swing at him. It connected painfully.

From the floor, Clayton heard him say that he had been waiting to get even for a long time. A moment later he made the mistake of revealing his identity: it was the former sergeant pilot from 405, and although he must have been aware of the dangers of revealing his name, he evidently couldn't resist.)

Clayton soon had 405 Squadron operating at peak efficiency.

XI

At the mouth of the river Arques, sheltered by the limestone cliffs of Normandy, lies the city of Dieppe. Once known as "the poor man's Monte Carlo," the city became infamous in 1942 when an appallingly unsuccessful raid – a so-called "reconnaissance in force" – was carried out, largely by Canadian troops.

In the cheerless predawn of August 19, an armada of more than two hundred vessels set sail from Portsmouth, Southampton, Shoreham, and Newhaven. Aboard were close to five thousand troops of the 2nd Canadian Division, plus more than a thousand British commandoes and fifty U.S. Army Rangers. Their mission was to travel seventy miles, across the Channel to Dieppe, arriving at dawn. They were then to storm ashore, do as much damage as possible to the defences and radar and power stations, seize landing barges, documents, and prisoners, then slip back to England.

The plan failed. Some five miles off Dieppe, the expedition ran into German naval forces. The vital element of surprise had been lost. So had any chance of success. By the time the assault troops stormed ashore – many in the wrong places – dawn had broken and the Germans were ready for them.

Above the beaches, a huge air battle quickly developed, involving several Canadian squadrons. John Godfrey of Toronto was flying with 412 Squadron. He had taken off during the morning from

Merston, a satellite of Tangmere, near Chichester, escorting Hurricane fighter-bombers to Dieppe. Their job was to attack gun positions to the left of the town. "Of all the jobs that could have been assigned to us, this undoubtedly was the worst," says Godfrey.

Over the coast, 412's Spitfires met the bomb-laden Hurricanes and headed out over the Channel "five feet above the waves and cruising quite slowly at about 200 mph. About five miles off the French coast, we gradually opened up so that we hit the French coast going flat out to the right of the town. There is quite a high hill here, which slopes down to the water. Up over the hill we went, right down to the deck. We were to the right of the Hurri-bombers, but the other squadron didn't come in, but waited a mile or so offshore for us to come out."

Godfrey's unit flew some three miles inland, weaving around tall trees at perilously low level, although, paradoxically, it was safer there than higher up, because, as Godfrey remarks, "you are over their heads and behind the trees before they can get a shot at you."

The aircraft turned back toward the beaches. They came across a slope, at the top of which sat a powerful flak position. "We were going so fast, we were on it before we realized it. All hell was breaking loose. There were at least six heavy ack-ack guns, and I don't know how many machine-guns blazing away at us at point-blank range. We had come right up a funnel, completely exposed."

Godfrey's leader, twenty-five-year-old John Brookhouse, from Magog, Quebec, took hits. Suddenly, shockingly, his aircraft staggered. The entire tail unit disintegrated, vanishing in a shower of fragments. The fuselage broke in two behind the cockpit. "His kite seemed to go slowly over on its nose," Godfrey says. He didn't see the stricken aircraft hit the ground, for he had already sped past, weaving wildly, somehow still untouched by the ferocious fire. Over another ridge he went, the ground blurring along only a few feet beneath him. The beach swept into view. Beyond it, the sea. And escape! As the fighters streaked across the battle-torn beaches, ground batteries kept up a continuous hail of fire. Godfrey glimpsed clusters of splashes all around him where the enemy's shots smacked the water. "Why I wasn't hit, I don't know," he says.

It was the start of a busy day for John Godfrey. Early in the afternoon, 412 Squadron received orders to escort more Hurri-bombers to the same target; the guns were still firing, according to the troops. After their experiences earlier in the day, the pilots were relieved to be told that they weren't required to stay with the Hurri-bombers; instead they were to remain over the beach and cover their withdrawal. "When we were about a mile offshore from Dieppe, we climbed to 500 feet. There were FW 190s all over the place at around 2,000 feet, and we were the only Spits at our height. Some 190s started to dive down on the Hurris. We tore after them and they started to break away. Just then someone yelled, 'Red section, break!' There were some 190s on our tail. We went into a steep turn to the right and shook them off. I lost the others for a few seconds. The flak started to come up at us in great volume. Red balls were shooting past my nose, uncomfortably close."

Remarkably, the squadron returned to base without casualties. Godfrey himself had a lucky escape. A chunk of shrapnel hit the fuselage of his aircraft immediately beneath his seat, sliced through the structure, and ended up lodged in the folded silk of his parachute on which he was sitting.

For George Hill, of Antigonish, Nova Scotia, Dieppe was his baptism of fire. The twenty-four-year-old Hill had been serving as an instructor in Canada for the past two years. Now at last he saw action, shooting down an FW 190 during the first of his four trips to Dieppe that day with 403 Squadron.

Don Morrison of Toronto was serving with 401 Squadron at the time. The unit moved to Lympne, near Folkestone, for the Dieppe "show":

We woke up early in the morning to the sound of gunfire, which could be clearly heard across the Channel. Although we were keen to go, we were held back until we took off at

0935 to escort 24 Fortresses. Their job was to knock out Abbeville, the main Luftwaffe base in the Dieppe area. They flew in through heavy flak without fighter opposition, dropped their bombs right on the aerodrome. . . . We stayed with them until they were well on their way back across the Channel, and then our squadron dived for Dieppe. We could see the smoke and the bursting shells and the ships offshore, which all seemed to be turning in high-speed circles, leaving long white wakes.

As we got closer to Dieppe, we could see that there was a real hive of air activity. Almost as soon as we arrived over the area, we got into action. . . . I saw an FW 190 alone about 1,500 feet below me, so I did a slipping barrel roll to lose height, levelled out about 150 yards behind the Hun, opened fire, and closed to a range of about 25 yards. Pieces of the 190 about a foot square flew from around the cowling. Just as the enemy ran into a cloud, he blew up with a brilliant flash of flame and black smoke. My windshield and hood were smothered in oil, and there was a terrific clatter as pieces of the FW 190 struck my plane. I broke away, hardly able to see through the hood. Afterwards, my No. 2 told me that one of the pieces I saw break off the enemy aircraft was about ten feet long.[60]

Morrison's Spitfire had been more seriously damaged in the encounter than he realized. After paroxysms of coughs and shudders, his engine stopped.

"I took off my helmet," Morrison later wrote, "undid my straps, and opened the hood since it would not jettison. Then I crouched on the seat and shoved the stick forward, but in some way my parachute became caught and I figured that I was only about 250 feet above the water when I got clear."

He was remarkably lucky, his chute snapping open a moment before he hit the sea. He spent about fifteen minutes in the water before an air-sea rescue launch picked him up. For the rest of the day, he had a grandstand view of the battles at Dieppe:

> We saw a heavy bomber attack on our fleet beaten off by AA [anti-aircraft] fire. We saw the explosion of two aircraft colliding head-on. We could see the gunfire from both the ships and the shore, and we watched aircraft laying smoke-screens. Later in the afternoon, two FW 190s passed over us at 1,000 feet, and they attacked and set on fire another rescue launch. We raced off to get help from a naval boat, but as we went back toward the burning launch, we saw another rescue launch going to its assistance. Suddenly four more FW 190s set the second launch on fire. Then Spitfires arrived. We signalled to them where the trouble lay ahead, and they went on to find it. No sooner had the Spitfires left us than six more FW 190s dived on us. I am afraid our guns did not have much effect on them, but I think the 20-mm cannon fire from the naval boat shook them quite a bit. Only when they had run out of ammunition did the FW 190s fly off. We and the naval rescue launch then picked up the crews of the two burning launches. . . . When we finally returned to Newhaven, we had our first opportunity to talk to some of the troops who got back. It was only then that we realized the beating they had taken from the German troops who were well positioned on the heights and in many fortified positions.

"My own feeling," Morrison adds, "is that it was a costly but valuable lesson which saved many lives when we finally landed in Normandy in 1944."[61]

Keith Hodson had been CO of 401 Squadron for two months at the time of Operation Jubilee, as the Dieppe raid was known officially. Born in Jersey, the son of a Canadian army officer, Hodson had joined the RCAF in 1937 and was thus one of the very few

Canadian regulars in action that day. The twenty-seven-year-old Hodson led his squadron over Dieppe three times. The unit shot down one FW 190, probably destroyed three more, and damaged five. Hodson himself accounted for one 190.

416 Squadron, led by Lloyd Chadburn of Montreal, shot down three FW 190s without loss to themselves. Buck McNair, newly returned from Malta and now a member of 411 Squadron, claimed a "probable" after hitting an FW 190. "Nobby" Fee of Toronto, CO of 412 Squadron, and Norman Bretz, also of Toronto, who commanded 402 Squadron, both won DFCs that day.

Canadian twin brothers, Bruce and Douglas Warren, from Nanton, Alberta, were also present in the skies over Dieppe. Flying together in the same flight of 165 Squadron, an RAF unit, they patrolled the beach at Dieppe for about forty minutes before being relieved. "There were still some boats waiting offshore, it seemed, and there were many splashes around them from the German heavy guns," Douglas "Duke" Warren recalls. Around mid-morning, 165 Squadron returned to Dieppe. "The first fifteen minutes or so were uneventful. Then a terrific battle commenced as German fighter squadrons entered the area to provide cover for Dornier 217 and Ju 88 bombers, which were attacking Allied shipping below. Since this was really my first engagement with enemy aircraft, and there were so many of both them and us, I found it too confusing to track individual aircraft." Moments later, Douglas joined in an attack on a Do 217e, which was seen attacking landing craft, and "each of us in Yellow Section fired. The bomber was destroyed and the crew baled out. After this episode there was a series of small dogfights with inconclusive results on either side." Again the squadron returned to base to refuel and re-arm. Then it was time to take off once more and go back to Dieppe to cover the withdrawal of the hard-hit troops.

A mid-air collision between two 403 Squadron Spitfires killed both pilots: twenty-three-year-old John Gardiner of Ottawa, and nineteen-year-old Norman Monchier of Dartmouth, Nova Scotia.

It may have been the collision witnessed by Don Morrison from the air-sea rescue boat that had plucked him from the sea.

All pilots involved in the Dieppe expedition had been briefed that, in the event of forced landings, they should make for a former racetrack in Dieppe or an area of level ground at nearby Puys. The orders were to "blow up your aircraft and join the troops to fight your way out." As far as is known, only one Canadian pilot attempted a forced landing on either emergency landing ground, twenty-eight-year-old Paris Eakins, of Minnedosa, Manitoba. He crashed and was killed.

Although early estimates pointed to a great victory for the RAF, with nearly 300 enemy aircraft shot down, the sobering truth soon emerged. The Luftwaffe had lost 48, with 24 damaged. RAF/RCAF losses amounted to 106. It was a bloody day, both on the beaches and in the air.

The Luck of the Game (2): After completing his training in England, Eric Cameron received a posting to Malta, to fly in Wellingtons on night shipping strikes. On a day off, he journeyed into Valletta, taking a wristwatch that one of his fellow WAGs wanted repaired. When he returned, he learned that the duty flight commander had been looking for him to fill in for a sick WAG. Since Cameron couldn't be found, another man went – the very man whose watch Cameron had just taken in for repair. He didn't return, so Cameron paid the jeweller and wore the watch for the rest of the war years.

PART FIVE
1943

The Tide Turns

AVRO LANCASTER

"Fortune favours the brave." – Virgil

I

The conflict had reached a turning point. The ghastly mincing machine of Stalingrad swallowed an entire German army. The British Eighth Army entered Tripoli; Rommel was in full retreat. Mussolini would soon be out of office. In the Far East, the Japanese, after enjoying an almost unbroken string of successes, were at last feeling the weight of growing Allied strength. Churchill himself was convinced that victory was almost within reach: "It is a straight run in now . . ."[1]

But the cost would be cruel.

For more than three years, the RAF and Fleet Air Arm had been learning an intensely painful lesson. The aircraft with which they had gone to war were, with a handful of exceptions, quite inadequate. By 1943, most of the worst examples had been withdrawn from first-line units: the Battles and Blenheims, the Defiants, the Bothas and their desperation-measure replacements, the torpedo-carrying Hampdens, the egregious Lerwick flying boats (unable to float or fly, according to their crews), the lumbering Whitleys, the incendiary Manchesters, the paunchy Buffalos. New aircraft incorporating all the lessons learned at such cost – the superlative Mosquitoes and Lancasters, the Typhoons, the Mustangs and Mitchells, the Hellcats, the Corsairs, and the later versions of the Seafire and Spitfire – would make all the difference in the air war. But for some months, Allied crews would still die because they flew indifferent aircraft.

On May 3, a formation of twelve Ventura medium bombers of 487 Squadron set off from Coltishall to attack a power station in the north of Amsterdam. The Ventura, built by Lockheed and based on the Lodestar airliner, looked like a larger version of the successful Hudson, but was far less efficient. (A joke among aircrew posed the question: What can the Ventura do that the Hudson can't? The answer: consume more fuel. Air Chief Marshal Sir Basil Embry unhesitatingly described the Ventura as "thoroughly bad, being slow, heavy, unmanoeuvrable and lacking in good defensive armament."[2]) It is hard to imagine any aircraft less suited than the Ventura to a daylight operation against a heavily defended target such as the Amsterdam power station. Sheer bad luck compounded the attackers' problems. A convention of some of the Luftwaffe's best fighter pilots was taking place at nearby Schiphol. The *Experten* had been alerted by an earlier attack by Bostons. They were waiting for the Venturas.

A wing of three squadrons of Spitfires (118, 167, and 504) escorted the Venturas as they approached the Dutch coast. Sid Watson of Toronto was flying number two to the wing leader, the veteran Howard "Cowboy" Blatchford of Edmonton, now wearing the three rings of a wing commander. Watson recalls that the formation climbed to bombing height as the Dutch coastline passed below. "Then we received a warning from Control: 'Seventy-plus bandits approaching you. Keep lookout.'"

The enemy attacked moments later. FW 190s and Me 109s streaked down through the formation, scattering it, before zooming up to attack from below. The bombers were decimated, tumbling one after the other, streaming smoke and flame as parachutes dotted the sky. "It seemed to take only a minute or two," says Watson. "The Venturas were shot down in droves. It was a terrible fiasco." Cleverly, the Germans succeeded in separating the fighters from the bombers – just as the RAF had managed to do on many occasions during the Battle of Britain.

The Venturas had gone. The sky had emptied. Sid Watson tried to find his wing leader, Cowboy Blatchford. Blatchford had vanished, and so had everyone else. It happened again and again in aerial combat. One moment, a sky teeming with diving, turning aircraft; the next, no one to be seen. But Watson wasn't alone. An FW 190 suddenly appeared, heading straight for him. After firing a few rounds, Watson jammed his stick forward. His Spitfire, a clipped-wing Mark VB, hurtled a foot or two beneath the Focke-Wulf. To his alarm, Watson found himself rising, pulling his parachute and dinghy onto the edge of his bucket seat as the negative G-forces did their best to project him out through the cockpit roof. He remained there, perched on the edge of his seat, unable to slip back to his normal position. After a few minutes, the 190 dived away inland. The five-foot-seven-inch Watson returned to base, his helmet still jammed against his canopy, smiling to himself as he imagined how puzzled the German pilot must have been when his opponent suddenly assumed the proportions of a giant!

Cowboy Blatchford never did return. He is believed to have crashed into the sea off the Dutch coast. The first Canadian to have shot down an enemy aircraft in the war was thirty-one.

Only one of the unfortunate Venturas succeeded in getting back to base, seriously damaged, its crew wounded. The squadron had been virtually wiped out.

II

The best-known Canadian fighter pilot of them all, George "Buzz" Beurling, had had enough of bond drives and public appearances. Although his wounds had healed, he had become increasingly testy as it dawned on him how flagrantly the Canadian government was capitalizing upon his fame. It is a reflection of the naïvety of the man that he could ever have been unaware of it. In the previous few months his face had become familiar to just about every Canadian; he was the darling of the media, his handsome features beaming from stacks of newspapers and magazines. He was as famous and admired as Clark Gable – and just as good-looking, many female admirers contended.

Dave McIntosh, of Stanstead, Quebec, had just completed his training as a navigator on Mosquitoes, and was awaiting an overseas posting when Beurling arrived in Halifax on a War Bond drive. Beurling fascinated him: "Long nose, that great shock of corn-yellow hair. And those eyes . . . Even from the back of the hall, you could see those little flashing pinpoints. No wonder he could shoot like he did. We were transfixed."[3]

Beurling sometimes liked to horrify his audiences. On this occasion, he recounted how he had destroyed an Italian fighter: "When I fired, I didn't hit the plane itself. I hit the cockpit, just like I wanted. Blew the cockpit and the pilot's head right off. You should have seen the red blood streaming back over the white fuselage."[4] Beurling grinned when he saw his audience in open-mouthed shock.

Similarly, he loved to recount tales of how the RCAF had turned him down despite his pilot's licence, and how he had had to work his passage on a munitions ship to get to Britain and join the RAF. Now Beurling had decided – or was persuaded – to transfer to the Canadian air force. Protocol demanded the agreement of the RAF. It took several months. Meanwhile, Beurling recrossed the Atlantic, on the *Queen Elizabeth*. His rather childish sense of humour prompted him to tell correspondent Bruce West that he had just been married by the captain to a young American nurse he met on board. The news sped around the huge ship. Congratulations poured in. But no one seemed to have met the bride-to-be. No one ever did. The ship's public-address system gravely announced that, despite earlier reports, Flight Lieutenant George Beurling had not become engaged and that any inconvenience or embarrassment the earlier announcement might have made was regretted. Beurling himself seemed to find it all highly amusing, no doubt because he had started the rumours in the first place. An odd little quirk in his complex personality apparently compelled him to test the limits, to see how much he could get away with, both in the air and on the ground.

The moment Beurling stepped ashore in Scotland, reporters dogged him, eagerly swallowing any morsels he cared to toss their way. Obligingly, he fabricated stories, then contradicted himself in the next interview. It didn't matter. He was a star – at least, for the moment. The *Daily Express* was running his biography. Buckingham Palace received him, and King George VI pinned the DSO, DFC, and DFM and Bar on the lanky Canadian. Until that day, no member of the armed services had been decorated so lavishly on a single occasion. The king and Beurling exchanged a few words. The king asked him what he thought of Malta. Beurling replied that he enjoyed every minute of his time there.[5]

Still waiting for his transfer to the RCAF, Beurling found himself teaching marksmanship to young RAF fighter pilots at the Central Gunnery School. The job bored him. Besides, he knew the RAF was busy building up a huge fighter force for the impending invasion of Europe. He ached to be involved.

While he was teaching, Beurling managed to survive three more crashes. The first incident involved one of his students, who accidentally fired his machine-guns while engaged in a mock dogfight with Beurling. Beurling's aircraft plunged, out of control. According to legend, he made good his escape at little more than 1,000 feet. Not long afterwards, Beurling was practising "scrambles" in which the fighters retracted their gear the moment they became airborne. Beurling retracted his a moment too soon. The Spitfire thumped back to the ground, sustaining serious damage. Beurling clambered out unhurt. A month or so later, he survived a forced landing on the muddy flatland of The Wash.

In August, Beurling journeyed to Kenley, south of London, to talk to the leading British fighter pilot, Johnnie Johnson. At that time, Johnson was busy forming 127 Wing, the famous Kenley Wing, with its Canadian fighter squadrons. Johnson got along well with the Canadians; he liked them, although he felt that "they required a firm hand on the reins."[6] Higher authority wanted Johnson to take Beurling into the new wing. Johnson was impressed by Beurling's combat record, but he made it clear that he would tolerate no lone-wolf tactics from the individualistic Canadian.

"Okay, Boss," Beurling replied, smiling the famous smile that had worked its magic on everyone from pretty secretaries to prime ministers. He joined 403 Squadron, the unit in which he had briefly served more than a year earlier, before his adventures on Malta.

The squadron was equipped with the latest Spitfire, the Mark IX. Powered by the Merlin 61, the new Spitfire had been introduced in response to the Luftwaffe's alarmingly successful Focke-Wulf 190. Many pilots considered it the best of all the Spitfire variants. (When Johnnie Johnson first flew the new model, he exclaimed, "I'm going to live! I'm bloody well going to live now! We've got a machine that will see them off!"7)

Although he had the highest regard for the average Canadian fighter pilot, Johnson was less impressed by the RCAF's senior officers. He took over the Kenley Wing from a Canadian wing commander, who, Johnson says, "wasn't a very aggressive sort of chap." Formerly a wing commander in the British Commonwealth Air Training Plan, the Canadian lacked the aggressive instincts of a fighter leader. "That was one of the faults of the Canadians," observes Johnson. "They brought these middle-ranking chaps like wing commanders and group captains straight from Canada into operational jobs, and they usually fell down."8

After a few sorties with his Canadian pilots, Johnson was well pleased with the Kenley Wing. The only problem child was Beurling. No one questioned his ability, "but we couldn't make a team player out of him," Johnson admits. "The Wing would take off, but over France he would do a half-roll, disappear, come back, and say he'd shot this and that down – which he had, he wasn't a liar. He'd clobber some trains and come back with bloodshot eyes from having pulled a lot of G, and there'd be rivets popping out of his airplane. I could do nothing with him. I made him gunnery officer to see if he could teach the others how he did it. I said he'd get his own wing inside a year. He wasn't interested. We should have given him a long-range Mustang and said, 'Okay, go off and fight your own private war.'"9

The brilliant young Canadian might have been the model for the stubborn, maverick heroes of countless 1930s aviation movies, daring and successful on their own, frustrated when part of a team. However, if the senior officers of the squadron were uneasy about Beurling, the ground crew considered him the greatest. George Demare of Winnipeg was Beurling's rigger (airframe mechanic). He had a ride in a two-seat Magister piloted by Beurling. The ace took off and promptly buzzed a rugby game at ground level. "Down over the goal posts we flew," says Demare, "causing the startled players to hug the ground, then up over the other goal posts and away. Next we swooped down over a herd of cattle, then over a potato field, so low we had to climb to clear the hedge at the far end. ... For the grand finale, Beurling took us into a power dive – straight down at a horrendous speed. . . . Then less than 100 feet from the ground, Beurling executed a vertical hairpin turn and we were skyward bound. After a few more aerial manoeuvres, we came in for a smooth landing. When I emerged, smiling, Beurling patted my shoulder and said, 'Good flying!' I replied, 'Terrific!'"10

Beurling still yearned for the free and easy days on Malta. It was only a few months ago, yet it felt like years, another life. On that Mediterranean island he had found an air war that appealed to his every instinct. But here in England, it was all too organized, almost choreographed, leaving little to the initiative of individual pilots.

· During one routine sweep over the French coast, the wing received orders to intercept a formation of FW 190 hit-and-run raiders on their way to England. Beurling immediately set off in pursuit of a single aircraft at low level. The squadron CO, Hugh Godefroy of Toronto, was first furious and then worried, because he was convinced that Beurling was dead. He thought he heard the famous pilot grunting over the R/T that he had "had it." But the incredible Beurling luck held. A lone Spitfire turned up at the unit's base, Headcorn, Kent, long after the rest of the squadron had landed. It was Beurling. He rolled up to the dispersal, his aircraft in bad shape with popped rivets and metal skin twisted by the violent stresses imposed on it. Beurling had dived the immensely powerful Spitfire so steeply that he had nearly lost control. Only by working the trim tabs had he been able to ease the fighter out of its precipitous plunge. That he accomplished the task was remarkable; even more remarkable was that he did it without tearing the Spitfire's wings off.

Not long afterward, Canada's hero came near to being court-martialled. 403 Squadron had a Tiger Moth, used for short trips and odd jobs, and Beurling liked to fly it. Godefroy had no objection, but he expressly forbade aerobatics over the airfield. To Beurling, the order automatically became a challenge. Not long afterwards, Godefroy saw the Tiger Moth, its wingtip only inches from the ground, turning in tight circles and zooming low over the airfield buildings. Angrily, Godefroy called dispersal and demanded to know who was flying the Tiger. The answer came as no surprise.

"I was seething," Godefroy later wrote. "Beurling had purposely disobeyed me. . . . An hour later, when I had cooled down, Beurling slumped into the office with a sly grin on his face. He stood in front of me with his arms folded.

"'Buzz, why did you purposely disobey my orders?'

"'The Tiger Moth's in my flight; I'm going to fly it when and how I want to. You can't tell me what to do.'"[11]

Godefroy didn't hesitate. He placed Beurling under open arrest, in preparation for a court martial. Beurling protested that he was flying low only because of the conditions. He said he had taken the Tiger Moth to fly to another station to provide gunnery instruction. The cloud was only 300 feet on the return trip, so he had no choice but to fly low.

RCAF HQ cringed at the prospect of a court martial for the nation's number-one hero. Bad publicity. Out of the question. Mackenzie King wouldn't stand for it. The PM had, after all, done everything but crown Beurling during his recent tour of the country.

Beurling received a "grounding." The press didn't get hold of the story, so it all faded quickly away. But Beurling had tried the patience of the air force too many times, and his days were numbered. He had one more posting to a fighter squadron. This time it was 412, then commanded by George Keefer, an ace of the desert war. The squadron, which had just traded its aging Spitfire vs for Mark IXs, was based at the famous Battle of Britain field, Biggin Hill.

Beurling was appointed commander of "A" Flight, a key job in any squadron, and one he didn't relish for that very reason. Now the archetypical loner found himself responsible for half a dozen pilots, many of them fledglings, whom he had to prepare for the harsh world of aerial combat. He was their tutor, their leader, their father confessor. He was their link with their squadron commander and even loftier personages.

Remarkably, in view of his career to date, Beurling did the job conscientiously. Lloyd Berryman, of Hamilton, Ontario, served on Beurling's flight and remembers him with affection and respect.

When I arrived at Biggin Hill, the adjutant introduced me to the CO and other key personnel. I didn't meet Beurling until later in the day. He had a fantastic reputation at that time. The papers were full of him. The *Daily Express* had run his biography. He was treated like a movie star. To be honest, I would have preferred to be assigned to someone a little less Olympian. At the time, I felt very much like a new boy at school, insecure, not knowing anyone, being virtually ignored by everyone and speaking only when spoken to. Beurling came looking for me that evening. In the friendliest way, he introduced himself and asked about my air force career. He seemed genuinely interested and said how much he was looking forward to flying with me. Then off he went with a cheery goodnight. It meant a lot to me. He made me feel part of the team.

Beurling became a surprisingly good teacher. To the pilots of his flight, he was The Master, a genius in the art of aerial combat, an amazing man who possessed the remarkable faculty of anticipating what was going to happen at all times. Beurling also possessed phenomenal eyesight, as did countless fighter pilots. But where Beurling differed from the others was in the way he used his gifts. To the amazement of his pilots, he seemed to be able to see through thick cloud so that he could warn the flight of enemy aircraft above. It seemed magical. It wasn't; the pilot from Verdun had trained himself to pick up the merest suspicion of shadows on clouds, revealing the presence of aircraft above. He urged his fellow pilots to use the sun to their advantage, to get in close to their enemies before opening fire, and, most important of all, to become proficient in the art of deflection shooting, essential for success in Spitfires, which at that time were all fitted with the fixed "100 mph" gunsight.

According to Berryman,

Beurling undoubtedly had a computerlike mind. Equally important, he was a complete professional, he didn't leave things to chance. He had painstakingly figured out every conceivable combination of aircraft type, wing span, closing speed, and angle of attack. He liked to get the pilots out on the dispersal for "mental" drills designed to help them make instantaneous decisions in deflection shooting. "All right," he would say, "your closing speed is 100 mph; the angle is 30 degrees; it's an FW 190 — wingspan 34 feet — quick, what do you give him. . . . Okay, your two seconds have gone. Who said a ring and an eighth? Anything more or less and you've missed your chance!" So it would go. He knew it all by heart. He'd studied it to the point where he had absolute confidence that, given the opportunity to open fire, the odds were bound to be on his side.

Berryman adds: "The fact that on his own initiative he sought out every pilot to master the skills of deflection shooting dispels completely the notion that George Beurling was not a team player."

(Not long afterwards, the unit's Spitfires were equipped with the excellent new gyroscopic gunsight, which eliminated most of the difficulties of deflection shooting. Variations of speed, angles, wingspan, and so on, were accounted for when the guns were fired. However, in tight turns and other "violent" manoeuvres, the gyros were apt to "topple," compelling the pilot to resort to the fixed sight for short periods.)

A squadron-mate of Berryman's, Charley Fox, of Guelph, Ontario, also has fond memories of Beurling. After two years of instructing in Canada, Fox went overseas early in 1944. His first operational flight had the famous flier as leader. "It was a great comfort, having George in charge. He knew everything – even before it happened sometimes." On this particular trip, Fox felt a thump during his take-off. He and the number-three man in the section had strayed uncomfortably close to one another as they lifted off the runway, but no damage appeared to have been done. Fox checked his controls and systems; everything worked satisfactorily. On his return to Biggin Hill, Fox had a shock. When his propeller swung to a halt, he saw that it was too small! He had hit the runway during take-off and had neatly removed about eight inches from each of the blades. George Keefer, the CO, instructed Beurling, as Fox's flight commander, to censure him. Beurling was never happy with such assignments. He cornered Fox in the Officers' Mess, whereupon the air raid siren began to wail. The crack of bombs came nearer, and Beurling and Fox took cover under a billiard table. Crouched, wincing at every explosion, Beurling couldn't take the moment seriously. He grinned and told Fox not to do it again. Fox didn't.

Although he was in the main friendly and approachable, there were times when Beurling seemed aloof and preoccupied with his own thoughts, Berryman says. He was totally self-disciplined, keeping himself in superb physical condition. He was a splendid swimmer – and was not above putting on spectacular shows of diving, particularly if pretty girls were watching. Berryman recalls an incident at a local swimming pool, where the squadron had found refuge during a spell of bad weather. One of the swimmers, a local champion back home in Canada, announced that he was going to swim an entire length underwater. Responding immediately to the challenge, Beurling announced that he would swim *two* lengths without coming up for air. And he did.

Beurling used to take the pilots to briefing and back to squadron dispersal in the unit Jeep. He revelled in driving the vehicle as if he were competing in a demolition derby. Most of the pilots felt that their work was hazardous enough without being chauffeured about by Beurling. They preferred to walk.

In the summer of 1943, the squadron's principal job was to escort daylight bombers: medium bombers to targets, usually airfields, in France; and heavy bomber formations partway to their targets on the Continent. Beurling disliked escort work, calling it "taxi rides." He longed to go on "ramrods," flying the Channel at sea level to escape detection, climbing high enough at the French coast to avoid light flak, then shooting up a range of moving transport. If this motivated the Luftwaffe to come after him, so much the better.

Berryman flew as Beurling's wing man for several months. Then he had an accident, colliding with a Spitfire on the active runway after the other aircraft had inexplicably turned 180 degrees instead of swinging off the runway as rapidly as possible. His Spitfire on fire, Berryman struggled out of his cockpit, helmet and flying clothes aflame. He saw airmen running toward him. "They won't get to me in time," he found himself thinking dispassionately, as if it were a matter of academic interest. When the men did reach him, the impact "felt like a wall hitting me," he recalls. They knocked him down and smothered the flames. When the ambulance ("the meat wagon" in air force parlance) arrived, it was Beurling who picked Berryman up and handed him to the ambulance staff. "You're going to be all right, Lloyd," he declared.

When Berryman returned to the squadron, Beurling had gone, his air force career over. He returned to Canada. This time there were no press conferences, no parades, no public displays of hero-worship. Beurling was posted to fly as copilot in light transports. It is hard to imagine any form of flying to which the young man from Verdun was less suited. If the RCAF was hoping to drive him out of the service, it succeeded. In June 1944, Beurling resigned, citing a stomach injury as the reason. He left the RCAF and, although the words of farewell from various high-ranking individuals spoke glowingly of his admirable service record and his contribution to Canada's history, there could be no mistaking the relief of the air force at getting rid of their troublesome star. Beurling's RCAF file was closed, his day done, just as the Allies were about to embark on the biggest invasion in history. If any Canadians wondered why their great hero was not participating in this huge enterprise, they weren't told. Beurling had become a sort of non-person in the well-polished corridors of official Ottawa.

Beurling attempted to rejoin the RAF and was rejected. He offered his services to the Americans. They didn't want him either. After that, on the rare occasions that his name cropped up in the papers, it was tucked away in some inside story, never on the front page, until he met his death in a crash after the war.

Lloyd Berryman recovered from his burns and inherited Beurling's Spitfire, VZ-B. Prominent on its side, close to the cockpit, was a row of more than thirty swastikas, representing Beurling's victories. Berryman remembers the squadron landing at Manston on England's east coast to refuel after an escort operation. "When we pulled up to the dispersal, half the personnel came out to see who the super-ace was with all those kills!" Berryman, who had a respectable four confirmed victories to his credit – including three in one day – plus three "damaged," remarks that he lost little time in getting all those swastikas painted out.

III

In the fall of 1942, 404 Squadron RCAF had begun the process of exchanging its aging Blenheim IVs for the tough, powerfully armed Beaufighter. Designated a coastal fighter unit, the squadron was soon engaged in shipping strikes, principally in Norwegian waters, attacking flak ships and coastal gun batteries, clearing the way for the torpedo-bombers (often torpedo-carrying Beaufighters). The Germans floated balloons, and mounted flak guns – a range of weapons, usually 20-mm to 88-mm cannon, but occasionally great 105-mm cannon, plus a profusion of machine-guns – on ships to discourage low-level attacks. Most of the so-called "flak ships" were converted trawlers of about five hundred tons. They were capable of putting up veritable storms of flak. Casualties among Coastal Command squadrons were high, sometimes reaching critical levels.

Attacks demanded courage of a high order. The barrages of flak hosed the sky, darting, flashing specks of light, red and orange, the larger calibre guns firing shells that looked like red-hot tennis balls, every one of which was capable of killing you or destroying your aircraft. Ideally, three "anti-flak" Beaufighters attacked each escort vessel, all three approaching, from slightly different angles, firing continuously. Herb Hallatt, of Windsor, Ontario, who had encountered the "anti-colonial" captain on the ship coming to Europe, recalls that the most effective technique was to use the Beau's four cannon from about one thousand yards to "keep the gunners' heads down," then fire a salvo of rockets at about six hundred yards from the target. The rockets could be devastating. Hallatt recalls seeing Ken Gatward, the CO of the squadron, "blow a ship out of the water with a salvo of rockets." He feels the rockets were far more effective than torpedoes.

The coastal Beaufighters often encountered enemy aircraft. In July, a newly arrived Canadian pilot, Sydney Shulemson of Montreal, was flying on his first operation with his observer, Albertan Al Glasgow, when a Ju 88 put in an appearance. Shulemson's aggressive flying sent the 88 off to seek sanctuary in clouds. Moments later, a big three-motor flying boat, a Blohm und Voss BV138, hove into view. Shulemson attacked from below. The 138, with its power-operated gun turrets and 20-mm cannons for defensive armament, was a formidable opponent. Undeterred, Shulemson opened up with his four cannons. The big, twin-boomed flying boat streamed flame, ending up in the sea. Only one crewman escaped. When a second 138 appeared, a 404 Squadron flight commander, Al de la Haye, shot him down in flames. Incredibly, the squadron encountered two more of the rare birds that day, both shot down by Jim Keefe of Vancouver, who, like Shulemson, was on his first operation. In the engagement, Keefe suffered damage to one engine but made it safely back to base. He reported that he had been attacked by FW 190s. Fellow pilots were incredulous. FW 190s off the Shetlands? It was unbelievable, way beyond a 190's range! And indeed, the 190s turned out to be FAA Wildcats from the carrier *Illustrious*, attacking what they believed to be German aircraft. Fortunately, they broke off before opening fire. Interestingly, one of the Wildcat pilots was a Canadian, Lieutenant Digby Cosh, of Hamilton, Ontario; he and his two wingmen shot down the fifth Blohm und Voss 138. Thus the five flying boats, from the same maritime reconnaissance unit, all fell to Canadian pilots on the same day.

A Canadian squadron, 415, was at this time still operating as a torpedo-bomber unit equipped with Hampdens, outdated rejects from Bomber Command and grossly inadequate for the task. For some months, the hapless Hampdens had been flying on shipping strikes, usually without fighter escort. Although the unit flew relatively few operations, its losses were grim. From early November 1942 to the end of May 1943, the unit had made twenty attacks on shipping, losing eleven aircraft in the process. The notoriously efficient German flak was largely responsible. Soon the RCAF was suggesting that the squadron be reassigned and re-equipped. The Air Ministry assured the Canadians that new equipment would shortly be available for the squadron, but when the "new" equipment did arrive, it turned out to be the Fairey Albacore, a single-engined biplane originally designed for the Fleet Air Arm as a replacement for the antiquated Swordfish. The Albacores proved adequate, however, in the role to which 415 had been assigned: attacking German E-boats (*Eilboote*, often known as *Schnellboote*, high-speed boats usually mounted with two torpedo tubes and several guns) in the Channel and North Sea. The unit was still flying Albacores on D-Day, the following year, laying smokescreens. A few weeks after that, the squadron converted to Halifaxes and joined 6 Group as a heavy bomber unit.

IV

Casualty rates of Bomber Command's crews varied widely at different periods of the war. In the earliest days, it was not a particularly hazardous occupation, unless you happened to be attacking battleships on daylight sorties. It was later, when the German defences had become efficient, when the German night-fighters had radar, when the bombing campaign was hurting the enemy, that the odds became daunting. When losses of 3 to 5 or 6 per cent were being suffered by the bombers, the chances of surviving a thirty-trip tour were hardly encouraging. The Air Staff kept casualty statistics under wraps. "I am extremely anxious that statistical information relating to the chances of survival of aircrews in the various types of operational employment should be confined to the smallest number of people," wrote Charles Portal, Chief of Air Staff, in December 1942.[12]

In fact, the average airman had little interest in overall casualty

In February 1944, Mosquito bombers breached the walls of a Gestapo prison at Amiens, France, releasing condemned prisoners. Harry Godfrey of 400 (RCAF) Squadron took this remarkable photo of the scene a few days later. (Harry Godfrey collection)

PRU pilots knew about Hitler's much-vaunted "vengeance" weapons many months before they were first used on London and other cities. This launching site was photographed in the fall of 1943. Note the bomb craters. (Jack Myles collection)

A Barracuda hits HMS *Rajah*'s round-down at the carrier's stern, tearing off the tailwheel (below the starboard flap, disgorging hydraulic fluid). The aircraft went "over the side," but the pilot, the only occupant, survived. (Jack Myles collection)

A Barracuda crashes into the gangway on HMS *Rajah* during deck landing trials for pilots training to drop "Highball" bouncing bombs against the Japanese fleet. The weapons, a development of the "Dambuster" bombs, were never used. (Jack Myles collection)

In May 1945, a Kamikaze caused chaos on the flight deck of the British carrier *Formidable*, killing eight and injuring 47 crewmen. Three months later Robert Hampton Gray took off from this deck on the sortie that won him the VC. (Charles Butterworth collection)

The excellent Avro Lancaster proved to be the best British heavy bomber of the war. By mid-1943, Lancaster Xs, powered by Packard-built Merlin engines, were being produced in Canada. These Lancasters are with 419 (RCAF) Squadron. (Canadian Warplane Heritage Museum)

At Trappes, France, wrecked rolling stock is testimony to the success of Bomber Command's Transportation Plan, which set out to render the local French railway system inoperative by D-Day. The message (r) exhorts workers to "keep the wheels turning for victory." (DND)

The superbly versatile Mosquito was flown by many Canadians during the war years. The aircraft, built largely of wood, served as a bomber, PRU aircraft, day fighter, night fighter, intruder, mine layer, and high-speed transport. This aircraft is seen in D-Day invasion markings. (RCAF, RE-20420-3)

Arms, ammunition, and medical supplies are loaded aboard a 148 Squadron Halifax at Brindisi, Italy, in August 1944, bound for Warsaw. The second of two major uprisings in the city was being brutally suppressed by the Germans. (Carm Chase collection)

The Allison-powered Mustang I served the RCAF well on photographic and tactical reconnaissance sorties. The camera was mounted behind the pilot; markings on the wing and windows enabled him to line up correctly for oblique shots. (Harry Godfrey collection)

Conceived as an interceptor, the Hawker Typhoon found its metier in ground support operations. Powerfully armed, the aircraft caused havoc among German troops in the fierce battles following D-Day. Note the steel-matting on the emergency strip. (Bill Baggs collection)

Ground crew gather around Buzz Beurling's Spitfire IX, 412 (RCAF) Squadron, 1943. Note the impressive row of victory symbols; in all, Beurling shot down 31 enemy aircraft, with many more categorized as "probables." (Lloyd Berryman collection)

Always popular with ground staff, the remarkable Canadian ace George "Buzz" Beurling (*centre*) poses with airmen of 403 (RCAF) Squadron. At left, "Smitty" Smith, Beurling's fitter; photo taken by George Demare, Beurling's rigger. (George Demare collection)

Depth charges dropped by a Sunderland III, EK 591, of 422 (RCAF) Squadron
send U-boat U-625 to the bottom, March 10, 1944. The aircraft's skipper,
Warrant Officer W. F. Morton (*top photo*), was on his first operational sortie.
(Frank Cauley and Kip Johnston collections)

The Halifax II equipped 419 (RCAF) Squadron from November 1942 to April 1944. It was underpowered and had serious handling problems. Later versions were far more efficient; some crews rated them superior to the Lancaster. (Canadian Warplane Heritage Museum)

This Vought Corsair, operated by the Canadian Warplane Heritage Museum, bears the markings carried by Robert Hampton Cray, the Canadian Corsair pilot who won a posthumous VC for his heroism in the final days of the war. (Canadian Warplane Heritage Museum)

Dubbed the "Jug" (from "juggernaut"), the hefty Republic Thunderbolt possessed powerful armament of eight .50-inch machine guns, great strength, and exceptional range. Harold Benson of Calgary (*centre*) flew the Thunderbolt in Burma. (Harold Benson collection)

The rockets beneath the wings of a Beaufighter TFX of 404 (RCAF) Squadron are readied for action by plugging their "pigtails" into individual electrical sockets. The photo was taken in August 1944 at Davidstow Moor, Cornwall. (Herb Hallatt collection)

A German *Sperrbrecher* (literally, "blockade buster"), used to destroy magnetic mines, is torn apart by rockets from 404 (RCAF) Squadron Beaufighters. Note the trails of the explosive rockets. (DND, UK-14168)

Low-level photography by 400 (RCAF) Squadron shows the devastation in Hamburg after heavy bombing in the last days of the war. The campaign against Germany had cost Bomber Command some 55,000 aircrew killed, and nearly 10,000 bombers destroyed. (Harry Godfrey collection)

figures, even if they had been available. It was the losses suffered by his squadron that affected a man. *His* squadron, *his* crew; they were the realities in an airman's day-to-day existence. Everything else was too remote to be of much concern. The air force had, with rare good sense, left the formation of most crews to the individuals themselves. Clusters of pilots, navigators, air gunners, and other trades, congregated in hangars. Shyly and hesitantly, like young men asking for first dates, they exchanged a few words as they sized one another up. They mingled. They chatted. They looked one another over. They discovered connections: geographical, family, educational. A few demanded detailed examinations of logbooks; others relied on first impressions. It was, by any standard, a haphazard business. The odd thing was that it worked so well. Heavy bomber crews consisted initially of two pilots, an observer, wireless operator, and air gunner. Later, when the large, four-engined bombers came into service, the crews grew larger. The second pilot was replaced by a flight engineer. A bomb aimer also joined the crew. Later still, usually at their Heavy Conversion Unit (HCU), a second air gunner was added. It was at HCU that crews learned to fly and operate the type of heavy bomber they would be using on operations. Here, the seven strangers often became closer than brothers, putting their lives in each other's hands night after night. In most cases, their lives were as tightly enmeshed on the ground as in the air. Only the absurdities of the commissioning system kept members of crews apart on the ground, since most consisted of both officers and NCOs. Commissioned and non-commissioned aircrew lived in separate quarters and, particularly in RAF squadrons, were discouraged from socializing off duty. Indeed, on some units, officers were *ordered* not to associate with mere NCOs except when flying. Canadians generally ignored such edicts.

The loss of crew members was devastating. On July 29, 1943, the recently appointed CO of 424 Squadron RCAF, Wing Commander John Blane of Ottawa, elected to fly on an op against Hamburg. A permanent force officer, thirty-two-year-old Blane was typical of many Canadian squadron commanders of the period. He had spent several years in training and administrative jobs in Canada before being placed in command of 424. Many of the members of his squadron had far more operational experience than he did, and this seems to have troubled him, for he did his best to fly as many ops as possible. As a squadron commander, he had no crew of his own; he flew with whomever was available. On the night of July 29, Blane went to Hamburg with a crew whose regular skipper happened to be away for a few days. Two 6 Group aircraft were lost that night. Blane's was one. The airmen who flew with him had come within two or three sorties of completing their tours.

When the crew's skipper returned to the station, the news of what had happened temporarily unhinged him. Storming into the station commander's office, shoving his way past the adjutant and the orderly room sergeant, he tearfully bellowed at the group captain, calling him a murderer for letting Blane take his crew on operations. The adjutant made a move to call the service police, but the station commander waved him into silence. Sensibly, he summoned another officer to take the pilot to the mess for a drink to calm him down. At the same time, he arranged for the bereaved pilot to be screened from operations and posted away. Even senior officers with no operational experience comprehended the intense emotional involvement between members of a bomber crew and excused behaviour that in other circumstances might have resulted in severe disciplinary action.

Ken Fulton, from Truro, Nova Scotia, joined an all-Canadian crew at 82 OTU, Ossington, Lincolnshire, in December 1943. The individuals worked well together and felt they had made good decisions about their crewmates. But not for long. In January, the pilot, Dave Brown, from Fredericton, New Brunswick, was injured in a traffic accident. For a few weeks, the crew continued to train with any pilot who happened to be available. Eventually, however, an RAF sergeant pilot was assigned to the crew. He had some operational experience, having done two operations; his original crew had gone on an op with another pilot and hadn't returned.

As soon as the Canadians began flying with their new RAF skipper, they felt uneasy. Their pilot seemed to be one of those legendary characters who should have been "washed out" during pilot training but who somehow managed to squeeze his way through test after test. His handling of the aircraft during the endless circuits and bumps flown by every novice crew was anything but sure. Later in their training, they flew on a "Nickel" – that is, a leaflet-dropping trip to the French coast – to prepare them for actual operations. The trip went well. But as the Wimpy turned for home, the engines cut out. The pilot panicked. Fulton, who was the navigator, says:

> In a Wellington aircraft, the fuel gauges were not very accurate, so a nacelle tank holding fifty gallons of fuel was located on each wing. It was standard procedure when landing, regardless of the readings on the fuel gauges, to open the nacelle cocks. I reached behind me and turned on the gas cocks for the nacelle tanks, and both motors started again. A quick discussion with the pilot determined that he had failed to cut in his supercharger when climbing, at 10,000 feet, so when he were at 15,000 feet, we were on rich rather than lean mixture, using about 200 gallons per hour rather than 100 gallons per hour.

Fulton worked out a course for the nearest point of land, in East Anglia, all too aware that the aircraft had barely enough fuel to get there. After sending an S.O.S. and throttling back as much as possible, the crew got the Wimpy back to England, flopping down at Foulsham, a Beaufighter base. "We hadn't enough gas to get off the runway to the hangar," Fulton recalls.

After this, the crew hadn't *any* confidence in their skipper. He seemed incapable of holding an accurate course or altitude. While the obvious solution would have been an immediate replacement, it was not as easy as that. Despite his shortcomings, the pilot had already completed OTU and been posted to a squadron. To have failed him now would have been unprecedented, an admission that the system was at fault. Far better, the uneasy members of the crew were told, to complain when they got to HCU. Let them deal with it there. It was a classic case of military buck-passing.

At 1659 HCU, Topcliffe, the crew members (minus their pilot) followed instructions and relayed their concerns to the chief instructor and, later, to the CO. The reaction set them back on their heels. Every member of the crew was threatened with a court martial if he refused to fly with his assigned pilot. Fulton says that the crew's wireless operator and bomb aimer "caved in" and remained with the unsatisfactory pilot. They lost their lives over Hamburg. Fulton refused to change his mind, however, and soon found himself with a new crew of airmen who for various reasons – sickness, terms in a detention centre, or "glasshouse," and so on – had become "spares," odd, unassigned bods. While they may have felt unwanted, they found that together they made an excellent crew. The new pilot, Sergeant Hugh Thompson, of Zealandia, Saskatchewan, known to everyone as Tommy, soon demonstrated his ability with the Halifax. "We went up to about 15,000 feet and he feathered one engine and carried out a few banks and turns. Then he feathered a second engine and did more banks and turns. Then he feathered a third engine and carried out more banks and turns including several 90-degree banks into our 'dead' wing." It was a convincing demonstration and the crew developed great confidence in him.

Fulton recalls that Thompson flew a gentle corkscrew path while over enemy territory. It gave the gunners a good view all around and seemed to inform any enemy fighters in the vicinity that a vigilant crew was flying the aircraft. (Since the war, several former Luftwaffe night-fighter pilots have commented that they usually looked for potential targets among bombers flying straight and level, because, in all probability, such bombers had happy-go-lucky or downright inefficient crews and usually made easy victims.)

Fulton and the rest of his crew remained convinced of the advantages of constant weaving. On an op on the night of June 28 "enemy fighters were out in full force," says Fulton, "and we saw many fighter attacks and quite a few planes shot down. We continued our weaving and, while several fighters came near us, none found it to their advantage to hang around ... (probably due to our continuous weaving). On one occasion we saw a German fighter about twenty to thirty yards off our starboard bow, slightly higher, and travelling in the same direction. Tommy ordered the gunners to hold their fire and we eased away."

In general, bomber crews were wise to avoid combat whenever possible, since their rifle-calibre machine-guns were no match for the cannons of the night-fighters. The disparity between the armament of bombers and fighters was as wide as it had been at the beginning of the war, and although the press delighted in publishing photographs of four-gun turrets and talking about the "fatal sting in the tail of Bomber Command aircraft," the fact was, the fighters possessed all the advantages. Many gunners never fired a shot in their operational careers, preferring to keep out of trouble rather than to engage in an unequal contest of firepower. The crews who survived tours of operations were usually the crews who were vigilant, always on the lookout for fighters, always weaving or at least banking to give all the gunners a look in every direction. A few squadrons had guns (or in some cases, merely windows) installed in the bellies of their bombers, with gunners keeping a lookout immediately below.

Intense crew loyalty had its negative aspects. Crews often "closed ranks," keeping quiet about a crew member no longer pulling his weight. Larry Keelan of Regina, a former 429 Squadron pilot, candidly admits that he never expected to survive his tour of ops. His crew had begun their operational tour late in 1943 as the Battle of

Berlin was getting into its stride. By June of the following year, they had become one of the most experienced crews on the unit, having got through the Berlin campaign unscathed. But the accumulated strain of that tough series of costly raids had begun to tell. On D-Day, Keelan's crew would participate in a daylight bombing operation on enemy gun positions. The Halifaxes flew in a loose "gaggle," rather than the rigid formations favoured by the American B-17 and B-24 squadrons. During bombing, the mid-upper gunner's job was to watch for friendly aircraft getting too close, for there was a very real danger of being bombed by "friendlies" flying above. Keelan concentrated on his bomb run, confident that experienced eyes were watching what was happening above and behind. Suddenly he saw them: bombs! With a deadly bang, one hit the leading edge of the wing, then another walloped into the trailing edge. They didn't explode, and Keelan was able to fly the aircraft back to base. Afterwards, he demanded to know why the mid-upper gunner hadn't reported the other aircraft directly overhead. The answer wasn't unexpected: the gunner's nerve had gone; when the bomb hit he had been busy putting his parachute on with the intention of jumping. Although the crew might have been expected to get rid of the gunner, they didn't. They had been through too much together.

In general, Canadians got on famously with fellow aircrew, poorly with RAF administrative personnel. When the first batch of Canadian-trained sergeant wireless operator/air gunners arrived at Cranwell, Lincolnshire, for what was termed "vocabulary, technical, and procedures training," they were treated as recruits and sent on endless route marches in rainy weather. They refused to march. An apoplectic air vice-marshal arrived from the Air Ministry and referred to them as mutinous colonials.[13] The Canadian High Commissioner, Vincent Massey, had to be called in to sort out the mess. Thereafter, Canadians tended to be regarded by RAF personnel with some caution – liberally mixed with envy, because they all seemed to have friends in high places.

In 1943, the Canadians' presence became even more marked. They formed their own Group, the only non-British Group in the history of Bomber Command. No. 6 (RCAF) Group came into existence on January 1. It had not been an easy birth; Harris had fought it from the start. He wanted the Canadians to augment the existing units of Bomber Command, not create a brand new organization with all the attendant bureaucracy. Besides, like many senior British officers of the time, he thought of "colonials" as good fighters but questionable administrators. He doubted that the Canadians could run a large formation the size of a Group. And he had no hesitation in saying so, complaining vociferously about Gus Edwards and George Brookes, the senior Canadian commanders in Britain. But in the end, he had no choice. The political pressure from Ottawa couldn't be ignored.

Harris's fears about the Canadian Group were not entirely without foundation. To meet the purely arbitrary deadline for its formation, 6 Group had been cobbled together, the longer-established Canadian squadrons, 408, 419, and 420, having to give up many of their most experienced crews to form the nuclei of new squadrons 424, 425, 426, 427, and 428 (405 Squadron was nominally part of 6 Group but continued to operate with Coastal Command for several weeks). Although classified as a Canadian formation, 6 Group had large numbers of RAF aircrew and ground staff among its ranks. It would take many months for the new Group to become Canadian in fact instead of just in title. It would take many more months for the 6 Group squadrons to achieve a satisfactory level of operational efficiency. While the politicians in Ottawa may have congratulated each other on having had the vision to bring a major Canadian air force formation into being, it was the aircrews and station staff who had to make it all work. This wasn't easy, and it wasn't done without mistakes and heavy loss of life.

The morale of 6 Group sagged badly during its first year of operations, undoubtedly the result of high casualties and questionable leadership. The Canadians quickly discovered that it took more than the assembling of crews and aircraft to make a Group. The key indi-vidual in every squadron was always the commanding officer, who had to combine the best qualities of the technician, the fighter, and the commander. The trouble was, 6 Group simply hadn't been in existence long enough to develop a cadre of such individuals. Some officers who had been serving with the British Commonwealth Air Training Plan in Canada came to Britain to lead operational squadrons. Many did well; many did not.

6 Group reached its ultimate strength of eighteen squadrons when 434 Squadron was formed at Tholthorpe, Yorkshire, in June. The new unit had an unhappy introduction to operations, suffering high casualties and acquiring an unenviable reputation as a "chop" squadron. In its first six months of operations 43 aircraft and crews were lost, 313 aircrew in 364 sorties, a calamitous rate of 11.8 per cent. The squadron was, in fact, wiped out twice during its opera-tional career from August 1943 to May 1945.

Some regarded the choice of air officer to command the new Group as the biggest mistake of all. Forty-nine-year-old Air Vice-Marshal George Eric Brookes was an amiable man, well liked by his contemporaries, but he was sadly lacking in operational experience and tended to be "a fatherly type," with a "remote perspective" on operational losses, hardly the dynamic leader needed in this sensitive position.[14] A pilot in World War I, Brookes had been shot down early in his career and seriously injured. He was still in hospital, recuperating from his wounds, at the time of the Armistice. Between the wars, Brookes became widely known as a highly capable flying instructor. To many critics, he exemplified the Canadian senior air force officer of the era, the product of a small and intensely insular peacetime force, thrust into a job for which he had had no training. Scores of Brookes's most capable Canadian airmen had served in RAF groups, under officers who had learned their profession in the hard school of operational flying. Inevitably, comparisons were made. Equally inevitably, they seldom flattered the newly formed Canadian Group.

What always troubled the RAF, the thread of uneasiness that wove its way into every discussion and decision about Canada and Canadians, was their casual, almost contemptuous regard for rank and tradition. How could you run an air force full of men who talked in the same, easy way to station commanders and taxi drivers alike? To make matters worse, the Canadians seldom hesitated to criticize orders they regarded as ill-conceived. For instance, when Walter Thompson, of Vancouver, was ordered to go to a navigation instructors' school, he flatly refused. He had graduated first in his class with an "above average" pilot's rating, so it was obviously absurd to put him into navigation instruction. To the open-mouthed astonishment of his RAF CO, he said that if the order wasn't rescinded, he would resign his commission and join the Tank Corps. For two months, Thompson was confined to his quarters and the officers' mess, wondering what fate would befall him. "I had no doubt that my air force career was over," he says, "and that I might serve a little time in jail. But I thought to myself, We'll soon see if 'Theirs is not to reason why.' If I'm going 'to do and die,' I'll do it my own way!"[15] Eventually, after a hearing complete with witnesses, Thompson had to appear before the AOC, Training Command.

> Two RAF police officers took stations on either side of me; I felt like Lord Essex going to the Tower.... "Well," said the Air Vice-Marshal, looking at the charge sheet in his hand, "what's this all about? Don't want to be an instructor? Is that it, Thompson?"
>
> My voice was squeaky. "Yes sir," I said, standing rigidly to attention. There was no turning back now, and further words would have been superfluous.
>
> "Hmmph," said the Air Vice-Marshal. "Hmmph," and then a long pause which I awaited with anguish to terminate. Then he looked out of the window at the sky and said, as if to himself, "Commendable spirit, really." He looked directly

at me for the first time. "But you know you can't go around disobeying orders. I'm sending you out as a staff pilot at a gunnery school."[16]

There can be little doubt that Thompson was fortunate to have been an officer and a Commonwealth airman. Similarly charged, an RAF sergeant pilot would almost certainly have faced the prospect of being court-martialled, losing his stripes and flying badge, and probably ending up cleaning latrines. After a short spell flying Botha target-towing aircraft at Morpeth, Northumberland, Thompson went on to a distinguished career as a bomber captain with 106 Squadron, then commanded by Guy Gibson, later becoming a member of the PFF force and being awarded the DFC and Bar. He maintained his independent attitude. When he had completed the requisite number of ops as a PFF pilot, he received a letter from Don Bennett, the head of the Path Finders, authorizing him to wear the badge of his calling, a small gold eagle, on his left breast-pocket flap. Bennett added a codicil: the authority was only temporary, and further written authority was required from him before the badge could be worn after Thompson had left the PFF. Thompson remarked in his memoirs: "I took offence at this and refused for some time to wear the badge at all."[17]

V

Harris vowed that 1943 was to be Bomber Command's year. His force was slowly but steadily becoming as powerful and capable as most people thought it had been for years. The technical problems had largely been solved; the necessary navigational equipment now existed, even if it was not yet being manufactured in sufficient quantities to equip all of Harris's aircraft. The new four-engined bombers were coming off the production lines in impressive numbers, steadily replacing the obsolete twin-engined mediums that had so far borne the brunt of the bombing war. With the formation of the Path Finder Force, Bomber Command had the means to get the bombs on target. In many ways, Bomber Command was the *raison d'être* of the RAF. Although Fighter Command had won glory for the RAF in 1940, defence had always been seen as a secondary function for the air force. Its "real" job was to attack. Bomber Command could win the war on its own, Harris believed.

In the early spring of 1943, Harris launched a major new campaign: bombing the Ruhr. "Oboe" enabled bombers to hit their targets despite the thick ground haze that obscured the enormous industrial area from Duisburg in the west of the Ruhr valley to Dortmund in the east.

Essen, Duisburg, Bochum . . . all the major cities of the Ruhr were attacked by Bomber Command from March to July 1943. In general, results were good; the attacks forced the Germans to move some of their most important war industries to safer rural areas and bolster their defences around major cities. But the campaign was a costly one for Harris's squadrons. In all, 872 bombers were lost, 4.7 per cent of the 18,506 sorties dispatched. The Canadian 6 Group mounted 2,649 sorties and suffered the loss of 145 bombers, 5.4 per cent of those dispatched. The Group's early-return rate caused much concern initially, but it improved as aircrews and ground crews acquired more experience and confidence.

The Canadian 405 Squadron left Coastal Command and became a heavy bomber squadron again, attached to 6 Group. The commanding officer, twenty-six-year-old Pitt Clayton, embarking on his third operational tour, was asked for his two best crews. They were wanted for the Path Finder Force, it was explained. The order set Clayton thinking: Why not an entire squadron of Canadians for the PFF? And wouldn't 405, the "senior" Canadian bomber squadron, be the logical choice? Never one to temporize, he set off for Group HQ, Allerton Hall, near Knaresborough, Yorkshire, to suggest the idea to George Brookes, the AOC. Nothing came of it. Possibly the desire to have RCAF officers in the PFF (Clayton was still a member of the RAF) influenced the decision. In any event, Clayton left the squadron on April 19, to be replaced by former CO, Johnny Fauquier. Now the unit became part of the Path Finder Force and moved to Gransden Lodge, Bedfordshire.

There's no doubt that Harris had a blind spot as far as the PFF was concerned. Donald Bennett wanted to introduce a "Master of Ceremonies" on every raid, a highly experienced (and exceptionally brave) pilot who would fly around the target area while the bombing was in progress, checking on its accuracy, advising the main force crews by R/T. Harris wouldn't hear of it – yet he immediately gave his approval when the same concept was suggested for the famous Dambusters raid. Eventually, however, the Master Bomber idea became commonplace and did much to enhance the accuracy of bombing.

During 1943, observant airplane watchers were puzzled by the appearance of tear-drop protuberances beneath the rear fuselages of some Lancasters and Halifaxes. Most people thought that at long last Bomber Command was mounting belly turrets to protect its bombers from fighter attacks. In fact, the bulges housed what was undoubtedly the most important development in the radar war: H_2S. For its time it was a daringly advanced concept, a centimetric-wavelength radar that could "scan" the ground beneath the aircraft no matter how thick the cloud cover. At last the night-bomber could bomb accurately in any weather.

When first told about the new device, many navigators thought they would see on their cathode-ray tubes a sort of movie of the ground. They were disappointed and bewildered when confronted by patterns of quivering dots, none of which seemed to make any sense. Soon, however, the operators began to understand what the display represented and could compare the returns with maps of the area. With practice, they could "fix" their position with astonishing accuracy – provided the area being surveyed possessed identifiable features. Coastal targets were ideal; features of the coastline were recorded well by H_2S, since the sets' echoes were strongest from built-up areas, weakest from water. The contrast created precisely the right sort of conditions for H_2S. Far less satisfactory were large urban areas such as Berlin, which tended to show indistinguishable masses of echoes. In fact, the very first raid in the so-called Battle of Berlin, on the night of August 23/24, failed for precisely that reason. The PFF crews couldn't locate the aiming point even with the help of H_2S. According to some reports, the Germans had industriously altered the shorelines of the city's lakes with huge wooden floats to confuse the bomb aimers above.

In May, Bomber Command mounted its famous raid on the Ruhr dams: the Eder, the Sorpe, and the Möhne. The great dams, with their immensely thick concrete walls, stored hundreds of millions of gallons of water to produce hydro-electric power for nearby industries. The potential effects of destroying them excited the imagination of Barnes Wallis, the Vickers designer responsible for the Wellington. He soon realized that to do any damage he would have to come up with an entirely new type of bomb. He did. It looked like a huge oil drum and it had to be dropped at a suicidally low level.

Initially, Harris was not enthusiastic. Ever since he had taken over Bomber Command, a parade of persuasive individuals had been trying to convince him to destroy this target or that. If he had had his way, Harris would have dismissed the project. But Charles Portal, Chief of the Air Staff, liked the idea. Harris had no choice. Reluctantly, he gave the go-ahead to form a special unit of experienced crews to fly the trip: 617 Squadron, later to become famous as "The Dambusters." He selected as leader twenty-five-year-old Guy Gibson, one of the most experienced and capable pilots in Bomber Command, who had already completed an extraordinary total of 172 ops and had won the DSO and Bar and DFC. Predictably perhaps, 617 was part of the élite 5 Group.

The unit had specially modified Lancasters. Each bomb was mounted on transverse racks incorporating a pulley-and-belt mechanism to set the bombs spinning before release. If dropped from very low-flying planes, the bomb would, it was hoped, skip across the water surface, over any anti-torpedo nets that might be encountered. When the bomb collided with the hefty concrete wall of the dam, it would rebound, but the spin would force it back to the wall. Then it would sink and, at a depth of thirty feet, a pressure fuse would detonate the 6,000 pounds of RDX explosive. Effectively tamped by several million tons of lake water, the explosion would rip the dam apart. But only, the silent aircrews learned at briefing, if the bomb was dropped at precisely 240 mph, precisely 60 feet above the surface of the water, and precisely 425 yards from the dam wall. Precision bombing indeed. The bludgeon of Bomber Command was about to become a rapier.

For the crews, the raid was appallingly hazardous, calling for great skill and courage. It meant flying at low level across enemy territory, circling the dams in the face of steady anti-aircraft fire, lining up one after the other to drop the specially developed bombs at just the right height and speed. Guy Gibson himself directed the operation, talking to the crews by R/T, drawing ground fire again and again as he went in with each bomber. He watched several of his best friends die in monstrous explosions when their Lancasters were hit. Little wonder that eight of the nineteen aircraft participating were lost in this, one of the classic bombing raids of all time.

In all, 56 aircrew became casualties, only three surviving as prisoners. Twenty-eight of the aircrew were Canadians. Gibson's crew included two: Terry Taerum of Calgary, the navigator, and Tony Deering of Toronto, the front gunner. The others were scattered throughout the force and many lost their lives, including Vernon Byers, from Flin Fon, Manitoba; Harvey Glinz, of Winnipeg; Jim McDowell, of Port Arthur, Ontario; Frank Garbas and Abram Garshowitz, both of Hamilton, Ontario; Floyd Wile, of Scotch Village, Nova Scotia; Jim Arthur, from Toronto; Ken Earnshaw, of

Semans, Saskatchewan; Alden Cottam, of Jasper Park, Alberta; Robert Urquhart, of Moose Jaw, Saskatchewan; Vincent MacCausland, of Tyne Valley, P.E.I.; Lewis Burpee, of Ottawa; and Joe Brady, from Ponoka, Alberta.

Two of the three dams were destroyed, and it appeared that Bomber Command had delivered a paralyzing blow to German industry. Eventually, however, it became clear that the two dams, the Eder and the Möhne, were the least important of the three. Albert Speer commented:

> A torrent of water had flooded the Ruhr Valley. That had the seemingly insignificant but grave consequence that the electrical installations in the pumping stations were soaked and muddied, so that industry was brought to a standstill and the water supply of the population imperilled. . . . The British had not succeeded, however, in destroying the three other reservoirs. Had they done so, the Ruhr Valley would have been almost completely deprived of water in the coming summer months. At the largest of the reservoirs, the Sorpe Valley Reservoir, they [the RAF raiders] did achieve a direct hit on the centre of the dam. Fortunately the bomb hole was slightly higher than the water level. A few inches lower and the small brook would have become a raging river, and would have swept away this stone and earthen dam. That night, employing just a few bombers, the British came close to a success which would have been greater than anything they had achieved hitherto with a commitment of thousands of bombers. But they made a single mistake which puzzled me to this day: They divided their forces and that same night destroyed the Eder Valley dam, although it had nothing whatsover to do with the supply of water to the Ruhr.[18]

Nevertheless, the raid was a breathtaking achievement, one which made a national hero of Gibson. Although there had originally been talk of disbanding Gibson's 617 Squadron after the Dams raid, it was decided to keep it together, for use on special targets. Johnny Fauquier later became its CO.

The summer of 1943 was a period of high achievement for Bomber Command. All those predictions about the war-winning power of the bomber seemed to be coming true. In late July, Harris set out to wipe Hamburg off the map. As Germany's most important port and its second-largest city, with a population of some one and a half million, Hamburg was an enticing target, the centre of U-boat construction and home to oil refineries, chemical installations, and industrial plants of all shapes and sizes. Harris estimated that it would take ten thousand tons of bombs to destroy the city. He had intended to send his laboriously assembled thousand-bomber force there a year earlier. Bad weather had forced a change of target. Since then, Bomber Command had hit the heavily defended city many times, but never with the crushing force now envisaged. Harris coined a suitably sinister code name for the operation: "Gomorrah."

The aircrews heard all about it late on the afternoon of July 24. Hamburg was about to be hit and hit hard. Some eight hundred aircraft would do the job, the vast majority of them four-engined Lancasters, Halifaxes, and Stirlings. The only twin-engined bombers in the operation were 73 Wellingtons, twenty-one of them from the Canadian 429 and 431 squadrons (both of which units would soon convert to the Halifax).

None of the assembled aircrews had any illusions about Hamburg. By any standard, it was a tough target, and it would be defended with all the courage and determination of the German flak and night-fighter forces. But Bomber Command had a surprise in store. Code-named "Window," it was the simplest of devices: millions of strips of coarse black paper each 27-cm long and 2-cm wide, with aluminum foil on one face. When the bomber crews unloaded their packages of Window over Hamburg, they created a nightmare for the city's defenders. Their radar screens went haywire.

Suddenly, bewilderingly, they registered *millions* of targets! Looking for individual bombers was like looking for a single tree in the thickest forest. No one could sort out the genuine echoes from the false. One German night-fighter pilot remembers that the radio reports kept contradicting themselves: "Now the enemy was over Amsterdam and then suddenly west of Brussels, and a moment later they were reported far out to sea in Map Square 25. What was to be done?"[19] Not much, it seemed, at least for the moment.

Window had been in existence for more than a year, and Harris had been eager to use the device for many months. But the War Cabinet had said no, fearful of having it used against Britain's own defences. By mid-1943, however, the war situation had changed out of all recognition. The initiative had swung to the Allies. The politicians agreed. Window was approved for use.

Hamburg suffered badly that night, with about 1,500 citizens killed and widespread damage done. In the morning, the U.S. Eighth Air Force mounted an effective raid on the shipyards. Hamburg's agony had just begun.

On the evening of July 27, nearly eight hundred of Harris's bombers took off, eighty-one of them from the squadrons of 6 (RCAF) Group. The bombers flew through cloud over the North Sea, but as they approached the German coast, the skies cleared. The bomber crews experienced no difficulty in finding Hamburg. Fires from the earlier raids still burned; gigantic columns of black smoke rose, looking solid and permanent in the motionless summer air.

It was uncommonly hot in the city. At six o'clock in the evening, the temperature stood at 30 degrees Celsius. People sat in doorways or at open windows, dabbing their foreheads with handkerchiefs. The air raid sirens began to wail shortly after midnight. The first PFF markers went down about an hour later, shimmering lights in the sky, aerial signposts for the bomb aimers crouched in their compartments. The bombs followed, incendiaries then high explosive, as usual. Although bombing invariably conjures up images of enormous explosions wiping out entire cities, most damage was done by fire. The small, four-pound incendiaries started fires in roofs, while the larger, thirty-pound fire-bombs smashed through roofs and set off blazes within buildings. The job of the high explosive bombs was to blow out windows, doors, and walls to help spread the fires and to disrupt the work of rescue crews by wrecking streets, water mains, and power facilities.

That night in Hamburg, it all worked with horrific efficiency. The concentrated bombing set off scores of fires in the Hammerbrook district, which rapidly merged into one hideous conflagration. Soon the world witnessed a new and frightful phenomenon: the firestorm. It was a blast furnace gone mad. Its hunger for oxygen was insatiable. Blazing timbers and trees went spinning into the grasping flames, spreading the blaze. Ferocious winds swept people into burning buildings. Those who fell on sidewalks burned to death almost instantly and turned to charcoal as they lay there. The winds acquired incredible strength, screaming between blazing buildings, twisting and tormenting the flames. Roofs tore away, disintegrating while airborne; trees came ripping out of the earth. The air became tinder-dry in the merciless heat. Vehicles, buildings, even people, suddenly erupted in flame.

Smoke climbed far above the bombers, probably reaching about 25,000 feet before spreading to create a great, sombre ceiling over the devastation. Soot smeared the windows of the bombers. Crew members could smell the fires below. Bomb aimers winced as the heat from the city wafted into their cabins. They hardly knew where to drop their bombs. Crew after crew reported that the entire urban area was a mass of fire. "You had to see the place to believe it," said Al Avant, a Canadian pilot then on his first tour of a highly successful operational career. Harry Holland, from Biggar, Saskatchewan, was on his Second Dickey (copilot) trip, flying with an RAF skipper, Pilot Officer Rodwell: "It was incredible. The place was a great mass of flame. Halfway home, we could still see the smoke rising from Hamburg."

In the city, people crouched in cellars and ditches; some plunged into the Fleet canal or the Elbe river to escape the flames. Sparks darted angrily about the city, setting new blazes, adding to the terror and despair of the population.

Long after the last bomber had turned for home, the fires gradually began to burn themselves out. There was nothing left to consume. The screaming winds subsided. The smoke began to clear. The survivors wondered if anything of their city had been spared.

Bomber Command had at last delivered a truly cataclysmic blow against a major German city.

Crews observed that between the first and second raid on Hamburg – a matter of a couple of days – the surprise value of Window had begun to diminish. The tireless German radar operators had discovered subtle differences between the echoes produced by aircraft and those created by Window. It took a skilled eye, but it was possible, and it became easier with practice.

A third raid was mounted on the port on the night of July 29 by more than seven hundred aircraft. Because of thick clouds and lingering smoke, the marking was done by H_2S; it was not totally accurate, leading to heavy bombing in residential rather than industrial areas. Although more fires were started, there was no firestorm on this occasion.

Harris wanted to deliver the *coup de grâce*, the last great raid that would eradicate Hamburg from the German industrial scene. Then he would take on the other great German cities, wiping them out one by one. His bombers could do it, Harris was convinced. Even the stubborn Germans would be compelled to realize that the war was irretrievably lost.

Harris sent his force to Hamburg once more, on the evening of August 2, but the weather foiled him as it had done so many times before. A vast mountain range of storm-charged cumulus cloud blocked the way to the target. Flying through the stuff was like making your way through a gauntlet of mailed fists. Powerful updrafts and downdrafts battered the sluggish, overloaded bombers, and their crews had to fight to keep them the right way up and heading on course. The storm area extended for about eighty miles, a heaving ocean of blinding rain and lightning, ice and hail. In such conditions, the PFF had no hope of marking the target effectively. Walter Thompson, who had refused a navigation course with the RAF, remembered it as the worst storm he had ever experienced.

> I never saw a thing until we broke through the cloud at about 15,000 feet over the North Sea prior to our rendezvous point. Then as we passed between Cuxhaven and Bremerhaven at about 20,000 feet on the route in to the target . . . [I saw] huge balls of static electricity, two feet in diameter, headed down the fuselage beside me. . . . When approaching Hamburg, a dazzling display of lightning lit up two clouds directly ahead of us and between them a Lancaster was flying. I saw a flash of what appeared to be lightning across the gap between the two clouds and then was shocked to see the Lancaster blow up in an orange and black ball of flame. Whether it was hit by flak or whether the lightning had caused a fire I was not sure, because a white flash preceded the orange ball.[20]

Less than half of the Main Force crews succeeded in fighting their way through to the target area. Those that did could see little of the ground; they dropped their bombs and hoped for the best. Most of their loads landed miles from Hamburg. J. Douglas Harvey of Toronto, flying with 408 (RCAF) Squadron, was on that hopeless operation. "As I struggled with the ice-laden bomber to gain altitude it was clear we wouldn't get above 17,000 feet. By dropping the nose slightly and then pulling back on the controls it was often possible to nudge the bomber up fifty feet at a time. . . . Thunderstorms were all around us. Lightning was tearing and streaking through the cumulus nimbus [sic] clouds, lighting the sky and making it possible now and then to see what a wild night sat outside the cockpit window."[21] To add to Harvey's problems, his wireless operator panicked, believing the aircraft was breaking up, and baled out.

The hopeless operation cost thirty bombers, including four from 6 Group.

For Harris, the failure of the August 2/3 raid detracted little from the overall triumph of his campaign against Hamburg. His bombers had destroyed five hundred public buildings and more than two thousand commercial enterprises. Half the residences in the city were no more; most of the rest had been damaged. Initial esti-' mates of casualties ranged as high as 55,000, but official figures eventually put the dead at between 30,000 and 40,000. Nearly a million had been made homeless. Extensive damage had been done to the shipyards, with considerable impact on the construction of U-boats. Some 180,000 tons of shipping had been sunk in the harbour. According to clandestine reports, SS troops had to patrol the city to quell civic unrest.

In the weeks to come, however, Hamburg came back to life almost as rapidly as had Cologne more than a year earlier. The same spirit of initiative and adaptability triumphed. Rather than wrecking morale, devastating air raids seemed actually to *bolster* the will of the people. By the end of the year, a mere five months after the raid, some 80 per cent of the city's productivity had been restored.

Shortly after the Hamburg raids, Bomber Command mounted an attack on the top-secret experimental facilities at Peenemünde, on Germany's Baltic coast, near the Polish border. Here was the centre of research on rocket propulsion and other projects, including various forms of pilotless bombs. The War Cabinet, aware of German progress in this sphere, wanted the place destroyed as soon as possible. Bomber Command got the job. Harris knew it had to be done the first time, for any second attempt would be met by enormous numbers of flak batteries and fighter defences brought in to defend the important facility.

The raid took place on August 17. The crews had been told that they were attacking a secret radar plant making equipment designed to interfere with the RAF's bombing raids. The Master Bomber on the raid was a highly experienced bomber pilot, John Searby. His deputies were Wing Commanders John White and the Canadian Johnny Fauquier.

The target, a complex of offices, shops, and accommodations, was bathed in moonlight and clearly visible. Even so, the raid began to run into problems from the start. The PFF erred, dropping markers two miles south of the aiming point, and many of the Main Force aircraft had already bombed by the time Searby informed them of the error. In addition, unexpectedly strong winds kept taking the markers and blowing them away toward the sea. By the time the Canadian 6 Group aircraft released their bombs, the target was completely obscured by smokescreens.

As the last wave of bombers was leaving the target area, the fighters arrived. Turning away from the target, Walter Thompson saw "the first orange ball of an exploding bomber."[22] The Luftwaffe fighters shot down forty bombers, 6.7 per cent of the force. It was a serious loss, but one which may have been justified; according to reports, the raid delayed the V-weapon attacks on Allied cities, notably London, for several months, perhaps as many as six.

VI

In far-off Victoria, British Columbia, Reg Lane was the city's hero. The handsome young ex-Hudson's Bay shoe salesman had been away three years – three tough, long years – during which he had carved a reputation as a brilliant bomber pilot. When he left Victoria, he had been a pilot officer in a brand new uniform, just another young airman on his way overseas. Now his sleeve bore the two and a half stripes of a squadron leader, and beneath his pilot's wings could be seen the ribbons of the DSO and DFC. People remembered him as somewhat shy and diffident. Now, with two operational tours under his belt, he was assured, handling receptions and speeches with the aplomb of a veteran. He had flown on most of the toughest targets attacked by Bomber Command, first as a member of the RAF's 35 Squadron (his first flight commander was an unusually percipient officer named Leonard Cheshire, later the winner of a VC and the founder of the Cheshire Homes), then as one of the élite, a Path Finder. He had come through more than fifty operations. On one occasion, he took over a hundred hits in the fuselage. He came home on three engines at least a dozen times. An incendiary shell once passed through a couple of his fuel tanks but didn't explode.

When he returned to Victoria, in his honour the bells at Christ Church Cathedral were all rung simultaneously, or "fired," a measure of the city's highest esteem. The mayor presented the "blond, rosy-cheeked lad of 23" with a silver tray.[23]

Now the air force had a special job for him. The first Canadian-built Lancaster was nearing completion in the Victory Aircraft plant at Malton airfield, near Toronto. This most impressive product of Canadian technology was to be christened by Mrs. C. G. Power, wife of the air minister, on August 6, 1943. It would be a major media event, with Lorne Greene providing a stentorian commentary for the coast-to-coast radio audience. To Reg Lane went the honour of commanding the new bomber; after the ceremony he was to take off and head east, with a full crew of veteran Canadian airmen aboard. Newspapers breathlessly reported that the Lanc, dubbed the *Ruhr Express* and widely described in the press as a "battleship of the sky," would fly across the Atlantic and head straight into action. It wasn't to be. The much-photographed Lancaster, incorporating Merlin engines made under licence by Packard in the United States, as well as innumerable other items of equipment from a variety of North American suppliers, was host to countless "bugs," as might have been expected. When Lane and his crew clambered aboard at Malton, they found that the engine instruments were inoperative. The rest of the controls seemed to work, however, so Lane started the engines and, to the cheers of thousands, took off.

He landed at Dorval, where for a month the big bomber sat in a hangar while technicians swarmed over her, frantically trying to tame her mechanical peccadilloes in preparation for her trip over the ocean. Eventually, in September, the *Ruhr Express* got away; she arrived safely in England to a ceremonial welcome by Vincent Massey, the Canadian High Commissioner.

VII

Following the successes of the Dambuster raid and the attacks on Hamburg and Peenemünde, Harris's reputation among the war leaders and among his own crews was at a new height. During recent weeks, his force had demonstrated its awesome destructive power and also its remarkable accuracy. But now he embarked on a campaign that would test the courage and endurance of his crews as no other. He resolved to eliminate Berlin just as he had (he believed) eliminated Hamburg.

His desire to destroy Berlin flew in the face of his well-known contempt for "panacea targets." There seems little doubt that he thought he could win the war by wrecking Berlin "from end to end," as he put it. He calculated that his force was big enough, just. His crews had the necessary electronic equipment to find the target in almost any weather. His boys could do it. The Germans were equally convinced that their defences, the deadly flak, the probing searchlights, and their eager night-fighter pilots, would destroy them in the attempt. The lines were drawn. The massive battle was destined to be one of the most brutal aerial conflicts ever fought.

The first of the series of raids that later became known as the Battle of Berlin took place on August 23. Johnny Fauquier was the Master Bomber. A force of 727 bombers arrived over the city shortly before midnight. Although many of the crews reported excellent results, the raid failed, due principally to the limitations of their H_2S equipment. Even the most experienced operators found themselves unable to identify anything in the muddle of echoes that filled the radar screens. The bombs that had travelled so far at such risk fell to the south of the city, despite Fauquier's splenetic exhortations over the R/T. Walter Thompson flew on this raid, detailed to come in after the blind markers and drop green TIs (target indicators). "The target was so large," he says, "that all that could be seen by the H_2S operators was a blaze of light indicating a solid built-up area, and the searchlights were so dangerous that one simply could not map-read properly. This, combined with sometimes intense flak, made it almost impossible for a crew to say that they had visually identified the aiming point."[24]

The results were far from impressive. A few ships were sunk in the canals and some government buildings were damaged, but all in all it was a disappointing start to what Harris saw as the most important campaign of the air war. It was also costly. Fifty-six bombers didn't return, 7.9 per cent of the force. The Canadian 6 Group detailed seventy-six aircraft, but only sixty-eight took off. Eleven returned early. Two failed to find the target.

Several nights later, on August 31, 622 of Harris's bombers set off again for Berlin. Again the defences inflicted fearsome punishment. Forty-seven Bomber Command aircraft were lost, 7.6 per cent of the force. And again, the PFF couldn't locate the aiming point in the sprawling expanse of the city. To add to the attackers' woes, high winds sent markers scudding all over the area.

On September 3, a relatively small force of just over three hundred Lancasters set out for Berlin. It did little better than the larger forces that had suffered such losses in the previous two weeks. Twenty-two Lancasters failed to return, in exchange for minor damage to a few factories and houses. Walter Thompson later admitted in his memoirs that during the raid he never knew what part of Berlin was below him.

One hundred and twenty-five four-engined bombers had gone down to destruction in three raids on the German capital. Like many a commander before him, Harris had to shrug off the losses and press on with his offensive. Total war was not for the faint of heart. He prepared to mount another attack on Berlin on September 8. To the intense relief of his weary crews, bad weather forced him to cancel it. Then the new-moon period started, preventing any long-range operations.

Not until mid-November did the Battle of Berlin resume. On November 18, a force of 440 Lancasters and four Mosquitoes appeared over the city. None of the aircrews could see the city because of a thick carpet of cloud. Stronger-than-predicted winds scattered the bomber stream en route to the target. A PFF aircraft dropped a yellow TI in error, confusing the Main Force bomb aimers, who had been instructed to bomb on green TIs only.

The raid had to be chalked up as another failure. The only positive thing to be said was that casualties among the bomber crews were light by Berlin standards: nine aircraft, 2 per cent of the force. All the twenty-three bombers from the Canadian 6 Group returned safely.

On the 22nd, the crews in the briefing rooms groaned when they heard that they were to hit Berlin again that night. The very name was enough to chill a man's soul. Endless hours of slogging across enemy territory . . . God only knows how many flak batteries . . . swarms of fighters . . . a nightmarish place of markers and darting tracer, flares and stabbing searchlights nosing through the dense cloud like devils' eyes . . .

A force of 764 bombers took off, including 110 from 6 Group. Five PFF aircraft carried the new Mark III H_2S radar sets, which promised enhanced definition of ground echoes. Tonight the new equipment would be tested in action for the first time. Unfortunately, technical problems caused three of the five aircraft carrying the new H$_2$S sets to return to base shortly after take-off. Great underpinnings of cumulus cloud obscured the ground all the way from the Dutch coast. Icing became a problem near the target. Conditions were hardly promising, but they never *were* over Berlin. On the other hand, the bad weather kept most of the Luftwaffe night-fighters on the ground. The first of some 2,500 tons of bombs went down on the city shortly after 8:00 P.M. Crews prepared themselves for another savage conflict in the dark, wintry sky.

Surprisingly, in view of the conditions, this was a highly successful raid, the most effective attack on Berlin to date. The PFF marked the target with commendable accuracy. Light winds permitted the markers to remain in position long enough for the bomb aimers to drop their loads "on the nose." And losses were light: 26 aircraft, 3.4 per cent of the force. Part of the reason was that the bombers sped through the target area at the unprecedented rate of thirty-four per minute, their numbers swamping the defences. Bomber Command had at last succeeded in delivering a tremendous blow to the city, wrecking some three thousand industrial buildings and killing at least two thousand citizens. It was the sort of attack that Harris had been aching to inflict on the German capital; now he had done it. A few more such attacks and Berlin would indeed be smashed from end to end, a taste of the fate that would soon befall the entire Reich.

The first Canadian-built Lancaster, *Ruhr Express*, took part in this raid, its first, with Flight Sergeant Harold Floren, of Weyburn, Saskatchewan, in command. A reporter and photographer went along to record the event for the media in Canada. They were disappointed. The Packard-built Merlins began to lose power en route to the target. Floren had to dump the bombs and return to base. He arrived safely, then had to go through the ordeal of a fake debriefing to placate the story-hungry press.

The raid of November 22 marked the swan song of the Stirlings on German ops, reducing 3 Group to a mere two squadrons, both flying Lancaster IIs. Fifty Stirlings had set off for the German capital. Twelve had turned back with various problems; three had been shot down. Unable to fly at the altitude of the Lancasters and Halifaxes, the Stirlings inevitably suffered the heaviest casualties from ground defences. And they always ran the risk of being hit by bombs from above.

It was hardly surprising that the single-minded head of Bomber Command insisted on following up this operation with another for the next night. As if reluctant to meddle with a successful formula, he made the operation almost a carbon copy of the previous night's op. The same take-off time as the night before. The same route to the target. The same zero hour. The same section of Berlin. But because the Stirlings weren't available, and because a maximum-strength operation had taken place only twenty-four hours earlier, the force was relatively small: 383 bombers.

The raid differed from the previous night's operation in one other important respect: the bad weather that had grounded large numbers of Luftwaffe night-fighters had moved on. The result was that Harris's bombers suffered far higher losses proportionately than on the earlier raid: twenty aircraft, 5.2 per cent of the force. Most of the losses were victims of night-fighters, for the flak defences were uncharacteristically light.

The losses had topped 5 per cent again, Harris noted. Nevertheless, the attacks went on. On December 2, he sent 458 aircraft, most of them Lancasters, to Berlin. Forty didn't return, almost 10 per cent of the force. On this raid, Walter Thompson's H_2S failed en route to the target. He later admitted that he should have turned around and returned to base, but it went against the grain. He reasoned that if he brought the Lancaster home safely, he could not be criticized. If they didn't get back, the subject would be academic. Harris would have approved. As it happened, Thompson's H_2S came back to life before he reached Berlin, and he was able to drop his TIs and bombs accurately. His crew saw "more than twenty of our bombers exploding in the characteristic yellow-orange balls of fire on the route and out of the target area."[25]

On December 16, 483 Lancasters and ten Mosquitoes hit the German capital. Twenty-five Lancasters, 5.2 per cent of the force, were lost. But the official figures told only part of the story. In addition to the twenty-five bombers lost on the operation itself, *twenty-nine* more crashed in the fog that blanketed the bases on their return. As ever, such losses were categorized as accidents and didn't appear on the official tally of losses.

Berlin was again the target on December 23. As on November 22, bad weather over Germany kept many night-fighters grounded. By Berlin standards, the loss was not excessive: sixteen Lancasters, or 4.2 per cent of the force. But the results were no triumph, with most of the damage being limited to residential areas.

Much the same kind of weather conditions were encountered on December 29 when more than seven hundred Lancasters, Halifaxes, and Mosquitoes attacked the German capital. Twenty of their number failed to return: 2.8 per cent of the force.

The Battle of Berlin was proving to be dreadfully costly to Harris and his crews.

The Luck of the Game (3): Eric Cameron had completed his tour of ops on Malta and was scheduled to return to Britain aboard the *Empress of Canada*. A Hudson took Cameron and other tour-expired aircrew to Wadi Seidna, near Khartoum, in the Sudan. From there, the plan was to journey to Takoradi, West Africa, aboard a civilian BOAC Ensign. But the Ensign had been grounded with engine trouble. It took a week to fix the problem, and Cameron and his companions missed the *Empress*'s sailing. It was just as well, for the great liner was ambushed by three submarines off the African coast and torpedoed. Nearly two thousand passengers died. Many of the survivors were rescued by the elderly liner *Mauretania*, on which Cameron sailed after missing the doomed ship.

PART SIX
1944

The Road Back

DE HAVILLAND MOSQUITO

"We sure liberated the hell out of this place."
– U.S. soldier surveying remains of a French village,
quoted by Max Miller

I

Harris's all-out assault on Berlin was like some terrible malignancy that consumed the very substance of Bomber Command. It was all anyone seemed to talk about. Although Harris sent his bombers to other targets, it was the Berlin trips that everyone remembered. They couldn't be forgotten.

The New Year brought no relief from the sickening casualties (due, many claim, to the introduction of Window, which prompted the Luftwaffe to send their fighters "freelancing" among the raiders, resulting in a great increase in the number of German victories). On the night of January 1 – actually the first few minutes of January 2, due to delays caused by weather – a force of 421 Lancasters took off for Berlin. Twenty-nine returned early for various reasons. En route, several PFF aircraft became casualties, and their loss probably ensured the failure of the raid before it had even begun. Over the target, the marking was erratic. Most of the bombs fell in the southern part of the city and in the adjacent countryside. Twenty-eight Lancasters (6.7 per cent of the force) were shot down, mostly by fighters.

The following day, Harris again ordered his bombers to attack the German capital. The crews, still weary from the previous night's operations, could hardly believe their ears. Some openly questioned the common sense of the order. But they struggled into their flying gear and went out to their aircraft. 383 bombers set out for Berlin. Twenty-six Lancasters went down, 7 per cent of the force. The bombers did little damage: "Bombs were scattered over all parts of Berlin, with the local reports stressing that there were no large fires . . ."[1]

One has to wonder what Harris privately thought about the progress of his all-important campaign. In the attacks on the German capital since the previous August, he had lost a frightful total of well over 400 bombers, most of them four-engined aircraft, each manned by a crew of seven, each the ultimate in technological development of the period. The cost was mind-boggling. And it was achieving remarkably little, by most estimates. Harris appeared to be banging his head against a wall. It is, however, questionable whether anyone told him so, as Harris never encouraged criticism from his staff; it has to be rated as one of his major shortcomings as a leader.

For the crews, the strain of continuous operations was enormous. According to J. Douglas Harvey, of 408 Squadron, "The total losses made noticeable differences on the base. Our friends were disappearing at an alarming rate. New crews arrived and went missing before you had the chance to know them. They were merely names chalked on the order-of-battle board in the operations room; names erased and replaced each day."[2] One 156 Squadron pilot returned from leave to discover that almost the entire strength of the unit had been lost while he was away. He had become a virtual stranger in the mess. Many aircrew remember morale sagging badly at this period, the consequence of high casualties with poor results. On the other hand, in some units, morale remained high; it all depended on how *your* unit was faring in the conflict, and how *your* luck was holding up. Ewart Cooper, of East Kildonan, Manitoba, and his crew of 432 Squadron began their tour of operations early in 1944, when the Berlin campaign was at its height and casualties dauntingly high. The crew flew thirty-five operations before completing the tour, suffering no casualties and never firing a shot. The only damage inflicted on the crew's Halifax was the result of British gunners who identified it as enemy due to failure of the IFF (Identification, Friend or Foe) system, a forerunner of the modern transponder. The damage was insignificant; the crew completed their tour in good order.

A strange, almost surreal, aspect of the Berlin campaign was that no one outside Bomber Command seemed aware that it was taking place. Even airmen on Coastal Command or Fighter Command units knew little of what the bomber boys were undergoing.

Around the beginning of 1944, the Germans had begun to equip their aircraft with new radar: the SN-2, the latest development in the frantic game of measure and countermeasure played by the two air forces throughout the war. Providing improved long-range detection, the new radar worked on a frequency of 90 megacycles and was impervious to Window. The Germans also developed new tactics, guiding the fighters into the bomber stream by intercepting their H_2S radar activity; thereafter it was up to the Luftwaffe fighter crews to pick out their victims and attack. "Now the fighters had such a marked superiority over the bombers that bomber crews were instructed not to use H_2S, or to use it only for short periods when vitally required for navigation or for blind marking on long-range targets," Walter Thompson recalled.[3] It can have done Harris's ulcer no good for him to contemplate that the essential H_2S radar, which had taken so long to develop and perfect, was turning out to be too dangerous for his crews to use. In addition, Bomber Command had at last accepted what many of its operational airmen had been saying for months: that German fighters had adopted the practice of cruising beneath the bombers and firing up into their fuel tanks in the wings. Occasionally both hunter and hunted became victims when the bomb-filled bellies of the Allied planes exploded. The German fighters' upward-firing guns – code-named *schräge Musik* ("Jazz Music") – were yet another of the innovations that were decimating Harris's gallant squadrons.

The first few months of 1944 were the worst in Bomber Command's history. Ironically, most of the technical problems that had bedevilled the force for years had at last been solved. But it all meant nothing if bomber losses were intolerable. The strain on the young crews was appalling. Inevitably, some airmen found themselves unable to continue. They had volunteered with the best of intentions. The reality of it had simply proved too much. Curiously, few aircrew blamed those who quit flying; indeed, many remember admiring them for having the courage to admit to fears that beset everyone.

The air force, however, had a particularly scornful way of categorizing such airmen, declaring that they suffered from LMF, Lack of Moral Fibre. The Air Staff seemed to believe that if the slightest leniency were shown to aircrew who refused to fly, squadrons would soon be emptied of personnel. Thus, at most stations, aircraftmen with light patches on their uniforms, where aircrew brevets and stripes had once been proudly displayed, could be seen swabbing the latrines or cleaning out the pans in the kitchen grease pit. This sort of treatment, smacking as it did of the Duke of Wellington's army or Nelson's navy, infuriated most Canadians. John Harding, a 103 Squadron navigator from London, Ontario, recalls what happened to a mid-upper gunner on his crew who declared himself unable to fly: "In a few days a full station parade was held. The 'hollow square' was the term the old hands used. All ranks had to view this dishonouring rite. He was stripped of his sergeant's stripes and his brevet in disgrace. Later he'd be discharged and sent home. In about a week he'd be called up into the army. I felt we were like cardboard pawns in the hands of these unfeeling, la-de-dah, upper-class Englishmen who seemed to run the RAF. At times I felt that war was like a game with them. They would brook no battle fatigue, everything was blanketly labelled cowardice."[4]

During the assaults on Berlin, many airmen abandoned all hope of survival, convinced that they would "get the chop" sooner or later. It helped to create a certain detachment from reality. It was going to happen, so why worry about just when?

The assault on the German capital went on. Harris had once hoped that the Americans would join the RAF in the night-bombing campaign. He had warned them that by sending their bomber formations over Germany in daylight, they would suffer catastrophic losses. He was correct; the Americans did indeed suffer grievously. But, characteristically, they decided that the solution to the problem wasn't to switch to night-bombing, but to develop a fighter that would be able to escort daylight bombers to every corner of Germany. Astonishingly they succeeded in a matter of months by marrying the same Packard-built Merlin engine used in the Canadian-built Lancaster X to a low-level fighter, the P-51. The result was a superb aircraft with a phenomenal range. The Mustang undoubtedly did more than any other type to tip the balance in the air war over Europe, clearing the way for the invasion in June 1944.

Meeting at Casablanca, Churchill and Roosevelt dreamt up a combined bomber offensive of round-the-clock assaults on key centres, the USAAF by day, the RAF by night. In fact, things seldom worked out that neatly. Harris simply would not accept any directive that diverted his forces from what he regarded as their sacred duty: eliminating German cities from the face of the earth. If he didn't favour a particular target, he could always say the weather or some other factor prevented him from attacking it. So, in spite of the strategy formulated at Casablanca, the British and American bomber leaders cordially agreed to go their own ways.

On January 20, a major force of 769 Lancasters, Halifaxes, and Mosquitoes took off for Berlin. It was an unusually fine day for the time of year, but although poor weather often spoiled Harris's plans, good weather did little for them on this occasion. Much of the tonnage fell outside Berlin. Bomber Command lost thirty-five aircraft, 4.6 per cent of the force. A week later, another heavy raid and more disappointing results. Two days later, the same story. And again on January 30.

Then a pause in the battle. A time for rest and repairs. It lasted two weeks, during which there were several heavy snowfalls, one delaying the resumption of ops for two days. But on the night of February 15, the battle resumed. A force of nearly a thousand bombers set off for the German capital. Forty-three failed to return.

After several more days of unsuitable weather, Saturday,

February 19, promised good conditions. Harris had intended to bomb Berlin, but changed his mind and ordered his force to Leipzig. It was a catastrophe. The forecast was inaccurate. The bomber stream became badly extended in unexpectedly high winds and took a terrible beating from the Luftwaffe fighters. Over the target, the general confusion resulted in many collisions among the bombers. An appalling total of 78 were lost, including 18 of the 129 aircraft of 6 Group.

For Harris, the crucial battle was turning into the worst of nightmares. There seemed to be a very real danger of destroying Bomber Command, breaking the will of its airmen instead of breaking the will of Berlin's citizens.

Replacing lost aircraft was no longer a problem; Harris could regularly dispatch close to a thousand four-engined bombers to hit the German capital. But in spite of the ebullient reports from the crews, Harris knew that he still hadn't devastated Berlin as he had Hamburg. The city was like some gigantic creature that kept growing new limbs as soon as the old ones were destroyed. It refused to burn as Hamburg had done; its citizens had not broken, its defences were as dangerous as ever. Berlin had taken the worse Bomber Command could dish out, and still it functioned.

Harris ordered another maximum effort for March 21. The weather spoiled his plans. The op was rescheduled for March 24. It was to be an historic operation.

A force of 811 Lancasters, Halifaxes, and Mosquitoes took off. Fifty-three, 6.5 per cent, returned early. More than two hundred aircraft flew on diversionary operations, hoping to convince the German fighter controllers that the main effort was not headed for Berlin. Two years before, such a force of bombers would have been considered a major effort; now it was a mere diversion.

Harris demanded accuracy on this operation above all. The PFF were instructed to identify the aiming point by eye; H_2S marking was only to be used as a last resort. Two Master Bombers were to be employed: the outstanding Canadian bomber pilot Reg Lane of 405

Squadron, and his deputy, a navigator, Wing Commander E. W. Anderson. Lane was flying one of the new Lancaster IVs with uprated Merlin 85 engines, specially developed for use by Master Bombers, enabling them to fly well above the Main Force. Anderson flew reposing on cushions in the nose of a Mosquito of the Meteorological Flight.

Soon after the mid-evening take-off, the navigators aboard the labouring bombers became uneasy about the strength of the winds. Everything pointed to a remarkable increase in wind velocity since take-off; well over 100 mph, according to preliminary estimates. As usual, the most experienced navigators calculated the winds as they found them and passed the "gen" on to their wireless operators, who in turn sent coded messages conveying the information back to England. The data provided the raw material for regular updates on met conditions that were broadcast back to the bomber force. But on this occasion, the staff navigators at Bomber Command simply didn't believe the messages coming from the bombers. Winds up to 130 mph? It was fantastic!

In 1944, no one had yet heard of the jet stream, which was what the labouring bombers had encountered. In England, the navigation staffs worked out figures that satisfied the staff officers. Aboard the bombers, the wireless operators obediently copied down the coded numbers and passed them on to their navigators, thereby adding to the confusion of all but the most skilled. The best navigators were true professionals, totally confident of their calculations, experienced enough not to believe the nonsense broadcast from England. But few of the youngsters crouched over their vibrating navigation tables in the cramped interiors of Halifaxes and Lancasters could claim such confidence. They had little choice but to use the broadcast figures.

Inevitably, the bombers became scattered. Most of the aircraft flew far to the south, their crews confused and frightened. When the first bombers crossed the Danish coast, many were as much as thirty miles off track. The stream had disintegrated, and hundreds of heavily laden bombers wandered about over Nazi-occupied Europe, prime targets for the night-fighters. Once again, the weather had made a mockery of Harris's careful planning.

Over the target, Lane tried desperately to concentrate the attack. It was impossible. Ed Moore, of Edson, Alberta, a navigator with 426 Squadron of 6 Group, remembers the ferocious wind driving his aircraft far beyond the target and creating tough questions for the crew. Dump the bombs and hightail it for home? It was tempting. "We would be bucking high winds all the way home and thus would be short of fuel," says Moore. "Finally we would be travelling alone and vulnerable to fighters . . . we all agreed with the skipper: 'We've come this far; we'll drop the bombs in the right place.'"5 Bill Jackson, a Canadian pilot with 166 Squadron, wasn't satisfied with his first bomb run and decided to go around again. He was shot down during this second attempt to get his bombs on target. Five of his crew of seven were killed. Lane recalls the night as "terrible," although the spritely performance of the Lancaster IV helped: "I remember we returned home from Berlin at over 25,000 feet with an increased true air speed. Even though we were over Berlin for some twenty-five minutes, we were the second aircraft back to base due to the better performance of the Mark IV. It was a wonderful aircraft."

But the raid was a catastrophe. The bombing itself was badly scattered, causing little damage to industrial buildings.

In the end, Bomber Command had suffered its worst losses ever. Fifteen bombers had been shot down en route to the target and over it. But sixty more became casualties during the return to England (including three that crashed in England). Most of the losses appeared to be due to night-fighters. Despite all the progress that had been made in night-bombing technology, the force was still appallingly vulnerable to attacks by fighters.

This was the end of the series of operations that came to be known as the Battle of Berlin; but there was one more that has to be considered in the same context. On March 30, 572 Lancasters, 214

Halifaxes, and 9 Mosquitoes took off for Nuremberg, the city so intimately involved with the rise of Nazism. Early weather reports had indicated a protective layer of cloud for the journey to the target, and the city itself was expected to be clear for ground-marking. Although these conditions had become doubtful even before take-off, the raid went ahead as planned.

The Luftwaffe fighter pilots couldn't have asked for better conditions. Their crews could see huge contrails in the night sky, formed as steam from the bombers' engines condensed in the chill. They pointed unerringly to the hapless bombers. The journey to the target became an aerial massacre. One after another the bombers went down, burning, exploding, as parachutes fluttered in the crisp night air. In all, 82 Lancasters and Halifaxes went down en route to the target, with another 13 lost over the target and on the way home: 95 aircraft in all, a loss even worse than in the last raid on Berlin. If the raid had resulted in significant damage to Nuremberg, the dreadful cost might have been considered worth-while. But cloud covered the city by the time the bombers arrived, creating difficult bombing conditions. Two PFF aircraft mistook nearby Schweinfurt for Nuremberg and dropped markers. An esti-mated 100 aircraft bombed on the markers. The raid was, by any measure, a disaster, a shocking defeat for Harris and his crews.

Uncharacteristically, Harris attempted to downplay the ghastly raid. In his memoirs he noted: "In attacks on targets in Germany our loss rate for the first two operations in February was 7.1 per cent, and for the last three attacks in February 3.3 per cent. At the end of March our casualties went up again because on two opera-tions we ran into most abnormal weather and lost 10.5 per cent of sorties [actually, 8.9 on the Berlin op, 11.9 on the Nuremberg], so that the loss rate for the whole month's attacks on Germany was 5.1 per cent."[6] Averaging of the loss rate seems somewhat callous; the percentages he quoted represented young men's lives. Donald Bennett, the head of the PFF, took a more subjective view, writing that the Berlin battle was "the bitterest part of the war for me, for not only was it gravely important that we should succeed and thereby confirm the effects of Hamburg, but also it was bitter because of the great losses we suffered. So far as the Path Finder Force was concerned, these losses were particularly serious because they included a large proportion of very experienced and good Path Finder crews. . . . At one stage I thought that the backbone of the Path Finder Force was really broken."7

Surely Harris must have entertained similar thoughts about Bomber Command as a whole, but if so, he never admitted as much, at least, not publicly.

At about this time, Bomber Command created a new group: 100 (Bomber Support) Group, whose function was electronic counter-measures. Murray Peden, a Canadian pilot from Winnipeg, flew B-17s with 214 Squadron of 100 Group:

> Our primary role while accompanying the bombers was to blot out, as frequently as possible, the essential VHF communi-nication between the German night-fighter controllers and the fighter pilots themselves. Every minute's delay thus occa-sioned saw the bombers a few miles further on, and reduced the chance of an interception. With a number of our 214 aircraft spaced out in the stream, it was hoped that the traffic around the main fighter beacons could be greatly impeded. The special wireless operators were to achieve that objective by the use of a three-stage jammer code-named ABC (Air-borne Cigar). First the operator tuned his own receiver over the bands most frequently used by the German controllers. The moment he picked up a controller broadcasting instruc-tions, he set ABC to the same frequency and flipped the switch, jamming the conversation into unintelligibility. Going back to his receiver, the special wireless operator then began tuning again to see what frequency the German controller had moved to in an effort to re-establish contact.

As soon as he found the next frequency, on went the jammer again, driving the controller to yet another frequency. And so it went, until the controllers were virtually apoplectic in their frustration."[8]

II

A world away, in the suffocating jungles of Burma, the Allied Fourteenth Army began the formidable task of pushing the Japanese out of the country. The air force had new equipment. The old Mark I Hurricanes and the inadequate Mohawks had gone, replaced by four-cannon Hurricanes, Spitfires, Beaufighters, and five squadrons of Vultee Vengeance dive-bombers, which took over from the elderly Blenheims that had been in use since the first days of the Japanese invasion. (The remarkable Mosquito was rather less successful in the area because of the effects of the heat and intense humidity on its wooden structure.) The entire force, Commonwealth and American, now came under control of South East Asia Command (SEAC), led by Lord Louis Mountbatten.

By early 1944, the Allied air forces were inflicting severe punishment on the Japanese. Rocket-firing Beaufighters wreaked havoc on their lines of communication and supply, both land and water. The Japanese troops called the powerful Beaufighters "whispering death," since they invariably approached at treetop height and often couldn't be heard from the ground until they began firing.

A new fighter made its debut in Burmese skies. The massive P-47 Thunderbolt began to re-equip eight Hurricane units during the monsoon season of 1944. One was 146 Squadron, in which Harold Benson, of Moose Jaw, Saskatchewan, served. Benson found the Thunderbolt a formidable aircraft after the good-natured Hurricane, but he had nothing but praise for its capabilities, its great structural strength, impressive firepower (eight .50-inch machine-guns), excellent range when fitted with 137-gallon wing tanks, and its ability to carry two 500-pound bombs for dive-bombing. The big "T Bolt" was superbly suited to the difficult conditions found in Burma.

For years, the Allied troops and airmen in Southeast Asia had complained of being "forgotten warriors," fighting on a front that no one cared about, a foul part of the world where heatstroke, jaundice, dengue, and "Delhi Belly" were constant companions. In fact, sickness put far more Allied troops and airmen out of action than did the enemy, and the violent weather conditions probably destroyed more Allied aircraft than did the Japanese. "Upon intimate acquaintance the romance of the mysterious East rather faded in the reality," writes Canadian historian John Gwynne-Timothy. "It was disconcerting to discover plagues of six-inch centipedes in an aircraft but perhaps less so than having white ants eat the glue and the heat warp the wood on Mosquitoes. . . . Panels on Blenheims would shrink and pop out in the air."9

Despite these problems, it was a campaign that demonstrated what could be accomplished by air supply. The innovative British Brigadier Orde Wingate led so-called Chindit expeditions far behind the Japanese lines, which depended entirely on air supply for survival. (The name Chindit is a corruption of the Burmese *chinthe*, the winged lions that guard Burmese temples.) Such tactics would eventually become commonplace, but at the time they were revolutionary. In March, when Japanese troops launched a drive to capture Imphal, about 250 miles northeast of Mandalay, C-46s and C-47s flew in the Fifth Indian Division to bolster the Allied defences. The result: one of the worst defeats in the history of the Japanese army. Long-range sweeps by U.S. P-38s and P-51s kept Japanese fighters from making any serious attempts to interfere with ground operations.

This interservice cooperation and air power would prove to be the key to success in Burma, just as it had in the Western Desert.

The Japanese simply could not get the supplies they needed to maintain their attacks – or indeed, even to survive long in that merciless environment. Allied troops found Japanese dead and wounded looking like concentration camp victims; air power had cut their supply routes and was slowly starving them to death. By mid-1944, as the Allied armies were storming ashore at Normandy, the siege of Imphal was broken.

In those months were laid the foundations of the overwhelming Allied strength in the air. It ensured victory. The transport squadrons supplied the troops as they hacked their way through the almost impenetrable jungles, while the tactical units took care of the opposition. Their work was phenomenally successful. Other innovations caused headaches for the Japanese. Mitchells, Thunderbolts, and Hurricanes would combine to lay on "Earthquakes," combined fighter and bomber offensives. These would employ such subterfuges as dummy parachutists with "parafex," which simulated the sound of rifle fire, and "aquaskit," which sent up flares when it hit water, such devices being known collectively as "canned battle."

Air power took many forms in Burma. "Cab ranks" of fighters "hailed" by visual-control officers providing coordinates proved to be as effective as they would in Europe. But air attacks on ground targets were always dangerous. In April, James Whalen of Vancouver was shot down and killed during an attack on enemy positions in Huewi, Burma. Whalen, a member of 34 Squadron, had distinguished himself during the abortive Japanese attack on Colombo two years earlier, when he shot down three Japanese Val dive-bombers. At the time, Whalen had been recommended for a DFC, but it was not awarded until long after his death. Opportunities for fighter pilots to run up high scores were limited at this stage of the war as the strength of Japanese squadrons became depleted. Many pilots, Harold Benson among them, seldom saw any Japanese aircraft throughout their tours. An exception to this was Bob Day, of Victoria, British Columbia, who succeeded in shooting down three Japanese fighters in the spring of 1944 and two more some months later. Day had flown with Fighter Command in England for several months without scoring a victory. By the time he had arrived in India, he had honed his skills. He joined 81 Squadron, operating from Imphal on red-nosed Spitfire VIIIs. On February 15, 1944, he shot down a Zero fighter; an Oscar fell to his guns the following month, and a second Oscar a few days later. Day became CO of 67 Squadron, on Spitfire VIIIs, and shot down two more Oscars, bringing his score to five and making him an ace.

III

When Bob Dale of Toronto joined 1409 Flight of 8 Group for his second tour of operations, it was as if he had skipped about ten years of technological development. In his first tour, back in 1941, he had flown in fabric-covered Wellingtons that could barely attain 15,000 feet. He had navigated his way about Europe by means of dead reckoning and the occasional astro shot. Now he flew in speedy Mosquitoes at 30,000 feet or more, with an array of navigational devices to assist him: "No. 1409 was equipped with the aircraft everyone wanted to use, the Mosquito – and we had the Mark XVI, with two-stage Merlin engines and a pressure cabin. Not least, we were a Special Duty flight under the direct control of Don Bennett, the AOC of 8 Group. . . . Ours had to be the finest job in the RAF." The Flight carried out a variety of duties, from weather reconnaissance, photography, and master bombing, to diversionary raids with bombs and flares. As D-Day neared, more and more raids were mounted against military camps, munitions depots, oil refineries, and ports.

On the evening of June 4, with Eisenhower and his generals peering anxiously out at the leaden skies, fretting about their D-Day plans, Dale and his RAF pilot, Nigel Bicknell, DSO, DFC, AFC, set off on a lengthy weather reconnaissance trip. Never had they flown a more important one, for on their findings would depend the most critical decision of the year: to proceed with the invasion of Europe or to postpone it. The tiny Mosquito headed out into the Atlantic. Conditions looked bleak. Cloud piled upon cloud, creating great walls of grey as far as could be seen. The two occupants of the Mosquito's cramped cabin searched in vain for a break in the clag, a break that might herald better weather on the way. None was to be found. Disappointed, the airmen headed back to England. As they neared the coast, a signal diverted them to a fighter base near the south coast. There, a cluster of very senior Allied officers of all the services waited anxiously. Dale and Bicknell told them the bad news. Although Montgomery was all for proceeding as planned, Eisenhower postponed the invasion for twenty-four hours, to the morning of June 6.

When Dale and Bicknell returned to their base, they found ground crews busy painting the black-and-white invasion stripes on all the aircraft. The immediate future would turn out to be a hectic period for Dale. He was to fly thirty-six sorties during the month of June alone.

Preparations for the mighty endeavour had been going on ever since the United States entered the war. From the start, the Americans had recognized the Germans as the principal enemy. Their enthusiasm for getting to grips with them caused the British the deepest misgivings. Nearly five years of war had convinced most senior British officers of one unassailable truth: man for man, the German soldier was better trained, better led, and – incredibly at this stage of the war – better armed than his Allied counterpart.

On the other hand, the Allies possessed a crushing superiority in air power. In the thirties, Hitler's propaganda chief, Joseph Goebbels, had terrified the world with his stories about the strength of the Luftwaffe and the capabilities of its fighters and bombers. Now it was all coming home to roost. The Allies had in response created an air force of breathtaking strength and capability, the greatest air force the world had ever seen. In June 1944, it would be the deciding factor, the all-important edge that guaranteed victory.

Eisenhower, the Supreme Allied Commander, insisted that both British and U.S. air forces be integrated into the gigantic effort. Harris, the single-minded head of RAF Bomber Command, found to his dismay that he had lost his independent status. His bombers were to be used as tactical weapons, knocking out railway yards, military camps, ammunition dumps, gun batteries, radar stations. He protested that his crews hadn't been trained for such work and their aircraft weren't properly equipped. (To his surprise – and perhaps chagrin – his crews did an excellent job.)

The Americans had won the first battle of D-Day back in the winter when they decimated the German fighter force in a series of tumultuous aerial battles. There would be no Luftwaffe fighter force to attack the D-Day landing barges and their human cargoes as they came ashore on the Normandy beaches.

In the weeks leading up to the invasion, Allied aircraft roamed the length and breadth of France, strafing, bombing, and photographing every conceivable type of target, from artillery installations to "Noballs," the launching and storage sites of the robot missiles the Germans would soon start launching against London and other cities. Inevitably, the low-level attacks sometimes killed the wrong people. Warren Mackenzie, of Durham, Nova Scotia, was a navigator with 419 Squadron who survived being shot down in January 1944, only to die in Germany more than a year later, when a "friendly" aircraft shot up a group of POWs in error.

An impressive ground-attack fighter aircraft now equipped many RAF and RCAF squadrons. First flown as a prototype before the Battle of Britain, the immensely powerful Hawker Typhoon was a far cry from the light, agile Spitfire and Hurricane. The Typhoon typified a new generation of aircraft: tough, heavily armed, destined to battle ground targets rather than enemy aircraft. The Typhoon had originally been envisaged as a speedy interceptor, designed to take over when the Hurricane had to be replaced. It emerged from the factory with an alarming array of flaws and foibles. Its power plant – the source of many of its problems – was a huge 24-cylinder Napier Sabre engine with a proclivity for melting the sleeves of its many valves, leaking glycol, gassing its pilots with carbon monoxide fumes, and maddening its ground crews with the inaccessibility of its parts. The mighty Typhoon had structural troubles, too, regularly shedding its tail unit in flight. The troublesome fighter had an unimpressive rate of climb, but its performance at low level was indeed spectacular; it was the only RAF type capable of intercepting low-level Luftwaffe "hit-and-run" raiders in 1942.

When planning began for the invasion of France, the heavily armed Typhoon was seen as an excellent ground-attack and dive-bombing type instead of as an interceptor, although its in-line engine was dangerously vulnerable to damage by ground fire. Eventually – its tail reinforced, its engine modified, its pilots using oxygen before start-up – the Typhoon went on to do remarkable things. But pilots treated it with respect; it was, by any standard, a handful, weighing in at some seven tons, twice the weight of most fighters of the day. John Thompson, of Woodbridge, Ontario, first encountered the Typhoon at 59 OTU, Millfield. He had been training on the good-natured Hurricane. One day, he recalls, a flight of Typhoons arrived. The air force wanted to find out whether relatively inexperienced pilots could handle the new fighter, and Thompson's class was selected for the experiment. No dual-control Typhoons were available; the student pilots had to learn about their new mounts on the ground. The aircraft's size was enough to intimidate anyone. (Even the notable Battle of Britain veteran Hugh "Cocky" Dundas was taken aback; in his memoirs, he noted that he felt as though he was about to take off "in a steamroller" the first time he taxied out in a Typhoon.[10]) Every student was warned repeatedly about the tremendous torque of the huge 24-cylinder Sabre engine. Most of the students' first take-offs were snaky, uncertain hurtlings along the runway. Thompson did better than most. With the instructor's warnings still ringing in his ears, he fed in plenty of rudder as the big fighter accelerated along the runway. He took off in good order, feeling quietly pleased with himself. The Typhoon handled well in the air. Now confident of being able to handle the fighter, Thompson approached for his first landing, with wheels and flap down. Suddenly, a red flare streaked into the air, the signal for him to go around again. Automatically, he slammed the throttle wide open. He describes the result as "startling." The Typhoon set off sideways at high speed. "I was no longer flying it," he admits. "It was flying me." Despite the shock, Thompson succeeded in regaining control of the fighter and brought it in for a good landing. He had seven hours and forty minutes on Typhoons at Millfield and hated every one of them. Eventually, however, he and the Typhoon would reach an amicable understanding.

The RCAF Typhoon squadrons were dive-bombing units; the rocket-firing Typhoons flew with RAF squadrons, one of which Thompson would join shortly.

In the spring of 1944, aircraft of every type filled countless British airfields. The war had come full circle. Now it was the Allies who had the men and the equipment – and the initiative. The enemy waited. There could be no doubt that the long-awaited invasion was imminent. The question was when. And where.

In the weeks leading up to D-Day, the Allied bomber forces played a major part in convincing the enemy that the invasion would take place in the Pas de Calais area, where the Channel is narrowest. They dropped three times more bombs east of the Seine than to the west. The Allies also worked diligently to convince the Germans that they planned an invasion of Norway.

Although the Allies held absolute control of the air, no flight over occupied territory was without danger. Wing Commander Bob Davidson of Vancouver had taken over command of 143 (RCAF) Wing in the fall of 1943. (At the time, Wings were known, confusingly, as Airfields.) Davidson was an ace – and an unusual one, the only Canadian to have shot down aircraft from all the Axis powers. He had shot down two Japanese aircraft during the attack on Colombo, Ceylon, in April 1942; during the dismal Greek campaign, he had destroyed an Italian Cant seaplane and a Ju 52; later a second Luftwaffe machine had fallen to his guns. On May 8, Davidson led a gaggle of Typhoons to Douai, France. Surprisingly, there was no opposition, but Davidson's engine chose that moment to cut out. He managed to crash-land successfully and escaped through the French underground, at one time serving as a member of the Maquis. Once, while Davidson hid in a farmer's house, a German soldier turned up and asked for a meal. Displaying admirable sangfroid, Davidson joined him at the table, pretending to be a farm worker. He chatted with the German in faltering French, and the two parted on good terms. Davidson added a Croix de Guerre to his DFC.

The Second Tactical Air Force, under the command of that outstanding New Zealander Air Marshal Sir Arthur "Mary" (from "Maori") Coningham, of Desert Air Force fame, combined fighters and photo-reconnaissance units, night-fighters, and light and medium bombers into a single, highly effective force that operated in close cooperation with the army.

All the squadrons going to France had to be highly mobile. For several weeks prior to D-Day, the Tactical Air Force (TAF) personnel lived under canvas to prepare them for the conditions they would face on the Continent. "All it accomplished was to give everyone colds just before the invasion," remarks Harry Godfrey, of London, Ontario (no relation to John M. Godfrey of Toronto), who flew Mustangs with 400 Squadron. They would be flying from airfields bulldozed out of farmers' fields, with metal strips for runways. The bases could be operational in an amazingly short time. But the metal runways could be dangerous. A break in the metal strips sometimes led to burst tires, which could cause an aircraft to flip onto its back, often with fatal injuries to the pilot.

Dive-bombing became a major part of the fighter squadrons' duties. The pilots had to learn the techniques hurriedly, since few had received any instruction. An Air Ministry directive helpfully advised pilots to approach at eight thousand feet, turn and dive at sixty degrees – keeping the target in the gunsight – pull out at three thousand feet, count to three, and release the bombs. In practice, this method of dive-bombing was found to have serious disadvantages, for the bombs had a nasty habit of falling into the fighters' propellers, blowing up the aircraft in the air. Besides, the method was not as accurate as everyone had hoped. Misses of several hundred yards were not uncommon. The pilots experimented with other techniques and soon became skilled.

400 Squadron, which relinquished its Mosquito XVIs for Spitfires in May, painstakingly photographed every square mile of the area in which the invasion was to take place. Thus did the Allies maintain a ceaseless watch on the enemy.

"By the end of May," states the Official History, "the Germans had 891 aircraft in France, of which 497 were serviceable, to face the nine thousand the Allies could muster against them, five thousand of them fighters. Additionally, a coded order was supposed to throw almost all units defending the Reich into the anti-invasion battle, thus giving the Luftwaffe another six hundred aircraft – still a pitiful force – to fight off the Allies."[11]

It began shortly after midnight on June 6, 1944, when more than 20,000 British and American paratroopers landed on the flanks of what in a few hours would become world-famous as the Normandy invasion beaches. The British 6th Airborne Division landed east of the Orne, the U.S. 82nd and 101st Airborne divisions came down between Ste. Mère-Église and Carentan. During the night, Allied bombers in their hundreds flew across the Channel. When John Turnbull of 424 Squadron did so, his navigator, Earl Albert, reported "new islands" below. In fact, the echoes in the radar screen came from the almost-solid mass of landing barges making their turbulent way across the Channel.

At 0630, the first assault troops waded ashore. The largest invasion in the history of mankind had begun. The cloudy, windy morning of June 6 saw an armada of aircraft crossing the Channel, wave after wave of bombers and fighters, all bearing prominent black-and-white stripes identifying them as Allied. (Ron Cassels, of Warren, Manitoba, was a student navigator at Ossington OTU at the time and remembers being alarmed as his Wellington training aircraft climbed through thick clouds and was immediately surrounded by Lancasters on their way to the beaches.)

Spitfires of Canadian 401, 416, 441, and 443 Squadrons escorted the convoys across the Channel. They encountered no enemy aircraft. Others did. John M. Godfrey, who had had a busy time at Dieppe, was now Wing Commander Flying of 39 Fighter Reconnaissance Wing of 83 Group. In company with Jack Cox of 430 (RCAF) Squadron and another pilot, Godfrey flew low over the beaches. Troops swarmed across the torn and littered sand, which was punctuated by ugly spouts of artillery explosions. A moment later it was all behind the speeding Mustangs. Calm fields swept into view. Forests. Rivers. A village. The pilots scoured the landscape, searching for a hint of troop movements. At about 1,000 feet, they saw an enemy armoured column heading in the direction of the beaches. Simultaneously, they spotted four FW 190s – a rare sight on D-Day. "I heard Cox yell through the radio: 'Bandits attacking! Break left!' "

Godfrey swung his Mustang into a steep left turn and saw an FW approaching, guns blazing. In the strange tranquillity that often overtakes one at moments of extreme peril, Godfrey observed that the enemy pilot wasn't allowing sufficient deflection. His shots went streaking past Godfrey's Mustang, curving away harmlessly to the rear.

Then Godfrey was shocked to see that Cox had been hit by the deadly flak. Cox's aircraft twisted over onto its back and, streaming flame, spun into the ground a few miles northeast of Bernay. The twenty-three-year-old Cox, a resident of Brockville, Ontario, was killed instantly.

Godfrey pulled out just above the trees. Keeping close to the treetops, he escaped, returning to base, where he reported the presence of the armoured convoy.

The once powerful Luftwaffe did little to interfere with the invasion. It couldn't. Most of its veterans – the *Experten* – had gone to their deaths in hopeless fights against overwhelming numbers, more than two thousand pilots dying in the first six months of 1944. The Germans had no equivalent of the British Commonwealth Air Training Plan to replace such losses. And critical fuel shortages exacerbated the problem. "We were so short of fuel that we could give the incoming pilots only 3 ½ hours' flying training per week," declared Albert Speer in a postwar interview.[12] The replacements who did get through to the squadrons were no match for the exuberant Allied pilots. Few survived more than a handful of sorties.

Overwhelming air superiority meant not only the ability to bomb, strafe, and photograph the enemy almost without pause, but also to provide security from the enemy's prying eyes. "In the first six months of 1944," notes historian John Keegan, "only thirty-two Luftwaffe daylight flights over England were recorded; there was only one in the first week of June – on 7 June, a day too late – and this at a time when Allied intrusions into French air space were as common as the flights of swallows."[13]

A Canadian air gunner, Andy Mynarski of Winnipeg, mid-upper gunner of a 419 Squadron Lancaster, won the Victoria Cross a week after D-Day. It was the crew's thirteenth operation, and it took place on June 13. As the Lancaster approached its target, a German Ju 88 night-fighter attacked, knocking out two of the Lancaster's engines and starting a fire in the aft fuselage. The skipper, Art de Breyne, ordered the crew to bale out. Mynarski slid out of his turret and scrambled aft. He stopped in his tracks when he saw the rear gunner, the Canadian Pat Brophy, trapped in his damaged turret. Ignoring the wind-beaten flames that blazed about him, Mynarski tried to hack his way through to Brophy. He could make no impression on the twisted metal. He kept trying, even as his flying clothes began to smoulder. Brophy gestured for Mynarski to save himself while there was still time. He ignored him and continued to chop at the stubborn doors. Eventually, exhausted, even he recognized that it was hopeless. As flames took hold of his clothes and the Lancaster went careering down to destruction, he pulled himself erect and saluted Brophy. Then he jumped, vanishing into the darkness. Resistance workers saw him plunge, his parachute trailing flames. He fell into a swamp and was alive when he was dragged free, but he died shortly afterwards.

Brophy went down with the Lancaster, still trapped in his turret. He could do nothing but await death. Incredibly, he survived. He woke up, dazed and disbelieving, and looked about him. His turret lay a few yards away, mangled and twisted. Beyond it, he could see the remains of the Lancaster, now burning furiously. The bomber had hit the ground almost flat, the impact tearing the turret away and saving his life. All the crew, with the exception of Mynarski, escaped. The gallant air gunner received his posthumous VC in October 1946.

In the days after D-Day, invasion shipping still crammed the Channel. The Germans could have dealt the Allies a crippling blow if they had succeeded in getting through to the hundreds of heavily loaded ships. Allied ships and aircraft maintained nonstop patrols to ensure that they didn't.

One of the aircraft involved in this important work was a Liberator of 224 Squadron, commanded by Flying Officer Ken Moore of Rockham, Saskatchewan. The sea looked like velvet on the night of June 8, shimmering gently in the moonlight; the weather had improved since the turbulent conditions of D-Day.

Suddenly the atmosphere in the Liberator became electric. The radar had picked up a contact a dozen miles away. Such contacts often turned out to be fishing boats and other innocuous vessels, but with the biggest invasion in history going on just a few miles away, no fisherman in his right mind would be abroad tonight. Excitement mounting, Moore roared low over the sea. In a few moments they would see it in the glare of the Leigh Light . . . Yes, there it was! A U-boat, U-636, travelling at about twelve knots at right angles to the Liberator. Crewmen could be seen on the conning tower and on the gun platform, often known as the "band-stand," where anti-aircraft weapons were mounted on most U-boats. Moore's nose gunner opened fire, hitting at least two sailors as the depth charges tumbled from the Liberator. The charges hit the water on either side of the sub, a textbook attack. The ocean heaved, erupting in twin mountains of spray. A moment later, the U-boat rose, grey hull streaming, already in its death agonies. Rapidly, the sub broke up. In a few moments it had gone, leaving only an oil slick to mark its passing.

Delighted with their success, the crew resumed their patrol. Now Moore headed closer to the extreme western tip of the French coast. Only minutes after leaving U-636 to its fate, the radar picked up yet another contact. Hardly daring to believe his luck, Moore waited until the range had shrunk to only a couple of miles. In a moment the target would be visible. There it was! A huge grey slug, low in the water, crew members turning, startled, dazzled by the bright light. They reacted quickly and opened fire with their flak guns. The bomber's front gunner quickly took care of the gun crew as Moore lined up to drop his depth charges. Again a perfect attack! The U-boat's bow emerged from the churning sea. For a few bizarre moments it looked like a monstrous performing seal attempting to balance on its tail. Then, quietly, the U-boat's lengthy hull slid into the depths. Moore turned away. Two subs in twenty minutes! A phenomenon indeed!

At first it looked as if the entire crew had gone down with the hapless sub; but the Leigh Light revealed sailors struggling in the oily water. The next day, most of them were picked up by British patrol boats. Moore's feat earned him the DSO and the American Silver Star.

When aircraft took on U-boats at close quarters, the outcome was by no means certain. Most U-boats were heavily armed with single or multiple 20-mm cannon and machine-guns. While such anti-aircraft weapons made aerial attacks increasingly risky, they were in fact an indication of how vulnerable U-boat commanders felt they had become. Besides, as a Coastal Command publication pointed out, "if a U-boat engages with gun or cannon fire she is obviously not going to dive. If the U-boat is not going to dive there is no longer any need to attack in the shortest possible space of time. The aircraft can break off the attack before getting dangerously close, then fly round the U-boat at 800 yards' range and bring all guns to bear. These tactics usually produce a high mortality rate among the gun crews on the upper deck, resulting in a sudden deci-sion on the part of the U-boat captain to *zum Teufel gehen*, i.e., 'get the hell out of it,' leaving the aircraft with a 'sitter.'"[14]

It didn't always work out so satisfactorily. A few days after Moore's striking success, a Canso amphibian took off from the Coastal Command base at Wick, in northern Scotland. The skipper, Flight Lieutenant David "Bud" Hornell, thirty-four, of Mimico, a Toronto suburb, was on his sixtieth operation. For ten hours, the stately Canso patrolled, the crew fighting fatigue and boredom as they scanned the desolate ocean. Imaginations tended to take over during lengthy patrols, sometimes playing tricks on crewmen, particularly gunners. They saw friends riding bicycles across the ocean. They found themselves telling their skippers to steer around tall sailing ships that weren't there. They warned of non-existent mountains in the middle of the sea.

On this occasion, the hours passed quietly for Hornell's crew. Eventually, they set course for Wick, some thousand miles away. That was when they saw it: the U-1225 on the port beam. Hornell dived to attack, but the sub opened fire first – accurate fire, at that. In moments, Hornell's Canso streamed flame from the starboard engine and the fuselage. Flak had ripped through its wing. But Hornell wasn't deterred. He pressed home his attack, straddling the

U-boat with depth charges. His placement could hardly have been better. As the charges exploded, U-1225 quivered and heaved. It quickly went to the bottom, leaving a few crew members on the surface.

Under normal circumstances, the sub's destruction would have been the subject of noisy celebration, but the members of Hornell's crew were fully occupied in trying to keep the violently vibrating Canso in the air. After Hornell managed to get the flying boat up to an altitude of 250 feet, the blazing starboard engine fell completely out of the wing and tumbled into the ocean. The Canso was now almost uncontrollable. Hornell slapped it down on the water without delay. The crew sent S.O.S. signals, none of which was ever received, because of flak damage to the radio.

Now the Canso began to sink. Remarkably, none of the crew had been injured during the attack or landing, and all eight members were able to get out. But only one of the two dinghies had inflated. Six of the crew huddled in the dinghy, with two in the water, clutching at ropes. The weather worsened rapidly; the wind gathered strength and was soon ripping up angry waves. The dinghy bounced helplessly, the men in the water hanging on for dear life. Spirits rose when a Catalina appeared. It couldn't land in the ferocious conditions, but it stayed nearby, flashing Morse signals to the ditched airmen. A rescue boat was on its way, it told them; but minutes later it had to return to base with engine trouble. The sea became increasingly violent. It capsized the tiny dinghy, tossing the airmen into the sea. They managed to right it and clamber back into its dubious security. Their condition quickly deteriorated. One of the crew died. Hornell himself could no longer see. After sixteen hours, a Warwick air-sea rescue aircraft appeared and dropped an airborne lifeboat. Again the dreadful conditions dashed the airmen's hopes. The lifeboat fell too far away and was soon out of sight.

When, after twenty-one hours, a rescue boat picked up the crew, Hornell was in terrible condition, barely conscious and frighteningly weak. Despite the best efforts of the rescue crew, he died before the launch could get him back to shore. David Hornell won the Victoria Cross for his heroism; his Canadian copilot, Bernard Denomy, won the DSO, and several other crew members were decorated.

The days following the Normandy invasion were hectic for all operational units. Canadian fighters soon landed on the Continent. Lloyd Berryman of 412 Squadron was probably the first. After briefing one morning at Tangmere, Keith Hodson, the CO of 126 Wing, called Berryman over and told him of a troubling situation. The Germans were believed to be poisoning the water supply at a landing strip known as B-4. Hodson came straight to the point. Berryman was to recruit a couple of other pilots and arrange to have the aircraft's ninety-gallon "slipper" tanks – the jettisonable tanks attached beneath the aircraft's belly – steamed out. "Then," said Hodson, "have the Officers' Mess fill them with beer. At 20,000 feet it will cool quickly. When you're over the beachhead, signal to the others, drop out of formation, and land on the strip." He assured Berryman that he would experience no trouble finding the strip. "It's directly under the salvoes the *Rodney* is firing on Caen from the beachhead," he explained helpfully.

Berryman and the others set off. As their Spitfires passed beneath the great warship's salvoes, the pilots could indeed hear the roaring of the shells blasting their way to Caen. The landing strip was directly below, as promised. The trio touched down on the metal strip and trundled to a halt, propellers turning, choking dust rising in dense clouds. But where was the reception committee? Where were the thirsty souls waiting for the contents of the tanks?

Then, at last, a sign of life! A Canadian soldier appeared, peeping cautiously from behind a tree. He waited, glancing cautiously in every direction, then he dashed over to Berryman's Spitfire and jumped on the wing.

"What the hell are you guys doing here?" was his greeting.

"Delivering beer," Berryman told him.

Clearly the soldier thought the airmen had lost their minds. He pointed out a church about a quarter of a mile away. "The Jerries are sniping at us from there," he said. The crackle of rifle fire confirmed the truth of the statement. It took only a moment for Berryman to inform the other two pilots to drop their tanks and clear out . . . *at once.*

Hugh Godefroy of Toronto, by then the Wing Commander Flying, 127 Wing, also touched down in France at about this time. It was a day he would long remember.

> There was something triumphant about stepping down on French soil. For such a long time I had flown over this occupied territory. If I had done this four days ago, I would have found myself a hunted man. Burgess [aide to Air Vice-Marshal Broadhurst] and I went for a stroll. We walked in silence, kicking up dust from the ground – bared by the Army's earth-moving equipment. Two Sherman tanks were making their way up a rise of a corn field, the caterpillar tracks squeaking noisily as they went. Now widely separated, Burgess and I struck out through the tall corn in their direction. Suddenly I fell flat on my face. I found myself lying on the distended, blackened corpse of a German soldier. It was alive with blowflies and maggots wriggling from his nose and eyes. On his belt buckle was stamped *Gott Mit Uns.*[15]

The Germans still occupied farmhouses and other pockets of resistance. While he was talking to some Tommies, Godefroy heard a rifle shot and the whine of a bullet. The Tommies shrugged, explaining that it was "just the sniper in the village over there." The German had been there as long as the Allied troops, and had become an accepted part of the scenery.

Despite the intense aerial activity, opportunities for combat with the Luftwaffe were limited. For some pilots, this was a bitter disappointment. Wally McLeod, from Manitou Beach, Saskatchewan, made no secret of his ambition to become the leading Canadian fighter pilot. The single-minded young man of twenty-eight with the penetrating gaze ("A killer if there ever was one," according to Johnnie Johnson[16]) had already scored an impressive twenty-one victories. Few pilots could match McLeod's aggressive style in combat. He never wasted ammunition, preferring to close to within a few yards of his opponent before opening fire. In June 1944, McLeod shot down three enemy aircraft, a 109 and two 190s, firing only twenty-six cannon shells in the process. He was killed in September without having realized his ambition.

In the early days of the war, the crank-winged Ju 87 had, with its accurate bombing and the unearthly howling of its sirens, struck terror into the hearts of troops and civilians. Now the Typhoons had much the same effect on the German troops in the west. The Wehrmacht detested and feared them. The big fighters were everywhere, dive-bombing or attacking with rockets. So effective was the Allied "air umbrella" that major military formations were virtually helpless. Major-General Fritz Bayerlein, commander of the formidable Panzer Lehr division, would later say, "Our division was denied the use of main roads and our movements were totally interrupted by daytime, as a result of the heavy losses sustained after the terrible and repeated attacks made by rocket-Typhoons."[17]

But the deadly German flak made ground-attack operations appallingly costly. Although obsessive about avoiding army casualties, the British high command seemed to have no trouble accepting murderous losses among aircraft and airmen. One Typhoon unit, 609, had five COs killed in twelve months, all the victims of ground fire. Casualties among Typhoon pilots were far higher than the general public knew. For example, during the months of June, July, and August, 1944, the Typhoon units lost a staggering 128 per cent of the number they had been operating on D-Day. Yet decorations were few. Just before D-Day, Harold Freeman of Winnipeg, a Typhoon pilot with 198 Squadron, was recommended for the

Victoria Cross for his gallantry during a rocket attack on a radar station in the Normandy area. The recommendation was turned down. It seemed that virtually every ground-attack operation demanded courage of VC-calibre.

Hugh Godefroy and his unit escorted rocket-firing Typhoons of 184 Squadron on an attack against a marshalling yard southwest of Caen. Godefroy saw the Typhoon leader do three circuits, after which he rolled over to attack, the others following. Intense flak greeted them. In minutes, all three had been shot down. Later in the day, Godefroy visited a Typhoon wing. One of the squadrons had been given the job of knocking out the radar stations in Boulogne harbour.

> The operation called for eight rocket-Typhoons. A single aircraft without rockets was to fly 2,000 yards ahead of the main force. He was to draw the flak to give the others a chance to knock out the radar stations. They called for volunteers to take the lead. One pilot volunteered.
>
> The light flak in the harbour was concentrated in three places: one on the end of the jetty, and two more large batteries on the surrounding hills. On the attack the lead pilot silenced the battery on the jetty but was hit in the process. He flew on, attacking the batteries on the hills, and was hit again by both batteries. The seven rocket-Typhoons were able to knock out the radar stations without having a shot fired at them.[18]

The extraordinarily gallant lead pilot made it back to England, despite terrible injuries to his arms and legs. He received no medal.

Adding to the high casualties suffered by the Typhoons were American pilots who never seemed to be able to distinguish the big British fighters from FW 190s. At one point the loss rate became critical, and the call went out for Spitfire pilots to volunteer for service in Typhoon units. Not one pilot came forward.

IV

Bob McKee of Toronto was posted to 296 Squadron because, he was told, he had above-average ability in map-reading. McKee soon found that he had embarked on a Special Services career, dropping supplies and flying agents into occupied Europe. Transporting agents was a strangely impersonal business; the crew never knew the names of the individuals involved. In fact, there was little contact of any sort, except for assisting the mysterious passengers to clamber aboard the aircraft and indicating where they should sit, usually huddled in a corner until it was time for the jump. "We flew around in the dark," says McKee, "and when we received our signal from the ground – an Aldis light – we turned on our lights, circled, came in about 700 feet. . . . I was responsible for picking the drop zone."

The secret operations were usually timed to take place while a bombing raid was in progress twenty or thirty miles away. "We would sneak in at low level . . . maybe fifty to one hundred feet over the sea, and climb up over high tension wires when we reached the coast."

When McKee joined 296, Armstrong Whitworth Albemarles were in use. One of the first British aircraft to feature a tricycle undercarriage, the twin-engined Albemarle had a composite structure of steel and wood, to conserve "strategic" materials. Less than successful as a bomber-reconnaissance type, it eventually achieved a measure of fame transporting secret agents and towing gliders.

McKee served with the squadron for about two years. His admiration for the agents grew more intense with every sortie. Most of the female agents dropped in France were from Ireland, women who had been educated in France and knew the local idioms and colloquialisms. Their courage was inspiring. He says, however, "The most admirable person I ever saw was a little Jewish chap who was being dropped in the Miana area." Beneath his jumpsuit, his coat bore the hated large yellow star. McKee sometimes saw double agents, dressed as German officers, practising their Nazi salutes and checking the fit of their German uniforms.

Special Air Service "para-commandoes" invariably accompanied these men and women on their one-way trips, handing them weapons, but holding back any ammunition until they were about to jump. Neither he nor any of the crew ever conversed with any of their "customers," nor did they ever learn what happened to them.

Casualties could be daunting on these trips, McKee says. "When I arrived on the squadron there were thirty crews and by the time I left they had replaced thirty crews."

V

The first V-1s fell on London during the night of June 12. The pilotless bombs – officially the Fieseler Fi 103, known to the Germans as the *Vergeltungswaffe* 1, or Reprisal Weapon 1 – were simple, gyroscopically controlled aircraft packed with a ton or more of explosive and powered by an Argus As 014 pulse jet engine. They were twenty-seven feet long, with a wingspan of seventeen feet. The V-1s were not precision bombing devices. Before take-off, ground personnel set a timing device that would cut the engine at the predetermined moment. The nose went down, shutting off the fuel supply. The "doodlebugs," as they were commonly known, caused much damage and killed thousands of Londoners, although the authorities did their utmost to suggest to the world that the new assault on the capital of the Empire was little more than a minor inconvenience, a futile gesture of defiance by Hitler and his cronies.

It was as well that the Allies had such overwhelming numbers of aircraft at their disposal; they were able to put hundreds to work shooting V-1s out of the sky or bombing their launching sites. Both were tricky and dangerous jobs. The V-1 launching sites were well hidden and protected by the notoriously efficient light flak batteries. Shooting them out of the air was no safer, as Dave McIntosh, of Stanstead, Quebec, a navigator with 418 Squadron, soon found out. McIntosh and his pilot, Sid Seid, an American in the RCAF, were on patrol over the French coast near Le Havre when they spotted a v-1, a small red glow moving rapidly in the night sky. They gave chase, but the bomb was too speedy; it vanished in the distance. Seid decided on a different approach. He climbed to 10,000 feet and waited. Before long a second v-1 appeared. As soon as he spotted it, Seid thrust the control column forward, jamming McIntosh against his harness: "The sudden dive lifted me up hard against my straps," writes McIntosh, "and my guts came up with a thud against my heart." This time, it was Seid and McIntosh who were too speedy; they overtook the v-1.

> We'd been warned about this too. Jerry mixed 'em up. He'd send one over at 500 miles an hour, which we couldn't catch, and then poop off one at 200 miles an hour. Whether this was deliberate or not we didn't know, of course, but it drove us crazy. We climbed back to 10,000 feet; Sid was sore as hell. He took the two misfires as a personal affront to his flying ability.
>
> Another hour went by and we were thinking of doing one more stooge before heading home, when we spotted a third doodlebug. "By God, this time," Sid said.
>
> The speed went up as we went down. I looked at the clock. It read 350 mph. I looked out along the wing. It was flapping like a seagull working in a hurricane. My stomach gave another wrench. Christ, the wings will come off and we'll go straight in.
>
> Down, down, down. We were gaining some because the fire coming out of the ass end of the v-1 was growing bigger. . . . "We're too close," I screamed. I shut my eyes as the cannons began banging away. I was thrown hard against my straps because cannons going off cut the speed suddenly.

When the explosion came I thought I was going to be dead. The goddam thing went off right in our faces. I opened my eyes and caught a glimpse of things whirling around outside the window. Black things and blobs of smoke . . . "I got too close," Sid said.[19]

One Canadian fighter pilot found that V-1s could be downright helpful. Bill Baggs, of Hamilton, Ontario, a Typhoon pilot with 164 RAF Squadron, had had a hectic morning in a Cab Rank attack on the Reichwald forest in which four of the eight Typhoons in the formation were shot down. "The weather was poor, with a cloud base of 1,500 feet. The light and medium flak was murderous," says Baggs. He got away unharmed, "with instruments toppled and compass spinning." Relieved, he set course for base. A moment later his relief turned to amazement. "Suddenly, a V-1 buzz bomb filled my windscreen, coming at me head-on. I pushed the stick forward, diving, and missed the missile by a few feet."

Recovering from the shock, Bill Baggs shook his head like a driver admonishing another on the road. Dumb bastards! That crazy V-1 was heading the wrong way. Or was it? He gave the matter a moment's thought. Wasn't it more likely that *he* was the dumb bastard? Perhaps he was, in fact, headed straight for the heart of Germany. Without delay, he turned 180 degrees. The V-1 was still in sight, but pulling away steadily. Baggs followed. To his delight, the pilotless craft took him straight over his base, by now almost totally obscured by fog. Baggs landed safely.

Another Canadian squadron, 402, exchanged its Spitfire IXs for Mark XIVs (powered by the muscular Griffon 65 engine with two-stage supercharging and a five-bladed propeller). The new version of the superbly versatile fighter was as great an improvement over the Mark IX as the Mark IX had been over the Mark V. The new Spitfire was, in most pilots' view, a demanding airplane to fly – and to taxi, being notoriously nose-heavy – but it was capable of close to 450 mph at 25,000 feet and quickly became one of the air force's champion "doodlebug chasers."

Some pilots became adept at toppling the V-1s' gyros by nudging them with a wingtip, sending them spinning to destruction. The dangers of this were obvious, and enthusiasm for the practice diminished rapidly when the Germans started putting explosive charges in the V-1s' wings.

The summer of 1944 saw the climax of the campaign against the Germans' "Reprisal" weapons. The bombing of the V-1 sites had become a significant part of Bomber Command's responsibilities. Early in August, a force of nearly three hundred Lancasters, Halifaxes, and Mosquitoes attacked sites in the Bois de Cassan and Trossy-St-Maxim areas. They encountered ferocious flak. Two 6 Group Halifaxes went down over the Bois de Cassan. Near the target, two Lancasters fell victim to anti-aircraft fire. One was under the command of twenty-five-year-old Squadron Leader Ian Bazalgette of Calgary, a member of 635 Squadron. Bazalgette's Lancaster took hits in both starboard engines. Flames roared from the wing tanks and the fuselage. Inside the crippled aircraft, the bomb aimer writhed in agony, having had one arm and part of his shoulder blown away by cannon shells.

Bazalgette continued his bomb run, his Lancaster painting streams of black smoke across the sky. He released his bombs and markers. But he lost control of the crippled Lancaster as he flew out of the target area. The big bomber plunged, apparently doomed. Incredibly, Bazalgette managed to wrestle the blazing aircraft out of the dive. He gave the bale-out order. Four of his crew jumped, but two others, the badly wounded bomb aimer and the mid-upper gunner, apparently unconscious from smoke inhalation, couldn't extricate themselves. Bazalgette faced the situation that confronted so many Bomber Command skippers. He couldn't jump; crew members were still aboard. He remained at the Lancaster's controls as the cabin filled with flame and smoke. With astonishing skill, he brought the bomber in for a crash-landing. A few moments more and he might have made it. But just above the ground, the burning Lancaster blew up, vanishing in a cataclysmic explosion, shedding blazing fragments in every direction. Ian Bazalgette and his two comrades died instantly. Bazalgette won the Victoria Cross.

Later in the year, a little-known experiment in the fight against the flying bombs involved a Canadian Coastal Command squadron, 407. At the time, the unit was based at Chivenor, North Devon, engaged in U-boat patrols. As the V-1 launching sites were taken over by the armies of the advancing Allies, the Germans took to carrying the missiles beneath Heinkel 111 bombers, transporting them across the North Sea at night, at low level, usually in poor weather. They released the V-1s about a hundred miles from London. The routine rarely changed: an approach at 100 feet to slip under British radar, a rapid climb to 1,500 feet, launch, then a hasty dive back to 100 feet for the trip home. The bomber was detectable by radar for only six or seven minutes, which made it difficult for the defences to direct night-fighters to intercept. But the "boffins" of the Royal Radar Establishment (RRE) reasoned that if the centimetric ASV radar used on Coastal Command aircraft could detect the conning tower of a U-boat from more than twenty-five miles away, it should have no problem with the Heinkels launching V-1s.

The Air Ministry decided to try out the idea using a Mark XIV Wellington equipped with the long-range ASV radar and a Leigh Light. Once a Heinkel had been detected, if the Wimpy illuminated the Heinkel and its charge it should be easy for an accompanying Beaufighter or Mosquito to finish it off. The Canadian Flight Lieutenant "Mac" McLean and his crew of 407 received orders to fly to the RAF station at Ford, in Sussex. Ross Hamilton, of Peterborough, Ontario, was one of the three wireless operator/air gunners on McLean's crew. He recalls that a ground staff fitter and mechanic came along, accompanied by a collection of spare parts. None of the crew knew what they had volunteered for. "Our curiosity was only heightened when we landed at Ford for the first time," he says, "and our lone Wimpy looked somewhat out of place among the rows of Beaufighters, Mosquitoes, Black Widows, et al."

McLean's crew was soon busy, practising homing on Beaufighters at low altitude. Two boffins flew on every trip. The sorties were hard work for everyone involved. The aircraft had to fly at about one hundred feet in the foulest weather, since the Germans usually chose such conditions for their ops. "Dicey," Ross Hamilton called it. "However, one of the trusty boffins soon came up with a solution: a 'radio altimeter.' This consisted of a white lightbulb on the pilot's instrument panel which would illuminate at a height of 100 feet. Unfortunately, the aircraft could also be lower than this, and a lot of attention was needed on the controls to keep the light blinking on and off – but never on fully for any length of time." Hamilton admits, "It was rudimentary by today's standards, but it worked."

The patrols usually took place along the Dutch coast. "We were normally accompanied by a Mosquito or a Beaufighter, or a combination of both – one to get the Heinkel and the other the V-1 if it had already been launched. When the long-range ASV radar in the Wimpy registered a contact, the accompanying fighter would be given a course to steer to intercept the bogey."

The system worked well – well enough, in fact, for plans to be drawn up for a squadron specializing in such interceptions. The time of the V-1 was passing, however. The army overran the airfields in France from which the Heinkels operated. McLean and his crew returned to 407 Squadron. "Few of our colleagues at Chivenor knew where we had been for the past several months," writes Ross Hamilton, "and even less about what we had been doing."[20]

VI

Montgomery had intended to take the city of Caen on D-Day. But as June gave way to July, Caen was still in German hands. The British Second Army attacked again in July – with Montgomery demanding air support to clear the way. The bomb aimers made sure they missed the British troops on the outskirts of the city, but they also missed most of the German defenders. They demolished the city, however, once the ancient capital of William the Conqueror. The press in England, aided and abetted by the over-optimistic claims from Montgomery's HQ, talked of "breakthroughs" and of the British army, "in full cry," pursuing the fleeing Germans. It simply wasn't so. The Canadians in particular had suffered serious losses, and the Germans still controlled much of the city.

Montgomery's stock among his fellow generals kept slipping. The Americans were increasingly critical of him – indeed of the British in general, who vociferously demanded to be treated as equal partners in the struggle while going to extraordinary lengths to avoid infantry casualties. The waspish Montgomery was in a difficult position. As Max Hastings points out, Montgomery "was never allowed to forget that he was charged with responsibility for Britain's last great army, her final reserves of manpower in a struggle that had drained these to the limit. With the constant admonitions reaching him from England about casualties, he would have faced bitter criticism – from Churchill as much as any man – had losses risen steeply."[21]

Not until heavy bombers had practically wiped Caen off the face of the earth was it taken.

Twenty miles south of Caen, the town of Falaise became the fulcrum of a huge operation designed to encircle the Germans. It all began with one of Hitler's spur-of-the moment inspirations. He struck for the coast, seeing it as the best way of cutting off the American army's advance from Normandy into the narrow corridor between Mortain and the sea. It was an imaginative plan. Unfortunately for the Germans, the Allies knew all about it, courtesy of the Ultra decryption service. The German counter-stroke rapidly turned into catastrophe. "The surviving German infantry divisions, terribly reduced in numbers, were bunched into three groups, one group of seven divisions standing in the path of the British and Canadians advancing on Falaise, one group of five divisions scattered about in the path of the American break-out into Brittany, the remaining nineteen divisions still clinging to the collapsing perimeter of the bridgehead they had defended so stoutly since 6 June. All were in imminent peril of encirclement, as the British–Canadian 21st Army Group drove south to cut off their line of retreat to the Seine, while the American 12th Army Group swung eastward to meet it behind their backs."[22] Thus were the parameters of the killing grounds delineated.

The tank battle around Falaise was one of the war's titanic armoured clashes. It was a conflict of enormous manoeuvres, ten German armoured divisions locked in battle with approximately the same number of Allied divisions, over an arena of roughly eight hundred square miles.

The narrow French roads became clogged with traffic, as they had four years earlier. In 1940 it was refugees and fleeing Allied soldiery; now it was German armour and infantry. And instead of 109s and Stukas doing the attacking, it was Typhoons, Mustangs, Spitfires, Thunderbolts, and a vast weight of artillery. The results were horrific.

Monty Berger was senior intelligence officer of 126 Wing, consisting of three Canadian squadrons: 401, 411, and 412. During August, the Wing destroyed two thousand enemy vehicles. Towards the end of the month two pilots of 412 Squadron found more than a thousand enemy vehicles jammed into a wooded area near Argentan, a few miles southeast of Falaise. By the end of one day, the Wing had claimed: "220 enemy vehicles destroyed, 151 left smoking and 292 damaged. . . . Four tanks were left in flames, five smoking and fifteen damaged. Eight armoured fighting vehicles were destroyed, two probable and six damaged as well as a troop carrier and seventy troops and an ammo dump."[23]

It was mass slaughter, carried out with awful efficiency. The killing went on for several days. Roads and fields became littered with burned-out vehicles and the bloated bodies of men and horses. The stench became unbearable in the warm August sun; and above the carnage floated a trembling fog of uncounted millions of flies feasting on the corpses. The ghastly smell affected even pilots flying overhead. General Eisenhower paid a visit just after the last German troops were driven out of the area: "I was conducted through it on foot, to encounter scenes that could be described only by Dante. It was literally possible to walk for hundreds of yards at a time, stepping on nothing but dead and decaying flesh."[24]

The Canadian fighter squadrons had acquitted themselves well during the Normandy campaign, claiming 239 enemy aircraft shot down for the loss of fifty-eight Spitfire pilots killed or captured. Twenty-one became victims of German flak, seventeen were shot down by Luftwaffe aircraft, and twenty crashed because of mechanical faults or undetermined causes.

The three RCAF Typhoon squadrons lost twenty-five pilots, seven each from 438 and 439 squadrons, and eleven from 440. The reconnaissance units were luckier: 400 Squadron, flying high-altitude photographic sorties, lost no pilots, but 414 and 430 lost four and six pilots respectively.

After the war, Göring declared that the Allies owed the success of the invasion to the air forces, which prepared the invasion, made it possible, and carried it through. Without such overwhelming air power, the former Luftwaffe leader claimed, German reinforcements could have been brought to the front in time to defeat the Allies. General Jodl, chief of the operations staff of the German High Command, also maintained that the Allies' success in Normandy was due principally to the total air superiority they enjoyed.

VII

In August, King George VI visited Leeming, Yorkshire, and decorated many of the Canadians of 6 Group, including twenty-one-
year-old John Turnbull of 424 Squadron, whose navigator had seen
what seemed to be brand new islands in the Channel on D-Day.
Turnbull was the youngest of three brothers then serving in
Bomber Command. The Turnbulls hailed from the tiny prairie
town of Govan, Saskatchewan (population: 325), the sons of Mrs.
Cameron Turnbull; their father had died in 1932. Locals called them
The Flying Turnbulls. Eldest of the remarkable trio was Bob,
twenty-five, a tour-expired wing commander at nearby Topcliffe,
the only one who as a boy had indicated much interest in matters
aeronautical. At the time of the king's visit, he commanded 1659
Heavy Conversion Unit. Bob had enlisted in 1940 and flew two
tours of operations, the first with 78 and 76 squadrons, flying
Whitleys and Halifaxes, the second with 427 Squadron of 6 Group
on Halifaxes. He flew seventy-eight ops in all. In September 1943,
he became CO of 427, having enjoyed a spectacular rise in rank,
from sergeant to wing commander in less than a year. At that time
he was the youngest wing commander in the air force. He won the
DFC and Bar, the DFM, and the AFC.

Walter Turnbull joined the RCAF in 1942. An accountant, he
inevitably found himself slated for training as a navigator, which he
completed in 1943. He went overseas and joined the crew of
Chester Hull, later the CO of 428 Squadron of 6 Group. Walter
completed a full tour of thirty-one operations with Hull's crew,
earning the DFC.

John enlisted in September 1941, two weeks after his eighteenth
birthday. By August 1943, he had joined 419 Squadron of 6 Group,
at Middleton St. George, Durham. He completed seventeen operations before being posted to 424 Squadron in January 1944. Now

based at Skipton-on-Swale, Yorkshire, he completed seventeen more. In August, he journeyed to nearby Leeming to receive his DFC from the king. It was a proud day, but windy. It almost ended in disaster when the breeze turned up a corner of the carpet, tripping Turnbull and nearly depositing him in his monarch's arms.

All three Turnbulls came through the war unscathed. On comparing logbooks, Bob and John found that on at least five occasions they had both been operating over the same targets.

VIII

In September, 126 Wing landed at Brussels-Evere airfield. The Luftwaffe had vacated the place only an hour or two before. When the Canadians walked into the Officers' Mess, they found food and drink still on the tables, with uniforms and greatcoats hanging neatly in closets. Crowds of joyous civilians quickly swamped the airport. Almost delirious with glee at the departure of the Germans, they embraced the Canadian airmen, pressing bottles of wine on them, welcoming them as heroes. Dal Russel of Toronto, CO of the Wing, became concerned for the safety of his Spitfires parked around the dispersal. He ordered his pilots to draw their service revolvers to keep the celebrants at a safe distance. The measures did little to stem the outpourings of joy and gratitude from the Belgians: "Parties, dinner, receptions – all were the order in every home, from the poorest to the wealthiest. Soldiers and airmen were collared and brought into these affairs regardless of their rank. There was no refusing."[25]

For a short time Brussels-Evere airfield became one of the busiest in the world, with as many as forty aircraft in the circuit at once. There was scarcely a single Allied luminary who failed to drop in at Brussels-Evere at some time during those fantastic days in

September. Lloyd Berryman saw General Montgomery standing in the middle of the dispersal, quite unconcerned, while scores of aircraft taxied around him. A heady time indeed. The war was just about over, everyone said. The Germans were beaten. It was just a matter of picking up the pieces and driving on to Berlin.

To speed the process, Montgomery devised an imaginative plan to capture the bridges over the rivers and canals in Holland, thereby seizing a corridor to the Rhine: Operation Market-Garden. As the Official History points out, possibly the most extraordinary thing about the planning for the operation was that

> Second TAF [Tactical Air Force] was not allowed to enter the area while troops and supplies were being dropped and was banned from attacking targets of opportunity on the ground unless the enemy fired first – no doubt a precaution to avoid firing on friendly troops, but at the same time, a notable loss of firepower. As a result, the only Canadian fighter unit to be directly involved in the Arnhem operation was No. 402, which as an ADGB (Air Defence of Great Britain) squadron escorted some of the air transport missions. Complications did not end there, however, for the entire operation was controlled from London by U.S. General Lewis H. Brereton's First Allied Airborne Army headquarters, so that the airmen of No. 83 Group had no means of contacting the soldiers except through the latter's commanders in England. Thus the inevitable problems associated with air/ground operations were vastly compounded by the Allies' own organization.[26]*

---

*   Lewis Brereton had had a chequered career. He was the architect of the disastrous Ploesti raid in 1943; earlier, he had been in the Philippines with Douglas MacArthur, who, according to historian Geoffrey Perret, had no confidence in him, describing him as "indolent, party-loving, self-indulgent," and calling him and his staff "bumbling nincompoops."[27]

Russell Bassarab, of Moose Jaw, Saskatchewan, was a navigator with 299 Squadron at the time of the unfortunate operation. No. 299 had been formed in 1943, initially flying Venturas, later converting to Stirling IVs, using them principally for the dropping of secret agents in occupied Europe. For Market-Garden Bassarab's unit would be towing gliders and dropping supplies. Bassarab recalls that aircrews had been on readiness for two weeks prior to the big day. Hopes were high that Market-Garden would be the decisive, war-winning operation.

Three times during the early days of September, the crews of the Stirlings and the gliders assembled to be briefed. "Rusty" Bassarab remembers the very detailed briefings, including reams of "gen" on the route to be flown, the weather, petrol loads, landmarks, estimations of enemy fighter opposition, flak positions, supporting fighter escorts, runway disposition, glider loads, landing zone routine, aircraft maintenance, and seemingly a hundred more necessary items of information – and as many that seemed unnecessary. On each occasion, the operation was cancelled at the last moment.

Then, for the fourth time, the aircrews assembled. Briefing officers informed them that the operation would take place the following day. The airmen shrugged. They had heard that story before. This time it turned out to be true.

By 0700 on Sunday, September 17, the crews were dressed and ready for breakfast, all of them aware of what Bassarab calls a "ticklish sensation in the pit of the stomach." Navigators received a final briefing at 0800 to receive the latest data on wind direction and speed, tracks, distances, and times. On the airfield, fifty Stirlings flanked the runway, squatting on their long undercarriages, noses high, as if sniffing at the morning air. From each snaked a nylon tow rope about an inch thick connected to a Horsa glider. The troops, weighed down by weapons and equipment, clambered aboard the gliders, which stirred in the gentle breeze, creaking like ships at anchor.

The first Stirling took off at 1015; the others followed at one-minute intervals, thundering along the runway, engines howling at full power as they dragged their heavy loads aloft. Shortly after take-off, while the big formation was in the process of forming up, the entire tail unit of one Horsa broke away. Under the horrified gaze of hundreds of airmen and troops, the fully loaded glider snapped into a vertical dive. It plummeted into the ground, killing everyone aboard. Subsequent investigation suggested that one of the twenty soldiers aboard had accidentally detonated a hand grenade.

Nearing the coast, Bassarab could see streams of Dakotas and American Waco gliders, Halifaxes and British Horsa gliders, an armada of 477 aircraft and 334 gliders. Weather conditions were still pleasant, although some cloud had moved in. The Horsa pilots concentrated on keeping their heavy gliders well positioned behind their tugs, avoiding the slipstream as much as possible and keeping the towlines taut. If a glider pilot lost concentration, the line could sag, then be suddenly jerked taut by the tug. Such incidents frequently resulted in breaks. Bassarab saw several gliders going down into the Channel having lost their towlines.

Nerves tightened as the Dutch coast approached. Forty minutes to go. The formation encountered a formation of Flying Fortresses, heading home after a raid. "We flew along the estuary of the Scheldt and on toward our target rendezvous near Hertogenbosch . . . and still no enemy opposition. Barges plied the rivers and canals, but few people could be seen in the villages."

The low-flying formation offered a superb target, but the flak seemed lighter than anyone had expected. The landing zone drew nearer. The troops in the gliders prepared for the descent. Bassarab called the glider pilot. The response was a cheerful "Okay, old boy, thanks for the ride. See you soon." A moment later, the sky was cluttered with gliders, banking and angling as they set up their landing approaches. They came down in an almost dead calm. Many overshot the field as a result and were wrecked on landing, some cartwheeling into spectacular destruction. Landing speeds were relatively low, however, and many crashes that looked deadly did little more than shake up and bruise the occupants. The men in gliders carrying guns or other heavy equipment suffered the worst, since a crash was almost certain to snap restraining chains and send their loads tumbling about. Several glider pilots were crushed to death or seriously injured when their cargoes broke loose.

On the return trip, Bassarab saw an "unending line" of gliders and their tugs transporting more troops to the landing zone. Five hours and ten minutes after take-off, Bassarab's Stirling landed. It had been a piece of cake. But it was just the first of a series of trips to Arnhem.

That evening, the Stirlings were again marshalled beside the runway, with gliders attached. Bassarab recalls that his Stirling was scheduled to tow a glider carrying a Jeep, two trailers, and auxiliary equipment. The take-off process began shortly after 1100 the following morning. The operation was similar in most respects to the previous trip, except that the weather had deteriorated. Low clouds had moved in, and visibility was poor. Two gliders ditched in the Channel. One broke up on hitting the water, taking an artillery officer to his death. Thickening cloud forced the tugs and their gliders lower. One Canadian Dakota crew of 437 Squadron took flak hits that killed the pilot, Flying Officer Ed Henry, of Flin Flon, Manitoba. Warrant Officer Bert Smith, occupying the right-hand seat, was a map-reader, not a pilot. The navigator, an American in the RCAF named Harry McKinley, took over the pilot's seat. Although suffering the pain of an almost-severed finger as well as wounds in the left arm and side, McKinley flew the Dakota back to Britain. He and Smith brought the transport in for a spectacular landing at Martlesham Heath. They bounced their way along the runway, coming within a few feet of demolishing a row of parked P-47s, before squealing to a halt. McKinley became the first patient in a ward intended for Arnhem casualties. Incredibly, neither he nor Smith was decorated for their action.

On Tuesday, September 19, 299 Squadron fielded seventeen

Stirlings for yet another operation to the Arnhem area. This time, Bassarab's Stirling was carrying twenty-four containers and four large panniers. Two senior officers of the Airborne Wing rode as passengers. The cloud base was down to 1,000 feet and visibility hadn't improved. "After setting course from base for Hatfield, we found ourselves playing hide-and-seek in the clouds," Bassarab says, "so we decided that the wise move would be to climb above the clouds to avoid collisions."

Near the Belgian coast, the Stirlings descended and crossed into the Continent near Ostend. Flying low over the Dutch towns, "We could see people in the streets waving to us and giving us the 'V' sign."

Near the dropping zone, the Stirling ran into ferocious flak. Bassarab was intent on watching the ground and the markers set there to assist the release. He could hear "the thud of metal tearing through metal." It seemed like an eternity before the aircraft had cleared the dropping zone. One army officer was nervously mopping his brow and freely admitted to being shaken by the experience. One of the dispatchers had a wound in his leg. The aircraft itself had been thoroughly peppered by flak but still functioned. Back at base, the crews learned that three squadron aircraft had been lost on the op, including that of the CO, Wing Commander Peter Davis, DSO. He and his crew were killed when their cargo of fuel blew up after a direct hit by flak.

More supply drops were flown the following day. And again on Thursday, the 21st. For Bassarab and his crew that was the most eventful day. "As the last container dropped away . . . all hell seemed to break loose." The lumbering Stirlings were boxed in by heavy flak. The rear gunner's fire could be heard as a dry rattle above the din of flak and engines. The skipper, Davy Davidson, hurled the big Stirling about in his efforts to evade the murderous flak. He was only partially successful. The Stirling lurched as shot after shot struck home. Remarkably, no serious damage had so far been done.

Alarmed at the number of hits the Stirling was taking, Bassarab suggested diving to ground level. The ploy worked. The gunners apparently thought the Stirling had been shot down, for the firing ceased. Weaving vigorously, Davidson pulled out of his dive but kept the plane at treetop level until he was clear of the immediate area. "As we looked back," says Bassarab, "the area seemed to be full of flak and aircraft. It was a terrible spot and we were glad to be out of it. I wondered what sort of battle the airborne men were having, and I knew it must have been terribly tough."

When Bassarab and his crew landed, they looked with awe at the damage to their aircraft, hardly able to believe they had survived without injury. Their Stirling was out of action for days while its battle damage was repaired.

The squadrons engaged in troop-support had suffered severe losses. 437 Squadron, the RCAF's first overseas transport unit, had flown its first operation on the 17th. On the 21st it lost four Dakotas to intense flak around the dropping zone. A Canadian pilot with Bassarab's unit, Karl Ketcheson, of Parry Sound, Ontario, refused to drop his supply containers on his first run over the dropping zone, being dissatisfied with his approach. He tried again and was killed by machine-gun fire.

The Arnhem operation could have been a triumph. Instead, it became a disaster. On September 24, the British troops began their withdrawal. Just over two thousand managed to escape across the Rhine, some swimming to freedom. About one thousand airborne troops had died in the hapless action; an appalling total of about six thousand became prisoners. The 1st Airborne Division had been destroyed. Remarkably, the disaster failed to tarnish Montgomery's reputation in England. The bumptious field marshal (he was promoted just before Arnhem) was still Britain's greatest military hero.

A few weeks before the Arnhem débâcle, the Baltic Air Force had attempted to assist the Warsaw uprising by dropping supplies to insurgents in the city.* Carm Chase, of Peterborough, Ontario, was a bomb aimer with 148 Squadron at the time. He and his crew had been engaged in pathfinding duties in Italy with 614 Squadron; Warsaw was to be their first supply-dropping operation. It was vital, Chase recalls, to make drops accurate and compact. This necessitated extremely low flying, a singularly unsafe practice over Warsaw at that time, because of the city's heavy ground defences.

Halifax JP254 took off from Brindisi, Italy, at 1440 hours on August 14. "As we approached Poland across the Carpathian Mountains," says Chase, "a Jerry night-fighter made a pass at us from below. . . . He did not open fire. Neither did we."

The elderly Halifax (a Mark II with the old "arrowhead" vertical tail surfaces) reached Warsaw as daylight was fading. A gigantic pall of smoke hung over the city, blending with the approaching night. As they drew nearer, every structure in the city seemed to be on fire. A searchlight carved a tunnel through the darkness directly across their path. The pilot, "Taffy" Jones, hurled the big bomber into a tight 90-degree turn to starboard. It was as well that he did. Flak opened up, streams of tracer following the Halifax's every move, and Chase noticed a "cone" of tracer converging on the bit of sky the Halifax would have flown into had it not changed direction. Descending rapidly, Jones flew straight at the searchlight. The crew found themselves at rooftop height, hurtling between huge columns of smoke. Buildings sped below, all roofless, gaping shells devoid of life.

"We continued east," Chase says, "until we reached the Vistula River, then we turned to port and flew north to the aiming point, the main square in the centre of Warsaw. We dropped our supplies near

---

* This was the second of two major uprisings. The first had taken place in April 1943, a gallant but futile gesture of defiance that was brutally suppressed by the Germans. In August 1944, some forty thousand Polish insurgents again attempted to oust the enemy from the city. Ill-equipped, they appealed to London for arms, ammunition, and other supplies.

the clock tower." Jones kept the bomber nail-bitingly low. "It seemed to me that the clock face was at eye level off the starboard wingtip."

As the Halifax flew southwest across the city, Chase saw two more Halifaxes trailing flames from burning engines. Then a Liberator appeared through the immense columns of smoke, chased by a twin-engined fighter. The Lib blew up in a shattering orange explosion. Moments later, a parklike open area swept into view, every square foot of it seemingly occupied by artillery, all firing. Chase could hear the cracking of the guns over the roar of the aircraft's four Merlins.

"Christ, they've got us!" came a cry from the tail.

In fact, part of the starboard rudder had been blown away as the aircraft took hits near the rudder and elevator control rods. In spite of the damage, the Halifax still flew, and none of the crew had been hit. Jones pressed on, still at rooftop height. So low was the big aircraft that Chase had to warn him to pull up to avoid a power line that suddenly materialized through the roiling smoke.

Chase's Halifax landed safely back at Brindisi. Two of the six squadron crews that set off for Warsaw on August 14, 1944, weren't so lucky.

IX

Early in October, 401 Squadron encountered one of the new German Me 262 jet fighters over Holland. The jet pilot spotted the unit's Spitfires and dived away. Hedley Everard, of Timmins, Ontario, one of 401's most experienced pilots, gave chase. The speedy jet proved to be a formidable adversary. Diving at full throttle, Everard realized with some alarm that he was exceeding the Spitfire's safe flying speed. But he had no intention of abandoning the chase. The German began to level off.

It became evident that I must pull out of the dive more sharply to get within firing range. I "blacked-out" as the excessive gravity forces buffeted my aircraft. As vision returned, my aircraft gave a sudden lurch. Ahead, the strange twin-engined fighter filled my gunsight. Soon cannon strikes were seen in the right engine, which immediately streaked dense white smoke. A barely controllable skid occurred in my aircraft as I decelerated rapidly. A horizontal distance of some 100 yards separated our two aircraft when I glimpsed another Spitfire 200 yards astern, pouring cannon fire into the crippled Hun. In rapid succession three other Spits made high-speed passes, all registering strikes on the now flame-streaked fighter. As the last Spitfire began its attack, the German pilot tumbled out of his cockpit. Although we were about 700 feet above ground, which is marginal altitude for safe fighter bale-outs, the victim's parachute failed to open. Over my shoulder I saw both him and his burning aircraft hit the ground. The Nijmegen Bridge loomed ahead of me, and in minutes I limped into our airfield, narrowly avoiding a crash landing. Both wings of my Spit were wrinkled, and I knew it would never fly again.... At a long hectic debriefing it was recorded that we had shot down the first jet-propelled aircraft [destroyed] by British forces.[28]

The five Spitfire pilots shared the kill.

In the fall of 1944, the Germans made effective use of the speedy Me 262s in ground attacks, concentrating on Allied airfields. They succeeded in wrecking some aircraft and killing and wounding ground personnel, but they failed to halt the inexorable Allied advance. The German jets would probably have been better employed in attacks on the vast armadas of heavy bombers that daily invaded the steadily shrinking territory controlled by the Third Reich.

Everyone agreed that the Jerries were on their last legs. No one expected the Germans to choose that moment to counterattack. But they did, in mid-December, striking through the Ardennes, the same area that had seen the beginning of the Blitz in May 1940. Seven Panzer and thirteen infantry divisions broke the VIII U.S. Corps' lines, heading for the Meuse. Hitler's goal was to seize Antwerp, Eisenhower's main port, thereby cutting the Allied front in two. For several days, vile weather prevented the Allied air forces from assisting the embattled American forces. Just before Christmas, however, the weather cleared. Five days of intense aerial activity followed.

Jim Collier, of Portage la Prairie, Manitoba, the CO of 403 Squadron, became the first Canadian pilot to shoot down an Me 262 single-handedly. "At 150 yards," says Collier, "I fired a four-to-six-second burst and observed numerous strikes on the fuselage and port wing. The port nacelle began to throw considerable [amounts of] white smoke."[29] Despite this, the German jet still outpaced Collier's Spitfire. Determined to get the 262, Collier continued firing. At about five hundred yards, he saw strikes. But still the distance grew between hunter and hunted. More determined than ever, Collier aimed above the enemy plane. He saw more strikes as his shots hit home. The jet dived away, on a course of approximately 70 degrees. At about 10,000 feet, Collier ran out of ammunition, but he continued to follow his prey, capturing the action on his cine camera. To his delight, volumes of white smoke began to stream from the 262's port nacelle. A moment later Collier saw the aircraft half-roll to starboard. The pilot fell free, his parachute snapping open. The jet crashed six to eight miles east of Aachen.

A few days later, another 262 went down to a Canadian pilot of 411 Squadron, this one to the guns of Flight Lieutenant Jack Boyle of Toronto. In shooting down the jet, Boyle came close to eliminating his squadron's ground crew as they lined up for Christmas dinner. Boyle had been slipping off height in preparation for landing when the enemy jet streaked into view. Boyle opened fire. He hit the German's port engine, and it streamed thick smoke. Now robbed of its greatest asset, speed, the 262 dived for the deck. "I scored several more hits," Boyle recalled, "before he clipped some tall treetops and then hit the ground at an almost flat angle. His aircraft disintegrated in stages from nose to tail, ripping up the turf as it cartwheeled in a trail of smoke and flame." Boyle's base swept into view – and there, in the path of the cartwheeling jet, was a line of airmen waiting for their dinner. They "fell like a row of dominoes," according to Monty Berger, 126 Wing's senior intelligence officer.[30] Fortunately none was hit.

It was a period of remarkable achievements by Canadian fighter pilots. On December 29, eleven Spitfire IXs of 411 Squadron took off from Heesch, in the Netherlands, where a few days before Jack Boyle had come close to spoiling the appetites of the airmen lining up for Christmas dinner. The Spitfires were ordered to carry out a sweep of the Rheine area, some twenty miles west of Osnabrück, where enemy air activity had been reported.

Soon after they arrived, a controller directed the formation to turn west. The tireless eye of radar had detected the enemy. The Canadians quickly spotted an Me 262 and about a dozen 109s and 190s. They dived to attack.

Leading Yellow Section was twenty-two-year-old Dick Audet, of Lethbridge, Alberta. Audet had done a lot of operational flying, but, surprisingly, had never fired his guns in anger. Now, at a range of two hundred yards, he opened fire on a 109, which spewed great clouds of oily black smoke. Audet didn't wait to see it go down; he was already busy attacking an FW 190. He saw hits on the fuselage and cockpit area. He was close enough to see the German pilot slumped in his seat as flames took hold around him. There was no time to watch what happened next. A 109 materialized. To Audet's surprise, it zoomed into an almost-vertical climb whereupon the pilot baled out. Audet caught a glimpse of a shredded parachute fluttering impotently as the pilot plummeted to his death. Instantly, he spotted an FW 190 with a Spitfire on its tail – and a second 190 behind that one. Audet yelled a warning over the R/T as he closed in on his fourth victim. A burst at 250 yards turned the German fighter into a blazing torch. It dived straight into the ground.

Audet's section had been scattered by the violent action. As he was reforming it, he spotted yet another enemy aircraft, this time an FW 190, some two thousand feet below him. The German pilot saw the Spitfire approaching and turned to meet his adversary head-on. Audet fired first, a short, lethal burst. The Focke-Wulf crashed. Audet had accomplished the almost-impossible: five victories in one combat.

The young pilot could scarcely believe what had happened. When he landed he claimed only four destroyed and one damaged. His wingman knew better, having watched the whole action.

Audet won an immediate DFC. Two days later, he shot down a pair of 190s. A few days later, he shot down another and shared a third with Jack Boyle. Ten days after that, another 190 went down to his guns. Audet came close to disaster when his jettisonable long-range fuel tank took a direct hit and exploded. He was lucky; the tank fell away, and he managed to get his damaged aircraft back to base. The following day, he wrecked an Me 262 on the ground, and on the way home shot down another 262 as it approached to land near Rheine. In a matter of days he had joined the ranks of the Allied top-scoring fighter aces. Sadly, he would meet his death in combat early in the New Year.

The Luck of the Game (4): Recently returned to Britain, Eric Cameron was riding back to camp on his motorcycle when a U.S. Army Jeep ran him off the road, catapulting him through a hedge and into a pasture. Cameron suffered a concussion, and another wireless operator/air gunner had to take his place on a flight that evening. The aircraft flew into a hill. Remarkably, the crew suffered only one casualty: the man who took Cameron's place. He was killed.

PART SEVEN
1945

Victory

NORTH AMERICAN MUSTANG

"More than an end to war, we want an end to the beginnings of all wars." – Franklin D. Roosevelt

I

They stared in disbelief as the fighters roared in at treetop level, guns blazing. Bombs tumbled from wing racks. The thudding of explosions jarred the wintry air, mingling with the rattle of machineguns. It was a few minutes after 0900 on January 1, 1945. The Luftwaffe, the force that everyone said was moribund, had come back to life with a vengeance.

Eleven major Allied airfields in the Low Countries and eastern France bore the brunt of the attack. Scores of aircraft went up in smoke and flame. Airmen ran for cover, this way and that like startled deer, as the streams of attackers dinned their way across airfields, guns rattling, bombs streaking earthward. The air reverberated from the clamour of exploding shells and gunfire. Operation *Bodenplatte* had achieved the surprise the Germans hoped for.

The operation had been planned to take place in conjunction with the Ardennes offensive in mid-December. Poor weather forced the Germans to postpone. It undoubtedly worked to their advantage. By New Year's Day, vast numbers of aircraft crammed Allied airfields – or at least, those patches of dry ground remaining after heavy winter rains. As a result, hundreds of Typhoons, Spitfires, Thunderbolts, and Mustangs sat cheek-by-jowl, perfect targets for the ravaging fighters.

That the Luftwaffe could mount such an operation at this stage of the war amazed everyone. It was another of the Germans' remarkable conjuring tricks; again they had succeeded in assembling powerful forces out of the wreckage of shattered units. Almost all the Luftwaffe's surviving *Experten* were active that day, leading a rag-tag force of fledglings on a complex, low-level operation. A large proportion of the young German pilots had less than sixty hours in their logbooks; in any Allied air force, they would still have been in basic training. But the fledglings in their high-performance fighters acquitted themselves far better than anyone could have expected, raking the parked Allied aircraft with cannon and machine-gun fire and dropping fragmentation bombs. They caused extensive damage and many casualties – and considerable embarrassment for senior officers. No one can have relished the task of telling HQ that between two and three hundred aircraft had been lost in a matter of minutes to an enemy believed to be *in extremis*. Thus Allied accounts downplayed the raid, tending to describe it as the last hopeless gesture of a defeated enemy, a minor inconvenience for the Allies.

The Canadian squadrons, 438, 439, and 440, at Eindhoven, in the Netherlands, suffered the worst casualties. Sixteen aircraft were lined up ready for take-off when the attack commenced. All were destroyed. Ground crews were also busy preparing Typhoons for another operation. Those aircraft were wrecked, too. The newly appointed CO of 438 Squadron, Peter Wilson of North Vancouver, was hit while attempting to take off. He died later of his wounds. His tenure as CO had lasted precisely one day. Gordon Wonnacott, commanding 414 Fighter Reconnaissance squadron, returned from an early patrol to find his base being ravaged by German fighters. The Edmonton native immediately attacked, shooting down two Me 109s and damaging an FW 190, winning a Bar to his DFC. The CO of 143 Wing, Wing Commander Frank Grant, of North Sydney, Nova Scotia, whose "personal" Typhoon, RB205, had been destroyed in the attack, declared the wing non-operational. It remained so until January 4, when the squadrons were re-equipped.

One of the enduring myths surrounding the operation is that Allied airmen couldn't defend their fields because they were all still in bed nursing New Year's hangovers. Doubtless some were, but it was the element of surprise that made the difference. In any event, such was the Allies' overwhelming strength that the losses in aircraft and personnel could be replaced in a matter of days. Not that long before, the daring raid would have been a catastrophic blow.

II

In the early hours of January 3, a Lancaster approached to land at 419 Squadron's base at Middleton St. George, Durham. The crew was prepared for trouble; the undercarriage indicator showed only one wheel down and locked, although visual inspections indicated that all seemed well below. Hydraulic problems added to the crew's discomfiture. On the crosswind leg of the landing pattern, the flaps wouldn't hold ten degrees. However, when the pilot, Flight Lieutenant Al Warner, turned on to final approach and selected full flap, the Lancaster's change of attitude suggested that the flaps were working properly. They weren't. As Warner levelled off to touch down, he "lost" the flaps. Suddenly robbed of lift, the bomber thumped down on the runway – "the worst landing I ever made," commented Warner. An almighty series of bounces put the Lancaster far down the runway. By now it was too late to go around. Warner found himself running out of concrete. The big aircraft came to a halt fifty feet beyond the runway. Warner had to make a decision. He knew that a bogged aircraft was supposed to be towed rather than taxied. But two squadrons of Lancasters were landing behind him. Warner decided to drag the bomber out of danger with its own power. Unfortunately, in the darkness, he hit a ditch-digger. The Lancaster burst into flames and was quickly reduced to ashes. Although the crew escaped unhurt, and no ground personnel were injured, the accident wrote off a famous bomber, KB700, the *Ruhr Express*, the first Canadian-built Lancaster, which, eighteen months earlier, Reg Lane had flown from Toronto to the cheers of thousands.

At the time of the incident, Bill Dunphy was the chief engineering officer of 64 Base, which included Croft and Middleton St. George. He recalls that a few weeks after the loss of *Ruhr Express*, he received a number of requests from politicians and others for pieces of the famous aircraft. Unfortunately, by then the famous Lancaster had ceased to be, its remnants having been gathered up and sent to a smelter. No matter; ". . . there were plenty of Lancaster bits lying around," explains Dunphy. So a museum got a rudder complete with bullet hole, a senior politician got part of the landing gear. The AOC of 6 Group, Air Vice-Marshal "Black Mike" McEwen, had a dozen engine pistons made into ashtrays and suitably engraved with the message that they came from the *Ruhr Express*.

Not so, says Dunphy.

III

Unpleasant winter weather plagued Western Europe in the early weeks of 1945, restricting flying. Met flights went on as usual, however. At Ballyhalbert, Northern Ireland, 1402 Met-Reconnaissance Flight still operated an almost forgotten fighter, the Gladiator. Ralph Schenck, of Stratford, Ontario, flew one of the last operational sorties of an RAF biplane, on January 7, 1945, in Gladiator N5592. "These neat biplanes were then sent to the scrap heap," Schenck adds with obvious regret.

By mid-February, Allied air forces were again fully operational. No. 83 Group claimed its thousandth enemy aircraft on the 14th; 126 Wing's Spitfires flew a record 237 sorties the same day, and the Typhoons of 440 Squadron broke their own record with 55 sorties.

In the waning weeks of the war in the west, RAF Bomber Command dropped immense tonnages of bombs on Germany, the most famous (or infamous) raid of the period being that on Dresden, on February 13, 1945. It resulted in the second great firestorm of the war as dozens of individual fires merged some forty-five minutes after the first bombs fell. The ghastly phenomenon first seen at Hamburg in the summer of 1943 was seen again at

Dresden. The same screaming, hurricane-force winds as the blaze gobbled up fantastic quantities of oxygen, knocking people off their feet and sucking them into the holocaust. The same incredible temperatures. The same poisonous fumes and smoke that killed people in unventilated shelters. About 85 per cent of the old Baroque city centre was gutted. Initial estimates of casualties ran as high as 150,000, but the death toll was later placed at some 25,000 with another 35,000 never accounted for.

IV

By early spring, one last great hurdle remained before victory could be achieved: the crossing of the Rhine. Allied bombers dropped thousands of bombs on enemy airfields, although by now the Luftwaffe was hardly able to put up more than a token resistance. "By mid-March the Luftwaffe was in dire straits," asserts the Official History, "as casualties and emergency withdrawals to the east (where Soviet armies were no more than forty miles from Berlin in the north and pressing through western Hungary in the south) left it with less than 1,100 aircraft on the Western Front."[1] The once-mighty Luftwaffe, the force that had terrorized a generation of Western Europeans, had been reduced to virtual impotence.

The Allied armies crossed the Rhine and struck into the heart of Germany. While the Wehrmacht continued to defend every inch of territory with stubborn courage, the end of the European war was at last in sight. In Italy, the German defence began to crumble in April; Allied forces crossed the Po and advanced to the Venetian plains. On April 30, Venice fell.

In these last days of the war in Europe, two Canadian AOP (Air Observation Post) squadrons made their appearance. Operating small, light Auster aircraft, they might be described as the ultimate in army cooperation, since army officers flew the aircraft and RCAF ground crews maintained them.

During the last three months of 1944, RAF Bomber Command had dropped a total of 163,000 tons of bombs. In the first four months of 1945, another 181,000 tons of bombs went down on the Third Reich. Only about a quarter of the tonnage fell on targets related to Germany's oil supply, yet shortages of oil brought the German war effort to a virtual standstill in the closing weeks of the war. How much sooner it would have ended had all the strength of the USAAF and RAF strategic bombing forces been brought to bear on such targets is impossible to say. To the end, Harris stubbornly (and typically) continued to send most of his bombers to strike at German cities.

By the early spring of 1945, several RCAF units had established themselves on German territory, with all personnel armed and ready to deal with any attempts at sabotage.

An increasingly common sight was of large numbers of soldiers and airmen giving themselves up. The personnel of 400 Squadron watched one day as a German training aircraft landed at their base. The two occupants surrendered. They had taken off from an eastern base and had simply turned west as the Red Army overran their field, preferring to give themselves up to anyone other than the Soviets.

Bill Baggs of Hamilton – the Typhoon pilot who had found his way home thanks to a helpful V-1 – had completed ninety-two sorties with 164 Squadron and was told that he needed a rest. Baggs found himself posted as a forward control officer, attached to the Fourth Canadian Armoured Brigade in northwest Germany, working from a radio-equipped Sherman tank. An army officer selected targets, and Baggs worked them out in air force coordinates and passed on the information to his Typhoon confrères circling overhead. In many cases, rockets and cannon fire were hitting targets only a matter of yards from Baggs's Sherman. Whether he got any rest is arguable.

Early in May, with German resistance crumbling, Baggs and a couple of army officers wandered off on their own and managed to get to Wilhelmshaven, where the enormous battle cruiser *Nürmburg* was berthed. Somewhat to the Canadians' surprise, they were invited aboard the ship, where the captain formally surrendered to them. Baggs recalls the large numbers of German crewmen, all armed and looking sullen. None made any threatening moves, however. Baggs claimed a large Nazi flag from the ship and the captain's Mauser 7.65-mm automatic pistol. The Germans handed the items over without a word of protest.

The Nazi forces in the Netherlands surrendered on May 4. A few days later, on May 8, it was all over. From D-Day to VE-Day, 196 aircrew and ground crew had lost their lives with the fighter and fighter-bomber squadrons of the RCAF in Northwest Europe.*

V

The war in Europe was over. In the Far East it continued, as savage as ever, but with the Allies steadily gaining the upper hand. Their enemies fought tenaciously, often to the last man and the last round. The prospect of invading the Japanese mainland appalled everyone. The imagination boggled at the thought of dealing with a nation of Kamikazes. Would they all have to be slaughtered, every man, woman, and child?

---

* The Typhoon squadrons suffered the heaviest losses; some 60 per cent of their pilots had become casualties. No. 126 Wing was credited with 361 victories in the air and on the ground; 401 Squadron was the most successful unit, destroying 112 enemy aircraft. Canadian fighter pilots became skilled at their trade during the period. No. 412 Squadron's Don Laubman of Provost, Alberta, scored 14 ½ victories and 401 Squadron's Bill Klersy of Brantford, Ontario, 13 ½ victories.

By now, Japanese aircraft were seldom seen, but like the Germans, they had a nasty habit of appearing when least expected. Seven Dakotas of 435 Squadron RCAF were dropping supplies near Shwebo, Burma, when Zero fighters appeared on the scene. One of the Dakota pilots was Herb Coons, of Morrisburg, Ontario. Coons had completed a tour as an observer with RAF Coastal Command, aboard Sunderlands. He had learned the essentials of piloting the hefty flying boats during lengthy patrols over the Atlantic. On completing his tour, he remustered as a pilot. Now he was in command of one of the good-natured but not very manoeuvrable Dakotas of 435 Squadron.

As the Zero bored in, Coons hurled his heavy transport into a tight turn. The Zero skidded by. The Japanese pilot came back to the attack, and Coons repeated his tactic, exhibiting superb airmanship as he swung the sluggish transport into violent turns. Frustrated, the Zero pilot turned his attention to the other transports; but Coons kept drawing fire from the Zeros. The violent action had brought the aircraft down close to ground level. Coons hit a tree, which removed four feet of wing. Nevertheless, he succeeded in getting his aircraft back to base at Tulihal, India. He received a Bar to the DFC he had won during his stint with Coastal Command.

Close air support paved the way for the Fourteenth Army's great successes in Central Burma during the spring of 1945. Hurri-bombers and Thunderbolts pounded the Japanese forces by day, Beaufighters and Mosquitoes continued the job after dark, while medium and heavy bombers concentrated on larger targets and lines of communication. Japanese transport was bombed and strafed, choking off vital supplies and reinforcements. At the same time, Allied transports brought an average of some 18,500 tons of supplies and several hundred reinforcements to the battle every week.

Air power was the vital element in gaining total superiority over the enemy. The Japanese found it almost impossible to move men or supplies without attracting the attention of predatory Allied aircraft. Their attempts to make use of the country's waterways met with no more success. The deadly fighters, fighter-bombers, and bombers persistently tore into every conveyance the Japanese attempted to use.

In August, the Combined Third Fleet, commanded by U.S. Admiral William "Bull" Halsey, was operating off the Japanese coast. The powerful fleet consisted of eighteen carriers, with more than one thousand aircraft. Four British carriers sailed with the fleet: *Formidable*, *Implacable*, *Victorious*, and *Indefatigable*, all under the command of Rear-Admiral Sir Philip Vian. On *Formidable*, 1841 Squadron had among its pilots a young man from Nelson, British Columbia, named Robert Hampton Gray. "Hammy" Gray was cast in the mould of Cheshire and Gibson, Lane and Edwards: quiet and unassuming when not flying, fearlessly aggressive in the air. Gray had seen a great deal of action since joining *Formidable* in August 1944. At the time, the carrier was engaged in attacks on the German battleship *Tirpitz*, lying in Altenfjord, Norway. The Germans had mounted dozens of flak batteries on the shore surrounding the big ship. Any low-flying aircraft faced a deadly curtain of flak and dozens of smoke generators that could fill the narrow fjord in minutes. A Corsair pilot, Charles Butterworth of Ottawa, flew from the carrier in attacks on *Tirpitz* and recalls that the smoke was so intense in the fjord, with its almost perpendicular cliffs, that during attacks on flak positions he never saw the battleship. During that summer, the name *Tirpitz* had become as detested among naval airmen as that of Berlin among Bomber Command aircrew. Butterworth's unit, 1842, lost a quarter of its aircraft and pilots in their attacks on the *Tirpitz*.

In late August, during yet another attack on the German battleship, Gray had gone for his targets with his customary élan, boring in so close that his combat photos showed only the muzzle flashes of enemy guns. Most of his rudder disappeared, shot away by the intense flak. Gray managed to control his Corsair, however, and landed safely on the carrier.

In the spring of 1945, *Formidable* sailed east, becoming part of the newly formed British Pacific Fleet, operating as part of the Combined Third Fleet off the coast of Japan. Now, in early August, the fleet was off the Sanriku coast, about three hundred miles northeast of Tokyo. An operation was scheduled, then postponed because of bad weather. The following morning, at 0410 hours, some four hundred aircraft began to take off from the British carriers to attack targets in northeastern Japan. Gray, leading the second flight of 1841 Squadron, had been briefed to attack airfields. Just before take-off, a petty officer, Dick Sweet, rushed to his aircraft, threading his perilous way between spinning propellers on the deck. He jumped onto Gray's wing. A convoy had been spotted in Onagawa Bay, he told Gray; he was to attack the convoy instead of the airfields.

Gray acknowledged the message and took off, with two 500-pound bombs on exterior racks beneath the distinctive inverted gull wings of his Corsair.

At Onagawa Bay, on Japan's east coast, overnight clouds were beginning to dissipate when Japanese sailors first spotted the Corsairs, streaking in over the adjacent hills. Intense flak greeted them. Darting, twinkling lights peppered the sky. The Corsair pilots could hear the thud of cannon fire and the kettledrum *rat-a-tat* of machine-guns. The bomb-carrying Corsairs headed for their drops, flying low over the water, lining up on their targets, readying themselves for skip-bombing, literally bouncing their bombs on the surface of the bay and into the sides of their targets. It was an effective method, but perilous for the attackers, because they had to fly straight and level in the face of murderous flak, which some pilots claimed was more intense than German flak. Gray lined up to attack an escort destroyer, *Amakusa*.

Hammy Gray was just about to release his bombs when flak hit his Corsair. One of his two bombs went spinning out of its rack.

Undeterred, Gray sped on toward the *Amakusa*, skimming low over the water. Amid a storm of defensive fire from several ships, Gray released his remaining bomb. At the same instant his aircraft staggered, hit again and again. The first flickers of flame could be seen coming from the lower part of his engine. Now Gray roared over his target, trailing a plume of black smoke. His bomb struck home just below a gun platform on the *Amakusa*. Gray could hardly have chosen a better spot. The bomb burst into the ship's engine room and killed some forty sailors before blowing up the magazine. With much of her starboard side missing, the ship was doomed. She capsized and sank in minutes, taking more than seventy sailors with her.

Gray's Corsair headed for the open sea. In vain. The fire became an inferno. The Corsair rolled abruptly to starboard and, inverted, went straight into the bay, vanishing in an explosion of spray. Gray was posthumously awarded the Victoria Cross for his exploit.

Canadian naval aviators wrote a glorious chapter in their history at this time. Earlier in the year, another Canadian Corsair pilot with 1830 Squadron, Arthur Sutton of Saskatoon, flying from *Illustrious*, was hit while strafing an airfield in Java. Like Hammy Gray, he was perilously low when the flak scored. His Corsair on fire, Sutton flew straight into a hangar full of enemy aircraft, destroying them all. Although he was recommended for a VC, he received no award, perhaps because the authorities could not be sure that the action was deliberate.

Undoubtedly deliberate was the action of a Canadian naval aviator, Jim Ross of Truro, Nova Scotia, who was waiting to take off from *Formidable* when he discovered that one wing of his Corsair would not lock in position, despite the attention of the deck crew. Rather than delay the aircraft behind him, Ross took off. He must have known that there was little chance of the wing remaining in position. It didn't. He had hardly got clear of the carrier before the wing folded. Ross crashed into the sea and was killed.

The battle over Onagawa Bay resulted in damage to another

Corsair flown by a Canadian, Gerald Anderson, from Trenton, Ontario, a member of 1842 Squadron. His Corsair suffered serious damage, but he managed to fly the 150 miles back to *Formidable*. Landing on, Anderson slammed into the rear deck. Bill Atkinson, of Minnedosa, Manitoba, witnessed the incident from the carrier: "The aircraft broke in two at the cockpit, the rear section falling into the sea. Then for a few seconds the front half perched on the stern of the flight deck. The canopy was shut by the impact. Andy was slumped forward in the cockpit. Then the wreckage slid slowly back into the sea as we helplessly looked on. Of the seven Canadians who flew and fought off HMS *Formidable* only Lt. C. Butterworth of Ottawa, Ontario, and I survived."[2]

Charles Butterworth nearly didn't. He led another attack on Onagawa Bay later that fateful day, following a tested procedure of going over the bay at about three thousand feet, picking his target, swinging inland, and roaring down to treetop level. There followed a brief trip at zero feet along a river leading to the bay before lining up for the run to the target. The flak was ceaseless: "You just had to learn to concentrate on the job and ignore the shells coming at you."

In Butterworth's case it wasn't easy. As he pulled his bomb-release lever, two bullets smashed into his windscreen, filling his cockpit with particles of armoured glass. He was lucky, escaping injury despite having neglected to pull his goggles down over his eyes before attacking. His Corsair was damaged and his radio out of action, but he completed his assigned strafing before flying back to *Formidable*. He landed safely.

Butterworth had narrowly avoided becoming Canada's last casualty of World War II. He and Atkinson both won DSCs for their work in the Fleet Air Arm; Atkinson became an ace, shooting down five Japanese aircraft.

On the same day, August 9, at 1102 hours local time (1202 Pacific Fleet time) a B-29 flying from the Pacific island of Tinian dropped the world's second atomic bomb. It exploded about 1,600 feet above Nagasaki, reducing some 2.5 square miles of the city to ashes and instantly killing 73,884 people in one cataclysmic eruption of power.

The Luck of the Game (5): By May 1945, Eric Cameron, now a commissioned officer, was on his third tour of operations, serving with 407 Squadron based at Langham, Norfolk. During a patrol of the Dutch coast on May 4, the crew saw big fires in Holland as the Germans blew up supply dumps. "Returning to Langham," Cameron recalls, "we landed smoothly. But the Wimpy's speed did not decrease. Then brakes started screeching and smoking." The Wimpy hurtled off the runway and went careering along on the grass. Inside, crew members hastily scrambled for crash positions. "Suddenly the brand-new Wellington flopped on its belly, with a tremendous, rending crash plus the ear-splitting shattering of both props and nose Perspex. The kite slewed wildly, dug up turf and stopped."

Shaken but unhurt, the crew jumped out. The pilot started berating the crash crew's flight sergeant. "Where the devil *were* you guys?"

"Where we were supposed to be, sir. At the other end of the runway."

It seemed that the large white "T" indicating wind direction had been reversed while the Wimpy was on patrol. The Wimpy, loaded with depth charges, had landed downwind. The second pilot had saved the day by retracting the undercarriage during the landing run, bringing the big aircraft to an untidy halt yards away from a farmhouse. Not long afterwards, Cameron obtained his release from the air force. The first person he met was the wireless operator from Malta whose watch he had had repaired and had worn. He had just been released from POW camp. He wanted his watch back.

Epilogue

The world heaved a sigh of relief and counted the cost. The war, that monstrous aberration in human affairs, was finally, mercifully, over. It had taken some *fifty million* lives, about half of them in Russia. The war changed everything. It had made the world an infinitely more frightening place. In 1939, a whole generation had expected the bomber to destroy civilization. That fear had been proved to be exaggerated; but now the bomber was indeed capable of ending everything. Rocket-propelled missiles became a reality. Aircraft, now powered by jet engines, were close to achieving supersonic speeds. The warship, the very symbol of national might in 1939, had become an anachronism. Germany and Japan lay in ruins (only to dominate the world of commerce a few short years later). The misery and despair that lay over much of the earth's surface was so agonizing, so *real*, that it seemed capable of being measured.

More than a million Canadian men and women served in the country's forces. This book details the careers of a small proportion of them: the Canadians who flew. Compared with the Americans, the Soviets, the British, their numbers were not large; but their contribution to victory was immense. For most of them, the war was just an interlude, an untimely interruption in their lives. For some, it became a climacteric, the most significant event, the moment from which all other events were measured. "Before" or "after" – it made all the difference in the measure of a man's life. The transition from smooth-cheeked recruit to steady-eyed veteran took its toll on some; others seemed to thrive on the wear and tear.

The survivors counted their blessings and got on with the rest of their lives. In some cases, they were tragically short. Bill Klersy of Toronto, CO of 401 Squadron, took off in his Spitfire, RM785, a mere two weeks after Germany surrendered. He crashed and was killed. The twenty-two-year-old Klersy, who was awarded the DSO and DFC and Bar, had sixteen-and-a-half enemy aircraft to his credit. John Griffiths, one of the first Canadian airmen decorated in World War II, was killed the day after Germany's surrender, in a traffic accident. He was thirty-nine and had joined the RAF in 1926. The redoubtable George Beurling died in the crash of a Norseman en route to Israel in 1948. Bob Buckham of Golden, British Columbia, won the DFC and Bar and the U.S. DFC for his brilliant career in which he specialized in ground attack. He remained in the RCAF after the war only to die in the wreck of a Beechcraft Expeditor in the Yukon. Keith Hodson, who had commanded 126 Wing at the time of the invasion of Europe, was a regular officer of the RCAF. In 1960, while being checked out in a T-33, he baled out when the jet developed engine trouble. He became entangled in his parachute and was killed. An aircraft accident also claimed the life of Hubert "Cub" Keillor of Mitchell, Ontario, who won the DSO and DFC and Bar in Coastal Command. He died in 1949, flying an Auster aircraft. Bob Kipp, a notable night-fighter pilot from Kamloops, British Columbia, lost his life in July 1949 while practising low-level aerobatics for the Canadian International Air Show. The identical twins Bruce and Douglas Warren both survived the war, and both stayed in the air force. Bruce joined Avro Canada a few years later as a test pilot and was killed in 1951 in the crash of the second prototype CF-100.

Canada's two leading bomber pilots, Johnny Fauquier and Reg Lane, came through the war unscathed. Fauquier died in 1981 of natural causes. Bob Dale, Jack Watts, and John Iverach, all of whom served with distinction as observer/navigators, survived the war, although John Iverach died in 1992. Stan Turner, arguably Canada's greatest fighter leader, flew on ops continuously from 1940 to 1945, survived being shot down (over Malta), the sinking of a navy boat (on which he was an observer), and being blown up by a land mine. He was awarded the DSO, DFC and Bar. He died in 1985 while teaching children to swim at a YMCA pool in Ottawa. Len Birchall, the gallant "Saviour of Ceylon," stayed in the RCAF after the war, as did Stocky Edwards. Vernon Woodward remained in the RAF after the war, retiring in 1963 as a wing commander. The names go on: Julian Sales of Toronto, Path Finder *par excellence*; Don MacFadyen of Montreal, brilliant night-fighter pilot; Bob Hayward of St. John's, fighter pilot; Duncan Grant of High River, the great "train buster"; Pete Engbrecht, the incredible Russian-born air gunner who became an ace by shooting down five German night-fighters; Russ Bannock, the son of Austrian immigrants, who destroyed nineteen V-1s and more than a dozen piloted aircraft . . .

We remember them all with pride.

Notes

Note: PRO refers to the Public Record Office, London; DHist refers to the Directorate of History, Department of National Defence, Ottawa; "n.d." indicates no publication date listed.

Part One 1939: Chaos and Crisis

1. Robert Jackson, *The Fall of France* (London: Arthur Barker Limited, 1975), p. 15.
2. John Terraine, *The Right of the Line* (London: Hodder and Stoughton, 1985), p. 108.
3. John Harding, *The Dancin' Navigator* (Guelph: Asterisk Communications, 1988), p. 74.
4. PRO, Group Ops Order B60.
5. PRO, Air 14/99XC21832.
6. Ibid.
7. PRO, Air 2/3788

Part Two 1940: Tragedy and Triumph

1. Martin Gilbert, *Churchill: A Life* (New York: Henry Holt, 1991), p. 29.
2. This section is based on an article by Hugh Halliday, "Sunderland in Norway," published in *I'll Never Forget* (Willowdale: Canadian Aviation Historical Society, 1979), p. 7.
3. *Life*, April 1, 1940.
4. Max Arthur, *There Shall Be Wings* (London: Coronet Books, 1993), p. 94.
5. Ibid., p. 95.
6. *The Roundel*, May 1951.
7. Michael Fopp, ed., *High Flyers* (London: Greenhill Books in association with The Royal Air Force Museum, 1993), p. 182.
8. *Toronto Globe and Mail*, May 14, 1940.

9. *Hamilton Spectator*, May 20 and May 27, 1940.

10. Quoted in Les Allison, *Canadians in the RAF* (Roland, Manitoba: Allison, 1978), p. 10.

11. *Maclean's*, October 1, 1942.

12. Len Deighton and Max Hastings, *Battle of Britain* (London: Michael Joseph, 1990), p. 73.

13. *Toronto Globe and Mail*, May 14, 1940.

14. Reader's Digest, *The Canadians at War*, Vol. 1 (Montreal, 1969), p. 40.

15. Ibid.

16. Ibid.

17. DHist., Public Relations Release No. 561, July 12, 1942.

18. John Terraine, *The Right of the Line* (London: Hodder and Stoughton, 1985), p. 169.

19. Ibid., p. 174.

20. Quoted in Jean Brown Segall, *Wings of the Morning* (Toronto: The Macmillan Company, 1945), p. 111.

21. Len Deighton, *Fighter* (London: Jonathan Cape, 1977), p. 117.

22. Adolf Galland, *The First and the Last* (London: Methuen & Co., 1955), p. 70.

23. Johnny Kent, *One of the Few* (London: William Kimber, 1971), p. 69.

24. Ibid., p. 98.

25. Ibid., p. 114.

26. Reader's Digest, *The Canadians*, op cit., p. 69.

27. Ibid., p. 70.

28. Quoted in Richard Hough and Denis Richards, *The Battle of Britain* (New York: W.W. Norton & Co., 1989), p. 335.

29. Arthur Bishop, *The Splendid Hundred* (Toronto: McGraw-Hill Ryerson, 1994), p. 116.

30. Dave McIntosh, *High Blue Battle: The War Diary of No.1 (401) Fighter Squadron RCAF* (Toronto: Stoddart Publishing Co., 1990), p. 41.

31. Philip Kaplan and Richard Collier, *Their Finest Hour* (New York: Abbeville Press, 1989), p. 139.

32. Quoted in Hough and Richards, *The Battle*, op cit., p. 202.

33. Quoted in Segall, *Wings*, op cit., p. 116.

34. Quoted in McIntosh, *Blue Battle*, op cit., p. 38.

35. Quoted in Les Allison, *Canadians in the Royal Air Force* (Roland, Manitoba: Allison, 1978), p. 53.

36. Quoted in Hough and Richards, *The Battle*, op cit., p. 341.

37. Alex Henshaw, *Aeroplane Monthly*, September 1995.

38. Quoted in Segall, *Wings*, op cit., p. 121.

39. Quoted in Hough and Richards, *The Battle*, op cit., p. 387.

40. John Terraine, *The Right of the Line* (London: Hodder and Stoughton, 1985), p. 81.

41. Ibid.

42. Quoted in John Keegan, *The Second World War* (New York: Viking Penguin, 1989), p. 104.

43. H. A. Taylor, *Test Pilot at War* (London: Ian Allan, 1970), p. 140.

44. Bruce Robertson, *Beaufort Special* (London: Ian Allan, 1976), p. 8.

45. Keegan, *War*, op cit., p. 320.

46. Ibid., p. 85

47. Hugh Halliday, *Woody: A Fighter Pilot's Album* (Toronto: Canav Books, 1987), p. 70.

48. G. W. Houghton, *They Flew Through Sand* (London: Jarrold Ltd., 1942), p. 17.

49. Quoted in Arthur, *There Shall Be Wings*, op cit., p. 127.

50. Houghton, *Sand*, op cit., p. 20.

Part Three 1941: The Lonely Fight

1. Hugh Halliday, *Woody: A Fighter Pilot's Album* (Toronto: Canav Books, 1987), p. 86.

2. Ibid. p. 97.

3. Ibid. p. 110.

4. Quoted in Daniel Dancocks, *In Enemy Hands* (Edmonton: Hurtig Publishers, 1983), p. 17.

5. Quoted in *405 Squadron History* (Winnipeg: Craig Kelman & Associates, n.d.) p. 10.

6. The following story of Jim Kirk is based on an article by Harold Holmes, "The First of Many," in *Airforce*, April 1994.

7. Quoted in Dancocks, *Hands*, op cit., p. 9.

8. Jack Watts, *Nickels and Nightingales* (Burnstorn: General Store Publishing House, 1995), pp. 93-4.

9. Ibid., pp. 94-5.

10. Ibid. p. 96.

11. *Toronto Star Weekly*, July 15, 1944.

12. John Iverach, *Chronicles of a Nervous Navigator* (Winnipeg: Iverach, n.d.), p. 52.

13. Ibid., p. 54.

14. Ibid., p. 55.

15. Ibid., p. 67.

16. Ibid., pp. 83-4.

17. Ibid., p. 84.

18. Ibid., p. 84.

19. Omer Levesque, "Air Warrior!" in *Air Classics*, September 1979.

20. Hugh Godefroy, *Lucky 13* (Toronto: Stoddart Publishing Co., 1987), p. 110.

21. J. E. Johnson, *Wing Leader* (Toronto: Clarke, Irwin & Co., 1956), p. 80.

22. Godefroy, *Lucky 13*, op cit., p. 71.

23. Johnny Kent, *One of the Few* (London: William Kimber, 1971), pp. 165-6.

24. Brereton Greenhous, Stephen Harris, William Johnston, William Rawling, *The Crucible of War: The Official History of the Royal Canadian Air Force,* Vol. III (Ottawa: Supply and Services Canada, 1994), p. 212.

Part Four 1942: Nadir

1. John Slessor, *The Central Blue* (London: Cassell and Company, 1956), p. 277.

2. Quoted in John Melady, *Pilots* (Toronto: McClelland & Stewart, 1989), p. 127

3. Ibid.

4. Ibid.

5. Bruce Robertson, *Beaufort Special* (London: Ian Allan, 1976), p. 26.

6. Laddie Lucas, ed., *Out of the Blue* (London: Grafton Books, 1987), p. 230.

7. Ibid.

8. Ibid.

9. Kim Abbott, *Gathering of Demons* (Perth: Inkerman House, 1987), p. 119.

10. Ibid., p. 128.

11. Ibid.

12. Adolf Galland, *The First and the Last* (London: Methuen & Co., 1955), p. 158.

13. Abbott, *Demons*, op cit., p. 129.

14. Ibid., p. 130.

15. Quoted in John Iverach, *Chronicles of a Nervous Navigator* (Winnipeg: Iverach, n.d.), p. 134.

16. Ibid.

17. Ibid., pp. 136-7.

18. Ibid., pp. 144-5.

19. Ibid., pp. 170-2.

20. Brereton Greenhous, Stephen Harris, William Johnston, William Rawling, *The Crucible of War: The Official History of the Royal Canadian Air Force,* Vol. III (Ottawa: Supply and Services Canada, 1994), p. 439.

21. J. F. Edwards and J. P. A. M. Lavigne, *Kittyhawk Pilot* (Battleford: Turner-Warwick Publications, 1983), p. 26.

22. Ibid., p. 35.

23. Ibid., pp. 51-2.

24. Ibid., p. 52.

25. Ibid., pp. 56-7.

26. Christopher Shores and Hans Ring, *Fighters Over the Desert* (New York: Arco Publishing, 1969), p. 235.

27. Ibid., p. 234.

28. John Keegan, *The Second World War* (New York: Viking Penguin, 1989), p. 331.

29. Edwards and Lavigne, *Kittyhawk*, op cit., p. 119.

30. Allan J. Simpson, *We Few* (Ottawa: The Canadian Fighter Pilots' Association, 1983), pp. 52-4.

31. Edwards and Lavigne, *Kittyhawk*, op cit., p. 128.

32. Ibid., pp. 141-2.

33. Ibid., pp. 142-3.

34. Simpson, *We Few*, op cit., p. 60.

35. Ibid., p. 61.

36. Ibid., p. 63.

37. Ibid., p. 65.

38. Ibid., p. 66.

39. Edwards and Lavigne, *Kittyhawk*, op cit., p. 190.

40. Ibid., p. 195.

41. Ibid., p. 201.

42. Ibid., p. 209.

43. Ibid., p. 262.

44. Quoted in Laddie Lucas, *Malta: The Thorn in Rommel's Side* (London: Stanley Paul, 1992), p. 29.

45. Ibid., p. 30.

46. Ibid., p. 102.

47. Douglas Bader, *Fight for the Sky* (New York: Doubleday & Co., 1973), p. 156.

48. Lucas, *Malta*, op cit., p. 155.

49. *Toronto Globe and Mail*, October 17, 1942.

50. Ibid., November 4, 1942.

51. Ibid., November 10, 1942.

52. Quoted in Alfred Price, *Battle Over the Reich* (London: Ian Allan, 1973), pp. 28-9.

53. *405 Squadron History* (Winnipeg: Craig Kelman & Associates, n.d.), p. 27.

54. Greenhous et al, *Crucible*, op cit., p. 594.

55. John Terraine, *The Right of the Line* (London: Hodder and Stoughton, 1985), p. 487.

56. Vancouver *Daily Province*, June 1, 1942.

57. Greenhous et al, *Crucible*, op cit., p. 596.

58. D. C. T. Bennett, *Pathfinder* (London: Sphere Books, 1972), p. 175.

59. Quoted in *405 History*, op cit., p. 32.

60. Quoted in Don Morrison, "In Air and Sea at Dieppe '42," in *Airforce*, September 1982.

61. Ibid.

Part Five 1943: The Tide Turns

1. Quoted in Martin Gilbert, *Churchill: A Life* (New York: Henry Holt, 1991), p. 740.
2. Basil Embry, *Mission Completed* (London: Methuen & Co., 1957), p. 242.
3. Dave McIntosh, *Terror in the Starboard Seat* (Don Mills: General Publishing Co., 1980), p. 16.
4. Ibid.
5. Brian Nolan, *Hero* (Toronto: Lester & Orpen Dennys, 1981), p. 92.
6. J. E. Johnson, *Wing Leader* (Toronto: Clarke, Irwin & Co., 1956), p. 157.
7. Max Arthur, *There Shall be Wings* (London: Coronet Books, 1993), p. 249.
8. Ibid.
9. Ibid., p. 244.
10. George J. Demare, "The George Beurling I Knew," in *Airforce*, Spring 1996.
11. Hugh Godefroy, *Lucky 13* (Toronto: Stoddart Publishing Co., 1987), p. 226.
12. DHist., H81, Harris Papers, December 1, 1942.
13. Spencer Dunmore and William Carter, *Reap the Whirlwind* (Toronto: McClelland & Stewart, 1991), p. 154.
14. Brereton Greenhous, Stephen Harris, William Johnston, William Rawling, *The Crucible of War: The Official History of the Royal Canadian Air Force*, Vol. III (Ottawa: Supply and Services Canada, 1994), pp. 635-6.
15. Walter Thompson, *Lancaster to Berlin* (London: Goodall Publications, 1985), p. 25.
16. Ibid., p. 30.
17. Ibid., p. 133.
18. Albert Speer, *Inside the Third Reich* (New York: The Macmillan Company, 1970), pp. 280-1.
19. Wilhelm Johnen, *Duel Under the Stars* (London: New English Library, 1975), p. 62.
20. Thompson, *Lancaster*, op cit., pp. 129-30.
21. J. Douglas Harvey, *Boys, Bombs, and Brussels Sprouts* (Toronto: McClelland & Stewart, 1981), pp. 43-5
22. Thompson, *Lancaster*, op cit., p. 144.
23. *Toronto Star*, August 5, 1943.
24. Thompson, *Lancaster*, op cit., pp. 146-7.
25. Thompson, *Lancaster*, op cit., p. 154.

Part Six 1944: The Road Back

1. Martin Middlebrook and Chris Everitt, *The Bomber Command War Diaries* (New York: Viking, 1985), p. 463.
2. J. Douglas Harvey, *Boys, Bombs, and Brussels Sprouts* (Toronto: McClelland & Stewart, 1981), p. 155.

3. Walter Thompson, *Lancaster to Berlin* (London: Goodall Publications, 1985), p. 199.

4. John Harding, *The Dancin' Navigator* (Guelph: Asterisk Communications, 1988), p. 38.

5. Quoted in Spencer Dunmore and William Carter, *Reap the Whirlwind* (Toronto: McClelland & Stewart, 1991), p. 225.

6. Sir Arthur Harris, *Bomber Offensive*, (London: The Macmillan Company, 1947), p. 191.

7. D. C. T. Bennett, *Pathfinder* (London: Sphere Books, 1972), p. 209.

8. Murray Peden, *A Thousand Shall Fall* (Toronto: Stoddart Publishing Co., 1988), pp. 366-7.

9. John R. W. Gwynne-Timothy, *Burma Liberators* (Toronto: Next Level Press, 1991), p. 402.

10. Hugh Dundas, *Flying Start* (London: Penguin Books, 1988), p. 111.

11. Brereton Greenhous, Stephen Harris, William Johnston, William Rawling, *The Crucible of War: The Official History of the Royal Canadian Air Force*, Vol. III (Ottawa: Supply and Services Canada, 1994), p. 292.

12. Quoted in James Parton, *Air Force Spoken Here: General Ira Eaker and the Command of the Air* (Bethesda: Adler and Adler, 1986), p. 485.

13. John Keegan, *The Second World War* (New York: Viking Penguin, 1989), p. 379.

14. Quoted in John Terraine, *The Right of the Line* (London: Hodder and Stoughton, 1985), p. 435.

15. Hugh Godefroy, *Lucky 13* (Toronto: Stoddart Publishing Co., 1987), pp. 252-3.

16. Quoted in Arthur Bishop, *Courage in the Air* (Toronto: McGraw-Hill Ryerson, 1992), p. 219.

17. Quoted in Charles Demoulin, *Firebirds* (Washington: Smithsonian Institution Press, 1986), p. 223.

18. Godefroy, *Lucky 13*, op cit., pp. 251-2.

19. Dave McIntosh, *Terror in the Starboard Seat* (Don Mills: General Publishing Co., 1980), p. 66.

20. From interviews with Ross Hamilton and an article, "The First AWAK," in *Airforce*, January 1995.

21. Max Hastings, *Overlord* (New York: Simon and Schuster, 1984), pp. 241-2.

22. Keegan, *Second World War*, op cit., p. 404.

23. Monty Berger and Brian Jeffrey Street, *Invasions Without Tears* (Toronto: Vintage Books, 1994), p. 76.

24. Dwight D. Eisenhower, *Crusade in Europe* (Garden City: Doubleday & Co., 1948), p. 279.

25. Berger and Street, *Without Tears*, op cit., p. 91.

26. Greenhous et al, *Crucible*, op cit., p. 325-6.

27. Geoffrey Perret, "My Search for Douglas MacArthur," *American Heritage*, February/March 1996, pp. 81-82.

28. Hedley Everard, *Mouse in My Pocket* (Picton: Publishing Division of Valley Floatplane Service, 1988), pp. 375-6.

29. Quoted in Greenhous et al, *Crucible*, op cit., pp. 337-8.

30. Berger and Street, *Without Tears*, op cit., p. 149.

Part Seven 1945: Victory

1. Brereton Greenhous, Stephen Harris, William Johnston, William Rawling, *The Crucible of War: The Official History of the Royal Canadian Air Force*, Vol. III (Ottawa: Supply and Services Canada, 1994), p. 347.

2. Quoted in Les Allison and Harry Hayward, *They Shall Grow Not Old: A Book of Remembrance* (Brandon: Commonwealth Air Training Plan Museum, 1991), p. 11.

Bibliography

Abbott, Kim. *Gathering of Demons*. Perth: Inkerman House, 1987.

Allison, Les. *Canadians in the Royal Air Force*. Brandon: Allison, 1978.

Allison, Les, and Harry Hayward. *They Shall Grow Not Old: A Book of Remembrance*. Brandon: Commonwealth Air Training Plan Museum, 1991.

Arthur, Max. *There Shall Be Wings*. London: Coronet Books, 1993.

Bader, Douglas. *Fight for the Sky*. New York: Doubleday & Co., 1973.

Barker, Ralph. *The Thousand Plan*. London: Chatto & Windus, 1965.

Bennett, D. C. T. *Pathfinder*. London: Sphere Books, 1972.

Berger, Monty, and Brian Jeffrey Street. *Invasions Without Tears*. Toronto: Vintage Books, 1994.

Bishop, Arthur. *The Splendid Hundred*. Toronto: McGraw-Hill Ryerson, 1994.

———. *Courage in the Air*. Toronto: McGraw-Hill Ryerson, 1992.

Bowyer, Michael J. F. *2 Group RAF*. London: Faber & Faber, 1974.

Boyne, Walter J. *Clash of Wings*. New York: Simon & Schuster, 1994.

Brickhill, Paul. *Reach for the Sky: The Story of Douglas Bader*. London: Collins, 1954.

Dancocks, Daniel. *In Enemy Hands*. Edmonton: Hurtig Publishers, 1983.

Deighton, Len. *Blitzkrieg*. London: Jonathan Cape, 1979.

———. *Fighter*. London: Jonathan Cape, 1977.

——— and Max Hastings. *Battle of Britain*. London: Michael Joseph, 1990.

Demoulin, Charles. *Firebirds*. Washington: Smithsonian Institution Press, 1986.

Dundas, Hugh. *Flying Start*. London: Penguin Books, 1988.

Dunmore, Spencer, and William Carter. *Reap the Whirlwind: The Untold Story of 6 Group*. Toronto: McClelland & Stewart, 1991.

Edwards, J. F., and J. P. A. M. Lavigne, *Kittyhawk Pilot*. Battleford: Turner-Warwick Publications, 1983.

Eisenhower, Dwight D. *Crusade in Europe*. Garden City: Doubleday and Co., 1948.

Embry, Basil. *Mission Completed*. London: Methuen & Co., 1957.

Everard, Hedley, *Mouse in My Pocket*. Picton: Publishing Division of Valley Float-plane Service, 1988.

Fopp, Michael, ed. *High Flyers*. London: Greenhill Books in association with the Royal Air Force Museum, 1993.

Galland, Adolf. *The First and the Last*. London: Methuen & Co., 1955.

Gilbert, Martin. *Churchill: A Life*. New York: Henry Holt, 1991.

Godefroy, Hugh. *Lucky 13*. Toronto: Stoddart Publishing Co., 1987.

Greenhous, Brereton, et al. *The Crucible of War: The Official History of the Royal Canadian Air Force*, Vol. III. Ottawa: Supply and Services Canada, 1994.

Gunston, Bill, ed. *So Many*. Toronto: Macmillan Canada, 1995.

Gwynne-Timothy, John, R. W. *Burma Liberators*. Toronto: Next Level Press, 1991.

Halliday, Hugh. *Woody*. Toronto: Canav Books, 1987.

———. *242 Squadron: The Canadian Years*. Stittsville: Canada's Wings, 1981.

———. *The Tumbling Sky*. Stittsville: Canada's Wings, 1978.

Harding, John. *The Dancin' Navigator*. Guelph: Asterisk Communications, 1988.

Harvey, J. Douglas. *Boys, Bombs, and Brussels Sprouts*. Toronto: McClelland & Stewart, 1981.

Hastings, Max. *Overlord*. New York: Simon and Schuster, 1984.

Hough, Richard, and Denis Richards. *The Battle of Britain*. New York: W. W. Norton & Co., 1989.

Houghton, G. W. *They Flew Through Sand*. London: Jarrold, 1942.

Iverach, John. *Chronicles of a Nervous Navigator*. Winnipeg: Iverach, n.d.

Jackson, Robert. *The Fall of France*. London: Arthur Barker, 1975.

Johnen, Wilhelm. *Duel Under the Stars*. London: New English Library, 1975.

Johnson, J. E. *Wing Leader*. Toronto: Clarke, Irwin & Co., 1956.

Kaplan, Philip, and Richard Collier. *Their Finest Hour*. New York: Abbeville Press, 1989.

Keegan, John. *The Second World War*. New York: Viking Penguin, 1989.

Kent, Johnny. *One of the Few*. London: William Kimber, 1971.

Kostenuk, Samuel, and John Griffin. *RCAF Squadron Histories and Their Aircraft*. Toronto: A. M. Hakker, 1977.

Lucas, Laddie. *Malta: The Thorn in Rommel's Side*. London: Stanley Paul, 1992.

Lucas, Laddie, ed. *Out of the Blue*. London: Grafton Books, 1987.

McIntosh, Dave. *Terror in the Starboard Seat*. Don Mills: General Publishing Co., 1980.

———. *High Blue Battle: The War Diary of No. 1 (401) Fighter Squadron RCAF*. Toronto: Stoddart Publishing Co., 1990.

Middlebrook, Martin. *Arnhem 1944: The Airborne Battle*. London: Penguin Books, 1994.

Middlebrook, Martin, and Chris Everitt. *The Bomber Command War Diaries*. New York: Viking, 1985.

Moyes, Philip J. R. *Bomber Squadrons of the RAF and Their Aircraft*. London: Macdonald & Co., 1964.

Nolan, Brian. *Hero*. Toronto: Lester and Orpen Dennys, 1981.

Parton, James. *Air Force Spoken Here*. Bethesda: Adler & Adler, 1986.

Peden, Murray. *A Thousand Shall Fall*. Toronto: Stoddart Publishing Co., 1988.

Price, Alfred. *Battle Over the Reich*. London: Ian Allan, 1973.

Rawlings, John D. R. *Fighter Squadrons of the RAF and Their Aircraft*. London: Macdonald & Co., 1969.

Reader's Digest. *The Canadians at War*, Vol. 1. Montreal: Reader's Digest, 1969.

Richey, Paul. *Fighter Pilot*. London: Batsford, 1941.

Robertson, Bruce. *Beaufort Special*. London: Ian Allan, 1976.

Rohmer, Richard. *Patton's Gap*. Don Mills: General Publishing Co., 1981.

Segall, Jean Brown. *Wings of the Morning*. Toronto: The Macmillan Company, 1945.

Shores, Christopher, and Hans Ring. *Fighters Over the Desert*. New York: Arco Publishing Co., 1969.

Simpson, Allan J. *We Few*. Ottawa: The Canadian Fighter Pilots' Association, 1983.

Slessor, John. *The Central Blue*. London: Cassell and Co., 1956.

Speer, Albert. *Inside the Third Reich*. New York: The Macmillan Company, 1970.

Terraine, John. *The Right of the Line*. London: Hodder and Stoughton, 1985.

Wisdom, T. H. *Wings Over Olympus*. London: George Allen and Unwin, 1942.

Acknowledgements

Although official records and historical works provided invaluable data for this book, much of the contents are derived from the recollections of Canadian ex-airmen. The author is most grateful to all of those who went to so much trouble to provide notes and photographs and to answer so many questions. Unfortunately, space did not permit the use of every item and every word. Sincere thanks to the following, without whose generous help this book could not have been written:

J. K. (Kim) Abbott, Fallbrook, Ontario; Ken Adam, Malibu, California; Paul W. Adams, Mount Royal, Quebec; Les Allison, Roland, Manitoba; Eric Appleton, Barefoot Bay, Florida; William H. Atkinson, Surrey, B.C.

Bill Baggs, Mississauga, Ontario; Arthur E. Barnard, Burlington, Ontario; Russell Bassarab, Calgary, Alberta; Harold Benson, Calgary, Alberta; Lloyd Berryman, Burlington, Ontario; Malcolm Beverly, Willowdale, Ontario; Leonard Birchall, Kingston, Ontario; Chuck Brady, Kelowna, B.C.; Robert Brady, Mount Royal, Quebec; Cal Bricker, Edmonton, Alberta; Frank Buckley, Toronto, Ontario; Charles Butterworth, Ottawa, Ontario.

Eric Cameron, Toronto, Ontario; Lorne Cameron, Victoria, B.C.; Alex Campbell, King City, Ontario; Ron Cassels, Gimli, Manitoba; E. Douglas Craig, Truro, N.S.; Frank Cauley, Gloucester, Ontario; Ron Chadwick, Kelowna, B.C.; Carman Chase, Willowdale, Ontario; Fred Chittenden, Hepworth, Ontario; A. C. Pitt Clayton, Christina Lake, B.C.; W. H. (Butch) Cleaver, Kelowna, B.C.; Arthur S. Collins, Omemee, Ontario; Fred Crick, Kelowna, B.C.; Ewart M. Cooper, Calgary, Alberta.

Robert G. Dale, Toronto, Ontario; George J. Demare, Winnipeg, Manitoba; W. P. Dunphy, Toronto, Ontario; Cecil Durnin, Winnipeg, Manitoba.

J. F. (Stocky) Edwards, Comox, B.C.; Philip Ely, North York, Ontario.

Ken Fulton, Thornhill, Ontario; Jerry Fultz, Pleasantville, N.S.

Joseph Gibson, Don Mills, Ontario; Albert Glazer, Toronto, Ontario; Ian Glen, Sechelt, B.C.; Harry Godfrey, Oakville, Ontario; John M. Godfrey, Toronto, Ontario.

Allan Gordon Hall, Burlington, Ontario; Herb Hallatt, Flamborough, Ontario; Donald Haggart, Belleville, Ontario; Frank A. H. Harley, Osgoode, Ontario; Alan Helmsley, Ottawa, Ontario; Howard Hewer, Toronto, Ontario; Robert J. Hiscock, Jackson's Point, Ontario; Ash Hornell, Oakville, Ontario; Bert Houle, Manotick, Ontario; David Howe, Burlington, Ontario; H. James Hunter, Kanata, Ontario.

Don Inches, Rothesay, N.B.

Johnnie Johnson, Buxton, England; Lloyd (Kip) Johnston, Sydney, N.S.; Harlo Jones, Winnipeg, Manitoba.

Robert L. Kift, Peterborough, Ontario; Jim Kirk, Victoria, B.C.; Peter Koch, Kelowna, B.C.

Reg Lane, Victoria, B.C.; Homer Lea, Barrie, Ontario; Frank H. Leigh-Spencer, Salt Spring Island, B.C.; Omer Levesque, Aylmer, Quebec; Laddie Lucas, London, England.

Staff Marlatt, Toronto, Ontario; Neil McArthur, Markham, Ontario; Robert McKee, Kelowna, B.C.; Wilf Miron, Chatham, Ontario; Jim Moffat, Lachine, Quebec; Ron Monkman, Mississauga, Ontario; Jack Myles, Saint John, N.B.

Peter O'Brien, Toronto, Ontario.

Stan Paget, Dundas, Ontario; Les Perkins, Kelowna, B.C.; Wally Pethick, Burlington, Ontario; Raymond Prince, Montreal, Quebec; Rex Probert, Calgary, Alberta; Steve Puskas, Waterdown, Ontario.

Warren Quigley, Halifax, N.S.

Howard Ripstein, Montreal, Quebec; Jack Ritchie, Oakville, Ontario; Ken Roberts, Ottawa, Ontario; Maurice Robinson, Guelph, Ontario; James M. Roper, Moncton, N.B.

John Scammell, Nepean, Ontario; Ralph Schenck, Geneva, Indiana; Jim Seary, Halifax, N.S.; John D. Sheehan, Victoria, B.C.; Jim Smythe, Newmarket, Ontario; Alex Stittle, Weston, Ontario.

Ed Tandy, North Bay, Ontario; Cameron Taylor, East Kelowna, B.C.; Alan Tustin, Niagara Falls, Ontario; Lucien Thomas, Scottsdale, Arizona; John Turnbull, Willowdale, Ontario.

Douglas (Duke) Warren, Comox, B.C.; Sid Watson, Scarborough, Ontario; Jack Watts, Naples, Florida; Ken West, London, Ontario; John Wilson, Miami, Florida, Bill Warren, Nepean, Ontario; Cliff Williams, Don Mills, Ontario; Gaynor P. Williams, Ottawa, Ontario; Ralph Wood, Moncton, N.B.

In addition, my thanks to such helpful people as Peggy Iverach of Winnipeg, Gerry Beauchamp of Gloucester, Ontario, Earl Hewison of the RCAF Memorial Museum, the staff of the Directorate of History, Ottawa, and R. G. Helbecque of the Canadian War Museum, Ottawa. My sincere thanks also to the ladies of the Burlington Public Library who searched far and wide tracking down copies of out-of-print books, and to Al Lutchin and Darlene McKinnon of the Canadian Warplane Heritage Museum, Mount Hope, Ontario. And, as always, my thanks to the people of McClelland and Stewart, principally Doug Gibson, Publisher, and Alex Schultz, Editor.

Index